P9-CFO-374

Nuclear Politics in America

STUDIES IN GOVERNMENT
AND PUBLIC POLICY

Nuclear Politics
in America
A History and Theory
of Government Regulation

Robert J. Duffy

 University Press of Kansas

© 1997 by the University Press of Kansas
All rights reserved

Published by the University Press of Kansas (Lawrence, Kansas 66049), which was organized by the Kansas Board of Regents and is operated and funded by Emporia State University, Fort Hays State University, Kansas State University, Pittsburg State University, the University of Kansas, and Wichita State University

Library of Congress Cataloging-in-Publication Data

Duffy, Robert J.
    Nuclear politics in America : a history and theory of government
regulation / Robert J. Duffy
       p. cm. — (Studies in government and public policy)
    Includes bibliographical references and index.
    ISBN 0-7006-0852-4 (alk. paper). — ISBN 0-7006-0853-2 (pbk.: alk.
paper)
    1. Nuclear industry—Government policy—United States 2. Nuclear
power plants—Law and legislation—United States. I. Title.
II. Series.
HD9698.U5D76   1997
333.792′4′0973—dc21   97-19146

British Library Cataloguing in Publication Data is available.

Printed in the United States of America

10 9 8 7 6 5 4 3 2 1

The paper used in this publication meets the minimum requirements of the American National Standard for Permanence of Paper for Printed Library Materials Z39.48-1984.

Contents

Acknowledgments

I am grateful to the many people who assisted me during this project. Special thanks to Shep Melnick and Sid Milkis for their patience and guidance while I struggled to find a way to begin this project, and for giving generously of their time over the years. Both read the entire manuscript and offered many helpful insights and suggestions. Chris Bosso was kind enough to review the entire manuscript twice, and his advice was invaluable. I owe a special debt to Rick Matthews, who taught me at a relatively early age to question the shadows on the wall, and for being an endless source of inspiration, ideas, and good humor.

I would also like to thank Rich Harris and Michael Kraft, and the several anonymous readers who reviewed the manuscript for the University Press of Kansas, for their many helpful suggestions. Much of my initial writing took place while I was teaching at Albion College, and I would like to thank Myron Levine and Glenn Perusek for their friendship and advice. Thanks as well to my colleagues at Rider University for their support and encouragement.

I also thank Michael Briggs, Rebecca Knight Giusti, and Susan Schott at the University Press of Kansas, whose diligence, hard work, and good spirits improved this manuscript in countless ways.

Finally, mere words cannot express my gratitude to my wife, Debra, whose love and constant encouragement mean more to me than she may know, and to my mother and my late father for always trusting me to choose my own paths. This book is for them.

1
Nuclear Power and Political Change

The crisis consists precisely in the fact that the old is dying and the new cannot be born; in this interregnum a great variety of morbid symptoms appear.
—Antonio Gramsci

The conventional wisdom has long held that dramatic policy shifts are not to be expected in American politics. For decades students of American politics stressed its extraordinary continuity. In recent years, however, the conventional wisdom has been challenged by a growing body of literature that documents significant changes in decision-making institutions and processes as well as in the substance of public policy.[1] Some have even suggested that the changes were so fundamental that American politics has been "remade" into a "new American political system."[2] Among the most important developments were institutional reforms designed to open up government to greater citizen participation. These reforms, it is said, have made leadership more receptive to symbols and ideas, which now play a significant role in precipitating policy change. Although many of those who argue that the American political system has been "remade" believe that the transformation was beneficial, others are less sanguine, claiming that it breeds policy gridlock and stalemate.[3]

These studies of systemic change help explain the politics of commercial nuclear power regulation, which has changed dramatically over the years. For the two decades following World War II, the political relationships in this area clearly reflected subgovernment dominance. The Atomic Energy Commission (AEC), the Joint Committee on Atomic Energy (JCAE), and the highly concentrated nuclear power industry formed a classic policy subsystem and exercised a virtual

1

monopoly over the nuclear program. Limited participation, consensus, and stability were the norm. The next twenty years, however, were very different. By the early 1970s nuclear power had become one of the most controversial issues in American politics; within the span of a few years significant statutory, institutional, and procedural reforms transformed the politics of nuclear power. By the end of the decade the subgovernment had collapsed, and sharp disagreements, institutional upheaval, and policy shifts were the norm.

Of course, none of this information is exactly new—several excellent case studies have documented the decline of this subgovernment and the subsequent shifts in both politics and policy.[4] But these accounts are incomplete. First, while all agree that a subgovernment no longer dominates policy making, none have much to say about what type of policy community replaced it. The studies, in fact, say very little about nuclear politics after the early 1980s, in part because many of them were written shortly after the collapse, and it was simply too early to offer definitive assessments of policy making in the postsubgovernment era. The advantage of a decade of hindsight should, however, provide a firmer foundation to evaluate contemporary nuclear politics. Accordingly, this study addresses several questions. Is conflict or consensus the norm? If nuclear policy was once dominated by a powerful subgovernment, what type of policy community exists today? Is it a more open, dynamic, and fluid "issue network"? One or more "advocacy coalitions"? A much weakened subgovernment? Or something else entirely? The case of nuclear power offers an important opportunity to study change within a single, well-defined policy community over a period of fifty years.

Second, in focusing on the internal dynamics of a single subgovernment, many of the studies also overlook the external factors that contributed to similar transformations in other policy communities at the same time. Although internal events are clearly significant, I will argue that nuclear politics is best understood from a broader perspective that considers the effects of macropolitical trends in regulatory politics. Two trends warrant special attention here: the public lobby era of the late 1960s and early 1970s, when much of the so-called "new social regulation" was enacted, and the deregulatory backlash that began in the mid-1970s and grew stronger in the 1980s under Presidents Reagan and Bush.[5] Both periods were characterized by major reforms in both the substance of public policies and in decision-making institutions and processes. Moreover, activists in both eras knew that the policy outcomes they sought often depended on those structural changes. Few policy communities were immune to these broader efforts to restructure the institutions of regulatory policy. As Baumgartner and Jones have argued, it is "simple fact that certain periods of recent political history" have seen the creation of numerous subgovernments, while others have witnessed their destruction.[6] The reforms of the public lobby era, for example, were important factors in the demise of many policy monopolies, including the one in nuclear power. The case of nuclear power is thus of interest because its historical development indicates how institutions and policies can be modified as regulatory politics changes over time.

Many of the previous accounts overlook larger developments in American politics and tend to overstate the extent to which policy outcomes changed. My argument is not that nuclear policy failed to change in the 1970s; it surely did. Rather, my point is that the federal government remains, on balance, largely supportive of nuclear power, at least in part because the regulatory relief movement of the 1980s blunted efforts to remake the Nuclear Regulatory Commission (NRC) into an aggressive regulatory watchdog.

Policy change was also limited by unique historical factors. The NRC, like its predecessor, operates in an environment ideally suited for regulatory capture; it regulates the actions of a single centralized industry dominated by a small group of large and powerful firms. In addition, the nuclear power industry is itself the product of an unprecedented partnership between the federal government and private enterprise, and the industry owes its existence to decades of federal support and protection. As we will see, old attitudes, and old policies, die hard.

SUBGOVERNMENTS AND POLITICAL CHANGE

Among the concepts political scientists have used to analyze policy making in the American system, few have been as popular as the subgovernment model. Also known as subsystems, iron triangles, or policy monopolies, subgovernments are small, stable groups of actors, both public and private, that dominate policy in specific issue areas.[7] The typical subgovernment is said to consist of at least three elements: midlevel executive agency bureaucrats, congressional committees or subcommittees, and the client groups interested in a particular policy issue. Because each derives some tangible economic or political benefit from the program's success, the actors in subgovernments are assumed to have complementary goals. Furthermore, these shared interests create strong incentives to reach agreements among themselves. Consequently, decision making within such monopolies tends to be cooperative and is characterized by quiet negotiation and compromise. Incrementalism is also typical because significant policy shifts could attract the attention of those outside of the subgovernment, which could then jeopardize its autonomy. The chances of policy change increase when new actors, and new perspectives, are attracted to an issue.

Although the model was presumed to be descriptive of many policy areas, more sophisticated analyses suggested that subgovernment influence varied according to the type of policy involved. Dominance was assumed to be greatest in "distributive" issues that, because they involve government subsidies or benefits to a relatively small group of actors, are marked by low public visibility and high degrees of cooperation. Conversely, subgovernment influence is less pronounced in "regulatory" issues, where costs and benefits are more clearly perceived. As a consequence, "regulatory" decisions are more visible, attract a wider array of interests, and tend to be more competitive—all of which works against the coziness characteristic of subgovernments.[8]

The possibility that subgovernment influence within a single policy area might fluctuate over time has also been recognized.[9] Subgovernment collapse, however, was generally assumed to be a rare event, because policy monopolies are expected to employ any and every means at their disposal to ward off challenges to their authority. But that is not what happened in the case of the atomic subgovernment, perhaps the most powerful policy monopoly in the nation's history.

Indeed, the rapidity of the subsystem's collapse was overshadowed only by the lack of resistance displayed by its component parts. Congress adopted the Energy Reorganization Act of 1974 by overwhelming margins, abolishing the AEC and dividing its responsibilities between two new agencies: the Nuclear Regulatory Commission and the Energy Research and Development Administration (ERDA). Not only did the AEC fail to oppose the legislation, but all of the sitting AEC commissioners actually supported it. So, too, did the nuclear power industry and a nearly unanimous Joint Committee on Atomic Energy. In fact, the JCAE, once described as "the most powerful congressional committee in the history of the nation," suffered a similar fate a few years later.[10] How could this happen?

James Temples, one of several analysts who applied Ripley and Franklin's approach to the case of nuclear power, has argued that the nuclear subgovernment disintegrated as the nature of the nuclear issue was transformed from "distributive" to "regulatory." According to Temples, the shift was prompted by greater issue visibility and an expansion in the number and range of participants, and was accompanied by a dramatic increase in political conflict.[11] Although the fact that this change occurred is significant, the more interesting question is *why* it occurred at all. To argue that nuclear policy became more "regulatory" in the 1970s because there was an increase in the number of participants is merely to restate the question. What we really need to know, then, is why more people suddenly became interested in nuclear power, and how this development undermined the subgovernment.

The subgovernment approach is based on the observation that relatively small groups of actors dominate certain sectors of the political system. Clearly, some groups perceive it to be in their best interest to mobilize for action, while others do not. The explanation offered most frequently to explain this phenomenon is different intensities of interest. In the case of regulation, for example, those most interested are the regulated parties themselves, who perceive that their financial welfare can be significantly affected by the regulatory agency's decisions. The firms therefore have a powerful incentive to monitor and influence agency decision making. The general public, on the other hand, is in a much different situation; each individual's stake in the agency's decision is small while the costs of organizing for action are high. In such situations, intense minorities will often prevail over apathetic majorities.[12] The result is often a policy monopoly.

Similarly, it is often assumed that narrow interests dominate policy making because they possess greater resources and are simply able to overpower their opposition. This premise assumes, of course, that there is an opposition to overcome, which is not always the case; group influence may sometimes result from a lack of interest from other actors. For this reason, we should not be so quick to conclude that policy making is inherently biased in favor of narrow interests; it might be that such actors dominate because no one is mobilized to oppose them. Policy monopolies, in short, may result from high levels of public apathy and the absence of countervailing power.[13]

Those very traits make policy monopolies vulnerable over time. After all, the public may not remain apathetic forever. If the public suddenly develops an interest in a particular issue, there is no guarantee that a subgovernment can maintain its dominance. Schattschneider argued that "the outcome of every conflict is determined by the *extent* to which the audience becomes involved in it."[14] Political struggles almost always involve conflicts between those seeking to privatize conflict and those seeking to socialize it. Those who are dissatisfied with the existing state of affairs, or more simply those who are losing, will try to engage the audience because conflicts, Schattschneider says, "are taken into the public arena precisely because someone wants to make certain that the power ratio among the private interests most immediately involved shall not prevail." While the weaker side tries to involve the audience, the stronger side strives to keep it on the sidelines because when more actors become involved, "there is a great probability that the original contestants will lose control of the matter."[15]

ISSUE DEFINITION AND POLITICAL MOBILIZATION

Experience shows that policy monopolies sometimes fail to privatize conflicts. People who have been apathetic suddenly begin to pay attention to an issue and demand inclusion in the debate. Why does this change occur? Is it because more people come to perceive that a program affects them in some way? And what effect does it have on policy communities?

The answer to these questions lies in how issues are perceived or understood. Any given public policy issue or program can be understood in a variety of ways, some positive, some negative. Aid to Families with Dependent Children, for example, may be perceived as either a valuable part of our social safety net for the less fortunate or as a government handout to the undeserving. If people focus on a program's benefits and minimize or overlook its costs, the program may enjoy widespread support. On the other hand, a policy may come under attack if people perceive that its costs outweigh its benefits. The fate of programs often hinges on which understanding is dominant among policymakers and the attentive public.

Perceptions of issues can also change over time. Programs that were once quite popular may become the target of discontent if problems arise or if costs increase. Similarly, an issue that was once ignored may attract considerable attention if enough people perceive its negative aspects.

The key to attracting the attention of the previously apathetic or "creating a public," writes Christopher J. Bosso, "lies in shaping popular perceptions" about issues.[16] Issue definition is a critical part of politics, and political conflicts, we are told, are often characterized by struggles over the definition of issues.[17] Policy entrepreneurs seek to define issues in ways that further their own policy goals; they thus have strong incentives to shape perceptions of issues. Subsystem actors, for example, try to promote apathy by showing that their issue, or their handling of the issue, has mostly beneficial consequences. Or they may try to define the issue narrowly, as a technical issue for example, to limit public interest. Those seeking to challenge a policy monopoly, on the other hand, must attract the attention of either the general public or policymakers in other institutions. The attempt to mobilize new actors can be accomplished by highlighting a program's problems or by showing others that they also have an interest in the issue. The definition and redefinition of policy issues, in short, is a political process that affects the mobilization of interests.[18]

Some types of issues are easier to redefine than others. As Baumgartner and Jones note, "Those wishing to mobilize broad groups attempt to focus attention on highly emotional symbols or easily understood themes, while those with an interest in restricting the debate explain the same issues in other, more arcane and complicated, ways."[19] Broadly defined issues, especially those with an element of drama, admit a wide range of participants and often become the focus of widespread political debates, while those that are narrowly defined restrict participation to a small group and often give rise to policy monopolies. When narrow issues become defined in broader terms, new groups of policymakers are attracted to the issue. Actors who once called the shots find their influence diminished as these new policymakers and institutions claim jurisdiction over issues that had previously been of little interest. The result can be dramatic policy change.

We would expect that actors within a subgovernment would try to limit awareness of their programs, just as those seeking to change policy outcomes try to increase it. The amount and quality of information the public has about an issue or program are important determinants of political activity surrounding that issue. Bosso has shown that one of the factors driving the expansion of the conflict over pesticides policy was the spread of information and knowledge about pesticides. The more people who perceive a problem, he says, "the more who wish to get involved."[20] This result has political consequences because more participants also means more viewpoints. Actors within subgovernments, for example, have complementary goals and typically share a common perspective; the introduction of new actors therefore threatens consensus. For these reasons, writes Bosso, subgovernment actors will try to manage the flow of information concerning their programs. The availability of information, in fact, is an important aspect of issue definition and the spread of political conflict. Information can be used by policy entrepreneurs to encourage audience involvement and to expand the range of actors in policy disputes. As we will see, information is frequently used in an advocacy fashion to shape people's understandings of public policy issues.[21]

In other instances, according to John Kingdon, a "focusing event" such as a crisis or a revelation of misconduct or incompetence among subgovernment actors may facilitate the flow of information.[22] Issues may then be understood in new ways. Similarly, when enough information, or when enough information of a certain type, becomes public, it may even change the nature of the issue itself, redefining it in the process. Once this transformation occurs, the terms of the conflict may change in some fundamental way. Schattschneider remarked that "everything changes once a conflict gets into the political arena—*who* is involved, *what* the conflict is about, the resources available, etc."[23] When an issue changes in such a way, alliances shift and the focus of the debate changes. How an issue is defined thus has important political implications, because issue definition determines what the debate will be about, which in turn goes a long way toward explaining the mobilization of forces in any given policy sector.

There are, claim Baumgartner and Jones, two distinct types of mobilizations. Drawing on the work of Anthony Downs and E. E. Schattschneider, they demonstrate that new actors may be mobilized during either a wave of enthusiasm or a wave of criticism. Each type of mobilization leads to different policy outcomes, because each leaves a distinct institutional legacy. More specifically, waves of enthusiasm lead to the buildup of policy subsystems, while waves of criticism lead to their demise.[24] Which type exists at any given time explains whether a policy community is stable or not.

Mobilizations that occur amid waves of enthusiasm are marked by overwhelmingly positive understandings of policy issues and by the creation of institutions designed to enhance and support subsystem hegemony. Positive images or perceptions are important in most such mobilizations because they encourage the delegation of power to experts and subsystem insiders. Typically, only program supporters are organized, and there is little or no organized opposition.[25] Subsystem proponents try to insulate themselves from the rest of the political system by designing new laws, new institutions, and new procedures that structure participation and ensure privileged access to program supporters.[26] Even after the initial enthusiasm fades, policy outcomes may remain stable for long periods because the institutions remain, protecting policies from outside challenges. But as Baumgartner and Jones note, this stability is quite fragile because it depends on two things: the existing structure of political institutions and the definition of the issues processed by those institutions. A change in either one can destabilize the other and lead to dramatic policy change.[27]

Waves of criticism, on the other hand, are marked by increasingly negative policy understandings and are identified by the efforts of opponents of the status quo to expand the conflict.[28] Critics attempt to redefine the issue by highlighting bad news about the program. During waves of criticism, more groups mobilize for political action, and other institutions become involved, destroying the policy consensus that had sustained the subsystem. Intense criticism, note Baumgartner and Jones, gives new policymakers an incentive to claim jurisdiction over the issue. Furthermore, criticism is directed not just at the substance of policies, but at the institutions and procedures that make them possible. In fact, institutional turbulence is characteristic of this type of mobilization, and it can lead to subsystem destruction and dramatic policy change.[29] According to Baumgartner and Jones, periodic institutional changes "can explain why policies may be relatively stable during long periods while the institutions are stable, but then change dramatically during those periods when the institutional revisions occur."[30]

Describing similar phenomena, Schattschneider suggested that "the outcome of all conflict is determined by the scope of its contagion. The number of people involved in any conflict determines what happens; every change in the number of participants, every increase or reduction in the number of participants affects the result."[31] In addition, the scope of conflict over an issue influences the type of political activity characteristic of that policy area; as a result, the politics of controversial issues will differ from those with a narrow scope. Furthermore, changes in the scope of a conflict are presumed to lead to different policy outcomes, because every change in scope has a bias. According to Schattschneider, three factors influence the scope of issue conflict: the degree of competition over the issue, the visibility of the issue to the public, and the role of government.[32] A conflict with a broader scope is characterized by active competition among an increased number of interested parties, greater issue visibility, and greater participation by governmental actors.

INSTITUTIONS AND POLICY CHANGE

Issue redefinition and broader mobilization by themselves, however, are not enough to explain the demise of subsystems or political change. After all, issues may be prominent for extended periods before any significant government action takes place. A more comprehensive account of political change must also explain how other government agencies claim jurisdiction over aspects of policy issues.

Therefore, in examining change within a single policy community, we must also look at the question of access. Access, after all, is a critical factor in determining policy outcomes. Those who are excluded from policy-making circles have little opportunity to secure their policy goals, while actors with privileged access have a tremendous advantage in shaping the statutory and regulatory framework in which policy is made. Naturally, if new actors gain access, their influence will increase, which means that others will see their influence diminished. For this reason, special attention must be paid to whether institutional changes affect the conditions for access.

Perhaps no other criticism of pluralist theories is as famous as E. E. Schattschneider's oft-repeated comment that "the flaw in the pluralist heaven is that the heavenly chorus sings with a strong upper-class accent."[33] A large body of work has been produced supporting Schattschneider's contention that some interests are systematically underrepresented in the political process. Clearly, the unequal distribution of status and resources within society undoubtedly has something to do with determining who has access to the policy-making process. But there is something else that helps account for the priveleged position of certain groups in our society and political system: the structure, rules, and processes of government. Institutions and procedures condition access to policy making; access, in turn, affects political influence and thus policy outcomes.

Many pluralist and group theorists have been accused of minimizing or neglecting the role that government plays in the political process. Pluralists, in particular, have been criticized for casting the government in the role of a neutral referee, whose responsibilities were limited to ensuring that all legitimate interests in the group competition were treated fairly.[34] Others have countered that view, arguing that governmental institutions and processes are anything but neutral; rather, they can be thought of as "gate-keepers," facilitating access for some interests while hindering others.[35] Policy outcomes, in this view, are shaped by the principles and rules that govern decision making. In any governmental system, the existing rules will benefit some actors and issues and will hurt others.

Moreover, governmental institutions and procedures also determine who has access to information and decision makers and under what conditions. In the words of Schattschneider, the "rules of the game" matter because they "determine the requirements for success in the political process."[36] The bias inherent in these rules can therefore have a powerful influence on how receptive the political system is to new interests and issues. The mobilization of new actors in a particular policy area may be of little consequence if the rules of the game exclude them from policy-making circles. In addition to knowing which actors became interested in nuclear power, therefore, we also need to look at how open the political system was to these new actors.

We should also refrain from thinking of our current political values and institutions as "eternal" and "immutable." The rules of the game can and do change and, therefore, so may the bias inherent in every policy-making arena. Going further, changes in the rules of the game will benefit some interests and harm others. It should be apparent, Rosenbaum adds, "that a conflict over what rules shall prevail for making decisions in governmental bodies is actually a contest to determine which array of interests will be favored by governmental decisions."[37] Structures and rules that discriminate against "outsiders" may become less restrictive over time, creating opportunities for those who had once been excluded to participate in the making of public policy. The reorganization of executive branch agencies, for example, or changes of jurisdiction among congressional committees can enhance the influence of new actors. So, too, with changes in an agency's internal structure or decision-making process: certain offices within an agency may find that their influence has been enhanced by new procedures. As a case in point, Melnick has argued that by requiring the EPA to disregard costs in formulating certain standards, the courts have strengthened the position of advocates within the agency, helping them resist efforts by agency economists to employ cost-benefit analysis in the standard-setting process.[38]

Each governmental institution, of course, has its own rules and procedures and thus its own biases. At any one time, some branches of government will be more receptive to the demands of certain groups and will fashion their procedures in such a way as to facilitate the access of those groups. This is important to know because rules and procedures may direct groups to certain policy-making arenas. And "where a decision evolves," says Bosso, "can be critical to what decision emerges."[39]

An examination of the various structures and processes involved in the nuclear issue, then, may shed some light on why certain groups press their demands in one arena and not another. Accordingly, it is not enough to say that more actors gained access to the debate over nuclear power in the 1970s. We need to be more specific in the questions we ask: access to whom, and why? Asking these additional questions will allow us to avoid the error of believing that all we need to know is that a certain group gained access to policy making. Furthermore, we should be conscious of the fact that the policy-making process is composed of several stages; there is a fundamental difference, for example, between gaining access to the arenas that formulate policy and to those that implement policy.[40] Put simply, some types of access may be more valuable than others.

POLICY COMMUNITIES AND MACROPOLITICAL TRENDS

Policy monopolies were once thought to be relatively autonomous and enduring, but there are times when external conditions force them to adapt. Even though they operate independently of particular policies and programs, large-scale shifts in the broader political or social environment may induce changes in institutions or policy-making processes. These changes, in turn, may alter the operating rules of subsystems. If monopolies prove unable to adapt to the new environment, they may grow weaker or even disintegrate. Ripley and Franklin claim that "subgovernment disintegration may occur because the subgovernment loses jurisdiction over its issues (either because of a reshuffling of congressional or bureaucratic boundaries or because of a redefinition of the issue as nondistributive), or because it has been weakened by repeated losses on a series of individually minor challenges, or because it has collapsed in the face of a major challenge."[41]

Although this book is a study of political change in a single issue, an adequate explanation of shifts in nuclear politics must look beyond the confines of one policy community. Policy making takes place in a dynamic social and political environment; even the most powerful policy monopoly does not operate in a vacuum. During certain periods, the institutions that structure participation in the policy-making process undergo important changes. These changes, moreover, affect the strength of policy communities because they alter the structures of bias. New actors gain access to policy making, others see their influence diminished. Hence, periods of significant institutional change may see the rise and fall of many subgovernments.

The 1960s and 1970s were one period that witnessed dramatic systemic changes in the structures of bias. This period was a time of great change in American politics. There were changes, for example, in the substance of government policy. Beginning with civil rights in the early 1960s, the agenda of the national government expanded dramatically; the list of domestic issues for which the federal government eventually assumed responsibility included health care, urban renewal, consumer protection, and the environment. In most instances, federal "responsibility" meant new laws, new institutions, or new programs. One manifestation of this responsibility was the "new social regulation," much of which was aimed at protecting the health and safety of the public.[42] The changes of the 1960s and 1970s went beyond the types of policies the federal government confronted, however, to include reforms in policy-making institutions and processes themselves. For example, campaign finance reforms and changes in the presidential nominating process contributed to the continuing decline of political parties. Similarly, congressional reforms, such as the decline of the seniority rule, increases in individual and committee staff, and the growth in the number and power of subcommittees, exacerbated the dispersion of power within that institution. At the same time there was a veritable explosion in the number of interest groups lobbying in Washington; this growth was especially pronounced among groups claiming to represent the public interest. Finally, there was a marked increase in demands for more meaningful citizen participation in the political process. It was during the 1960s, says Anthony King, that "it came to be thought good for both the participating individuals and the polity that ordinary men and women should have a direct say not merely in the choice of public office holders but in the making of public policy."[43]

THE PUBLIC LOBBY ERA

A number of political scientists have argued that many of these changes can be viewed as products of a reform movement intent on "opening up" the political process in an effort to render it more representative and more democratic.[44] Although the "public lobby" reform movement was itself an amalgamation of several distinct movements with different agendas, they did share some common themes. One was that narrow interests were unduly influential in the political process; another was that government had become too big and impersonal and was too far removed from the understanding and control of average citizens.[45] Furthermore, many of the reformers expressed a profound distrust of big business and big government and believed that the two had forged a mutually rewarding alliance that left little room for consideration of the public interest in the policy-making process.[46] Although Americans have traditionally expressed an antipathy to concentrated power and bureaucracy, antibureaucratic sentiments were especially pronounced in the 1960s and 1970s. According to Richard A. Harris, many reformers believed that after the New Deal the focus of American politics had shifted from Congress to the administrative process.[47] This change was not a problem so long as Congress was willing to provide effective oversight or to enact statutes specific enough to limit the discretion of administrators. But Congress, faced with an increasingly large and complex set of issues, began delegating authority to administrative agencies in very broad terms, which meant that many of the details of programs would be resolved in the relatively inaccessible administrative process. The dilemma, as perceived by reformers, was that organized interests were represented in the administrative process while the public was not. All too often reform advocates from earler periods had assumed that the battle was over once Congress had acted, overlooking the fact "that those vanquished in the legislative arena can, and often do, resort to the administrative forum where they successfully undercut the effectiveness of policy at the point where it is interpreted and applied."[48] The subsequent imbalance of interests created an environment that left agencies vulnerable to capture by the very interests they were supposed to be regulating.[49] It became increasingly apparent to many reformers that "vigilance over administration" was "the price of victory in the policy process"; if they were to achieve their policy objectives, they would have to ensure that programs would be faithfully implemented.[50] In short, reformers in the 1960s and 1970s recognized that successful policy reform depended on reforming the administrative process itself.

Perhaps the most frequently recommended reform was to expand public participation in administrative proceedings. The public lobby movement was distinguished by a genuine commitment to what has been called "participatory democracy." It was widely believed that citizens should participate in the policy process on a regular basis, especially on those decisions that affected them directly. Similarly, it was thought that one way to counteract the influence of business interests in the administrative process was to open up administrative institutions and processes to the public. Expanded public participation in administrative processes was intended to accomplish several objectives. First, it would presumably rectify the imbalance of interests represented in the administrative process by facilitating access by new groups. At the very least, administrators would be required to consider other perspectives in making decisions. Second, greater public participation was intended to limit the discretion of agency administrators. An alert and involved citizenry, according to many reform advocates, would be able to monitor the actions of administrators to minimize the possibility of capture or inefficiency.

One way to accomplish both of these goals was to require elaborate new procedures that would expand the representation of public interest groups in the administrative process.[51] In theory, the introduction of these new groups into the administrative process would counter the influence of business groups. Although reform advocates were highly critical of the administrative process, they were not alone; Congress and the federal courts often joined reformers in efforts to check administrative discretion and autonomy. In this sense, the drive to "open up" the administrative process was not simply a product of increased interest group activity; many of the new procedures were, in fact, mandated by government agencies.[52] The 1970s were a time when a number of actors—interest groups, Congress, and the courts—became actively involved in administrative oversight. Furthermore, this convergence of new ideas and new actors produced significant political change.

For example, in the 1970s Congress repeatedly passed legislation imposing strict procedural obligations on agencies and agency administrators. Much of the new social regulation contained detailed provisions aimed at opening up the process to public participation. Among other provisions, agencies were required to hold public hearings before promulgating new regulations or revising old ones; to provide opportunities for interested parties to comment on proposed rules; and to publish reports or studies that were used in formulating agency decisions. A number of other statutes, such as the National Environmental Policy Act of 1969 (NEPA), allowed citizens to sue federal agencies. The Freedom of Information Act provided citizens with access to agency documents. Still other laws required many executive agencies, advisory committees, and even committees of Congress to open their meetings to the public.[53]

The courts also imposed new procedural obligations on executive agencies, reinforcing the efforts of public interest groups and Congress to check administrative discretion. Not only did the courts relax "standing" requirements, but they began to engage in more stringent reviews of agency decisions; judges demanded that agency decisions be based on a record, that the record be reviewable, and that agencies give "adequate consideration" to competing viewpoints.[54] Again, the point of such actions was to limit the discretion of administrators by expanding public participation. The rationale behind most of these new procedural obligations was that if agencies were subject to rigorous oversight they would be less susceptible to capture by special interests.

What are we to make of these reform efforts? Some have argued that reforms of this period represented a broad-based effort to restructure the principles, institutions, and processes of American politics in such a way that policy would be more responsive to "the public interest." Much of the new social regulation, according to this view, constituted an attempt to restructure, but not eliminate, the institutions of regulatory policy. Although the reformers were hostile to centralized power, there was, as Sidney Milkis argues, a certain tension in their prescriptions. On the one hand, the reformers believed that bureaucracy was unresponsive to the public interest, but they often relied on the effective use of the administrative process to achieve their policy objectives. Consequently, even though big government was part of the problem, reformers also saw it as part of the solution.[55]

Public lobby advocates were also aware that policy shifts often depended on institutional and procedural change. More specifically, they knew that successful policy reform depended on changing the policy process in such a way as to redistribute political influence in their favor. Reformers, then, were not simply hostile to administrative power; rather, their task was to devise new institutions, or reorient old ones, to create new centers of power that would be more responsive to the public interest. In other words, many of the reforms were designed not to diminish administrative power but to redirect it. What reform advocates were trying to do, suggests Milkis, was recast administration as an agent of democracy.[56]

MODELS OF POLICY COMMUNITIES

Many of these changes have prompted scholars to search for alternatives to the subgovernment model. Some have argued that policy communities are broader, and conflict among participants greater, than traditional subgovernment models admit. The subgovernment approach has also been criticized for overlooking the function of ideas in policy debates, neglecting the often critical role of state and local governments, and perhaps most important, its inability to explain policy change. These shortcomings have prompted a growing number of observers to conclude, in the words of Hugh Heclo, that the subgovernment model "is not so much wrong as it is disastrously incomplete."[57] In searching for narrow iron triangles, says Heclo, researchers tend to overlook "the fairly open networks of people that increasingly impinge upon government."[58] Jeffrey Berry contends that in addition to being overly simplistic, the approach "is no longer descriptive of most policy communities."[59] According to Berry, numerous changes in the political system in the 1960s and 1970s, such as an explosion in the number of organized interest groups and institutional reforms in Congress, altered traditional patterns of interaction between agencies, committees, and interest groups. His argument is not that subgovernments have completely disappeared from American politics; rather, it is that American politics has changed in such a way that many subgovernments have lost their dominance.[60] Subgovernments, he argues, simply cannot function in today's more open and conflictual political environment. Berry's claims are supported by several excellent case studies in pesticides, agriculture, and water policy that have documented the transformation over time of particular subsystems into more conflictual patterns of decision making.[61]

Heclo, Berry, and others have suggested that the issue network model more accurately describes the complexity of contemporary policy making. Issue networks consist of the actors who form the core of subgovernments plus legislative aides, academics, consultants, and other persons with specialized knowledge of the relevant policy. Issue networks are "shared knowledge" groups, and "the exchange of information is what makes individuals who share expertise part of a network."[62] Subgovernment participants, by contrast, are united by a direct economic or political stake in the given policy. Although restricted participation is characteristic of policy monopolies, issue networks tend to be larger, less exclusive, and grant access to a broader range of participants. These same traits increase the likelihood of conflict, which varies from network to network and over time within a single network. Conflicts can become intense. Furthermore, issue networks are dynamic and "lack the stable set of relationships that characterize subgovernments"; therefore, alliances are often temporary.[63] Participants move in and out of networks with such ease that, according to Heclo, "it is almost impossible to say where a network leaves off and its environment begins."[64]

Nevertheless, claims Berry, issue networks are not merely large subgovernments with greater levels of conflict and participation. Rather, the two models are based on different assumptions about political behavior. Subgovernment theories assume that actors have complementary goals and thus have a strong incentive to cooperate; the issue network approach, on the other hand, recognizes that actors may have competing goals and that "there is often much to be gained from pursuing a strategy of conflict." Policy-making styles also are very different because issue networks have a wider range of interests, which works against the cooperative and accomodationist styles typical of many subgovernments. Bargaining, negotiation, and coordination are therefore more difficult in issue networks.[65]

Christopher Bosso offers a less sanguine assessment of contemporary policy making in his study documenting the transformation of a pesticides policy community from an iron triangle into an especially conflictual type of issue network he labels "presence politics." The distinguishing feature of this model is that members of the policy community are essentially permanent players in policy debates; their interest in issues does not rise and fall with shifts in public or media attention. "Year after year," he says, "the same organizations, and, often, the same faces, appear. Everyone in attendance knows one another, and, more important, one another's views. They may not like each other, and they certainly don't agree, but all seem to accept each other as permanent and legitimate players in the game."[66] Bosso claims presence politics has its roots in the structural changes of the 1970s, which made the American political system far more open and less exclusive than it had been. Consequently, a far broader range of demands and views are now included in policy debates. Indeed, that is precisely the problem; it seems the system is now so permeable that almost everybody has access, which all too often leads to "exhaustive policy warfare" between permanently mobilized factions and ultimately to policy stalemate.[67] If Bosso is correct, presence politics would appear to produce incrementalism, much like subgovernments. Yet there is an important difference. In policy monopolies, incrementalism is the result of limited participation; presence politics, on the other hand, claims that unlimited participation leads to policy stasis.

Advocacy coalitions represent yet another type of policy community. As described by Sabatier and Jenkins-Smith, advocacy coalitions consist of "actors from a variety of public and private institutions at all levels of government who share a set of basic policy beliefs (policy goals plus causal and other perceptions) and who seek to manipulate the rules, budgets and personnel of governmental institutions in order to achieve those goals over time."[68] Information is used strategically, in an advocacy fashion, to mobilize supporters or undermine opposing coalitions. Policy change, claim Sabatier and Jenkins-Smith, is best understood as the product of competition between advocacy coalitions. Significant policy shifts "require the replacement of one dominant coalition by another, and this transition is hypothesized to result primarily from changes external to the subsystem."[69] Levels of conflict will vary depending upon what is at stake, with conflict naturally being greater when coalitions disagree on "core beliefs."[70]

Although there are important similarities, advocacy coalitions differ from issue networks in several ways. First, the advocacy coalition model assumes that "shared beliefs provide the principal 'glue' of politics," not self-interest, and that actors' core beliefs are resistant to change. Consequently, "on major controversies within a policy subsystem when core beliefs are in dispute, the lineup of allies and opponents tends to be rather stable over periods of a decade or more."[71] Issue networks, on the other hand, were said to be fluid and dynamic, with persistent cleavages the exception. Second, advocacy coalitions aggregate "most actors within a subsystem into a manageable number of belief-based coalitions, whereas Heclo views individuals as largely autonomous and thus risks overwhelming both himself and the reader with an impossibly complex set of actors."[72] Sabatier and Jenkins-Smith contend that in most policy communities, there will be two to four politically significant coalitions, although "in quiescent subsystems there may be only a single coalition."[73] Third, other models focus on national politics and "dramatically underestimate" the importance of state and local agencies; an important premise of advocacy coalitions is that policy communities "must include an intergovernmental dimension."[74]

Richard A. Harris, on the other hand, argues that contemporary policy making is sometimes less combative than the various other approaches predict. Although acknowledging that evidence for his model, known as "neocorporatism," is "fragmentary and anecdotal," Harris cites the decline of contentiousness in some areas of social regulation in the 1980s as a sign that issue networks no longer describe all areas of contemporary policy making. Neocorporatism, as described by Harris, is not intended as a comprehensive description of the political system; rather, it refers to "an emergent set of institutional relations specific to the realm of regulatory policy and, even more particularly, to the realm of the new social regulation."[75] More specifically, neocorporatism is a pragmatic "system of interest intermediation" through which competing interests attempt to resolve policy conflicts. Neocorporatism is characterized by collaborative decision making, where the emphasis is on problem solving rather than confrontation. In fact, says Harris, "Without the added dimension of collaboration in policymaking, the concept of an issue network would be an adequate representation of interest interaction."[76]

Neocorporatism has its roots in the business sector's response to the new social regulation of the 1970s. According to Harris, the many institutional and policy reforms of that era transformed issue networks by politicizing corporate managers, effectively forcing them to become directly involved in regulatory politics. Although the initial result was an "endemic contentiousness" consistent with Bosso's "presence politics," businesses seeking certainty in their regulatory environments eventually accepted the underlying principles of the new social regulation and became effective participants in social regulatory issue networks. This acceptance gave corporate managers credibility with regulators and public lobby groups and, in conjunction with their integration into regulatory decision making, diminished the confrontational character of regulatory politics that had characterized the early 1970s. As business and public lobby groups interacted more frequently and in greater depth, their relationships grew less adversarial. "Politicized management," concludes Harris, "has begun to push issue networks beyond consultation and participation to actual collaboration."[77]

Despite their many differences, all of these models claim that powerful forces of change have opened up the American political system to a wide array of contending interests. With the exception of neocorporatism, each also seems to suggest that these changes are permanent. Such a conclusion is premature. Institutions and processes that were "remade" once can be "remade" again, fundamentally altering the mobilization of bias. The American political system certainly became more participatory in the 1960s and 1970s, but there are no guarantees that it will remain that way.

All of the models also raise important questions about citizen participation and democratic governance. Although each agrees that policy making today is more open than the subgovernment model suggests, most hold that meaningful participation is still limited to organized groups. What we have today, they suggest, falls well short of full-blown participatory democracy. Given the specialized nature of many contemporary policy debates, that conclusion seems justified. Nevertheless, it may be the case that citizens play a more meaningful role in policy making than these models assume, at least when it comes to issue definition and agenda setting. Citizen participation in these processes, for example, could help ensure that government is responsive to public concerns.

CONCLUSION

The search for one all-encompassing model of policy communities is misguided; no one model explains all issues at all times. As Baumgartner and Jones rightly note, at any given time there exists a great variety of policy communities in the United States in various phases of change. The American political system, they say, is a "mosaic of continually reshaping systems of limited participation."[78] This is certainly true of nuclear power.

Although many question whether the subgovernment model accurately depicts contemporary policy making, it was clearly applicable to nuclear power policy in the twenty years after World War II. Indeed, if the model ever had any utility, it was in this issue: the AEC, JCAE, and nuclear industry formed an archetypical policy monopoly whose autonomy was rooted in, and enhanced by, the high attention levels and positive understandings associated with a wave of enthusiasm. The creation of supportive laws and institutions structured political participation for decades, limiting meaningful access to program supporters. This one-sided mobilization was reinforced by public and elite perceptions of this unique policy. Nuclear energy was highly complex, potentially lethal, and shrouded in the secrecy of national security. Policy was made by an exceptionally small and cohesive cadre of true believers committed to the development and utilization of nuclear energy.

Despite its unique powers and traits, the policy monopoly was transformed in the 1960s and 1970s. Changing perceptions of the issue were a crucial factor in this transformation, as mounting concerns about the potential environmental and safety consequences of nuclear power led to an expansion in the scope of conflict. The introduction of new actors shattered the consensus on nuclear power; the ensuing disagreements made the issue more visible, attracting more actors.

All of this enhanced interest in nuclear power may not have mattered if governmental institutions and processes had not also been remade. Through much of the 1950s and 1960s, the arena of nuclear power was notable for its exclusivity. For the most part, all roads lead through the AEC and JCAE, who acted as vigilant gatekeepers by limiting participation for anyone outside the subsystem. But changes in institutions and processes, such as the abolition of the AEC and the joint committee, decentralized control over nuclear power and made it much easier for critics to gain access to policy-making circles. These changes, along with others from the public lobby era, contributed to the transformation of the atomic subgovernment and altered the nature of political activity surrounding the nuclear issue. In that sense, the case of nuclear power offers an example of how it is possible to modify particular programs during times of fundamental regulatory change. More important, these reforms were cumulative and reinforcing. With each reform, new actors entered the debate, and the scope of conflict expanded even further.

Although the changes in nuclear politics and policy were significant, they were not as extensive as the reforms enacted in some other policy areas. That result is due, in part, to the strength of the atomic subgovernment and to the essentially moderate reforms suggested by antinuclear activists. It is also a consequence of the fact that the effort to reform the politics of nuclear power, for a variety of reasons, got started too late. By the time antinuclear forces won their biggest battles in the mid-1970s, the wave of reform that typified the public lobby era had already crested.

The remainder of the book is organized as follows. In Chapter 2 I examine the early years of nuclear energy policy with an eye toward understanding the origins and underpinnings of a nuclear subgovernment. Special attention is paid to the unique government–private sector partnership that gave birth to the nuclear power industry and then nurtured it for the next twenty years. In Chapter 3 I explore the actors and conditions that made the nuclear power issue the focus of a highly charged political controversy and document its transformation from a narrowly defined national security issue to a broadly defined environmental and safety issue. Changes in the commission's licensing and rulemaking procedures are the focus of Chapter 4, while the events leading to the abolition of the Atomic Energy Commission and the Joint Committee on Atomic Energy and the efforts of other governmental institutions to claim jurisdiction are discussed in Chapters 5 and 6. In both chapters I also trace the effects of the public lobby era reforms on this policy community. Nuclear politics and policy in the immediate aftermath of these organizational and procedural reforms are examined in Chapter 7, while the focus of Chapter 8 is presidential efforts to provide regulatory relief to a beleaguered industry. In the final chapter I review the current status of nuclear power politics and offer some conclusions concerning policy communities, regulatory politics, and political change.

2
Subgovernment Dominance, 1945–65

From its inception, the private nuclear power industry in the United States was promoted, subsidized, and insulated heavily from political and economic shocks by the federal government. Well into its third decade, the industry and its governmental regulators collaborated to make management of the "peaceful atom" the work of a largely invisible and unassailable subgovernment whose components included congressional committees responsible for nuclear power policy, the federal regulatory agency responsible for controlling the nuclear power industry, the trade associations representing the manufacturers of the technology, and the scientists in institutions, public and private, working on the program.

—Walter Rosenbaum

In many respects, the atomic energy program in the twenty years following World War II was the archetypical subgovernment. A small, cohesive, and stable group of actors exercised considerable autonomy in policy making. Each of the participants involved in nuclear policy making during this period had either an economic, political, or organizational stake in the development and utilization of atomic energy. There is, however, one highly unusual aspect of this policy community. Unlike the familiar example of subsystems in which governmental actors had been "captured" by the very business interests they were supposed to monitor, with nuclear power there was no industry "client" group until the government created one. It was only after policymakers in the mid-1950s took steps to overcome the serious technological, economic, and political obstacles confronting the generation of electricity from the fission process that one could even begin to speak of a commercial nuclear power industry. James R. Temples has written that the nuclear industry "is unique in that the federal government itself is largely responsible for creating as well as sustaining it," while Bruce L. Welch rightly claims that nuclear energy "is wholly and completely a product of government design, promotion, and subsidy."[1] This unusual government-industry relationship is crucial to understanding the nuclear subgovernment.

This subgovernment was endowed with additional prestige and power because of the atomic energy program's identification with national security issues.

The actors in this tightly knit monopoly were united by a conviction that the development of atomic energy, first as a weapon but later as a means of generating electricity, was both necessary and desirable for the nation's welfare. Indeed, this commitment was enthusiastically embraced by those involved in formulating and implementing policy and drove the atomic program for over twenty years. For the most part, this consensus meant that decision making would be extraordinarily accommodative and that policy would be quite stable. The important decisions concerning the atomic program were made with little public debate by this small set of participants "behind the scenes." In fact, few outside the confines of the subsystem were interested in atomic energy. Atomic regulation during the 1950s and early 1960s, according to two researchers, "was largely invisible, intangible, and undramatic."[2]

In this chapter the factors and conditions that contributed to the rise of this subsystem will be examined. Unlike an "iron triangle," this policy community was actually composed of four sets of actors: the Atomic Energy Commission (AEC), the Joint Committee on Atomic Energy (JCAE), the nuclear power industry, and the scientists and engineers working on the program in universities and national laboratories. Following Baumgartner and Jones, I argue that a "wave of enthusiasm," marked by overwhelmingly positive perceptions of nuclear power and by the creation of supportive laws and institutions, paved the way for the creation of a powerful subgovernment that would dominate policy making for twenty years. Atomic energy first came to public attention as a new and terrible weapon of mass destruction, but these negative images soon gave way to the seemingly infinite promise of the "peaceful atom." Visions of clean, cheap, and boundless energy, rather than mushroom clouds, soon occupied the dreams of most Americans. New laws and institutions assisted this remarkable image transformation. The new laws granted broad statutory authority to the two governmental bodies, the AEC and JCAE, and directed them to develop and promote a nuclear power industry. These new laws and institutions also structured participation in ways that rendered the issue relatively inaccessible to all but a small group of boosters who controlled program information, access to decision making, and policy outcomes.

Their control was bolstered by the widespread perception, diligently nurtured by them, that atomic energy was primarily a national security issue, which meant that very few actors would have detailed knowledge of the program. Atomic energy was also a highly complex and scientific issue that further reduced the number of actors who understood its details. For all intents and purposes, only supporters of nuclear power were mobilized for action. Presidents rarely involved themselves in the program, Congress readily deferred to the advice of the Joint Committee on Atomic Energy, and, with the exception of the nuclear industry, interest group activity was virtually nonexistent. This one-sided mobilization ensured that government policy during this period was characterized by generous subsidies and the absence of political conflict.

THE EARLY YEARS, 1940–46

The atomic program began under conditions ideally suited to the formation of subgovernments. Almost from the outset, public understanding of atomic energy was overwhelmingly positive. But it could have been very different, given that the initial interest in the atom stemmed from its use as a terribly destructive instrument of war. Years later, in fact, perceptions of nuclear power would change, and the public would recognize more of the program's potential costs. In the early years, however, supporters of atomic energy used their control of strategic junctures in the political system to construct a positive policy image, one that stressed the atom's tremendous potential as a cheap and plentiful energy source and minimized fears about mushroom clouds and radiation.[3]

From its birth in the highly secretive Manhattan Project, atomic energy was defined and perceived in military terms,[4] which naturally meant that information regarding the bomb was subject to elaborate security precautions. This concern with maintaining the "secret" of the atom set the tone for the atomic program far into the future. From the beginning, access to information involving atomic energy would be severely restricted.

The task of designing and constructing an atomic bomb required scientific knowledge and resources that the government simply did not possess. Thus, the army turned to the private sector to perform much of the vital research and development work. A considerable amount of the wartime research, for example, had been contracted out to scientists in universities and private enterprise. DuPont was hired to construct and operate a large plutonium production facility at Hanford, Washington. Similarly, the headquarters of the Manhattan Engineering District at Oak Ridge, Tennessee, was the location of two major production facilities, one operated by the Monsanto Chemical Corporation, the other by Carbide and Carbon Chemicals Corporation, a subsidiary of Union Carbide.[5] These initial projects, which yielded dividends for all involved, marked the beginning of a strong government-business partnership in atomic energy; in fact, the partnership is one of the subsystem's distinguishing traits and accounts for much of its durability.

When the war ended, the sense of national emergency that had driven the atomic program disappeared, and many of the top scientists who had worked on the bomb project returned to their positions in universities and the private sector. With virtually no stockpile of atomic weapons at the war's end, government officials worried that if the atomic program ground to a halt, the nation's security would be threatened. A vigorous weapons program, it was believed, was essential to the nation's defense and security, especially because it was widely recognized that the American monopoly on atomic weapons would not last forever.

THE ATOMIC ENERGY ACT OF 1946

In pursuit of these general goals, Congress in 1946 passed the Atomic Energy Act, which established the institutional framework within which atomic energy decisions would be made for approximately the next thirty years.[6] The legislation, also known as the McMahon Act, created the Atomic Energy Commission, which inherited ownership of all atomic materials, facilities, and information from the Manhattan Project; the General Advisory Committee (GAC), which was to advise the AEC on scientific and technical issues; and the Joint Committee on Atomic Energy, which was to oversee AEC operations.

The Atomic Energy Commission

Section 2 of the Atomic Energy Act of 1946 established the Atomic Energy Commission, which was to have five civilian members appointed by the president, subject to Senate confirmation, to five-year terms. After giving consideration to a single administrator for the proposed agency, Congress decided that the highly technical nature of the subject matter would be too much responsibility for one man. The new and evolving technology, it was claimed, would best be controlled by a five-person commission, with each of the members having different backgrounds and experiences. The AEC was to be the primary actor in formulating the nation's atomic energy policy. Its principal duties, as defined by Congress, were the production of atomic weapons and the fissionable materials required for their manufacture. Assisting the five AEC commissioners would be a general manager, who would be responsible for managing the day-to-day affairs of the commission.[7]

Seeking effective management, Congress tried to create an "expert" agency that would be insulated from the political pressures that could conceivably distort its decision-making processes. The structure and position of the AEC, as well as the fixed tenures of AEC commissioners, indicated congressional intent that the AEC be independent of the president, thereby making it more susceptible to legislative influence.[8] Moreover, this independence reduced presidents' effective control of, and interest in, the program. Indeed, lack of presidential interest and involvement was a staple of the atomic program throughout much of its history. Given the program's identification with national security concerns, however, the lack of presidential support was not a real problem for the commission. On those occasions when the AEC did need political support, it turned to the Joint Committee on Atomic Energy.[9]

In addition to establishing the AEC, the McMahon Act mandated a government monopoly in atomic energy. Congress stipulated that responsibility for all atomic programs and information be transferred from the army to the AEC. Furthermore, the AEC was granted ownership of all fissionable materials and all facilities that utilized or produced fissionable materials.[10] This responsibility was significant because at the time of the transfer, more than 2,000 military personnel, 4,000 government employees, and 38,000 contractor employees were involved.[11] The facilities the AEC inherited from the Manhattan Project were spread across the nation and included all research laboratories, weapons production plants, and administrative offices. The size and scope of the AEC's operations, together with the sweeping powers granted by Congress, clearly indicated that it was intended to be a powerful agency. Indeed, one account of the AEC's early years concluded that "during the first two years of its existence, the Commission had exercised its extraordinary powers almost in a vacuum. Behind the security barriers the Commission's staff and its contractors lived in a world of their own, a world unknown to most of the nation. The President caught only fleeting glimpses of this world, and the Congress was almost totally excluded."[12]

As a further illustration of the primacy of military concerns, the Atomic Energy Act of 1946 established programs for the control of scientific and technical information concerning atomic energy. Section 10(a), for example, directed that "it shall be the policy of the Commission to control the dissemination of restricted data in such a manner as to assure the common defense and security." The term *restricted data* was defined as "all data concerning the manufacture or utilization of atomic weapons, the production of fissionable material, or the use of fissionable material in the production of power." As a practical matter, this definition meant almost all information regarding the program. The McMahon Act also prohibited the AEC from exchanging information with other nations with respect to the use of atomic energy for industrial purposes until "Congress declares by joint resolution that effective and enforceable international safeguards against the use of atomic energy for destructive purposes have been established."[13] These provisions clearly indicate that development of the peaceful uses of the atom would take a backseat to assuring the common defense and security.

The classification of almost all information pertaining to the atom meant that for the next twenty years, the atomic program would be shrouded by a blanket of secrecy. These conditions all but guaranteed that an exceptionally small set of governmental actors, in this case the AEC and the JCAE, would have access to information concerning the atomic program. The legacy of secrecy would persist when the atomic program's emphasis later shifted from defense to the commercial generation of electricity.

The responsibility for managing such an important project, especially one that involved a new and sophisticated technology with implications for national security, is perhaps one reason there were remarkably few disagreements among AEC commissioners throughout these early years. Initially, the AEC perceived that its goal, or "mission," was to build and maintain a strong program for the production of atomic weapons, because such a program was seen to be in the national interest. The "sense of mission" made the commission an exceptionally cohesive body; indeed, unanimity was the rule and not the exception for commission decisions. During its first three years, the AEC rendered more than 500 formal decisions, and all but 12 were unanimous. Moreover, this trend continued well into the next decade. During the 1953–58 period, for example, there were 1,531 unanimous AEC votes, while only 70 were split.[14] These figures suggest a remarkable degree of consensus within the commission on basic policy matters, which is not surprising given the broad bipartisan consensus on foreign policy issues that characterized the period. The commission's first chairman, David E. Lilienthal, once explained the basis of this consensus, saying, "The one thing I have worked hardest to accomplish—because without it this job can become too unpalatable to be borne—is to cultivate a brother-feeling among the members of the Commission."[15] From its inception, then, the commission was committed to presenting a united front to outsiders. Unanimous decisions, it was thought, would lend credibility to AEC actions as well as reassure outsiders that the commission was making sound policy decisions.

The General Advisory Committee

The 1946 act also created the General Advisory Committee, empowering it to advise the AEC on "scientific and technical matters relating to materials, production, research and development."[16] The General Advisory Committee was to be composed of nine "top" scientists appointed by the president. As an indication of the prestige of the GAC in this period, among its original members were renowned scientists J. Robert Oppenheimer, Enrico Fermi, and Glenn Seaborg. For the next three years, the GAC would serve as the AEC's chief source of scientific and technical advice. Because their staffs were relatively small and inexperienced, the AEC and JCAE relied almost exclusively on the GAC for guidance on the formulation of policy. Reinforcing this trend was the fact that most of the early AEC and JCAE members had little or no training in physics or atomic energy. Members of the AEC, for example, were chosen for their broad experience, not for their scientific expertise. As a result, they were inclined to defer important policy decisions to the more scientifically experienced and renowned members of the GAC. Such behavior, although not inevitable, is commonly found in science and technology policy arenas.[17]

The Joint Committee on Atomic Energy

Similarly, scientific expertise was not a factor in the selection of the first members of the JCAE. Rather, many early committee members were chosen for their backgrounds in defense and security issues. Constituency considerations also appear to have played a major role in JCAE membership, because states with national laboratories or atomic production facilities were disproportionately represented on the committee throughout its existence. For example, the JCAE was populated with members from New Mexico (Los Alamos), Tennessee (Oak Ridge), California (Livermore), Illinois (Argonne), and Washington (Hanford). As might be expected, membership on the joint committee could be a valuable base to those seeking to provide their constituents with visible benefits. This information suggests that aside from the consensus on the value of the program as a defense issue, the JCAE also supported the program because of the obvious pork-barrel possibilities.[18]

Composed of nine members from each chamber, the Joint Committee on Atomic Energy was clearly intended to be a powerful committee. It was, for example, the only joint committee created by statute rather than by the rules of both houses. The JCAE was also the only permanent joint committee granted the full legislative and investigative powers of a regular standing committee. Its formal status alone suggests that Congress intended to exercise control over atomic energy in general and over the AEC in particular. Leaving no doubt as to congressional intent, the McMahon Act required the AEC to "keep the Joint Committee fully and currently informed with respect to the Commission's activities."[19] It has been suggested that the inclusion of this language "broke new ground" and was "intended to give the JCAE a unique capacity for legislative surveillance."[20] The act also mandated that all bills concerning the atom were to be referred to the JCAE, and it set no limits on the number of staff members or consultants the joint committee could hire.[21] Congress, in other words, was not about to abdicate responsibility for this new program to the executive branch. These sweeping and unusual grants of power, along with the JCAE's status as a special joint committee with exclusive jurisdiction over a glamorous and highly technical issue, made the committee one of the most powerful congressional committees in the nation's history. Indeed, in their comprehensive study of the JCAE, Green and Rosenthal claim that the joint committee was "in terms of its sustained influence in Congress, its impact and influence on the Executive, and its accomplishments, probably the most powerful Congressional committee in the history of the nation."[22]

Although the JCAE was granted exclusive jurisdiction over all bills pertaining to atomic energy, it tended to exercise its influence primarily through continuous participation in AEC deliberations rather than through legislation. The provision of the act that required the AEC to keep the JCAE "fully and currently informed with respect to the Commission's activities," for example, allowed the joint committee to involve itself in the day-to-day affairs of the AEC. By getting involved at an early stage, the JCAE could resolve any disagreements with the AEC before an issue was formally considered and before any conflict emerged in public. Decisions could be made behind the scenes, thereby avoiding the spotlight of public discussion or open congressional debate. Such behavior, in which issues are resolved in secondary arenas, is typical of subsystem politics.[23]

The JCAE's influence within Congress was enhanced because it was a *joint* committee, with exclusive jurisdiction over the atomic program.[24] In practice, the JCAE would normally issue identical reports—one each for the House and Senate—on pending legislation. This monopoly created a situation in which Congress would have the opportunity to review or discuss only one bill—that of the JCAE. And if either chamber amended the bill, the joint committee acted as the conference committee. In essence, that meant the scope and extent of public and congressional debate was reduced; one bill rather than two meant fewer choices for Congress and fewer chances for outsiders to have any input. A contributing factor to the unity and influence of the JCAE was that the committee had only one staff, which reinforced the committee's tendency to speak with one voice to the rest of Congress. Indeed, in the early years of the program, the joint committee, as Green and Rosenthal suggest, "*was* the Congress" on atomic energy matters.[25] With respect to atomic energy, for the next two decades all roads led to the JCAE.

The normal tendency of Congress to defer to the advice of its specialized committees and subcommittees was reinforced in the case of atomic energy by several additional factors. First, atomic energy was largely perceived and justified as a defense program, with primary emphasis on military applications. In 1948, for example, over 80 percent of all funds spent on atomic energy were earmarked for programs with military applications. As late as June 1961, approximately two-thirds of all research and development and construction activities of the AEC's reactor program continued to serve weapons and military applications.[26] The definition and perception of the atomic program as primarily military in character lent credibility to both the program and the joint committee and legitimized its exclusive policy-making role.

Because the United States was the only nation with the atomic "secret," security was considered to be an essential part of the effort to retain the atomic monopoly. As mentioned earlier, many of the first members of the JCAE had backgrounds in defense issues, having been members of military and security committees. Not surprisingly, during the late 1940s, the JCAE was primarily interested in security matters. Approximately three-quarters of the JCAE's meetings in the 1947–51 period were held in executive session due to security requirements.[27] Hall argues that this circumstance occurred because most members of the JCAE did not understand the scientific principles of atomic energy, but they could understand security. Since they were unable to determine the relative significance of much atomic information, the JCAE's inclination, like that of other security and defense committees, was to keep most information classified.[28] With its exclusive control over atomic energy matters in Congress, the committee was able to dominate the legislative aspect of policy making in these early years. The security restrictions meant that the atomic program was obscured by a blanket of secrecy that effectively limited the number of participants in the atomic program. Within Congress, only JCAE members had access to atomic information.

The JCAE, as the exclusive guardian of the atom, was a prestigious committee and soon became an elite congressional group. On many issues, Congress readily deferred to the JCAE. In the words of Senator Brien McMahon (D-Conn.), this situation placed the Congress as a whole at a relative disadvantage: "Congress has only the most general idea of what the atomic package contains. . . . So far as atomic energy is concerned, Congress simply lacks sufficient knowledge upon which to discharge its constitutional duties."[29] Furthermore, members of the JCAE recognized that much of their power and status derived from their monopoly of atomic information. The joint committee would be relatively immune to challenge so long as access to information concerning the atomic program was limited to JCAE members alone. The committee's position was also protected by the perception, which the committee itself helped reinforce, that one had to be "qualified" to participate in discussions of atomic energy policy. The AEC, seeking to maintain its own influence, often joined the JCAE in suggesting that an understanding of scientific or technological principles was a prerequisite to admission to policy-making circles.

THE ATOMIC SUBGOVERNMENT

The complexity of atomic energy facilitated the formation of a subgovernment. The technology was new, exciting, and potentially dangerous; it also affected national security. The institutions created to handle this unique problem were thereby distinguished by their special tasks. Only a handful were allowed access to atomic information; therefore, only a handful were capable of understanding the program or even discussing it. Given these conditions, it was only natural that the perception of a special assignment would generate a sense of unity and "mission" within and among the new institutions. Green and Rosenthal contend that the "essence of the Joint Committee on Atomic Energy is its positive sense of mission. It has a philosophy of atomic energy, it has definite objectives, and it has a program." Furthermore, because of their common task, members of the JCAE often had more in common with members of the AEC and GAC than with other members of Congress.[30]

Like much defense policy at the time, atomic energy policy was characterized by bipartisanship. In an era of bipartisanship, no one, especially members of Congress, wanted to be portrayed as being opposed to the nation's security. In their study of the early years of the atomic energy program, Dahl and Brown noted the equation of the program with an "overriding national interest"; they also commented that criticisms of the program "appear to many minds as an almost unpatriotic attempt to play politics at the expense of national security."[31] President Truman illustrated this very point during a 1948 controversy over legislation that fixed the terms of AEC commissioners, declaring that "politics and atomic energy do not mix."[32] The military character of the atom during these early years shielded the program from outside congressional scrutiny and from most partisan disagreements. To be sure, there were conflicts among Democrats and Republicans on important issues, such as the pace of reactor development, but on the question of the desirability of atomic energy itself, there was a deep-seated agreement by joint committee members of the program's intrinsic value. In their study of the JCAE, Green and Rosenthal remarked, "The Joint Committee, probably more than any other Congressional group, has carefully cultivated a tradition of nonpartisanship. . . . Members have claimed to be above party so frequently that the claim itself has become something of a shibboleth and has exerted independent influence."[33] It should not be surprising, then, to find a consensus in a program that was defined and justified as being instrumental in securing the nation's future. The cold war, the prevailing faith in science, and the recognition that the atomic monopoly could not last all contributed to such a consensus. According to Kaku and Trainer, this belief led those involved to believe "that their work was linked to a vital national interest or at the very least, national prestige. Such thinking led to a situation where the term 'national interest' could be used to promote almost anything pertaining to nuclear power."[34]

Furthermore, the perception of a common purpose helped overcome differences in institutional goals, and the overwhelming commitment among subsystem actors to atomic energy lent a consistent pattern to policy making. Policy making was largely bipartisan and cooperative because the AEC, GAC, and JCAE were united in the goal of developing a self-sustaining atomic program. A strong atomic program would benefit everyone involved: it would increase the demand for scientists and engineers, it would help the AEC justify its existence, and it would enhance the positions of JCAE members by providing their constituents with tangible benefits. Proponents of the program became committed to its defense and were reluctant to raise questions for fear of harming, or being charged with harming, the national interest. Criticism of the program could only attract unwanted attention. As a result, cooperation was the rule and not the exception in the program's early years.

A strong atomic program was also believed to be good for human welfare. Following the rapid and stunning success of the Manhattan Project, there developed a tremendous faith in science and scientists among both the general public and government policymakers. It was assumed that science, given the time and adequate resources, could solve many of mankind's most pressing problems. To a significant extent, scientific progress was equated with social progress. Beginning with the Manhattan Project and continuing until well into the 1960s, there were predictions of a world made better by science. According to one observer, "leading scientists, turned into celebrities by the national news media, were looked upon as the high priests of a state religion that promised social progress by means of made-to-order technological advances." Expressing a similar faith in science and in the atom, then AEC chairman Lewis Strauss stated in a 1955 article for *Reader's Digest* that atomic energy had the support of a "higher Intelligence."[35]

If scientists in general were held in high regard, then nuclear scientists in particular were especially lauded. According to Ralph Lapp, a scientist who was involved in the atomic program, "The atomic scientist, to single out one species of the new order, seemed an extraordinary person. Before the war the public had rarely heard about a nuclear physicist; after Hiroshima he became a celebrity, but he was also regarded as something of a mental freak. Here was a man whose mind touched at the innermost wellsprings of nature's secrets, and the layman became inclined to view every physicist as much a genius as Einstein. They were all high priests in the Temple of Science."[36]

Furthermore, it was believed that nuclear energy could revolutionize the nature of industrial society by providing a relatively cheap and abundant source of power. In the early 1960s, AEC Chair Glenn Seaborg commented that nuclear scientists would "build a new world through nuclear technology."[37] Nuclear energy could lead to the discovery of new production techniques, it was said, and provide cheap electricity to areas where supplies were scarce.[38] The promise of cheap electricity was especially attractive to southern Democrats, because electricity was seen as a key to economic growth in the South. It was also claimed that nuclear power could drastically reduce the costs of production, leading to increased economic growth and an improved standard of living. In short, a vigorous atomic energy program was thought to be necessary for a nation seeking to exert military, economic, and technological leadership in the postwar era. The national interest seemed to demand that the nation explore the atom's many possibilities.

Very few people had reasons to challenge this position. That the issue was defined and perceived in military terms severely limited the number of decision makers. That the program involved sophisticated scientific concepts and complex technologies served to further reduce the number of participants. The end result was that from the outset decisions concerning atomic energy were made by a small elite in what Dahl and Brown called a "political void."[39] What little debate there was would be framed in scientific or technological, not "political," terms. Only a very small group of actors, then, those considered to be "experts," were thought to be qualified to debate policy options. Those who lacked such technical or scientific abilities or knowledge—which meant, in essence, those outside of the subsytem—were considered to be ill-equipped to rationally debate and resolve such complex issues. This technocratic ethic, it can be argued, bolstered the autonomy and political legitimacy of subsystem actors by making it difficult for outsiders to challenge their decisions. And it seems likely that subgovernment insiders consciously reinforced this belief as part of an effort to limit debate on the atomic program. Green and Rosenthal conclude that during the period in question "the JCAE did not conceive its mission to be one of informing Congress or stimulating Congressional and public discussion of atomic energy. On the contrary, the Committee's attitude seemed to be that the atomic energy program could be debated in Congress only by those with immediate responsibility who were already privy to atomic secrets—in effect, only by members of the JCAE."[40] By defining the issue in a particular way, members of the subsystem were able to control who had access to information about atomic energy, and under what conditions. Because subgovernments thrive under conditions of limited information, the subgovernment's exclusive possession of atomic information enabled it to maintain and strengthen its own position within the policy arena.[41]

The general public, for the most part, was not interested in the atomic program, because the program did not appear to have any direct impact on their lives.[42] Of course, if the public had been aware of problems stemming from the fallout that resulted from testing in Nevada, it seems safe to say more would have been interested in the atomic program. Nevertheless, at this time there were only a few atomic facilities, mostly located in remote regions, and the bulk of information about the program was classified. Few individuals or groups were in a position to gain or lose much from AEC or JCAE decisions. Therefore, few were interested in the atom, and as a consequence interest group activity, aside from the scientists and contractors working for the AEC, was negligible.

THE EARLY 1950s

With the dawn of the new decade there was a subtle but significant shift in the nation's atomic energy plans. The principal focus remained on the atom's military aspects, but government officials recognized that the so-called "peaceful uses" of the atom could also serve a variety of important objectives in both domestic and foreign policy. Although the cold war dictated that the program's primary purpose would continue to be weapons production, the joint committee began to urge the AEC to put more emphasis on developing and promoting the peaceful uses of atomic energy. At the time, the most likely prospect for peaceful applications was the production of electricity from atomic fission.

Despite this subtle shift in the program's avowed goals, it was still largely justified by national security arguments. The national interest, it was argued, demanded the development of a viable nuclear power industry. For example, it was widely acknowledged that it was important for the United States, which emerged from World War II as a military and economic superpower, to keep ahead of the world scientifically. Science, after all, had forever transformed the nature of modern warfare with the splitting of the atom, and there were compelling reasons to believe that the peaceful atom would have a similarly revolutionary effect on society. For the United States to develop the peaceful atom would be an effective mechanism both for retaining its edge in the atomic field and for solidifying the nation's scientific reputation. AEC Chair Gordon Dean expressed this sentiment to the joint committee when he remarked that "it would be a major setback to the position of this country in the world to allow its present leadership in nuclear power development to pass out of its hands."[43]

Aside from enhancing the nation's reputation and providing an abundant source of energy, finding a constructive use for the atom would also further the nation's postwar geopolitical aims. The explosion of the Soviet atomic bomb in

1949 punctuated the end of the American nuclear monopoly. American officials worried that the Soviets would try to develop the "peaceful" atom before the United States in order to reap the propaganda benefits; they were also concerned that the Soviets would try to exploit the situation for political gain. This prospect was not a pleasant one for those responsible for managing the nation's atomic program. In the words of joint committee member Chet Holifield, "We cannot be indifferent to the enormous psychological advantage that the Soviets would gain if they demonstrated to a tense and divided world the ability to put the atom to work in peacetime civilian pursuits. . . . The United States will not take second place in the contest."[44] In much the same vein, in 1953 AEC commissioner Thomas Murray warned that U.S. interests would be harmed if the Soviets built the first nuclear power plant, because the peaceful atom could translate into real foreign policy gains. The *London Times* quoted Murray as saying, "Once we become fully conscious of the possibility that power-hungry nations will gravitate towards the USSR if it wins the nuclear power race, it will be quite clear that this power race is no Everest-climbing, kudos-providing contest."[45]

Although American officials were preoccupied with the USSR, they were also concerned that other nations would try to develop their own atomic capabilities. The events of 1949 had shown that the United States no longer had a monopoly on the atom, and that the knowledge and ability to build atomic weapons would inevitably spread to other nations. It was commonly accepted, for example, that it was only a matter of time before Great Britain and France would join the "atomic club." Other nations would surely do the same and launch their own atomic programs whether the United States wanted them to or not. Faced with this reality, the United States wanted to be in a position to control nuclear proliferation to ensure that it was compatible with American perceptions of world order. Government decision makers recognized that in order to avoid losing influence around the globe the United States would have to assert its leadership and share some atomic information, and secrets, with other nations.[46]

With these objectives in mind, in a speech to the United Nations in December 1953, President Eisenhower launched an initiative that came to be known as "Atoms for Peace." The program was clearly an effort to distinguish between the peaceful and military applications of the atom while identifying the United States with the peaceful applications. Although the rhetoric of the proposal was crafted to improve the reputation of the United States, in reality the Atoms for Peace plan served a number of American foreign policy goals.[47] The Atoms for Peace proposal, according to two researchers, was "in fact nothing less than a coherent global strategy for protecting Western Europe from Soviet domination." A strong and free Western Europe was seen as essential to the containment of Soviet expansionism and, therefore, to the maintenance of world order. If the United States could develop the atom as a source of power, it was argued, it would be a boon to Western European industries and economies while helping to contain the Soviets. In this sense, it is accurate to think of Atoms for Peace as an "atomic Marshall plan."[48]

The Atoms for Peace proposal had the added attraction of assisting American industry by providing access to potentially rewarding markets. According to the terms of the bilateral agreements signed pursuant to the Euratom program, which was essentially the legislative enactment of Atoms for Peace, European nations contracted with American firms for all atomic technologies and materials. The attraction of these agreements, as one Babcock and Wilcox official wrote to the joint committee, was that they were "a means of securing a good and early foothold in Euratom countries for American pressurized and boiling water reactor types."[49] Furthermore, there was an assumption that the European market would be a lucrative one: a panel appointed by the joint committee in 1955 reported that "the potential demand may represent a $30 billion market."[50]

INDUSTRY AND THE ATOM

There were some significant changes in the objectives of subsystem actors in the early 1950s. First, more time and resources would be devoted to the peaceful applications of atomic energy. More specifically, a greater emphasis would be placed on developing atomic reactors for the purpose of producing electricity. Second, it was widely acknowledged that the United States, for the reasons already discussed, would have to exchange atomic information with its allies. In practice, achieving these objectives would require greater participation by private industry in the United States and greater access to information by allied nations. This approach was well understood by government officials. The JCAE held hearings in 1953 for the purpose of reviewing the McMahon Act. The overwhelming consensus among those who testified was that the Atomic Energy Act of 1946 would have to be amended if commercial nuclear power was to become a reality, and that government assistance would be an integral part of that effort.[51] The elaborate security restrictions of the McMahon Act, together with the government monopoly on all atomic information and materials, impeded both the proposed Atoms for Peace program and the development of the atom as an energy source.

Although American firms were expressing an interest in atomic power, the calls for revising the Atomic Energy Act of 1946 to allow for greater industrial participation came primarily from the U.S. government and not from American industry, which was not prepared to assume the full responsibility for development because of the financial risks involved. In contrast to coal plants, the initial costs for nuclear plants would undoubtedly be high, profits uncertain, and the technology new and potentially hazardous. In addition, projected demand for electricity in the early 1950s provided utilities with little incentive to build additional generating capacity. Furthermore, there were no reliable estimates of the possible damages stemming from a serious reactor accident. Nevertheless, development of the peaceful atom was assumed to be vitally important to addressing a number of "problems" confronting the United States in the 1950s.

Energy requirements, the need to control nuclear proliferation, the desire to contain the Soviets, and the determination to maintain the nation's leadership position in the atomic field lent a sense of urgency to the atomic program. If the nuclear industry would not take the necessary steps to solve these problems, the U.S. government would. In fact, it is misleading to even speak of a "nuclear power industry" before 1954, because properly speaking none existed. To be sure, a number of firms had been involved with the atom since the Manhattan Project, but the Atomic Energy Act of 1946 prohibited private ownership of atomic materials and facilities and allowed only the most limited access to atomic information. Atomic energy was, for all intents and purposes, a government monopoly. Subsystem actors, however, believed there was a need for commercial nuclear power, and they were committed to satisfying that need. The "solution" to the government's "problems" was the Atomic Energy Act of 1954 which, in effect, created both commercial nuclear power and a commercial nuclear power industry. In this sense, the development of commercial nuclear power is unusual in that it emerged from an effort initiated by government rather than by private industry.[52]

THE ATOMIC ENERGY ACT OF 1954

According to the McMahon Act, only the AEC could own fissionable materials and utilization facilities, and only the AEC, for national security reasons, had access to all relevant atomic information. In order to open the door to greater industrial and international participation, Congress loosened the restrictions on access to previously classified information, permitted the private ownership of nuclear facilities and allowed the private use of fissionable materials through a system of AEC licensing, liberalized patent laws in the atomic energy field, and offered a number of economic incentives to private industry.[53]

The Atomic Energy Act of 1954 can be viewed as an attempt by the U.S. government to give, in the words of joint committee chair Sterling Cole (R-N.Y.), "a material and substantive start in law to a new atomic industry."[54] In pursuit of that goal, the act revised the patent laws in the atomic energy field to permit the patenting of nonmilitary inventions, because normalized patent laws were thought to be a necessary prerequisite for large-scale industrial participation in reactor development.[55] Much of the congressional debate on the 1954 act centered on the patent issue, with many corporate spokesmen testifying in favor of a liberalization of the patent laws. Republican members of the JCAE favored restoring the atomic energy field to the normal patent system immediately, believing it would spark inventive effort in reactor development. Otherwise, they argued, an inventor would have no incentive to invent, and as a result the reactor program would not move ahead. On the other hand, Democratic members of the joint committee, as well as the AEC, believed the federal government had a responsibility to see that firms that had been involved in the atomic program from the beginning did not have an unfair advantage in the newly created nuclear power industry. According to this view, these firms could use the knowledge and experience they had obtained while under contract with the government to preempt any competition. Fearing a "giveaway" to these firms, a coalition of JCAE Democrats and the AEC pushed for a five-year transition period to normalized patent laws, hoping that this stipulation would prevent the formation of private nuclear monopolies. Their position prevailed, but given the amounts of capital involved in the research and development of nuclear technology, the revised patents policy by itself could not prevent the eventual formation of a private nuclear monopoly.

Although the Atomic Energy Act of 1954 reflected the consensus among subsystem actors on the stated objective of encouraging "the development and utilization of atomic energy for peaceful purposes," there were disagreements as to the best means of achieving that goal. Generally, Democrats on the joint committee wanted the government to be more actively involved in developing reactor technology, while joint committee Republicans, along with the president and the AEC, favored a larger role for the private sector, arguing that private business offered the best means of developing atomic power. This issue, along with the larger issue of public versus private power, would be a source of conflict within the joint committee and between the joint committee and the AEC for years to come.[56] Lewis Strauss, chairman of the AEC, was an ardent advocate of free enterprise and private power.[57] Strauss's outspokenness often put him at odds with JCAE Democrats such as Chet Holifield and Clinton Anderson, who were enthusiastic proponents of public power. Public power advocates, especially those on the JCAE, viewed the generation of electricity from the atom as a key to economic growth in rural areas. The hope was that nuclear electricity would provide the same benefits to other areas as the Tennessee Valley Authority (TVA) had for many regions in the South. For the business-oriented Eisenhower administration, on the other hand, the TVA symbolized everything that was wrong with the New Deal. Not surprisingly, the public versus private power controversy was often quite bitter and was the notable exception to the absence of conflict among subsystem actors during the 1950s.

The Atomic Energy Act of 1954, as a consequence, contained a number of compromises concerning this dispute. The act allowed public power agencies, such as the TVA, to build and operate reactors, but it prohibited the AEC from going into the power business itself.[58] Section 44 of the new Atomic Energy Act, for example, was intended to encourage the growth of a private nuclear power industry. This provision, while granting the AEC authority to construct large-scale reactors for research and development purposes, prohibited the agency from building reactors for the sole purpose of selling or generating electric power; in effect, it reserved the area for private enterprise.[59]

Section 2 of the act made the AEC responsible for developing, promoting, and regulating nuclear power.[60] From the outset, this statutory conflict of interest would be problematic as it became apparant that the AEC would emphasize its promotional and developmental responsibilities at the expense of its regulatory duties. Although the joint committee at one point considered creating separate agencies for development and regulation, at the time there were good reasons for combining the two tasks in one agency. The supply of qualified technical personnel was presumed to be so limited that it would have been difficult to staff two separate agencies. Second, because atomic technology was so new and there were still many unknowns, it seemed unwise to create separate regulatory and developmental agencies. By combining the two tasks in a single organization, it was assumed that each branch of the agency would benefit from the other's presence. Information obtained by the development staff often would be useful to the regulatory branch and vice versa. In addition, at this early stage the regulatory and developmental roles seemed like two sides of the same coin. On the one hand, if the AEC's efforts to encourage atomic development were unproductive, the scope of the regulatory program would be diminished. On the other hand, the AEC recognized that a reactor accident would hinder the development of an atomic industry, and that an effective regulatory program was therefore essential to program growth.[61] The problem facing the commission was how to perform its developmental and regulatory functions simultaneously.

Congress, through the Atomic Energy Act of 1954, offered little guidance on how to resolve this dilemma. The act delegated a considerable amount of authority to the AEC, leaving it to the AEC to determine how to most effectively implement its regulatory and developmental programs. The Atomic Energy Act of 1954, for example, directed the AEC "to protect the health and safety of the public," but the statute contained little guidance as to how to achieve that broadly defined goal. Although such an expansive grant of authority was not unusual, it would prove to be a problem as the atomic program moved into its commercial phase. The legislative history also provides little evidence as to the meaning of this vaguely defined goal: although the act contains thirty-one references to "the health and safety of the public," there are none in the legislative history.[62]

In passing the Atomic Energy Act of 1954, Congress provided the AEC with little guidance on establishing regulations or defining safety objectives. The act did make clear, however, that Congress did not want the AEC to impose burdensome regulations during the early stages of the development process. Section 104b, under which all of the reactors in the AEC's Power Reactor Demonstration Program were licensed, instructed the AEC to "impose the minimum amount of such regulations and terms of license as will permit the Commission to fulfill its obligations under this Act to promote the common defense and security and to protect the health and safety of the public."[63] Additionally, the JCAE and the industry made it clear that they wanted regulations to be as simple as possible to encourage private participation in the atomic industry. Under section 202 of the Atomic Energy Act of 1954, the JCAE was required to hold annual hearings to assess the industry's progress. At the first "202" hearings, JCAE members commented frequently on the need for the AEC to keep licensing regulations and procedures simple.[64] This environment reinforced the agency's inclination to consider the potential impact of proposed regulations on the development of the atomic industry. At the same hearings Lewis Strauss told the JCAE that regulations "should not impose unnecessary limitations or restrictions upon private participation in the development of the atom's uses." Consistent with his fervent belief in private enterprise, Strauss noted at another time that "the AEC's objective in the formation of regulations was to minimize government control of competitive enterprise."[65] In much the same vein, Kenneth Nichols, then the AEC general manager, claimed that the principles of AEC regulations were to "get into the licensee's business as little as possible."[66] These comments indicate that from the beginning the AEC gave extensive consideration to the effect its proposed procedures and regulations would have on the young industry. The problem for the AEC was that such an approach, while acceptable at this early stage of the industry's development, would lead to problems when the industry and the technology were more mature.

Although the Atomic Energy Act of 1954 gave the AEC the responsibility of balancing the goal of stimulating industry growth with the need to assure public health and safety, its actions during the 1950s and 1960s displayed a consistent emphasis on promotional rather than regulatory issues. According to one study of the AEC's regulatory procedures and organizations, the conflict between promotion and regulation was accentuated in these early years by two factors. First, the technology was new and complex, so it was difficult for either the industry or the AEC's regulatory branch to establish precise standards because technology was changing so rapidly. Second, reactors were not economically competitive with fossil fuel plants, so electric utilities did not have the normal incentives to construct reactors. As a result, the AEC had to offer a variety of incentives, including economic assistance, to the nuclear industry.[67] In a sense, the AEC was to build an industry it would then have to regulate.

The Atomic Energy Act of 1954 created a built-in conflict of interest by giving one agency the responsibility for regulating and promoting the atomic industry. In its efforts to balance the two tasks, the AEC consistently gave precedence to its development programs, which is not surprising given the AEC's own conception of its primary mission and the constant pressure from the joint committee to expand its reactor development programs. Congress, after all, had directed the AEC to impose the "minimum amount" of regulation consistent with assuring health and safety and, with the passage of the Atomic Energy Act of 1954, created a regulatory framework conducive to the development of a commercial nuclear power industry. In carrying out its duties, the AEC tried to minimize the financial risks and maximize the opportunities for profit in the private sector in order to induce firms to pursue the nuclear option. The AEC, responsible for developing and regulating the same industry, was forced to seek a balance, but the need to encourage development seemed more pressing.[68]

One example of how the AEC used its substantial discretion to emphasize its promotional responsibilities involves the granting of licenses for utilization facilities. The Atomic Energy Act of 1954 established two classes of licenses for such facilities. All of the reactors licensed by the AEC in these early years under its Power Reactor Demonstration Program received the less restrictive "class 104" licenses, which were intended for reactors used in research, medical therapy, and power demonstration. In issuing class 104 licenses, the AEC was instructed "to impose the minimum amount of such regulations and terms of license" that would allow the commission to fulfill its obligations to protect public health and safety.[69] The issuance of class 104 licenses to early reactors was an indication that the AEC and joint committee did not want to burden the nuclear industry by imposing regulations that could impede advances in atomic energy.[70] Such behavior was also an early indication that the AEC would emphasize its developmental efforts rather than its regulatory duties.

The 1954 amendments also gave the JCAE the power to authorize AEC appropriations, something it lacked under the 1946 statute. Although this authority was not unique, it was unusual, since in the case of most government agencies with programmatic responsibilities Congress has reserved the right to authorize activities by statute before funds could be appropriated. The JCAE became increasingly dissatisfied because the House Appropriations Committee often ignored its advice and cut programs and the AEC's budget. If the JCAE had the power to authorize expenditures, on the other hand, it would be able to exert greater control over the AEC and therefore over the pace and scope of reactor development programs.[71] Section 261 of the revised act required specific legislative authorization of all appropriations for "acquisition or condemnation of any real property or any facility acquisition, construction, or expansion."[72] In 1957, when the AEC interpreted the term "facility" to exclude from the authorization process certain experimental reactors, section 261 was amended to make it clear that authorization was required for any nonmilitary experimental reactor designed to produce more than 10,000 kilowatts of heat or to be used in the production of electric power. At the same time, it was amended to require authorization for any AEC cooperative program involving the use of AEC funds directly or indirectly for development and construction of demonstration reactors.[73]

THE POWER REACTOR DEMONSTRATION PROGRAM

Despite the stated intentions of the Atomic Energy Act of 1954 to encourage the development of the peaceful uses of atomic energy, private industry was reluctant to jump into the business of reactor development. As a result, the joint committee and AEC created a number of programs and subsidies to induce participation by private firms. Examples of such incentives include the provision of reactor technology research and development; the legalization of private ownership of nuclear facilities and fuels; government subsidies for fuel costs, reprocessing, and waste disposal; favorable tax policies; and liability limits in the event of a nuclear accident.[74]

In early 1955 the AEC announced one such effort—the Power Reactor Demonstration Program (PRDP). The PRDP was designed to encourage industry participation in the commercial power program by subsidizing the construction of reactors. The PRDP encouraged research on a number of reactor designs in the hope that it would provide the government and industry with valuable information that could spur the achievement of economically competitive power. The AEC sought competitive proposals for cooperative projects from applicants who were willing to assume the risks of construction, ownership, and operation of nuclear reactors. According to the terms of the program, the AEC would assist the privately financed projects by waiving for seven years the charges for the loan of source and special materials; by performing in its laboratories, free of charge, certain research and development work; and by agreeing to purchase technical and economic data from the participants under fixed-sum contracts.[75]

The AEC, by encouraging research on a variety of reactor designs, hoped to determine which designs were most promising from both a safety and economic standpoint. As initially formulated, the AEC announced a 1 April 1955 deadline for industry proposals. Only four were received. The tepid response was an indication that private enterprise remained skeptical about nuclear power. More specifically, private utilities viewed the PRDP as a "smokescreen" for federal support of publicly owned utilities.[76]

After a similarly muted response to the program's second round, the joint committee grew increasingly dissatisfied with the AEC and the pace of its reactor development program. In particular, JCAE Democrats believed that the reactor development program was stagnating, and that the AEC was not doing enough to encourage progress in the field. Indeed, the JCAE was frequently urging the commission to accelerate its commercial power programs. Against this backdrop, in January 1957 the AEC announced a third round of industry proposals, which was designed to encourage private utilities to finance the construction of advanced reactor designs.[77] Still, Democrats on the joint committee wanted the government to play a larger role in reactor development. Two joint committee Democrats, Chet Holifield of California and Albert Gore of Tennessee, sponsored a bill that called for authorizing $400 million for the AEC to construct, own, and operate six full-scale demonstration plants. The Gore-Holifield bill, opposed by the administration and the AEC, set off one of the most bitter conflicts in the program's history, splitting the joint committee along partisan lines. Although the bill passed in the Senate, it was defeated on the floor of the House and was one of the rare occasions that partisan differences intruded on atomic policy debates.

The Atomic Energy Act of 1954 contained several additional provisions to overcome industry's reluctance to enter the field. The AEC would provide fuel for the reactors free of charge for a seven-year period, provide assistance for research and development of possible reactor designs, and conduct its own research in the AEC's national laboratories to aid in reactor design. In fact, the AEC employed a mixture of threats and incentives to induce industry interest.[78] For example, even though the AEC retained ownership of all fissionable materials, through a system of AEC licensing the Atomic Energy Act of 1954 made these materials available to firms, including both the fuel for nuclear reactors and the fissionable materials produced by nuclear reactors. Because there was still a "shortage" of fissionable materials for atomic weapons, the AEC agreed to purchase all of the plutonium produced in private reactors at a guaranteed price. According to the 1954 act, in setting this price the AEC was to "take into consideration the value of the special nuclear material for its intended use by the United States and may give such weight to the actual cost of producing the material as the Commission finds equitable."[79] In other words, the AEC had the discretion to base the price of plutonium on its value as a weapon rather than on its actual cost to the reactor owner. This provision gave the AEC a great deal of leeway, and in general the prices it established were significantly below the actual cost of production.

The Atomic Energy Act of 1954 also allowed the AEC to waive charges for materials used in power reactors. Section 53(c) of the act only requires the AEC to exact a charge for materials from the owners of "commercial reactors." Since most power reactors at the time were deemed not to be of practical value under section 104, they were not commercial, and hence the fuel charges could be waived.[80]

THE PRICE-ANDERSON ACT

Even with these subsidies, the nuclear industry was reluctant to assume complete responsibility for the risks involved with nuclear power. The underlying reason for this reluctance was the fear that they would be held liable for any and all damages resulting from a reactor accident. Although the AEC had an impressive safety record with its reactors, the technology was new and largely untested. Furthermore, there were no guarantees that the industry would remain accident-free in the future, and because the potential damages from an accident were unknown, the reactor vendors and electric utilities were unwilling to make a full-scale commitment to nuclear power. The industry wanted some form of government protection from liability claims before proceeding with their reactor plans.[81] The problem was that the potential liability from a reactor accident was so large it was unlikely that either nuclear vendors or utilities would be able to obtain the necessary insurance from private insurers. The fear of financial disaster led the industry to seek legislation limiting their liability in the event of an accident.

The AEC and the joint committee were also concerned about this potential obstacle to the development of an atomic energy industry and, after industry prompting, began to study the insurance question. In 1956 industry witnesses at the JCAE's annual hearings on the development, growth, and state of the atomic energy industry testified on the need for insurance protection in the event of a reactor mishap. Walker Cisler, representing Detroit Edison, told the joint commmittee that "the absolute necessity of insurance against a catastrophe involving extensive public liability, in adequate amount, cannot be overstressed."[82]

In March 1956 the JCAE held an informal seminar with representatives from the AEC, reactor vendors, electric utilities, and the insurance industry. Representatives of the utilities and reactor vendors emphasized that the protection provided by the insurance industry would likely be inadequate. Because the potential damages from an accident could be so high, they argued that indemnification, in which the government would give general protection to the atomic industry against uninsured liability to the public, was needed to allow development to proceed. Representatives from the insurance industry indicated that they opposed some of the other proposals under consideration, most of which involved some form of government insurance. The reason was simple: the insurance industry did not want the U.S. government to enter the insurance business. The AEC had also expressed a preference for indemnification rather than insurance. In the end, the seminar reached a consensus in support of some legislative action to guarantee government protection above that offered by private insurers.[83]

The joint committee then went to work on drafting legislation. The problem of what type of protection—indemnification or government insurance—was easily resolved because none of the interested parties opposed indemnification. Rather, the problem was to determine how much protection the government would offer. Private insurers had already agreed to provide $60 million of protection for each nuclear facility, which was far more than had been made available to any other industry. It was entirely possible, however, that damages from a reactor accident would far exceed $60 million. As a result, the AEC favored unlimited indemnity for the nuclear industry. The joint committee, on the other hand, recommended that the government offer limited indemnity of up to $500 million above any third-party liability insurance provided by the insurance industry. The $500 million figure was not based on any reliable scientific evidence or calculations; rather, it seems to have been based on political expediency. According to one account, JCAE staff director James Ramey suggested the number because it was halfway between zero and one billion dollars.[84] Another account claims the figure was chosen because it satisfied the industry's demands for liability protection without offering the industry a "blank check," and because it was large enough to suggest to the public that something was being done but not so large as to "frighten the country and the Congress to death."[85] In total, then, the JCAE recommended a liability ceiling of $560 million in the event of an accident.

The joint committee bill was introduced in Congress in May 1956. Named after its sponsors, Melvin Price in the House and Clinton Anderson in the Senate, the Price-Anderson bill reflected the years of study devoted to the insurance question. The bill was a classic example of legislative compromise hammered out between the insurance and nuclear industries, the AEC, and the joint committee. The insurance bill would eventually be approved by Congress in 1957, but not before undergoing some important revisions.

During deliberations, three key amendments were added to the Price-Anderson bill. The first called for granting statutory standing to the Advisory Committee on Reactor Safeguards (ACRS). The second required ACRS reports to be made public, and the third mandated public hearings on every reactor application. The AEC disliked these amendments but decided not to oppose them because of the need for the indemnity legislation.[86] Representatives from the nuclear industry supported the proposed changes because they believed the amendments would increase the public's trust in the licensing process, and because the industry did not want to jeopardize the insurance portions of the bill. These amendments would later prove to be critical factors in the subgovernment's demise; opponents were able to take advantage of the changes to obtain program information and gain access to policy deliberations. Nevertheless, in hearings before the joint committee, Francis McCune, vice president of General Electric, testified that the proposed law had the support "of almost every group in any way connected with atomic activities." Calling the absence of liability protection a "major obstacle" to private participation in the atomic program, he went on to say that a recent poll by the Atomic Industrial Forum revealed that the liability question "was rated second only to the lack of economic incentives as a roadblock to further progress."[87] Sponsored by two members of the JCAE, the Price-Anderson legislation was passed by a voice vote in the House; there was no debate on the legislation in the Senate. President Eisenhower signed the bill into law on 2 September 1957.[88]

That such a remarkable bill could be passed in both chambers of Congress with such ease illustrates the influence of the joint committee. It also reflects the consensus in government on the unquestioned desirability of commercial nuclear power. Significantly, like the Atomic Energy Act of 1954, the Price-Anderson bill was an effort by subgovernment insiders to remove certain "obstacles" to the development an atomic energy industry. The "problem" of atomic insurance was of interest only to those involved in the atomic program; it was not an issue that received much attention from the general public or the press. In the words of Mazuzan and Walker, the "basic purpose" of Price-Anderson was "to reduce a significant impediment to the development of the atomic industry"; even the regulatory amendments "were partly an effort to promote the industry, since building public confidence in the licensing process" was considered to be "essential" for the development of an atomic industry.[89]

After the adoption of the Price-Anderson Act, private participation in nuclear power slowly picked up. Although the liability limit eased industry fears, reactor orders remained at low levels for the next few years because nuclear electricity was still much more expensive to generate than electricity produced by conventional fuels like coal and oil. However, the words and actions of government officials convinced the nuclear industry that in the future there would be nuclear power in America, with or without the participation of private enterprise. Many private utilities decided to purchase reactors in order to gain an advantage for the future; others bought reactors because they wanted to keep the federal government out of the power business. The big fear of many utilities was that the federal government would build reactors on its own and give the power to public corporations. Consequently, the fear of public power led utilities to invest in reactors before they were economically competitive. The AEC and JCAE were cognizant of this fear and used it to influence the industry's actions. For example, Lewis Strauss, then AEC chairman, invoked the specter of public power as a thinly disguised threat to private utilities in a much publicized speech, saying, "It is the Commission's policy to give the industry the opportunity to undertake the construction of power reactors. However, if industry does not, within a reasonable period of time, undertake to build the type of reactors which are considered promising, the Commission will take steps to build the reactors at its own initiative."[90]

The government's commitment to the development of reactor technology is well documented. By 1962, the AEC had spent over $1.2 billion to develop reactor technology; this figure was double the amount spent by private business. One Department of Energy study concluded that without the federal subsidies nuclear electricity would be 50 percent more expensive. These calculations did not include federal tax write-offs for utilities nor did they include money spent on programs with possible military implications.[91]

It would be some time before the AEC's regulatory program became more rigorous. The commission continued to emphasize its developmental and promotional responsibilities, and as of 1960, members of the commission estimated that they devoted only one-sixth to one-third of their time to regulatory matters.[92] The preoccupation with development makes sense when one considers that the only parties interested in the agency's actions, the atomic industry and the joint committee, were strong advocates of development. During this period the general public, if they expressed any opinion about atomic energy at all, also supported greater development. Another reason the commission devoted so little time and resources to regulatory issues was because there were few facilities to regulate. Although utilities were becoming more interested in the nuclear option, electricity from atomic fission was not yet competitive with that generated from burning fossil fuels. By the mid-1960s, in fact, there were only six operating nuclear plants, all producing less than 265 MWe, which was less than 1 percent of the total electricity-generating capacity in the United States at the time.[93] As a consequence, aside from the controversy over the PRDC, the commissioners were rarely confronted with regulatory matters, so it is not surprising that they emphasized developmental tasks.

Because the regulated industry is directly affected by the agency's decisions and thus has a strong incentive to pay attention to the agency's actions, it is often argued that regulatory agencies are overly responsive to the interests of the regulated industry. The general public, on the other hand, may not perceive that its interests are affected by the agency's decisions and therefore may not closely monitor its actions. The asymmetry between public and industry interests is especially pronounced with regard to agencies that regulate only one industry,[94] which appears to be the case with the AEC. Aside from the JCAE and the nuclear industry, who both supported the development of nuclear power, no one was paying much attention to AEC actions during the 1950s and early 1960s. Consequently, the AEC had only one constituency group and one source of political support. This asymmetry was compounded in the case of the AEC because the agency was also responsible for promoting and developing the use of atomic energy.

Eventually, the AEC recognized that a stronger regulatory organization and a more efficient licensing process would be necessary in the future, when more reactors would be licensed. Accordingly, in an effort to increase public confidence in both the agency and its reactor review process, the AEC revised both its regulatory branch and its licensing procedures in the late 1950s and early 1960s.[95] Since so few utilities thus far had applied for reactor licenses and because there were only a handful of reactors in operation, the AEC's regulatory staff was small and inexperienced. According to L. Manning Muntzing, the AEC's director of regulation at the time, the AEC's regulatory staff was so small during this period that "the standards zealots could meet in a phone booth."[96] Furthermore, because there were only a few reactors, there was little operating experience to determine if reactor designs assured public health and safety or if the AEC's few existing reactor safety criteria were adequate. Not only was the lack of operating experience a problem, but the job of establishing adequate safety regulations and standards, for example, was made even more difficult by the many uncertainties about the new technology. In many respects, the AEC's staff was forced to make judgments based on either incomplete information or unproven theories and assumptions. Under these circumstances, the staff and the industry believed regulations and standards should be flexible enough to encourage innovation. The staff was also cognizant of the need to avoid burdening the industry with unnecessarily stringent regulations, because industry success is typically one of the criteria by which regulatory agencies are evaluated.[97]

Detailed involvement in an industry's affairs is frequently a source of clientelism. In these years, the AEC's regulatory and development staffs worked closely with one another and with applicants for construction permits and operating licenses to resolve outstanding safety questions. Because the AEC's staff was small and inexperienced, however, it often depended on the nuclear industry for technical assistance and information concerning reactor design and safety standards.[98] On one level, this approach made sense: who knew a proposed reactor better than those who designed it? Seen from another perspective, such behavior amounted to self-regulation.

In this early developmental period, the licensing process was conducted in an informal, ad hoc manner because both the nuclear industry and the AEC staff were operating in uncharted territory. Owing to the rapidly evolving technology, during this period no two reactor applications were the same, which meant in essence that the review process for each application for a reactor license was different and that the AEC would proceed on a case-by-case basis. In reviewing the application, the AEC's staff would work closely with the applicant. The licensing review, conducted in a cooperative manner and characterized by informal negotiations, was frequently a learning process for both parties. Part of the explanation for the cooperative atmosphere stemmed from the parties' similar goals: both the staff and the applicant wanted to expedite the licensing of nuclear plants. For example, any major differences on safety issues between the staff and the applicant were usually resolved during this informal review process. Indeed, the vendor and the applicant had considerable access to the regulatory staff during the early stages of the review process. This almost continual access was instrumental in developing a good working relationship with the staff, but it would later lead to charges that the AEC's licensing process was biased in favor of the applicant and against any intervenors opposing the plant. With the exception of the PRDC's Fermi reactor, however, all reactor applications until the summer of 1962 were uncontested by members of the public.

An important year in the atomic energy program was 1962. Following the election of John F. Kennedy, Democrats on the joint committee were optimistic that the atomic program would receive greater support. Accordingly, JCAE chairman Chet Holifield wrote to President Kennedy on February 13, urging him to increase funds for the AEC's reactor programs. Holifield also told Kennedy that it was time to "begin some practical demonstrations" and that "we have invested almost a billion dollars in atomic power development and have only a relatively short way to go to achieve economic nuclear power."[99] Holifield had a supporter in the new chairman of the AEC, Glenn T. Seaborg, a chemist with extensive experience in nuclear research and a strong advocate of atomic energy. In an effort to obtain greater support for his agency, Seaborg suggested that Kennedy ask the AEC for a report that would take a new look at the role of atomic energy in the nation's future. Entitled *Civilian Nuclear Power—A Report to the President,* the study claimed that fossil fuel supplies would be depleted in seventy-five to two hundred years. It therefore recommended supplementing fossil fuels with other energy sources where possible. Not surprisingly, the AEC re port concluded that nuclear power was "on the threshold of being competitive with conventional power" and "with relatively modest assistance by the AEC," nuclear energy could "and should make an important and, eventually, a vital contribution toward meeting our long-term energy requirements." The report optimistically predicted that nuclear power could contribute up to half of the nation's generating capacity by the end of the century.[100] By some accounts a "promotional paean" designed to win support for the AEC's development efforts, the AEC's study was significant because it marked the end of the developmental stage of nuclear power and the beginning of a stage of rapid expansion.[101]

CONCLUSION

Commercial atomic energy began under conditions almost ideally suited to the formation of a subgovernment. As we have seen, public attention to atomic energy was high, and public understanding was mostly positive. Policymakers rushed to capitalize on this "wave of enthusiasm" by establishing laws and institutions to support the program. Actors in these institutions, in turn, worked to reinforce the positive perceptions. After the initial burst of enthusiasm, public attention faded, but the laws and institutions remained intact and restricted participation to program supporters. The result was a small but powerful policy monopoly.

The atomic energy program during this period supports Schattschneider's claim that every form of political organization has a bias in favor of some interests and against others.[102] Here the structure was biased in favor of the development and utilization of atomic energy. The combination of laws, institutions, and procedures established in these early years stacked the deck in favor of the "peaceful atom" for decades to come. The Atomic Energy Acts of 1946 and 1954, for example, formed the statutory framework for atomic energy decision making and provided generous government subsidies for commercial nuclear power. The Atomic Energy Act of 1954 essentially "created" a nuclear power industry and directed the AEC to take a number of steps to enhance the industry's prospects for survival. Similarly, the Price-Anderson legislation removed some of the economic obstacles to commercial development. Throughout this period, in fact, the AEC and JCAE consistently supported the development and utilization of atomic energy. The AEC and the joint committee were so supportive of the atomic program that Bupp and Derian referred to them as "soapboxes" for the nuclear industry.[103]

This case illustrates how those controlling important junctures in the political system may consciously structure the opportunities for access to the policymaking arena. In the case of atomic energy, subsystem actors first limited access by fostering the perception that atomic energy was a defense issue; in later years, access was restricted by the carefully tended notion that nuclear power was a highly technical issue suitable only for those with specialized knowledge. Program supporters also crafted decision-making rules and procedures to exclude outsiders.

Although the atom received a great deal of popular attention after the war, the atomic program itself, because it was a defense program, was shielded from outside scrutiny by stringent security restrictions. In addition, subsystem insiders often claimed that because the program involved complex scientific and technical information, only scientific "experts" should be admitted to policy-making circles, which further reduced the number of interested observers. Moreover, the number of operating reactors was quite small until the mid-1960s. Consequently, few in American society perceived any immediate direct costs or benefits from the atomic program; therefore, few had any incentive to pay much attention to it. To the extent that the American public even thought about the program at all, the predominant perception was that its benefits far outweighed any potential costs. This perception resulted in a situation where only a few found the program relevant. Those who were interested in the program—the AEC, the JCAE, the atomic scientists and engineers, and the nuclear industry—shared a belief that atomic energy had an almost unlimited potential. All were committed to the development and utilization of atomic energy, and all had a direct stake in the program's success. Not surprisingly, the relationships among these participants was usually characterized by a high degree of cooperation. According to Bupp and Derian, the case of nuclear power was a "textbook illustration" of how to guarantee the triumph of narrow interests over the public interest.[104]

Atomic energy during the 1950s and 1960s was also characterized by a high degree of policy stability. In their study of deregulation, Derthick and Quirk argued that status quo policy often results less from one group's overpowering influence in Congress than from a longtime absence of effective opposition from other actors.[105] This scenario appears to be the case with nuclear power during the 1950s and much of the 1960s. Only supporters were mobilized. Although the members of the atomic subgovernment were certainly powerful, the atomic energy program received little oversight from either the executive branch or from Congress. Nor did atomic energy receive much attention from interest groups. Indeed, for the twenty years following World War II, nuclear power was a nonissue for all except the AEC, the JCAE, and the nuclear industry. Effective access to decision making was open only to those with a direct economic or political stake in the development and utilization of atomic energy.

Despite its presumed autonomy, the subsystem was built on a more fragile foundation than many recognized. Installed nuclear capacity in 1965 was minimal—there were only a handful of small reactors operating around the country. But as Steven Del Sesto points out, while the complex nature of high technology generally confines decision making to the subsystem level, the ultimate use of a technology always spreads its effects throughout society.[106] As the atomic energy program shifted into its commercial phase and the number of nuclear plants increased, more persons came to perceive that their interests were potentially affected and began to demand access to policy-making circles. In the next chapter it will be shown how changing perceptions played a critical role in transforming the politics of nuclear power. An influx of new participants destabilized the subsystem and paved the way for its eventual collapse.

3
Redefining Nuclear Power

It must be considered that there is nothing more difficult to carry out, nor more doubt-ful of success, nor more dangerous to handle, than to initiate a new order of things.
—Machiavelli

In 1965 the politics of commercial nuclear power was of little concern to anyone not having a direct stake in the program's success. By the middle of the next de-cade, however, the policy-making arena was crowded and complex, and few issues in American politics were more visible or controversial. In this chapter I explain the roots of that transformation and confirm Baumgartner and Jones's claim that new understandings of policy issues attract the attention of new actors and thus contribute to the destruction of policy monopolies.[1] My contention is that the atomic subgovernment lost influence because commercial nuclear power came to be understood in new, less positive ways. Long perceived as a national security issue, in the late 1960s nuclear power came to be seen in the context of debates over environmental protection, public health and safety, and energy supplies. Eventually, it became part of even larger debates about government regulation of business, citizen participation, and democratic governance. As a result of these changing perceptions, subgovernment members lost the power to define the issue and control the parameters of debate. The subgovernment was soon radically transformed.

As understandings and perceptions shifted and became increasingly nega-tive, new actors were drawn to the nuclear issue. The new participants included other federal agencies, officials from state and local governments, and a number of prominent "public lobby groups." Many of the new participants would be critical of nuclear power. The influx of new participants, who brought their own opinions, shattered the consensus that had existed within the small atomic subgovernment. As one might expect, the mobilization of previously uninvolved interests disrupted the traditional patterns of policy making within the subsystem.[2] In short, when perceptions of the costs and benefits attending the nuclear program changed, so did the politics of nuclear power. So why did perceptions change?

Part of the answer is that information about nuclear power became more widely available. The autonomy of policy monopolies, we are told, is a factor of their ability to control information about their particular programs. Indeed, one observer concludes that "subgovernments thrive under conditions of minimal information."[3] Typically, subgovernments are small and actors have complementary goals; it stands to reason that the introduction of new actors and new viewpoints would threaten this consensus. We would therefore expect actors within a subgovernment to seek to shield their activities from outsiders to maintain the consensus. As we saw in the previous chapter, subgovernment members kept a very tight lid on program information for twenty years.

But as the nuclear industry entered its commercial phase during the 1960s, it became very difficult to maintain exclusive control of program information. With more reactors being licensed and built, more people became aware of and concerned about nuclear power. Many came to believe that nuclear power affected them and could even harm them, and as James Q. Wilson points out, it is the perceived distribution of costs and benefits rather than the actual distribution that shapes the way politics is conducted.[4] The amount of information the public has, then, is an important factor in shaping perceptions of an issue. In other instances, a "focusing event" such as a crisis or a revelation of misconduct or incompetence by policymakers may facilitate the flow of information, thus casting an issue in a new light.[5] When enough information, or information of a certain type, becomes public, perceptions of an issue may change, redefining it in the process. This is what happened in the case of nuclear power: there was an increase in the amount of information about nuclear power and a dramatic change in the nature of that information.

Perceptions of issues can also change as a result of deliberate political action, that is, someone may consciously seek to alter public or elite perceptions of an issue by highlighting its negative implications. In this case, local citizens' groups and several national environmental organizations tried to alter perceptions by calling attention to the potential environmental and safety consequences of nuclear reactors. As we shall see, they found willing allies among officials in state and local governments. Their actions offer a good illustration of E. E. Schattschneider's notion of the "scope of conflict." According to Schattschneider, every conflict consists of two parts: the few who are actively engaged and the larger audience who could potentially become engaged.[6] Politics thus almost always involves struggles between those seeking to privatize conflict and those seeking to socialize it, and issue definition is crucial to these battles because it can determine whether or not the audience seeks to become involved. In most cases, those who are unhappy with the existing state of affairs try to engage the audience because they hope that taking the dispute public will alter the balance of power among private interests. On the other hand, those seeking to defend the status quo, such as members of a subgovernment, strive to keep the audience on the sidelines and thus maintain their influence. Perceptions matter, and everyone knows it. Once perceptions change, policy making may change in some fundamental way; alliances may shift and so may policy outcomes.

NUCLEAR POWER IN THE 1960s

In December 1963 Jersey Central Power and Light signed a contract with General Electric to purchase a 515-megawatt boiling water reactor for a plant in Oyster Creek, New Jersey. This agreement seemed to herald both the arrival of nuclear power as a viable alternative for generating electricity and the beginning of widespread commercial acceptance of nuclear power in the United States. The Oyster Creek reactor was to be the first built without any direct government subsidy, and Jersey Central Power and Light claimed the plant would be more economical to operate than conventional power sources within five years.[7] Although utilities began to order reactors in increasing numbers, in reality the generation of electricity through nuclear fission was not yet economically competitive with fossil fuels, primarily because of the higher capital costs for nuclear plants. In fact, the plant was a "loss leader" designed to persuade electric utilities of the viability of light water reactor technology. The reactor was sold under a turnkey contract, in which General Electric agreed to absorb all the costs of designing and constructing the reactor for a fixed price, so that all the utility would have to do was "turn the key" to begin producing electricity. In the words of Bertram Wolfe, vice president of General Electric's nuclear division, "The turnkeys made the light water reactor a viable product. They got enough volume in the business that we could build an engineering staff, standardize our product, and put up facilities to mass produce things so that cost went down."[8] General Electric was not alone among reactor vendors in choosing this path; Westinghouse, their chief competitor, also sold a number of turnkey plants. Although it has been estimated that the two companies lost between $800 million and $1 billion on these plants, the strategy worked—utilities began purchasing increasing amounts of nuclear generating capacity.

The utility industry's sudden interest in nuclear reactors can be attributed to several factors. First, demand for electricity in the 1960s was growing at an annual rate of 7 percent; at that rate of growth, demand would double every ten years. Utilities, as a result, needed to order new plants to meet projected demand. At the same time, many public utility commissions were lowering prices, which further increased demand for electricity. Next, because utility profits are determined by

Table 3.1. The Great Bandwagon Market

Years	Number of Reactors Ordered	Total Nuclear Capacity (MWe)
1955–59	5	777
1960–64	7	3,650
1965–69	81	70,099
1970–74	142	157,078
1975–79	13	15,232

Source: Energy Information Administration, *Commercial Nuclear Power 1991: Prospects for the United States and the World* (Washington, D.C.: Government Printing Office, 1991), 105–10.

the size of their rate base, utilities had an incentive to build additional generating capacity and expand their rate base. Nuclear power was an especially attractive option because it was by far the most capital-intensive source of electricity.[9] Furthermore, the conventional wisdom in the utility industry was that larger plants would yield impressive economies of scale and result in cheaper electricity. Utilities therefore had a number of incentives to build nuclear plants. Consequently, there was a rapid increase in both the number and size of plants ordered after Oyster Creek. For example, American utilities ordered seventy reactors between 1963 and 1967, with approximately 80 percent of the orders being placed in 1966–67 (see Table 3.1). During that same period, the average capacity per reactor jumped from 550 MWe to 850 MWe. By 1972 the average capacity of new orders was 1,100 MWe. In fact, in 1967 nuclear power accounted for slightly more than half the total generating capacity ordered that year. The market for nuclear reactors was so good that some observers refer to this period as the "Great Bandwagon Market."[10]

But the Bandwagon Market was based on exceedingly optimistic projections and expectations of construction costs and operating performance. Because commercial generation of electricity from nuclear fission was in its infancy and still largely untested, there was little in the way of hard data or analyses concerning actual costs or performance. In these early years of the commercial program, the utilities, the commission, and the joint committee lacked the technical resources to assess the projections of reactor costs and efficiency offered by the reactor vendors. Not only did they lack the resources, but the AEC and JCAE also lacked the desire to carefully examine the vendors' claims. In their rush to commercialize light water reactor technology, the cost and efficiency estimates offered by reactor vendors were uncritically accepted by both the utilities and the AEC.[11] For their part, reactor vendors were eager to realize a return on the massive amounts of capital they had invested in the development of light water technology.

As in many subsystems, the flow of information resembled a "closed loop," with the vendors, utilities, and AEC citing the same estimates and numbers, leading one scholar to note that in this period the "distinction between promotional prospectus and critical evaluation became progressively more obscure."[12] Indeed, the distinction vanished completely. Bupp and Derian, in their study of the development of the light water reactor, note that "government officials regularly cited the nuclear industry's analyses of light water plants as proof of the success of their own research and development policies. The industry, in turn, cited those same government statements as official confirmation of its own claims about the economic competitiveness of its product. The result was a circular flow of mutually reinforcing assertions that apparantly intoxicated both parties."[13] Bupp and Derian conclude that "systematic confusion of expectation with fact, of hope with reality, has been the most characteristic feature of the entire thirty-year effort to develop nuclear power."[14]

This "systematic confusion" had very real consequences for the nuclear industry in general and reactor vendors in particular. Not only did the circular flow of economic claims intoxicate all involved, but it also "decisively altered the commercial strength" of the reactor vendors.[15] Electric utilities in the United States and abroad, caught up in the flood of good news about nuclear reactors, purchased more nuclear reactors and fewer fossil plants. According to the *New York Times,* by 1971 utilities in the United States were ordering equal amounts of nuclear and conventional plants, even though there was little operating experience on which to judge reliability.[16] The rush to nuclear power on the basis of the reactor vendors' early and exceedingly optimistic price estimates eventually came to haunt utilities that had purchased nuclear plants. It would eventually become apparent that many utilities did not possess the technical staff and resources needed for building or operating nuclear reactors. It would also become clear that nuclear plants were not as efficient or reliable as vendors had claimed. The optimistic predictions for nuclear power thus succeeded in establishing a market for the technology, but they also set the stage for the future economic problems that would ravage the industry.[17]

Such mutually reinforcing behavior is not unusual in subgovernments. Reactor vendors clearly had reason to produce analyses detailing the competitiveness of their product, while the AEC and the joint committee had strong institutional incentives to rely on the industry's estimates. After all, both were working toward assuring a viable nuclear power industry, and for the next few years at least, it seemed they had largely succeeded. Certainly, the subsystem had created a vast constituency for the program. According to one estimate, by the early 1970s the AEC had contracts with 538 corporations and 223 colleges and universities. Furthermore, private firms with AEC contracts employed approximately 125,000 workers.[18] One of the consequences of this liberal distribution of contracts and grants from the AEC was that in creating this constituency it reinforced the degree of consensus about the program. As in earlier years, knowledge of the nuclear program was available only to those who benefited from it, and the recipients of the subsystem's largesse had little incentive to criticize the program. For much of the 1960s, then, the nuclear power program was still characterized by low levels of participation and a high degree of consensus on its value. It was not until the emergence of the environment as a national issue that significant opposition to nuclear power emerged.

Early opposition to nuclear power was localized and emerged as a response to the potential environmental impact of particular reactors. Within a few years, however, local activists were joined by national environmental groups in a more general criticism of the environmental effects of nuclear reactors. By the early 1970s, critics were voicing significant concerns over a variety of potential safety problems at nuclear reactors, and questions were raised about the disposal of nuclear waste. Eventually, opponents of nuclear power broadened their attack to include objections to the political and social implications of nuclear technology. Although it had been unthinkable just five years before, by 1972 the atomic subgovernment found itself in the midst of a full-blown debate not only over the future of nuclear power, but over the future of nuclear politics as well. With each successive stage of the debate, the conflict over nuclear power escalated, introducing new participants and new issues.

THE ENVIRONMENT

The boom in the market for nuclear power plants coincided with the rise of the environment as an issue of national importance. A number of events, including the publication of Rachel Carson's *Silent Spring* and environmental disasters such as the oil spills off Santa Barbara in 1969, catapulted the environment into the nation's consciousness.[19] The two oil spills, for example, galvanized public attention with vivid pictures of despoiled beaches and dying animals covered in oil. Although a concern for the environment was certainly not unique to the 1960s, what was different was the widespread attention given to the issue by citizens, the press, and public officials. During the 1960s more people recognized that human activities had environmental consequences, many of which were harmful to human health and safety. The Santa Barbara oil spills hammered this message home.

The growing concern with environmental values was initially perceived by subsystem members as a boon to the prospects of nuclear power. The AEC and the nation's utilities actively promoted the notion that nuclear power was cleaner than coal and other sources of electricity. In fact, utilities often cited nuclear power's projected environmental superiority as one of the key factors in their decision to build nuclear plants.[20] This makes it all the more ironic that the first consistent opposition to nuclear power emerged in response to the potential environmental consequences of reactors.[21] For the most part, the early opposition to nuclear power was essentially local in nature, being directed at particular reactors and not at nuclear power itself. More specifically, concern during this period tended to focus on the thermal pollution caused by nuclear plants' discharge of heated water into nearby lakes and rivers. In the early 1960s, environmentalists were ambivalent about nuclear power: they believed it was cleaner than coal but were concerned about the loss of scenic areas as well as the potential environmental effects of radiation. The emergence of the thermal pollution issue transformed this ambivalence into outright opposition. In addition to being the first issue to raise widespread doubts about nuclear power, the thermal pollution controversy paved the way for future disputes over nuclear power, including the debate over reactor safety, and opened the door to participation by state and local governments. Moreover, the AEC's inept handling of this issue helped undermine its credibility with Congress and the American public.[22]

Although thermal pollution was a problem at all generating plants, it was especially pronounced at large nuclear plants, which produced more waste heat than conventional fossil plants because they were less efficient at converting steam into electricity. The discharge into rivers and lakes of large amounts of water that had been heated as much as ten to twenty degrees Fahrenheit was thought to have harmful short- and long-term effects on aquatic environments and marine life. Some species of fish and plant life, for example, were extremely sensitive to temperature changes. Recognition of the problem increased after several fish kills in the years 1962–67 were attributed to thermal discharges from fossil plants. One highly publicized incident in the Sandusky River in Ohio in 1967 resulted in the loss of over 300,000 fish.[23]

Largely as a result of these and similar incidents, fishermen, biologists, several government agencies, including the Department of the Interior's Fish and Wildlife Service (FWS), and state and local governments began to take an interest in thermal pollution. Although the FWS recognized that thermal pollution was a problem, it lacked statutory jurisdiction. In fact, every federal government agency seemed to lack jurisdiction over thermal pollution. Enforcement of water quality standards had traditionally been a function of state governments, but thus far most states had shown little inclination or ability to act. Meanwhile, the AEC insisted that it lacked the statutory authority to regulate the nonradiological effects of nuclear power, including the environmental effects of thermal discharges.[24]

The commission's refusal to consider the environmental effects of thermal pollution can be attributed to its well-developed sense of mission. As James Q. Wilson has argued, agencies frequently resist taking on new tasks if they are seen as incompatible with the agency's own conception of its mission.[25] In the case of the AEC, the agency did not believe environmental concerns were part of its mandate; rather, the AEC believed its primary goal was to encourage the development and use of nuclear power. To the extent that consideration of the environmental effects of nuclear reactors detracted from that goal, the AEC had little incentive to take them into account. Furthermore, the AEC was adamantly opposed to any thermal pollution measures that would apply to nuclear plants but not to fossil plants. The commission believed that such measures would place the nuclear power industry at a competitive disadavantage by forcing nuclear plants to meet more stringent environmental requirements.[26]

During the mid-1960s, the FWS labored to convince the AEC to assume responsibility for thermal pollution at nuclear plants, but the commission continued to claim that it lacked statutory authority over nonradiological environmental matters. In 1966 the dispute emerged publicly in a disagreement over an application for a construction permit for the Millstone Nuclear Power Station in Connecticut. In November of the preceding year, the AEC, as it customarily did, sent the FWS a copy of the application for review and comment. In a move that surprised and alarmed both the commission and the JCAE, FWS head Clarence Pautzke notified the AEC that the service would no longer accept the commission's denial of jurisdiction and asked for a Justice Department review of the matter. Pautzke's challenge of the AEC's position brought the thermal pollution issue out into the open and attracted the attention of other federal agencies and some members of Congress. After an internal review of its legal position at the behest of the joint committee, the AEC reaffirmed its stance.[27]

By this point several members of Congress were becoming exasperated by the impasse and introduced legislation explicitly subjecting the AEC to the provisions of the Fish and Wildlife Coordination Act, which required all federal agencies to consult with the Fish and Wildlife Service if they licensed actions in which water would be substantially affected. The AEC opposed these measures for several reasons. First, the commission did not want to cede any of its autonomy to either the FWS or the Department of the Interior. Second, the commission believed that in singling out nuclear plants the proposed bills would place an unfair burden on the nuclear industry. The AEC still resisted any solution that required it to regulate thermal discharges from nuclear plants unless fossil plants were subject to the same standards.

As the impasse dragged on, public and congressional concern grew. By 1967, thermal pollution became an issue in almost every contested licensing proceeding. The controversy reached a peak in 1966, when a Vermont utility applied to the AEC for a construction permit to build a nuclear reactor on the Connecticut River. The utility, the Vermont Yankee Nuclear Power Corporation, proposed a design utilizing "once-through cooling," in which the water that had been diverted from the river would be used to cool the steam in the condenser and then returned to the river. A group of local citizens, joined by the Vermont Department of Fish and Game, the state's attorney general, and the neighboring states of New Hampshire and Massachusetts, intervened in the construction permit proceeding, arguing that the proposed discharge of water into the river would raise the water temperature and irreparably harm fish and plant life. They also objected to the AEC's refusal to consider thermal pollution in its review process, and they demanded that the utility redesign the reactor to mitigate the consequences of its thermal discharge.

More specifically, the Vermont attorney general demanded that the utility install cooling towers, which cool the water from the condenser by creating a natural draft. The waste heat would then be vented into the atmosphere as the water in the cooling towers evaporated. Eventually, the utility relented and announced plans to use "open-cycle" towers in which the water from the condenser would be diverted to the cooling towers before being discharged into the river. This design would enable the plant to meet Vermont's water standards, established under the Water Quality Act of 1965, but not those of New Hampshire and Massachusetts. Whereas Vermont's standards allowed the river to be heated four degrees Fahrenheit at the point of discharge, New Hampshire and Massachusetts prohibited any river heating at all, in effect requiring the installation of a "closed-cycle" cooling system. Closed-cycle systems differed from open-cycle systems by returning the water in the cooling towers to the condenser rather than discharging it into the river. The utility refused to adopt the closed-cycle system because it was more expensive to install and because it significantly reduced plant efficiency.

Meanwhile, entrepreneurial members in both houses of Congress had seized upon the thermal pollution issue. In 1966, for example, Representative John Dingell (D-Mich.) held widely publicized hearings in which he accused the AEC of providing "grossly inadequate protection" for fish and wildlife.[28] The controversy over the Vermont Yankee plant attracted the attention of Senator Edmund Muskie (D-Maine), who was already establishing his reputation as a leader in environmental issues. Muskie, who was chair of the Subcommittee on Air and Water Pollution of the Committee on Public Works, wrote to AEC Chairman Glenn Seaborg in 1967 questioning the commission's refusal to consider the thermal effects of nuclear power. Muskie contended that the Water Pollution Control Act of 1965 required all federal agencies to take steps to reduce water pollution from any of their actions. Dissatisfied with Seaborg's response, Muskie continued to pressure the AEC and held hearings in Vermont where public officials from that state, New Hampshire, and Massachusetts denounced the AEC.[29] Even Chet Holifield, chairman of the joint committee, recognized the need for action and introduced legislation to give the AEC authority for regulating thermal discharges. But because the commission vigorously opposed the measure, it was never reported out of the JCAE.

In December 1967, the AEC licensing board dismissed the intervention and issued the construction permit, contending that under the Atomic Energy Act the commission had no authority to consider nonradiological issues. The intervenors appealed the ruling to the commissioners, who agreed with the licensing board. Still not satisfied, the state of New Hampshire filed an appeal in federal court. The First Circuit Court of Appeals upheld the AEC's decision in January 1969 but noted that it had the "utmost sympathy" with the intervenor's arguments that the commission had adopted a narrow interpretation of its statutory responsibilities. Despite upholding the AEC's position, the court said that it did so "with regret that the Congress has not yet established procedures requiring timely and comprehensive consideration of non-radiological pollution effects in the planning of installations to be privately owned and operated."[30]

Although the AEC had been vindicated in court, the thermal pollution controversy did not go away. In fact, it got worse. Exactly one week after the court announced its decision, *Sports Illustrated* published an article highly critical of the AEC and its handling of the thermal pollution issue. According to J. Samuel Walker, the article "clearly broadened and called attention to the thermal pollution controversy more than any previous discussion had done."[31] Members of Congress inserted the article into the *Congressional Record*. More and more, the AEC was perceived as an agency that was shirking its environmental responsibilities.

Shortly thereafter, Muskie introduced legislation requiring applicants for federal licenses to present certification from state agencies showing that the plant could meet the state's water quality standards. When the AEC learned that the bill would apply to fossil plants as well as nuclear, it announced its support of the measure. Clearly, the AEC was growing tired of the thermal pollution controversy and the damage it had done to the agency's public image. A revised version of Muskie's bill was adopted by Congress in March 1970. Together with the recently enacted National Environmental Policy Act, the Water Quality Improvement Act of 1970 ensured that federal agencies, including the AEC, would consider thermal pollution issues in the course of their licensing reviews.[32]

Although the furor over thermal pollution eventually died down, the controversy fundamentally altered the course of nuclear politics. It was the first critical step in the redefinition of the nuclear power issue; nuclear power was increasingly understood as an environmental issue, not a national security matter. Public perceptions of nuclear power, and of the AEC, would never be the same. Equally important, the controversy marked the beginning of the end of the federal monopoly on nuclear power. When nuclear power was perceived as a national security issue, it was naturally seen as the responsibility of the federal government. As an environmental issue, however, state, county, and local governments could claim jurisdiction through their powers to regulate land use, which is, in fact, what transpired. As we will see, over the next two decades state and local agencies played an increasingly prominent role in nuclear policy.

The thermal pollution issue was also responsible for convincing many environmentalists to oppose nuclear reactors. Still, much of the early opposition to nuclear reactors was temporary in nature, disbanding after its concerns had been met or rebuffed. Soon, however, activists began organizing more permanent local and regional antinuclear groups, such as the Carolina Environmental Study Group, the Conservation Society of Vermont, and the Environmental Coalition on Nuclear Power. Most of these organizations were loose alliances of groups who agreed to consolidate their efforts to oppose particular plants. These more permanent arrangements would become significant when the nuclear issue heated up in the 1970s, although opposition to nuclear power remained primarily local in nature.

By the end of the 1960s, national environmental organizations such as the Sierra Club, the Natural Resources Defense Council (NRDC), and Friends of the Earth (FOE) were joining local groups in opposing specific plants, particularly if they saw a chance to establish a precedent-setting victory.[33] But not all of the national environmental groups were interested in the same aspects of the nuclear controversy. The Environmental Defense Fund (EDF), for example, tended to focus its efforts on assuring compliance with the procedural requirements of statutes like the National Environmental Policy Act, while the Natural Resources Defense Council was more concerned with the issues of nuclear waste disposal and fuel transportation.[34] As the number and scope of environmental issues grew from the initial focus on thermal pollution to include a concern with a wide variety of land, air, water, and even aesthetic issues, more groups became involved in the fight against nuclear power. Changing understandings of the nuclear issue brought an end to the one-sided mobilization of interests that had existed for twenty years.

THE RADIATION CONTROVERSY

Another issue that attracted a considerable amount of attention from new actors involved radioactive emissions from nuclear power plants. As with the issue of thermal pollution, the AEC soon found itself embroiled in controversy, but this time it was for very different reasons. Whereas in the case of thermal pollution the AEC denied that it had any jurisdiction over the issue, in this instance the commission argued that it had exclusive jurisdiction. The seeds of the controversy were sown in 1965 when Congress adopted the Water Quality Act, which required states to establish their own water quality standards.

Up to that point, the AEC had established regulations for radioactive emissions in the air and water. But some states, concerned about the possible long-term effects of radiation, wanted to impose more stringent emissions standards than the AEC. The state of Minnesota, for example, announced that a reactor being built by the Northern States Power Company would have to emit much lower levels of radiation than the AEC allowed as a condition of receiving a discharge permit. Despite the fact that the technology existed to control releases at much lower levels than it required, the AEC balked, arguing that states did not have the authority to regulate radioactive emissions. Nevertheless, Minnesota issued the new standards in 1969, prompting the utility to file suit. In its complaint, the utility argued that only the AEC had the authority to regulate radiological matters. The case eventually reached the Supreme Court, which decided in favor of the utility and the AEC.[35] Despite the fact that they had again prevailed in the courts, the AEC's victory was yet another empty one. In resisting efforts to allow states to adopt more stringent standards, the AEC had painted itself into a familiar corner and was once more on the defensive. Intervenors began to challenge the standards on a regular basis in licensing hearings in the late 1960s and early 1970s.

In a sense, the debate over radiation was not really a new issue but rather a continuation of a much older fear of radioactive fallout from the nation's atmospheric testing of nuclear weapons in the 1950s and early 1960s. The commission's constant reassurances that radiation from nuclear reactors was "nothing to worry about" undoubtedly rekindled memories of similar claims it had made a decade before.[36] Unfortunately for the AEC, their efforts to reassure the public were just as unsuccessful. Following so closely on the heels of the thermal pollution debate, which had raised serious doubts about the agency's performance and credibility, the emerging radiation controversy only fueled suspicions that the AEC was again being less than honest with the public.

If the general public had not yet made a conscious connection between reactors and weapons fallout, Dr. Ernest Sternglass soon made it for them. In 1968 Sternglass, a professor of radiation physics, was capturing headlines with his claims that there was a strong positive correlation between fallout and infant mortality rates; he later argued that there was a similar correlation between infant mortality rates and emissions from nuclear power plants. Seeking to rebut Sternglass, the AEC asked John Gofman and Arthur Tamplin, two scientists working at the Lawrence Livermore Laboratory, to study the matter. What the AEC did not count on was that Gofman and Tamplin would conclude that although Sternglass had overstated his case, there was nevertheless evidence that the AEC's existing radiation standards were indeed seriously inadequate. Gofman and Tamplin claimed that the existing standard would result in 16,000 excess deaths, a figure they later revised upward to 74,000 deaths. The two scientists accordingly urged that exposure levels be reduced to one-tenth the currently allowable level, but the AEC rejected their arguments and set out to discredit them.[37]

The damage, however, had already been done. Gofman and Tamplin presented their conclusions to the joint committee and to Senator Muskie's Subcommittee on Air and Water Pollution. Gofman, Tamplin, and Sternglass made the talk show and lecture circuit, drawing attention everywhere they went. For the next several years, a debate over the health effects of radiation raged in both scientific journals and in the popular media.[38] Over the protests of both the AEC and the joint committee, the responsibility for regulating radioactive emissions was eventually transferred from the AEC to the newly created Environmental Protection Agency (EPA). The EPA promptly lowered the allowable exposure levels from 170 millirems per year to 25.[39] In the controversy over radiation the AEC once again appeared to be reluctant to take action that would harm the nuclear power industry, even in the face of signs that public health and safety might be endangered. The AEC's credibility suffered yet another blow.

The criticism of nuclear reactors on environmental grounds was significant because it introduced new actors and concerns to the nuclear issue. In addition to environmental groups, new government agencies such as the Environmental Protection Agency and the Council on Environmental Quality assumed responsibility for some aspects of nuclear policy. In his study of iron triangles, J. Leiper Freeman notes that issues escalate out of the subsystem and into the larger political setting in several situations. One of those situations is when the issue assumes considerable and increasing relevance for a large segment of the public, as the environment did during the 1960s. Freeman adds that when this escalation occurs, " 'little policy' can grow into 'big policy' and move from subsytem toward system,"[40] which began to happen to nuclear power in the 1960s. The emergence of the environment as a major issue altered the nature of nuclear policy making, since subsystem members could no longer control the debate. The commercial nuclear program was now seen by many as a potential health threat; it was no longer simply a defense or security issue of little relevance to everyday life. This change in the nature of the nuclear issue was a crucial factor in the subgovernment's eventual demise, because it allowed outsiders to shape the parameters of the debate over nuclear power.

SAFETY CONCERNS

The emergence of the environment as a national issue certainly played a key role in creating a debate over nuclear power, but the most significant factor in the expansion of that debate and in the demise of the atomic subgovernment was the development of reactor safety as a prominent issue. The controversy over safety energized the opposition to nuclear power and thrust the nuclear issue into the media spotlight, making it difficult for public officials to ignore. Even before the accident at Three Mile Island in Pennsylvania, public opinion surveys showed that when asked about nuclear power, the American public mentioned safety as their biggest concern.[41] This response reflects the fact that at some point the dominant understanding of the nuclear power issue had changed. Nuclear power was now a public safety issue.

The safety issue emerged and developed in much the same way the environmental issue had—as a response by local citizens to particular nuclear reactors—before rapidly expanding to include questions about the safety of nuclear plants in general. But concerns over the safety of nuclear reactors attracted more attention and generated more controversy than other environmental issues, in large part owing to the characteristics of nuclear technology, which were still relatively new and unfamiliar to the American public. For many Americans, especially those reared on cold war rhetoric, it was difficult to distinguish the civilian and military aspects of the atomic program. The mere mention of the words "atomic energy" conjured images of nuclear bombs, mushroom clouds, and terribly destructive forces.[42] At a time when the nuclear sector was rapidly expanding, fears of reactors releasing invisible clouds of radiation to the atmosphere were very real. In addition to linking the various antinuclear groups together, the fear of radiation was also their most effective mechanism for attracting attention to the nuclear issue. The knowledge that radiation resulting from a large-scale accident at a nuclear plant could contaminate very large areas enabled opponents to argue that the nuclear issue was something more than a "local" concern. So when questions of reactor safety emerged, the dramatic nature of the potential consequences of reactor accidents lent the nuclear issue a sense of drama and urgency that earlier concerns about thermal pollution could not. Furthermore, because the issue was so dramatic, it captured the attention of the national media. Shortly thereafter, the conflict over the safety of nuclear reactors occupied a prominent position on the public agenda.

This case illustrates that one issue can have both positive and negative images. The key is which image is dominant at any point in time. In the first twenty years of the atomic program, positive understandings dominated. Supporters carefully tended the image, stressing the atom's potential as a source of cheap, clean energy. In later years, however, critics succeeded in raising questions about the safety and environmental consequences of reactors and about the honesty of government officials responsible for the program. As perceptions changed, alliances shifted and so, too, did the politics of nuclear power.

It would be misleading, though, to speak of the concern with safety as a "debate" until the AEC's public hearings on emergency core-cooling systems (ECCS) in 1971. Although questions about reactor safety had been raised before, even as early as 1956 with respect to the Fermi reactor near Detroit, never had they been raised so publicly. In fact, the hearings, which ran approximately two years and produced a hearing record of over 22,000 pages, were the catalytic event that thrust the nuclear safety issue into prominence. The ECCS controversy started in July 1971, when the Union of Concerned Scientists (UCS), a public lobby group concerned about the impact of advanced technology on society, held a press conference at which they issued a report detailing the potential consequences of ECCS failure.

The report, based on information leaked to the UCS by AEC staff members at Oak Ridge National Laboratory (ORNL), revealed that AEC tests conducted at its Idaho test facility failed to demonstrate the adequacy of current AEC regulations. The press conference, which was reported by two of the three television networks on their evening news as well as by a significant number of major newspapers, caused a "sensation."[43] News stories detailing shortcomings in reactor design, construction, and operation became prevalent, as did stories charging the AEC with regulatory neglect. The influential journal *Science*, for example, ran a series of articles critical of the AEC and the nuclear industry in the months following the UCS revelations, charging that the AEC had suppressed studies that raised questions about reactor safety.[44] The AEC, which by this time was under attack on many fronts because of its dual mandate to promote and regulate nuclear power, decided to hold public hearings on the issue as a way of defusing the controversy and restoring its credibility as an impartial regulator. Public hearings, it was thought, would effectively counter the charges that the AEC had something to hide or had been trying to "cover up" reports unfavorable to the nuclear industry. The strategy backfired.

In the first month of the ECCS hearings, the intervenors revealed considerable disagreements on the significance of some technical issues among researchers at the AEC's national laboratories, the AEC's reactor safety staff, and the commissioners. Although the agency had worked very hard to create the impression that there was widespread agreement on the adequacy of emergency core-cooling systems, according to Robert Gillette the ECCS hearings uncovered a "welter of dissent inside the AEC" regarding the agency's handling of emergency core-cooling research.[45] In fact, it was the AEC's efforts to suppress the internal dissent that led many scientists and engineers to communicate their concerns, through clandestine meetings and leaked documents, to members of the Union of Concerned Scientists.[46]

The ECCS hearings revealed serious disagreements between researchers at the commission's national laboratories and the AEC. Part of the disagreement was undoubtedly the result of the researchers' unhappiness with the more stringent oversight placed on their work by Milton Shaw, head of the AEC's research and development program. Under Shaw, the AEC's research program increasingly emphasized applied research and engineering, which did not appeal to the more theoretical scientists at the national laboratories. More important, though, some of the researchers, particularly those at Oak Ridge and Idaho, believed that the AEC was going too fast in its efforts to develop nuclear power and was failing to address some tough safety questions because they were reluctant to impose costly safety requirements on the nuclear industry.[47]

During this period researchers in the national laboratories were discovering dozens of potential safety problems and requested additional research funds from the AEC, but the AEC was slow to respond. Several tests conducted at both the Oak Ridge and Idaho facilities in 1970 and 1971 raised serious questions about the performance of the ECCS during a loss of coolant accident (LOCA).[48] One of the tests conducted at Oak Ridge, for example, showed that fuel rods did not behave as predicted during such an accident. Despite the potential safety implications of these findings, the AEC canceled the rest of the research on that project and reassigned the researchers to new tasks.[49] When news of both the test results and the disagreement over the safety research program was revealed at the hearings, the AEC's hopes for a quick resolution to the ECCS controversy were dashed. Similarly, Philip Rittenhouse, one of the Oak Ridge researchers, testified that he believed there was inadequate evidence that the ECCS would work as predicted; the *New York Times* reported the events in a story entitled "AEC Experts Share Doubts over Reactor Safety." The next day Rittenhouse revealed the names of thirty other scientists and engineers, some of them members of the AEC's own regulatory staff, who shared his doubts.[50] For many of the research scientists at the AEC and its national laboratories, the decision to speak out in public was prompted by what was perceived to be a violation of their professional norms by AEC administrators. Trained as either scientists or engineers, the researchers were reluctant to subordinate their safety concerns to the apparently politically motivated desire of their superiors to enhance the commercial prospects of nuclear power.

It would be difficult to overestimate the effect the emergence of expert critics like the Union of Concerned Scientists had on the safety controversy. Their contribution was so significant precisely because they were scientists. From the beginning, those involved in making nuclear policy had insisted that an issue so complex should only be decided by qualified experts. Those who lacked knowledge of the details of atomic energy were presumed to be incapable of making rational and informed decisions. Dixie Lee Ray, then AEC chair, expressed this sentiment in 1973, writing that "the fact is that in a social decision, when it is taken, any citizen has as valid an opinion as anyone else. But with a scientific and technical decision, this is not true, and an expert's opinion must carry more weight than that of non-experts."[51]

As far as those outside the subsystem could tell, there was unanimous agreement among the experts on nuclear power. All that changed with the ECCS hearings, and from that point on, the AEC was clearly on the defensive. The intervenors, helped considerably by reports and documents leaked to them by employees of the AEC and the national laboratories as well as by documents reluctantly released by the AEC under threat of Freedom of Information Act lawsuits, succeeded in making the ECCS controversy front-page news. Although media coverage of the hearings eventually diminished, the hearings dragged on for months.

When public criticism of nuclear power first developed, program supporters often argued that no reputable scientific experts opposed nuclear power, implying that those who did were either unqualified, misguided, or naive. As a case in point, joint committee member Craig Hosmer attempted to depict the UCS as a small bunch of disaffected naysayers when questioning a UCS staffer in 1973: "Then when we hear that the Union of Concerned Scientists is concerned about this or that or the other thing, it boils down to 12 to 20 people, is that right?"[52] The clear implication of Hosmer's remarks was that the testimony by the UCS was unrepresentative of the scientific community and therefore should not be taken seriously. Various other AEC and JCAE members characterized critics of nuclear power as "obstructionist," "reckless and irresponsible," and as having a "damaging effect" on the nation.[53]

Indeed, a review of many JCAE hearing records reveals that opponents of nuclear power were treated quite harshly by members, often being asked to justify their credentials, while industry representatives on the other hand received deferential treatment. The attitude of joint committee members toward the critics was shared by other subgovernment actors as well. In hearings before the joint committee in 1973, AEC chairman James Schlesinger compared critics of nuclear power to those who had earlier expressed "undue fears" of the iron plow and the first engines.[54] Such tactics were relatively successful, at least until scientists began to disagree. Once that happened, critics of nuclear power could not be easily dismissed as either romantic visionaries or reactionary Luddites. In fact, by impatiently rejecting the concerns of critics as "unenlightened," nuclear supporters unwittingly reinforced the perception that they were concealing the truth about nuclear safety.

Because the effort to commercialize nuclear power had created a situation in which virtually all nuclear engineers and scientists depended on the program's success for their livelihood, there were very few nuclear experts willing to side with the opposition, at least publicly. During this period, almost every nuclear expert was under grant or contract to the AEC or was employed by the AEC, the nuclear industry, or the national laboratories. Two observers wrote at the time that "the exclusivity of AEC sponsorship of reactor research and development" was "a basic and perhaps insurmountable obstacle to a free and open debate within the scientific community and therefore, in the public arena."[55] The apparent unanimity among scientific and technical experts lent considerable credibility to the safety claims of the AEC and the nuclear industry.

That credibility suffered, however, when experts began to disagree in public. Ironically, the scientific and technical dispute over reactor safety began *within* the AEC, when some scientists in the national laboratories, the ACRS, and the agency's technical staff began to question policy decisions made by the AEC's administrators.[56] The decision to speak out could not have been an easy one. Nevertheless, some scientists did speak out, and their actions may have been motivated by what they perceived to be their professional responsibilities as scientists. When safety tests revealed potential problems in emergency core-cooling systems and that there was simply not enough data to determine if the safety systems would work as planned, AEC scientists called for an expedited and upgraded safety research program. For the most part, these requests were either ignored or rejected, leading some of the scientists to conclude that AEC administrators were so eager to ensure the success of the nuclear industry that they were willing to overlook important safety issues. Because this overtly "political" decision was inconsistent with their professional training and norms, some scientists objected.

During this period the AEC's Division of Reactor Development and Technology, under the guidance of Milton Shaw, was responsible for both the reactor development and reactor safety research programs. Several studies have documented the division's emphasis on reactor development programs in general, and the breeder reactor in particular, at the expense of the safety research programs.[57] Despite the obvious need for independent research on safety systems, the AEC chose instead to subcontract such programs to reactor vendors, which meant the agency and its technical staff were relying on data from the very industry they were supposed to be regulating. In spite of protests from researchers at Oak Ridge, members of the ACRS, and AEC regulatory staff that this approach was unsound, the AEC persisted. By 1971 the doubts and concerns of these scientists were appearing in technical journals, which attracted the attention of the outside scientific community, most notably the Union of Concerned Scientists.[58] The UCS also obtained information about the dispute taking place within the AEC from several sources, including documents leaked to them by scientists at Oak Ridge. Eventually a much larger audience learned of the internal dispute when it was revealed that the AEC had tried to censor or cover up the staffers' criticisms. These revelations further impaired the agency's credibility while lending credence to the claims of nuclear opponents. In the process, the technical debate taking place within the AEC moved out of the agency and into the larger political arena.

Nelkin and Pollak argued that the legitimacy of the nuclear "establishment" was sustained by its expertise, and when the experts began to disagree, its legitimacy suffered.[59] Although this was certainly true, it is also clear that in addition to impairing the credibility of the subgovernment, the emergence of expert critics was crucial in establishing the credibility of the opposition. Although it had been one thing to dismiss early critics of nuclear power as dilettantes or eccentrics, it was quite another to refute the claims of experts, although supporters certainly tried. The fact that by 1976 a number of the more visible critics of nuclear power had once been employed by the AEC or the nuclear industry made it more difficult to portray them in such a light. That they had once been "insiders" made their charges all the more damaging to the subgovernment.[60] The importance of scientific and technical experts to their cause was not lost on the opponents of nuclear power. As an illustration, in 1975 a *New York Times* headline announced that "2,300 Scientists Petition U.S. to Reduce Construction of Nuclear Power Plants." The petition, presented by Henry Kendall of the UCS, urged cutbacks in the reactor program pending the resolution of unresolved safety matters. Among the petition signers were some famous and respected scientists, such as James B. Conant, George B. Kistiakowsky, and Victor Weisskopf. All had impressive qualifications; in fact, because all had been involved in the Manhattan Project, they could easily be seen by the press and the public as the ultimate "insiders." Kendall, who was a nuclear physicist, said at the time that the petition was significant because it destroyed the industry argument "that no reputable scientists had doubts about the safety of reactors."[61]

The conflict over nuclear power rapidly escalated once scientists began to disagree publicly. The Union of Concerned Scientists played the key role, but other groups such as the Scientists' Institute for Public Information (SIPI), the Federation of American Scientists, Common Cause, Critical Mass, and the Nader-affiliated Public Interest Research Group also raised questions about reactor safety. The press diligently reported the opinions of these groups, as indicated by these increasingly negative headlines from the *New York Times:* "Scientists, Citing Hazards, Urge Cut in Reactor Operating Levels" and "Atom Plant Perils Cited by Scientists."[62] Whereas for the previous twenty years scientists (and the press) had only good things to say about nuclear power, the signals reaching the general public suddenly shifted. Now, apparently, scientists could not determine if nuclear reactors were really safe. As Steven Del Sesto claims, "Nothing serves to escalate the conflict and debate among the public than a scientific and technical debate among the experts; for if the experts can't agree, how can the public decide?"[63]

The resignations of several employees of AEC contractors and reactor vendors and NRC staff also helped fan the flames of controversy. Carl Hocevar resigned in 1974 from the Aerojet Nuclear Company, an AEC contractor, to "be free to tell the American people the truth about the potentially dangerous conditions in the nation's nuclear power plants."[64] Hocevar, who announced that he planned to work with the UCS, was not the only nuclear "insider" to resign that year. In December 1975 three experienced General Electric managers resigned to express their concerns about reactor safety. The three men, Dale G. Bridenbaugh, Richard B. Hubbard, and Gregory C. Minor, had impressive credentials and had been employed with GE a total of fifty-five years.[65] Their actions, along with the February 1976 resignation of Robert Pollard, an NRC staff member, prompted the joint committee to hold hearings to investigate the charges made by the men. The hearings attracted considerable publicity, leading one committee member to express his wish that the press give as much attention to the AEC and industry responses as it had to the charges. Pollard, in his prepared statement to the committee, said he took the public resignation route in part because of "the widely-held and oft-expressed view by my NRC colleagues that if well-intentioned critics of nuclear power had even just a little expert technical advice, they could be successful."[66] The conflict grew wider as shortly after the hearings, *60 Minutes* broadcast a show detailing Pollard's charges that the NRC was concealing safety hazards.[67] Pollard eventually went to work for the Union of Concerned Scientists as a technical adviser on reactor safety issues.

Similar stories charging that the AEC had suppressed information and reports had appeared in the press earlier. For example, it was reported in November 1974 that a review of AEC documents showed that "for at least the last ten years," the commission had "repeatedly sought to suppress studies by its own scientists that found nuclear reactors were more dangerous than officially acknowledged or that raised questions about reactor safety devices." According to the story, in 1973 an AEC internal task force on the licensing process completed a critical study of AEC effectiveness. The report of the task force had been leaked to the UCS, which then released it to the press. The story went on to say that "the large number of reactor incidents, coupled with the fact that many of them had real safety significance, were generic in nature, and were not identified during the normal design fabrication, erection and preoperational testing phases, raises a serious question regarding the current review and inspection practices both on the part of the nuclear industry and the AEC."[68]

In addition to illustrating the role of the UCS in widening the scope of the conflict, this example shows the often symbiotic relationship between policy activists and the press that developed during the period. In their efforts to change regulatory policy, public lobby groups like the Union of Concerned Scientists frequently sought to bring pressure on decision makers by attracting publicity for their cause. An effective way of bringing this pressure to bear was by exposing instances of corruption or nonperformance by government officials. An even better tactic was to suggest the need for urgent action or to argue that unless immediate policy changes were effected, catastrophe was imminent. In a sense, public lobby groups were performing a communications function by making issues more visible and understandable to the public.[69] And in order for activists to perform this function effectively, they had to attract the attention of the press.

Because the media initially showed little interest in the nuclear issue, antinuclear forces had to bring it to their attention. The nuclear safety issue, with its scientific disputes and the potentially dramatic consequences of reactor accidents, was a good story. The story became even better when Ralph Nader became involved in the controversy. Nader, who eventually earned the title of the "nation's number one critic of nuclear power," first spoke out against nuclear power in testimony before the joint committee in 1973. At the hearings, Nader garnered headlines with his criticism of the committee and the AEC, accusing them of being "Siamese twins" with a "zeal for promoting nuclear power."[70] Later that year he joined the Friends of the Earth in a lawsuit against the AEC, asking the court to shut down twenty reactors because they presented a threat to life, health, and property.[71] As with so many other issues during the 1970s, Nader's participation was a significant factor in attracting media attention and in mobilizing grassroots support for opponents of nuclear power. In 1974, for example, Nader helped establish Critical Mass, which was an organization designed to coordinate the activities of local citizen groups by providing them with technical advice and support.[72] Critical Mass convened conventions in Washington in November of 1974 and 1975. In addition to providing an opportunity to devise a coordinated strategy for the fight against nuclear power, the conventions attracted a fair amount of attention to the nuclear issue. After the 1975 convention, Nader expressed his belief that citizen concern "made the organizing of a mass movement against nuclear power a practical and achievable goal."[73]

Indeed, it was Nader, and the organizations allied with him, that publicized the nuclear issue and helped push it into the electoral arena. It was the Critical Mass conventions that provided the impetus for launching many of the antinuclear initiatives, referenda, and legislation that were proposed in the mid-1970s. Largely in response to the nuclear controversy, numerous states enacted power plant siting laws. Many of the laws were quite similar, requiring utilities to submit long-range planning schedules for plant sites, to consider multiple sites, and to provide full public disclosure of relevant information. Maryland, for example, mandated a minimum two-year lead time between the time of application and the beginning of plant construction.[74] New York's siting statute required public hearings of "sufficient duration" to be held in the proposed site location and imposed a 180- to 210-day period between the initial application and the public hearing. New York also required utilities to submit detailed applications describing the site and facility, assessing the plant's environmental effects and estimated cost, and demonstrating the plant's compliance with state and local laws and regulations. Another requirement in New York was for utilities to provide $25,000 to state authorities to offset the expense of obtaining expert advice.[75] As many as twenty-eight states considered some type of antinuclear measures in 1975 alone.[76]

Some of the nuclear referenda attracted considerable attention, forcing candidates for a variety of elective offices to address the nuclear issue. In 1976 presidential candidate Jimmy Carter, for example, endorsed an antinuclear initiative in Oregon. Although none of the ballot initiatives passed, the nuclear industry, which had grown accustomed to the quiet, behind-the-scenes negotiations that had characterized the commercial nuclear power program since its inception, was forced to spend millions of dollars in a number of high-profile public relations campaigns to defeat them.[77] Although the industry was ultimately successful, the very fact that it was forced to respond in such a high-profile manner was an important indication of the extent to which the politics of nuclear power had moved beyond the exclusive province of the atomic subgovernment once the debate focused on reactor safety. It also illustrates how the degree of conflict within a policy community can shape the public's response to that issue. As Baumgartner and Jones have argued, consensual communities can foster a positive policy image and insulate themselves from outside interference, but communities split by internal conflict are more likely to be subjected to broad political debates.[78]

THE RISE OF ENERGY ISSUES

The Arab oil embargo in October 1973 and the ensuing "energy crisis" profoundly altered the perception of the nation's energy policies in the eyes of the public and government officials and catapulted the energy issue to the top of the nation's political agenda. At first glance this turn of events might have been expected to bolster the prospects of nuclear power. After all, the dramatic increase in the price of fossil fuels could only make nuclear power more attractive. Instead, the rise of energy issues to prominence subjected the subsystems that had developed surrounding the various energy sources—coal, oil, gas, and nuclear—to intense scrutiny. Once this happened, energy issues became the focus of a national debate. The group arena became more crowded as interests that had been complacent about energy issues as long as supplies had remained plentiful began to mobilize and express their concerns over the economic and environmental consequences of energy policy. With this increased scrutiny, energy interests were placed in direct competition for federal research and development funds; nuclear power, which had received the bulk of such monies over the years, would now face stiff competition. At the same time, government officials began to recognize the need for a comprehensive long-term energy policy to replace the fragmented and ad hoc decisions that were characteristic of energy policy making in the United States. As part of their efforts to manage energy policy in a more comprehensive fashion, policymakers responded by reorganizing both the administrative and legislative branches. These organizational changes would prove to be inconsistent with the continued domination of energy politics by subsystems.[79]

In addition, the effort to make energy decision making more comprehensive inevitably made it more complex as new actors entered the debate. By all accounts, the ultimate goal of the nation's policymakers during this period was energy self-sufficiency. This goal was not empty rhetoric; there was a tremendous amount of activity in the mid-1970s as both the executive and legislative branches reorganized themselves in an attempt to deal more effectively with questions of energy supply and demand. But reorganization of the government's energy apparatus served less lofty goals as well; it allowed new agencies and committees to stake a claim in a newly important policy area. By 1976 there were twenty-three committees and fifty-one subcommittees in Congress with some responsibility for energy issues.[80]

Rapidly rising energy prices also commanded the attention of state officials, thrusting public utility commissions (PUCs) into the spotlight and disrupting their once friendly relationship with utilities. In Vermont, for example, electricity prices quadrupled after the Vermont Yankee plant was ordered. Throughout the nation, public utility commissions faced political pressure to hold rate increases to a minimum during a period of rising energy prices. Previously routine rate making proceedings were now contested as utilities seeking rate increases were opposed by alliances of antinuclear activists, consumer advocates, and large industrial users of electricity, who all sought lower rates. Responding to demands from opponents, some PUCs refused to allow utilities to pass on to ratepayers the costs of construction work in progress until the plants were completed. In New York, for example, the PUC disallowed Long Island Lighting Company's request to allow $1.4 billion of the $4.7 billion cost of its Shoreham plant to be included in its rate base. Compared with earlier periods, fewer rate increases were granted in the 1970s, creating financial problems for many nuclear utilities. New Hampshire's refusal of an emergency rate increase for one of the owners of the Seabrook plant led to the company's bankrupty in 1988.[81] These rejections forced utilities to find other revenue sources. Many turned to borrowing, but inflationary pressures forced them to pay high interest rates. As a result, utility debt increased and bond ratings declined. As we will see in Chapter 7, mounting financial problems eventually undermined the nuclear industry. It is enough here to note that state governments, which had played a minimal role in regulating nuclear power, were now prominent actors, and utilities had to deal with a growing number of state agencies responsible for rates, siting, the location of transmission lines, and so on. As at the national level, the new regulatory environment was fragmented and time-consuming.

All of this institutional upheaval meant that policymakers in a number of energy subsystems were forced to operate in new and unfamiliar political environments, which were frequently crowded and politically charged. In short, the rise of the energy issue to the top of the nation's agenda demonstrates that events in the macropolitical arena can penetrate the normally closed world of subsystem politics and lead to fundamental changes in decision-making processes.[82]

CRITICISMS OF THE AEC LICENSING PROCESS

Antinuclear partisans in the late 1960s and early 1970s were extremely critical of the AEC's licensing procedures, arguing that the agency's rules of practice exhibited a bias in favor of utility applicants. In their view, the bias was primarily the result of the conflict of interest inherent in the commission's statutory mandate to promote, develop, and regulate nuclear power. To many of its critics, the AEC had clearly chosen to emphasize its promotional and developmental roles at the expense of its regulatory responsibilities and had shown neither the ability nor the inclination to fulfill its duty to protect the health and safety of the public. What was needed, according to many opponents of nuclear power, was to force the AEC (and its successor, the NRC) to be more aggressive in regulating the nuclear power industry.

In general, critics charged that AEC procedures tended to preclude meaningful public participation in agency proceedings while granting the nuclear industry privileged access to AEC personnel, especially in the critical early stages of the licensing process. Additionally, critics claimed that AEC regulations were primarily responsive to the desires and needs of the industry, reflecting the commission's enthusiasm for building and licensing reactors. Perhaps most important, critics charged that the decision to approve reactors had usually been made by the time citizens were given an opportunity to register their opinions, and that the AEC's public hearings, the principal forum in which citizens were allowed to participate, were nothing more than "stacked-deck" proceedings designed to foster the illusion of citizen input. In testimony before the joint committee in 1974, Harold P. Green, then a law professor at George Washington University, said that "from the standpoint of meaningful public participation" the AEC's licensing hearings were "at best a charade and at worst a sham."[83] If nothing else, the frequent charges that citizens were helpless before "expert elitism" and the "steamroller of big government" clearly reflected the distrust many antinuclear reformers felt toward the AEC and its proceedings during this period.[84]

More specifically, critics often argued that the AEC's licensing process presented a number of institutional barriers to effective public participation. For example, citizen groups often complained that their ability to intervene in an effective manner at individual licensing hearings was hindered by their lack of technical and scientific expertise. The reality was that almost every scientist and engineer familiar with nuclear power at this time was either employed by or under contract to the AEC or the nuclear power industry. With the exception of a very small number, these experts were reluctant to bite the hand that fed them. In describing the situation facing citizen intervenors to the Senate Committee on Interior and Insular Affairs in 1971, Edward Berlin, an attorney who had represented the Sierra Club and the National Wildlife Federation in the *Calvert Cliffs* court case, testified that citizen groups typically operated with "an extreme paucity of expert assistance."[85]

One of the consequences of this shortage of technical and scientific assistance was that citizen groups and their attorneys rarely knew what type of information could be useful to them in presenting their case to the licensing boards. Similarly, intervenors frequently had little knowledge of which documents or reports to request from the AEC or the applicant and were therefore forced to rely on the cooperation of the commission or applicant for information. Moreover, lacking technical or scientific sophistication, many citizen groups also had a difficult time evaluating the importance of the information that was available to them.[86]

The imbalance in technical and scientific expertise had other consequences as well. AEC regulations prevented intervenors from challenging the validity of the commission's rules, regulations, or standards. Interventions could only be concerned with whether or not the proposed reactor satisified the AEC's rules. In the eyes of some, this requirement prohibited intervenors from raising the issues that most concerned them and instead forced them to contest licenses on technical and scientific grounds, which they were ill-equipped to do.[87] Barred from challenging the adequacy of the commission's rules in individual licensing proceedings, intervenors could not directly confront the question of whether the reactor in question was safe. Consequently, they had to find ways of raising the issue indirectly. Typically, this process involved trying to uncover discrepancies in the testimony of AEC and utility witnesses during cross-examination. In other instances intervenors relied on documents leaked to them by sympathetic AEC scientists or engineers. By emphasizing technical issues, the commission's licensing proceedings thereby placed a premium on technical and scientific expertise; because of their difficulty in obtaining such expertise, intervenors were thus forced to debate the issue in an unfamiliar language. It was not a debate they could expect to win.

The bias toward technical issues was also reflected in the AEC's rules of practice, which defined an expert as "a qualified individual who has scientific or technical training or experience."[88] This definition was important because only those individuals recognized as experts by the commission's hearing boards were permitted to act as technical interrogators in licensing hearings. Moreover, intervenors were burdened by an AEC rule that limited cross-examination to areas within the expertise of the person conducting the questioning.[89] Because the typical intervenor group was fortunate to have even one or two technical "experts," this requirement strictly limited their ability to conduct a searching cross-examination of the numerous witnesses testifying on behalf of the AEC and utility applicant.

The paucity of expert advice was not the only problem facing citizen groups at this time. Another barrier to effective participation was the formidable cost of intervening in nuclear plant licensing decisions. According to AEC regulations, "any person whose interest may be affected by a proceeding and who desires to participate" could file a written petition to intervene.[90] Although this provision seems to invite citizen interventions in licensing proceedings, in reality local citizen groups often operated under severe financial constraints and had a difficult time raising the money to hire the legal and scientific assistance needed to intervene. On the other hand, a utility applying for a construction permit or operating license typically could devote considerable economic resources in support of its position, setting aside hundreds of thousands of dollars for legal and technical advice. Unequal resources, then, placed intervenors at a distinct disadvantage in commission proceedings.

A number of those critical of the AEC's licensing process also believed that the public was deliberately excluded from that process until a very late date, when the proposed reactor was already in an advanced stage of planning and had developed considerable economic and institutional momentum. Typically, a utility seeking a construction permit for a reactor would submit a safety analysis and a preliminary application to the AEC's regulatory staff for review. This preapplication review was not a public proceeding. In most circumstances neither the AEC nor the utility issued a notice informing the public that the utility had plans to construct a reactor at a particular site. Therefore, because the public was usually unaware of the utility's plans, there was no opportunity for interested citizens to participate in these early stages.[91]

Even if opponents of nuclear power had been aware of the proposal at an early date, they would not have learned much. Until the early 1970s, the information contained in preliminary documents was usually quite general and imprecise, reflecting the rapidly changing technology, the utility's relative lack of experience in building nuclear power plants, and the lack of standardized design requirements. In what was typically a fairly informal process, the commission's regulatory staff would review the utility's plans to detect potential safety problems; after this review the utility applicant and the regulatory staff would work together to correct any problems. After those problems presumably had been resolved to the satisfaction of the staff and the Advisory Committee on Reactor

Safeguards (ACRS), the utility would then file a formal application for a construction permit. Only at this point, after many months and sometimes even several years had elapsed, would the public learn that a utility planned to construct a reactor at a particular site. Myron Cherry, an attorney who represented citizen groups in several licensing interventions, complained to the AEC that the public's inability to obtain information earlier in the commission's environmental proceedings was "a particularly harsh burden in light of the fact that adequate preparation for the intervenors over the long months we have participated in this case has been thwarted by the failure to let us in the process early. . . . The realization is that the collective efforts of the utility and the AEC have taken nine months to prepare their position on environmental issues and yet we are asked to duplicate that effort in less than a month without having the information available. We cannot see the fairness in such a procedure."[92]

Not only did opponents of nuclear power claim that such procedures were unfair, but many believed that as a practical matter the procedures skewed subsequent events by making it appear as if the primary goal of intervenors was to delay the licensing process. Certainly, in some instances intervenors did seek to delay licensing proceedings in the hopes of driving up the cost of the reactor, but many others did not. Yet even those who intervened in "good faith" were viewed with skepticism by the AEC's hearing boards. In the words of Edward Berlin, an attorney for the National Wildlife Federation, "When the notice of hearing is filed, all the parties, except the intervenors, are ready to begin the hearing and there is no patience with an intervenor who seeks to obtain this underlying data and the time to study it thoroughly."[93] The exclusion of the public until this late stage was perhaps the single most important barrier to effective public participation in the licensing process. At the root of this belief was a perception that the decision to issue the permit or license had already been made by the time public hearings were announced and that the outcome of the hearings were, in the words of two researchers critical of the commission's licensing procedures, "for all intents and purposes predetermined."[94] Such fears were not unfounded, because the informality of the AEC's licensing review process, especially in the initial preapplication stage, encouraged frequent contact between the applicant and the commission's regulatory and development staffs. It has been commonly acknowledged that the relationship between the two parties during the 1960s was collegial and supportive, which is understandable given that the staff and the applicant were both working toward the same goal—the development of nuclear power as a viable source of electrical energy.[95] Lending further credence to the intervenor's concerns was the fact that public hearings were not announced until the regulatory staff and the ACRS had decided the application satisfied the commission's regulations. By the time the public was notified that a utility was planning to construct a nuclear reactor, then, the two branches of the AEC that were responsible for reviewing the proposal had already concluded it was sound. Critics believed this procedure was unfair and pointed out that by excluding the public until the staff had concluded its safety review, the commission effectively guaranteed the issuance of the permit or license.

The consequences for the conduct of public hearings, according to critics, were quite clear. The commission's licensing boards, aware that other branches of the AEC had already given the project the stamp of approval, would be inclined to accept the staff's recommendation and grant the construction permit or operating license to the applicant. This practice placed the burden of proof in public hearings on the intervenors, even though the commission's rules of practice stipulated that unless otherwise ordered by the presiding officer, the applicant had the burden of proof on all issues.[96] In actuality, however, the staff had already concluded the plant was safe and tended to assume the role of an "ally of the applicant" in licensing proceedings,[97] which meant that intervenor groups had to overcome the judgment and expertise of the regulatory staff, the ACRS, and the utility applicant.

At the public hearings, the licensing boards were usually limited to consideration of the issues placed in contention by the intervenors. The AEC's rules of practice stated that "as to matters not pertaining to radiological health and safety which are not in controversy, boards are neither required nor expected to duplicate the review already performed by the regulatory staff and ACRS, and they are authorized to rely upon the testimony of the regulatory staff, the applicant, and the conclusions of the ACRS, which are not controverted by any party."[98] The licensing board's role, according to the AEC's rules, was to determine if the regulatory staff's review had been adequate to ensure that the plant could be built and operated without undue risk to the health and safety of the public.[99] Critics argued that these rules, as interpreted by the boards, required them to prove that the plant was unsafe rather than requiring the staff and the applicant to make a positive safety finding. In other words, the burden for raising safety issues was placed on the intervenors rather than on the staff or the board, because the staff had already determined that the reactor could be built and operated without undue risk to the health and safety of the public. Again, intervenors were placed in the unenviable position of opposing the accumulated technical and scientific judgments of the regulatory staff, the ACRS, and the applicant.

Opponents of nuclear power also claimed that the AEC's licensing boards often were composed of individuals with long ties to the AEC who were therefore predisposed to issue a construction permit or operating license. Their study of the AEC's public proceedings led Ebbin and Kasper to conclude that "it is precisely the predisposition of Licensing Boards (and the AEC) to grant licenses and permits based on their preconceived support of nuclear power which constitutes the gravest and most meaningful threat to real citizen participation in the decisionmaking process."[100] In conclusion, it seems apparent that critics of nuclear power believed that the AEC's licensing process was both undemocratic and unfair, and that the commission had failed to fulfill its statutory mandate to regulate the nuclear power industry to ensure the health and safety of the public.

Nuclear activists urged numerous changes in the AEC's licensing and rule-making procedures. Reformers believed that a more open and democratic licensing process, one that would enable citizens as well as Congress, the courts, and the press to perform an oversight function, could also work to ensure that the commission was fulfilling its regulatory mandate. As we shall see, these goals reflect the fundamentally moderate and liberal nature of nuclear reformers. Like other policy activists of the time, they demanded changes in decision-making processes of government agencies, believing that the attainment of adequate procedural rights would somehow lead to the attainment of some substantive right. In the case of nuclear reformers, the substantive right in question was the health and safety of the public. In pursuit of this goal, nuclear reformers urged increased citizen access to the AEC's licensing and rulemaking proceedings. They also demanded more timely access to information concerning proposed reactors, which would allow citizen groups to intervene more effectively in contested cases. Comprehensive and timely disclosure of documents and records, they argued, would alert citizens and government officials to potential safety problems before construction began. In the words of attorney Edward Berlin, the utilities "must, at the first possible moment, openly and frankly communicate their future construction plans and invite and encourage frank public discussion which must be predicated on the full disclosure of all relevant information in their possession."[101]

This is not to suggest that nuclear reformers viewed the participatory measures merely as instruments of policy reform. Certainly the critics saw many of these reforms as a means to policy change, but they also believed that greater citizen participation in public affairs was in itself desirable.[102] That is what public interest attorney Anthony Roisman tried to tell the joint committee in 1974 during its consideration of several measures that would have limited the number of opportunities for citizen participation in AEC licensing proceedings. Roisman claimed that "in addition to the important and substantial contribution which public participation has made there is the incalculable benefit of public participation per se, even when the position advanced by the public is rejected. It is the cornerstone—really the whole foundation—of a democracy that the people must be allowed and encouraged to actively participate in the decisions which affect them."[103] Like many policy activists of the time, nuclear opponents believed that participation in politics would have a beneficial effect on the participants. In their eyes, participation in public affairs was more than a means of protecting private interests and ensuring good government; many believed the central function of participation was an educative one. By participating in politics, citizens would learn to widen their horizons and to distinguish between their own individual impulses and desires and those of the larger community. In short, through active participation in politics the individual could learn to be a public as well as a private citizen.[104]

CRITICISMS OF THE POLITICAL PROCESS

By the middle of the 1970s, the subgovernment had lost its ability to define the nuclear issue; consequently, the debate over nuclear power had widened to include a variety of new issues. Some opponents of nuclear power were suggesting that rather than being only a technical matter, the nuclear issue also involved social, political, and moral questions. As such, scientists and engineers possessed no special ability to resolve those types of questions. To be sure, the nuclear power issue did require some understanding of complex matters, but antinuclear forces did not believe it an insurmountable problem. They believed that citizens, as with other social and political issues, could learn enough about nuclear power to participate in a responsible manner if given the opportunity. They also believed that citizens had a right to participate meaningfully in decisions that affected their lives, particularly if the decisions involved significant risk.

Ralph Nader expressed these sentiments in his testimony before the joint committee, saying the nuclear power issue was "not just a technical problem but a moral issue of the greatest gravity." Members of the JCAE heard similar ideas from Ann Carl, a spokesperson for the Lloyd Harbor Study Group, a group opposed to the licensing of the Shoreham nuclear power plant on Long Island, who claimed that nuclear power was "a social problem as much as it is an engineering problem."[105] In attempting to redefine the nuclear issue as essentially social or political in nature, the opponents were simultaneously challenging the subgovernment's exclusive authority by suggesting that others be admitted into policy-making circles. In the words of one nuclear critic, "there is a myth that only technical experts are capable of forming valid judgements as to scientific and engineering applications in public policy issues."[106] Critics of nuclear power were tired of what they perceived to be the subgovernment's "papa-knows-best tendencies" and "technological arrogance and hubris," and they demanded to be included in the decision-making process.[107] Similarly, the conviction that the nuclear debate was really a political question provided a foundation for demands for greater citizen involvement, leading some to state that "what is at issue in contested proceedings is whether or not society is willing to accept the inherent risks and the detrimental impacts on the environment; the difficulty of answering the question of what constitutes 'too great' a risk or environmental impact is the reason that public involvement in the decision-making process is essential."[108]

In this way, antinuclear forces were able to link their concerns about nuclear safety to more general concerns about accountability and responsiveness in government. In expressing this antipathy toward both the decision makers and the decision-making process, the critics of nuclear power were able to capitalize on the sharp increase in negative feelings toward institutions that characterized this period.[109] With liberalism deeply embedded in the political culture, Americans have traditionally feared concentrated power and have therefore been distrustful of large and powerful institutions. But the period from 1965–80 was exceptional for the enormous growth of distrust in both business and government. During this period it was commonly accepted that government institutions were overly responsive to organized interests, leaving citizens with little or no say in important matters. More specifically, there was increasing hostility toward *big* business and *big* government, which were perceived to be working in tandem at the expense of the common good. Furthermore, when asked to identify specific industries where power was too concentrated, a far larger percentage named utilities and oil companies than any others.[110] Moreover, only the largest corporations possessed the technical and economic resources needed to design and construct nuclear reactors, while the technology's significant risks mandated a large federal role in regulating the industry. Not surprisingly, then, the charges by opponents of nuclear power that the nuclear industry had formed an alliance with the AEC and JCAE hit home for many citizens who were already feeling disenchanted and disenfranchised. The nuclear enterprise, in short, seemed to symbolize bigness run amok.

Subgovernment members, however, seemed oblivious to the changing environment and were no longer capable of shaping perceptions of their program. Ironically, by arguing that specialists should make nuclear policy, nuclear insiders were urging citizens to trust them at a time when the public was increasingly less willing to do so. The nuclear industry, in particular, was composed of engineers and scientists whose work consisted of devising solutions to technical problems; they were "scientific optimists" whose training and experience convinced them of the potential solubility of such problems.[111] Additionally, most nuclear supporters were convinced that nuclear power was in the public interest, believing that more nuclear power meant more energy, which meant greater economic growth, which meant, in turn, a higher standard of living. Expressing this view, John Nassikas, chairman of the Federal Power Commission, remarked that "in the future, as in the past, man's economic and social progress will be closely dependent on the provision of increasing amounts of energy for his use."[112]

For these reasons, subsystem members were reluctant to consider views from those critical of nuclear power, especially if the critics were not scientific or technical experts. In many respects, such behavior is typical of those with specialized knowledge: experts are trained to perceive and interpret information through their own particular profession's perspective. In the words of Harold Laski, expertise often "has a certain caste-spirit about it, so that experts tend to neglect all evidence which does not come from those who belong to their own ranks."[113] But in claiming that participation in the nuclear issue demanded specialized knowledge, nuclear insiders, according to Bupp and Derian, "contributed to the identification of nuclear power technology with something that many citizens in these countries dislike and distrust about their societies. Moreover, it is this dislike and distrust which is the driving force behind the nuclear safety controversy and the principal cause for the dissolution of the nuclear dream."[114]

As the conflict over nuclear power grew, it came to resemble a "dialogue of the deaf" because both sides approached the issue from fundamentally different points of view.[115] Antinuclear forces were reacting to the perceived dominance of the political process by a cloistered technocratic elite. They were afraid that if experts were allowed to depict social and political issues as technical choices, citizens would be forced to accept policies, and risks, to which they had not consented. The solution, from their perspective, was to recognize the essentially political character of nuclear policy and allow citizens greater input into the policy-making process. Only an informed and active citizenry, they argued, could provide the rigorous oversight that is "at the heart of the democratic process in an open society."[116] For their part, supporters of nuclear power believed the controversy stemmed from their inability to communicate the scientific "facts" about nuclear power to the public. The problem, from their perpective, was to overcome the "erroneous assumptions and misrepresentation of facts" communicated by nuclear critics and the press; they were convinced the controversy would disappear once the public learned the "truth" about nuclear power.[117] AEC commissioner William Doub illustrated this sentiment in hearings on the status of reactor safety before the JCAE: "I think we have probably been deficient in not informing the public sufficiently as to the technical aspects of nuclear energy. We have assumed—I think to a degree erroneously—that it is too complicated for the public to understand. This has led to the kind of dramatization by obstructionists which concerns the public because they don't know the facts. I think we have to speak out, we have to inform the public, we have to give them the facts. I think when the public has the facts, they will make the correct decisions."[118] By the middle of the 1970s, then, pro- and antinuclear forces were struggling to shape understandings of the nuclear issue. Subsystem members tried to restrict the debate to narrowly drawn technical and scientific questions, while critics of nuclear power sought to transform the nuclear issue into a full-scale debate over how policy decisions ought to be made in a democratic society.[119] At stake was the future of commercial nuclear power.

CONCLUSION

The issue of nuclear power had been fundamentally redefined by the middle of the 1970s as attention shifted to the potential negative consequences of its use. An important factor in this transformation was the success of outsiders in gaining access to information about nuclear power and then publicizing it. Indeed, battles for control of program information were intense because all parties knew how crucial it was for shaping public perceptions of nuclear power.

Once outsiders succeeded in redefining the issue, the subgovernment lost its ability to frame the debate and control access to policy making; in the end, the atomic subsystem lost its monopoly on power. Put another way, the subgovernment fell apart because it could not keep the outsiders "out." As a result, the arena of nuclear policy making became more open, crowded, and conflictual. The inclusion of a broader range of participants meant a broader range of views, which destroyed the unanimity that had reigned for over twenty years.

Similar developments in other issue areas suggest that the case of the nuclear power subgovernment was not an aberration. As a case in point, Bosso documents how the gradual cumulation of knowledge and awareness of the potential hazards of pesticides eventually led to the downfall of the pesticides subgovernment.[120] Similarly, Derthick and Quirk show how growing awareness of economic critiques of regulation attracted the attention of policymakers and contributed to efforts to deregulate the airline, trucking, and telecommunications industries.[121]

As perceptions of issues change, new groups of policymakers are drawn to them and others become less important. In the process, "little" policy becomes "big" policy. Moreover, such changes in image are often used purposefully to attract the attention of policymakers in new institutions or "venues."[122] Usually, it is those who are on the losing side of political debates who seek to expand the conflict in this manner, hoping to alter policy outcomes by bringing the issue to the attention of new actors with different views. Critics of nuclear power were no exception. They were aware that policy shifts often hinged on institutional change. More specifically, they knew that substantive policy change could be facilitated by convincing new governmental actors to claim jurisdiction over nuclear power, thereby expanding the conflict.

As we have seen, the perception of nuclear power as a national security issue helped create and sustain the atomic subgovernment. But as the issue was redefined to include environmental and safety questions, other actors, including state and local governments, claimed jurisdiction. The federal monopoly over nuclear power was over, and actors in these new venues proved to be more responsive to certain aspects of the nuclear issue. Policy images and venues are clearly linked, and as Baumgartner and Jones note, different venues are responsive to different sets of policy images.[123] Responding to constituent concerns about the environment and reactor safety, state officials used their land use powers to regulate power plant siting. Similarly, public utility commissions were responsive to concerns about electricity rates rather than questions of national security. Different actors focused on different aspects of the issue. As indicated in the next three chapters, public interest groups and state and local governments were not the only new participants. Dramatic institutional changes sweeping through Congress and the AEC would introduce others and fundamentally transform the nuclear subgovernment. Nuclear politics would never be the same.

4

The Courts, Licensing Reform, and Venue Shopping

I know of no safe depository of the ultimate powers of the society but the people them-
selves; and if we think them not enlightened enough to exercise their control with a
wholesome discretion, the remedy is not to take it from them, but to inform their discre-
tion.

—Thomas Jefferson

For over two decades industry representatives and other nuclear power supporters enjoyed unrivaled access to the JCAE and AEC; at the same time, however,
critics of nuclear power were effectively screened out of policy making. When the
debate over nuclear power heated up in the 1970s, nuclear activists were forced to
do what those on the losing side of policy debates often do—turn elsewhere to
achieve their goals. One of the first places they turned was to the federal courts.[1]
Somewhat later, as is shown in subsequent chapters, other actors—from all levels
of government—began to encroach on the policy monopoly once enjoyed by the
AEC and JCAE. Committee reforms in Congress, for example, granted jurisdiction over some aspect of nuclear policy to multiple committees and allowed opponents to challenge the dominance of subsystem members, particularly the joint
committee. With other governmental actors playing more important roles, nuclear reformers eventually secured significant changes in the AEC's licensing and
rulemaking procedures, which in turn provided them with valuable access to
both policymakers and program information. Some of the jurisdictional changes
were the result of shifting perceptions of nuclear power; others were products of
broader developments in American politics. Regardless of their origins, the jurisdictional changes were key factors in the subgovernment's fall.

Having lost the battle over issue definition, subsystem members became
trapped in the critics' story of thermal pollution, radiation, and unsafe reactors.

The outcome of the image battle had significant institutional consequences as well. According to Baumgartner and Jones, image change frequently leads to venue change, as new understandings of issues lead other governmental actors to claim jurisdiction.[2] Both sides understood this effect, which explains why they struggled so intensely to shape elite and public perceptions. Subsystem members fought to maintain their policy monopoly by stressing the issue's complexity and by suppressing studies critical of nuclear power, while opponents purposefully highlighted problems that would surely attract the attention of actors in new institutional venues. Antinuclear activists, claim Baumgartner and Jones, "followed the classic pattern of expanding the conflict by altering the institutional venue."[3]

Not only does image change often lead to venue change, but they also build on each other in a cumulative and reinforcing manner. "With each change in venue," write Baumgartner and Jones, "comes an increased attention to a new image, leading to further changes in venue, as more and more groups within the political system become aware of the question. Thus a slight change in either can build on itself, amplifying over time and leading eventually to important changes in policy outcomes."[4] In this case, "as the venues of nuclear power policy expanded, image degradation accelerated."[5] More specifically, Baumgartner and Jones argue that "a variety of institutional changes followed, each of which reinforced the negative image of the industry and gave greater access to opponents in the policymaking process. Combined, these changes in venue and in image lead to the destruction of this once-powerful subsystem."[6]

To be sure, many of the venue changes resulted from the conscious efforts of antinuclear activists, who recognized that such shifts could facilitate substantive policy reform. Other venue changes, however, resulted from developments unrelated to nuclear power. Some, for example, were products of a broader reform movement that swept through the American political system and contributed to the more or less simultaneous collapse of many policy subsystems.[7] One manifestation of this development was the "new social regulation," much of which was aimed at so-called "quality of life" issues, such as protection of consumers, the environment, and public health and safety.[8] Underlying much of the new social regulation was a conviction that narrow interests were unduly influential in American politics while others were routinely and systematically excluded. Part of the solution, from the point of view of policy activists, was to restore a sense of balance or fairness to the administrative process; only by expanding the number and range of interests represented could agencies become more responsive to the public interest.

But policy activists, aware of the importance of effective implementation, also knew that the success of their programmatic reforms depended on more than correcting an imbalance in the number of interests formally represented in the political process. History had shown all too frequently that well-intentioned policy reforms were often subverted during implementation. Reformers in the 1970s concluded, therefore, that the administrative process itself needed reform.

Only by democratizing and "opening up" administrative agencies could citizens ensure that administrators faithfully performed their congressionally authorized tasks. Accordingly, many of the reforms proposed by policy activists in the 1970s were designed to increase citizen participation in, and control over, agency decision making.

Public lobby groups provided the vehicle for many of the activists' reform initiatives. Many of these groups, including some of those opposed to nuclear power, relied on highly visible revelations of corruption or scandal to attract supporters. The Union of Concerned Scientists, for example, used this approach quite effectively. The more perceptive groups knew that influence gained from glaring headlines in the *New York Times* would be fleeting, while the type of long-term influence they sought was contingent upon better and more effective access to commission proceedings. With these goals in mind, activists set out to expand and institutionalize their own access to all phases of the administrative process. They were joined in their efforts by Congress and the courts, who deliberately created many new procedural arrangements to facilitate the participation of public lobby groups in agency deliberations.[9] Central to the reformer's desire to play a more direct role in the policy-making process was the notion of procedural rights. In fact, during this period Congress and the courts expanded both the public's right and opportunity to participate in agency decision making. Citizen participation, it seemed, was an idea whose time had come.

In this chapter I will show that venue changes involving the courts provided antinuclear activists with an important wedge to crack open the subsystem's policy monopoly. Judicial action was predicated on the perception that many regulatory agencies had been insufficiently aggressive in carrying out their statutory responsibilities.[10] Seeking to remedy the situation, judges imposed numerous procedural reforms designed to encourage agency administrators to be more responsive to nonbusiness interests. Many of these reforms thus increased citizen access to administrative files and proceedings, which had the added benefit of providing more effective oversight of agency decision making. At the same time the federal courts were imposing strict procedural mandates on administrative agencies, requiring them to conduct their licensing and rulemaking proceedings with greater formality. The courts also required agencies involved in rulemaking to seek additional information before making decisions, to allow all interested parties to examine information and data, and to clearly explain the basis of their decisions. Moreover, the courts encouraged agencies to grant broad hearing rights, which were seen as a means for the public to have an effective and meaningful voice in decision making. In some instances, the courts insisted that agencies involved in rulemaking adopt procedures traditionally associated with more formal adjudicatory hearings; in others, the courts forced administrators to promulgate new regulations or revise existing ones. By the middle of the 1970s, the new procedural arrangements fashioned by this institutional partnership of policy activists, Congress, and the courts had created a more open policy-making arena.

THE COURTS AND THE ADMINISTRATIVE PROCESS

For most of the late 1960s and early 1970s, persons or groups seeking to participate in the formulation of nuclear policy were consistently rebuffed by both the
AEC and the joint committee. In a textbook case of venue shopping, critics of
nuclear power turned to the courts for assistance. Schattschneider was correct in
arguing that it is the losers in any political dispute that seek to expand the conflict
by shifting it into a different arena. But the ability to change political arenas depends on a variety of resources that are distributed unevenly among social interests. In the case of nuclear power, litigation was an attractive strategy because it
allowed reformers to expand the conflict without using too many of their scarce
resources. Reformers also believed that judges, who tended to be policy generalists, would be more receptive to the concerns of critics than the more scientifically
and technologically oriented AEC had been.[11] The commission's proceedings, after all, placed a premium on technical expertise. Moreover, antinuclear forces believed litigation would allow them to frame the legal issue and pick a more sympathetic decision-making forum. Repeated references by members of the JCAE
and AEC to "fear-mongers," "Nervous Nellies," and "unreasoning critics" led nuclear activists to believe, not incorrectly, that the courts might give their claims
more serious consideration.[12]

Certainly one of the most important developments in American politics in
the 1960s and 1970s was the increasingly active role of the judiciary in many policy issues. Nowhere was this judicial activism more apparent than in the area of
administrative law, as the federal courts played a leading role in reforming the
administrative process. According to Melnick, the courts' activism was based on
the premise that business groups exercised too much power in the regulatory process and often succeeded in capturing bureaucratic agencies.[13] The courts' solution to this particular type of regulatory failure was to ensure a "fair representation" of all affected interests in the administrative process.[14] Moreover, the courts
began to insist that agencies live up to their mandates to protect the public interest by encouraging the participation of "nontraditional groups," especially those
claiming to be advocates of the public interest.[15] In some instances the courts
urged administrators themselves to become more aggressive in defending and
protecting the public interest. In a case involving the Federal Power Commission,
for example, the Court of Appeals for the Second Circuit told the FPC that it was
not "to act as an umpire blandly calling balls and strikes for the adversaries appearing before it; the right of the public must receive affirmative protection at the
hands of the Commission."[16]

The courts also began to devote considerable attention to agency oversight.
During this period the courts generally tightened their review of agency decisions and encouraged agencies to restructure their rulemaking and adjudicatory
proceedings. The courts required agencies to explain their actions in greater detail and to show that they had solicited and considered many different points of

view. In some instances, the courts struck down regulations because agencies did not comply with certain procedural requirements; in others, the courts required agencies to reconvene rulemaking sessions for the purpose of considering alternative courses of action. The rationale for this increased oversight was not so much to limit the power of executive agencies as it was to ensure that the agencies were responsive to a broader range of societal interests. Additionally, in building citizen participation directly into the administrative process, the courts hoped to improve the quality of agency decision making: an agency that had considered many points of view would presumably make better decisions.

The extent of public participation in agency decision making often depends on whether an agency is engaged in adjudication or rulemaking. Formal procedures for both are established by the Administrative Procedures Act. The ostensible purpose of adjudication is to resolve disputed facts in a particular case, while rulemaking is designed to allow public input to more general policy issues. Typically, an adjudication is a formal process in which the agency's decision must be made on the record of a trial-type hearing. As in trials, parties to adjudicatory proceedings are allowed to submit evidence, engage in discovery, and conduct cross-examination. Agencies involved in adjudicatory proceedings must provide a statement of "findings and conclusions" on all of the issues placed in contention by the interested parties, and their decisons can be reviewed and reversed by the courts if the record does not support the decision.

Rulemakings, on the other hand, are traditionally much less formal. The Administrative Procedures Act requires agencies seeking to issue, amend, or rescind rules to give advance notice of their intentions in the *Federal Register* and to invite comments from the general public. Public hearings are generally not required, so interested parties participate in the rulemaking through the submission of written statements or arguments. If rulemaking hearings are held, they usually follow a legislative-type format, where each party is allowed to present oral testimony but has no rights of discovery or cross-examination. Rulemakings may be initiated by either the agency or by petition of interested parties.

The AEC's rules of practice established the agency's procedures for both adjudications and rulemakings. For adjudicatory proceedings such as a public hearing for a construction permit or operating license, the AEC would publish a hearing notice in the *Federal Register.* Within sixty days after the hearing notice had been published, the Atomic Safety and Licensing Board would convene a special prehearing conference in order to consider all petitions to intervene, to identify key issues, to begin discovery, and to establish a schedule for further action.[17] The AEC's rules also stated that within sixty days after the completion of discovery, a second prehearing conference would be held to consider "simplifications" or "clarifications" of the issues, to obtain stipulations and admissions of facts, to verify the authenticity of documents, and to establish a hearing schedule and a list of witnesses.[18] Pursuant to the Administrative Procedures Act, every party to the public hearing was granted the right to present such oral or documentary evidence and conduct such cross-examination as was "required to fully disclose the facts."[19] The rules also stipulated that the licensing board's initial decision must be in writing, based on the whole record, and supported by "reliable and substantial evidence."[20]

The commission's rules of practice for rulemaking proceedings were considerably less formal.[21] According to AEC regulations, rulemaking could be initiated by the commission, on the recommendation of another government agency, or on the petition of interested parties. Interested parties could also petition the AEC to issue, amend, or rescind any rule or regulation. Again pursuant to the Administrative Procedures Act, the AEC would publish a notice of its intent to convene a rulemaking. The notice was to include the terms or substance of the proposed rules as well as the issues involved. Interested parties were invited to participate in rulemaking through the submission of statements, information, and arguments in the manner stated in the rulemaking notice. The AEC's usual method was to solicit comments in writing. Finally, when the commission formally adopted a rule or regulation, it was required to issue a general statement of the rule's basis and purpose and publish both the statement and the new rule in the *Federal Register.*[22]

In the mid-1960s, judges began to impose additional procedural requirements on agencies engaged in informal rulemaking. Judges were concerned that "notice and comment" rulemaking was an insufficient check on administrative discretion, but they were reluctant to impose specific procedural requirements on agencies, preferring to leave that determination to the agency's discretion. As a general rule, judges deferred to agencies on questions of fact and rarely overruled administrators on the merits of decisions. For the most part, courts have limited themselves to the question of whether an agency's factual findings were supported by a record. In the 1970s, however, judges began to subject agency decisions—and procedures—to more "searching and careful" review to ensure that the agency had given "adequate consideration" to all relevant factors and had provided genuine opportunities for interested parties to present their views. If they had not, the courts proved quite willing to set the decision aside.[23] In this way, judges forced agencies to produce a more complete record supporting their actions. In practical terms, though, this practice created a strong incentive for agencies to go beyond the requirements of "notice and comment" rulemaking; in many instances, agency lawyers urged administrators to adopt more elaborate hearing and rulemaking procedures in an effort to compile an administrative record that would withstand judicial scrutiny.[24] More often than not, this process entailed increased public participation in agency deliberations.

At the same time, the courts were contributing to the blurring of the Administrative Procedures Act's distinction between adjudication and rulemaking. In an effort to cope with rapidly increasing workloads, administrative agencies were expanding their use of informal rulemaking in place of the more formal adjudicatory proceedings, even though the two proceedings were intended to serve different purposes. Issues that had previously been perceived as more appropriate subjects for adjudication became the focus of rulemaking proceedings. The problem confronting administrators—and judges—was how to resolve factual disputes in such a setting. Typically, informal notice and comment rulemaking failed to generate an adequate record that would allow judges to review the merits of agency actions. The solution many agencies seized upon, with the encouragement of the courts, was the creation of new "hybrid" proceedings that involved elements of both adjudication and rulemaking.[25]

The AEC's 1971 rulemaking for emergency core-cooling systems was a perfect example of the new type of hybrid proceeding. Because the issue was highly controversial, the AEC decided to convene a legislative-type public hearing to accommodate all those interested in participating. For the most part, parties submitted their testimony and arguments in writing, but the AEC also granted parties limited rights of discovery and cross-examination. This experimental proceeding was thus more formal than a typical rulemaking but less formal than a full adjudication. Thus, rulemaking proceedings tended to become more formal and adversarial.

Regulatory agencies typically have broad discretion in prescribing the procedures to be used in their decision-making process. In addition, an agency's choice of procedures is not neutral. Inevitably, some interests gain when certain types of procedures are adopted, while others lose. For example, it has been noted that the reliance of many agencies on case-by-case adjudication, as opposed to rulemaking, may benefit industry interests. When agencies rely on adjudication, regulatory policy tends to develop incrementally as a result of the accumulation of decisions in individual cases. Thus the outcome of any particular adjudication is likely to be of limited significance to most government officials and the general public. Moreover, formal proceedings tend to be expensive, which discourages participation by interests with limited resources. Rulemakings, on the other hand, are generally less expensive and are capable of producing broader policy effects. Therefore, public lobby groups, who were traditionally short of resources, were said to prefer rulemaking because it allowed them to use their scarce resources more efficiently.[26]

For the most part, the AEC preferred to rely on case-by-case adjudication rather than rulemaking in its licensing review process. Regulatory policy thus evolved in an ad hoc manner through decisions handed down by the commission's licensing boards. Consequently, opponents of nuclear power were forced to raise their objections time and again in proceedings that placed a premium on legal, technical, amd economic resources. Because opposition to most nuclear plants in the early 1970s was localized, intervenors were usually outgunned. Furthermore, the commission's preference for adjudication discouraged participation by national environmental organizations, who preferred to pursue other political strategies that promised larger policy effects.[27]

The commission continued to rely predominantly on case-by-case adjudication throughout the decade, although it began to make more frequent use of the rulemaking option as time went by.[28] The AEC first used the rulemaking option for a controversial issue in the ECCS proceedings in 1971; in the next few years, the commission convened a number of other rulemakings to consider "generic" safety issues, which were problems affecting more than one reactor. Although antinuclear groups liked the generic rulemaking option in principle, they were concerned that the commission was using it not as a means of resolving important safety problems, but as a convenient mechanism for removing troublesome issues from individual licensing cases in order to avoid licensing delays. According to the commission's rules, once a particular issue was labeled "generic," it could no longer be contested in individual licensing cases. Moreover, most of the commission's generic rulemaking proceedings were held in Washington, which severely limited the opportunities for local intervenor groups to attend. In their study of the AEC's licensing process, Ebbin and Kasper noted that an increased reliance on generic hearings "could easily become a means for frustrating citizen participation by considering important issues in a relatively inaccessible forum, for all intents and purposes hidden from public view."[29]

During the 1970s the concerns of reformers and judges converged with respect to the administrative process. Both sought to open up the process to greater citizen participation and to improve the quality of agency decision making. In bringing their complaints to the courts, antinuclear forces concentrated their attack on the AEC's licensing and rulemaking procedures. Edward Berlin, one of the attorneys involved in the *Calvert Cliffs* case, told the joint committee that intervenors were not upset with the substantive determinations of the AEC but with "the complete absence of procedural due process in the decision-making scheme."[30] These appeals for due process were warmly received by judges seeking to democratize administrative decision making. Indeed, the federal courts handed down several decisions in the 1970s that greatly enhanced the access of antinuclear forces to the commission's records and proceedings. However, the basic format of commission decision making remained intact, with policy evolving incrementally through case-by-case adjudication.

CALVERT CLIFFS COORDINATING COMMITTEE V. AEC

On 23 July 1971 the Court of Appeals for the D.C. Circuit issued the single most important decision in the history of the atomic energy program.[31] In a case with far-reaching implications for other federal agencies, antinuclear forces won an impressive victory that helped transform the AEC's decision-making procedures. In its decision the D.C. Circuit told the commission that it could no longer engage in narrow, incremental decision making, and that it must consider the environmental consequences of its actions at all stages of its licensing review process. Largely as result of the increased regulatory workload stemming from the ruling, the AEC issued no new contruction permits or operating licenses for a period of seventeen months.

The *Calvert Cliffs* decision actually involved two separate cases that had been consolidated for argument by the D.C. Circuit. In one case, the Calvert Cliffs Coordinating Committee, a group of local environmentalists, joined by the Sierra Club and the National Wildlife Federation, claimed that certain aspects of the AEC's environmental regulations violated the National Environmental Policy Act (NEPA). In the second case, the same groups challenged the application of those regulations in a construction permit hearing for the Calvert Cliffs, Maryland, nuclear plant. The D.C. Circuit, in a scathing opinion written by Judge Skelly Wright, agreed with the environmental groups and ordered the AEC to make fundamental revisions in its licensing process. According to the court, the AEC would have to conduct detailed environmental reviews for all nuclear plants licensed after 1 January 1970. Furthermore, the commission would have to consider the environmental consequences of its actions at all stages of the licensing process and would have to "balance" environmental concerns along with other values that had traditionally received consideration in the decision-making process. In the words of one attorney involved in the case, the decision established "the principle that important administrative decisions . . . are to be made frankly, openly, and with the public permitted to participate." An attorney for the Natural Resources Defense Council commented that "on almost every issue he took up, Skelly Wright's language couldn't have been better if the environmentalists had written the opinion themselves."[32]

Indeed, Judge Wright's opinion echoed many of the same criticisms of the administrative process expressed by public lobby groups. Wright was clearly concerned with the problem of administrative discretion, fearing that the AEC was either unable or unwilling to consider alternative points of view in its licensing review process. If that were the case, it would be up to the courts to monitor the agency's decision-making process to ensure that all relevant issues and parties were given "adequate consideration." In arguing their case to the court, the Calvert Cliffs intervenors claimed that several provisions of the AEC's environmental regulations violated NEPA. Because the case was one of the first judicial decisions involving the new law, it had implications for many federal agencies. Judging from the tone of the opinion, the D.C. Circuit apparently wanted administrators to know that they should take their NEPA responsibilities seriously. Prior to the passage of NEPA, the AEC had frequently argued that it lacked the statutory authority to consider the environmental consequences of its actions.[33] The AEC's attitude was not surprising given its zealous promotion of nuclear power, but it was precisely that sense of mission that NEPA was intended to challenge.

According to the court, in passing NEPA Congress hoped to convince federal agencies that "environmental protection is as much a part of their responsibility as is protection and promotion of the industries they regulate."[34] Drawing upon the act's legislative history, the court argued that NEPA "makes environmental protection part of the mandate of every federal agency" and required the AEC "and other agencies to *consider* environmental issues just as they consider other matters within their mandates."[35] According to Wright, the AEC was not only permitted to consider the environmental consequences of its actions, it was compelled to do so. Furthermore, the responsibility for ensuring that NEPA's promise was fulfilled rested with the courts, who "must assess claims that one of the agencies charged with its administration has failed to live up to the congressional mandate. Our duty, in short, is to see that important legislative purposes, heralded in the halls of Congress, are not lost or misdirected in the vast hallways of the federal bureaucracy."[36] In his opinion, Wright argued that NEPA set a high standard for administrative agencies, and it was a standard that would have to be enforced by the courts. In arguing its case before the court, the AEC had claimed that NEPA's mandate was vague and thus allowed agency officials considerable discretion in implementing its various provisions. Wright disagreed. In a signal to agencies everywhere, he noted that although the act's substantive policy was flexible, its procedural provisions were designed to see that all federal agencies did in fact exercise the substantive discretion given them. NEPA's procedural provisions, said the court, created "judicially enforceable duties" and established a "strict standard of compliance."[37]

In the opinion of the court, NEPA envisioned "a rather finely tuned and systematic balancing analysis" of environmental, economic, and technical factors.[38] To ensure that this analysis was faithfully conducted, NEPA required agencies to prepare detailed environmental impact statements to assess the environmental consequences of proposed actions as well as alternatives that could minimize those consequences. According to the court, the legislative intent behind NEPA's procedural requirements was to improve the agency's decision-making process by ensuring that each administrator "has before him and takes into account all approaches to a particular project." "Only in that fashion," continued Wright, "is it likely that the most intelligent, optimally beneficial decision will ultimately be made."[39]

The AEC's environmental regulations implementing NEPA had gone into effect in December 1970.[40] The environmental groups objected to a provision that prohibited licensing boards from considering environmental issues in licensing proceedings unless they were contested. The AEC rule stated that when parties to a proceeding failed to contest environmental issues, such issues would not be considered by the Atomic Safety and Licensing Board. Rather, under such circumstances the applicant's environmental report, comments thereon, and the detailed environmental statement would "accompany" the application through the commission's review process, but they would not be received into evidence by the licensing board, and the "Commission's responsibility under the National Environmental Policy Act of 1969 will be carried out in toto outside the hearing process."[41] Upon examining this rule, the court found that "the Commission's crabbed interpretation of NEPA makes a mockery of the Act." In colorful language chiding the commission, the court characterized the rule as "ludicrous" and asked "what possible purpose could there be" in requiring the detailed statement to accompany proposals through the agency review process "if 'accompany' means no more than physical proximity?"[42] According to the court, the word "accompany" in section 102 (2)(c) of NEPA must be read "to indicate a congressional intent that environmental factors, as compiled in the 'detailed statement,' be *considered* through agency review processes."[43] Finding that NEPA was addressed to entire agencies and not just their professional staffs, the court argued that environmental impact statements must be considered at "every stage where an overall balancing of environmental and nonenvironmental factors is appropriate and where alterations might be made in the proposed action to minimize environmental costs." For the AEC, this stipulation meant that its licensing boards would have to examine the environmental statement to determine whether the regulatory staff's review was adequate. The court's rationale for imposing this new requirement on the AEC was that independent review by the licensing boards would provide "a crucial check on the staff's recommendations."[44]

In ruling that licensing boards would have to consider environmental factors in both contested and uncontested proceedings, the court noted that the agency had an affirmative obligation to consider the environmental effects of its actions and could not rely on intervenors to take the initiative. Moreover, it would be "unrealistic" to assume that there would always be an intervenor with the ability and inclination to contest the staff's environmental review. In the eyes of the court, NEPA established environmental protection as an "integral part" of the AEC's basic mandate: "The primary responsibility for fulfilling that mandate lies with the AEC. Its responsibility is not simply to sit back, like an umpire, and resolve adversary contentions at the hearing stage. Rather, it must itself take the initiative of considering environmental values at every distinctive and comprehensive stage of the process."[45]

Although the comments of the D.C. Circuit were specifically addressed to the AEC, it was abundantly clear that the court was putting other agencies on notice that they would have to pursue aggressively their NEPA mandates as well. The court went to great lengths to point out that while it could probably not reverse an agency's substantive decisions under section 101 of NEPA unless it could show that the decision was somehow arbitrary or clearly inadequate, it would not hesitate to enforce NEPA's section 102 procedural requirements. Noting that NEPA's language required agencies to fulfill their procedural duties to the "fullest extent possible," the court enthusiastically embraced the responsibility for enforcing the performance of those duties, saying that "if the decision was reached procedurally without individualized consideration and balancing of environmental factors—conducted fully and in good faith—it is the responsibility of the courts to reverse."[46]

A second issue before the court was an AEC rule that prohibited the licensing boards from conducting an independent evaluation and balancing of certain environmental factors if other government agencies had already certified that their own environmental standards were fulfilled. More specifically, the AEC had indicated that it would defer to water quality standards devised and administered by state agencies and approved by the federal government under the Water Quality Improvement Act. Accordingly, the commission's rules prohibited licensing boards from independently considering water quality issues, which in the court's view was "perhaps the most significant impact of nuclear power plants." Arguing that the AEC's rule would cause NEPA procedures to "wither away in disuse," the court struck down the rule as an "abdication" of the commission's responsibilities under NEPA.[47] Relying extensively on the legislative history of NEPA, the D.C. Circuit ruled that because the AEC was the only agency with overall responsibility for nuclear power, it would therefore have to conduct its own "individualized balancing analysis" to ensure that "the optimally beneficial action [was] finally taken."[48] As a result, the court held that the commission could not rely upon the environmental determinations of other federal agencies.

The *Calvert Cliffs* case was widely perceived as a stunning defeat for the AEC, yet the commission decided not to appeal the decision. In announcing that decision, the commission's new chairman, James Schlesinger, said it was the AEC's intention to be more responsive to the concerns of conservation and environmental groups. As a result of the decision, the commission added environmental specialists to its regulatory staff and licensing board panels. The addition of personnel trained in environmental sciences introduced new—and potentially conflicting—professional norms into the AEC staff and led to greater sensitivity to the environmental effects of nuclear reactors. The *Calvert Cliffs* decision thus enhanced the position of environmental advocates *within* the commission by institutionalizing an environmental perspective in the commission's decision-making process.

On the same day that Schlesinger announced the AEC would not appeal the *Calvert Cliffs* decision, the commission convened a meeting with environmental groups and industry representatives to discuss new environmental regulations that had been drafted by the regulatory staff in response to the court's decision. The AEC published a revised policy statement on 9 September 1971 in which it specified its new procedures for carrying out NEPA requirements.[49] Reaction from environmental groups to the new rules was generally positive, but there was a consensus among industry representatives that the AEC had "overreacted" to the court's ruling.[50] The AEC's new rules required the regulatory staff to prepare a cost-benefit analysis of the facility, taking into account the environmental consequences of the reactor; they also required the regulatory staff to prepare environmental impact statements for both construction permit and operating license reviews. The rules also established NEPA hearing procedures for licensing board consideration of environmental issues. Furthermore, applicants were required to submit more detailed information in their environmental impact statements to the staff as part of the licensing review process.

As a result of these new requirements, the AEC's licensing process came to a screeching halt. The commission issued no new construction permits or operating licenses for a period of seventeen months. According to Nathaniel Goodrich, chairman of the commission's Atomic Safety and Licensing Board Panel, the new environmental hearing and impact statement requirements, in conjunction with the large number of applications being received by the licensing staff, contributed to a "logjam" in the licensing process.[51] In an effort to put the licensing process back on track, the AEC hired additional environmental staff and shifted personnel from other tasks to the preparation of environmental impact statements.

The new environmental regulations produced some substantive changes in commission policy as well. In December 1971, for example, the AEC published new rules concerning the types of site preparation activities applicants for construction permits could engage in while their application was pending. Although the AEC's old rules had prohibited the applicant from pouring foundations or installing any portion of the nuclear reactor building before the permit had been issued, they did allow excavation, road building, the installation of railroad and transmission lines, and the construction of certain nonnuclear facilities. The new rules, however, prohibited preconstruction permit clearing of land, excavation, and other "substantial action that adversely affects the natural environment."[52] Other regulations resulted in significant design changes at nuclear plants. The owners of the Indian Point Two and Peach Bottom plants were forced to redesign their water intake structures and reactor cooling systems; the radioactive waste recovery systems at the San Onofre and Vermont Yankee reactors had to be upgraded; and Consumer's Power Company, the owner of the Midland, Michigan, plant, was forced to reroute the plant's transmission lines.[53]

The *Calvert Cliffs* case was not the only example of the D.C. Circuit's increased scrutiny of the commission's decision-making process; nor was it the only instance where the commission suffered defeat. In the *Quad Cities* case, for example, the Court barred the AEC from authorizing an interim operating license before the commission had completed its NEPA 102 (2)(c) procedures. In 1973 the Scientists' Institute for Public Information (SIPI) brought suit against the AEC, claiming that the commission had failed to fulfill its NEPA responsibilities with respect to the proposed liquid metal fast breeder reactor. SIPI argued that because the breeder reactor would produce plutonium, the commission should consider the environmental consequences before it began construction. The D.C. Circuit agreed, saying the unique hazards of plutonium warranted "the most searching scrutiny under NEPA." Similarly, in 1975 the court ordered the commission to perform an individualized analysis of the costs and benefits of reducing routine radioiodine emissions in accordance with the commission's own regulations.[54] Quite clearly, the Court of Appeals for the D.C. Circuit was paying a great deal of attention to the commission's proceedings.

NATURAL RESOURCES DEFENSE COUNCIL V. NRC

In two decisions handed down on 21 July 1976, the D.C. Circuit again served notice that it would closely monitor the commission's decision-making procedures to ensure that it was fulfilling its statutory mandates under NEPA and the Atomic Energy Act.[55] In both decisions the court stressed that agencies were to consider a broad range of views when contemplating any significant actions. The court hoped that forcing agencies to produce a detailed record of their actions would not only make agencies more accountable but would result in better decisions. The court also paid particular attention to the procedures used by the commission in its licensing and rulemaking proceedings and emphasized the commission's obligation to adhere to the standards of due process.

In the *Natural Resources Defense Council v. NRC case,* the D.C. Circuit set aside the waste management and reprocessing portions of the NRC's uranium fuel cycle rule and remanded the Vermont Yankee Nuclear Power Station operating license to the commission for further consideration pending a review of the rule.[56] In rendering its decision, the court held that the NRC's rule was not adequately documented or explained. The court's majority seemed to think that the inadequacy of the record reflected the inadequacy of the procedures used by the licensing board to develop the rulemaking record.[57] To remedy the situation, the NRC was advised to make a "sensitive, deliberate" use of fact-finding procedures going beyond the requirements of "notice and commment" rulemaking as set forth in the Administrative Procedures Act. This decision was later reversed on appeal by the Supreme Court in the landmark *Vermont Yankee* case.[58] Nevertheless, the case was significant because cautious administrators often adopted the more stringent procedural measures to avoid the threat of being overruled by the D.C. Circuit, which handled far more regulatory cases than the Supreme Court. According to Antonin Scalia, the D.C. Circuit functioned as a "resident manager," while the Supreme Court was more of an "absentee landlord." As a result, it was the court of appeals that had to be satisfied on an everyday basis and not the Supreme Court.[59] Accordingly, rational administrators, because they do not like having their decisions overturned, would seek to please the D.C. Circuit.

In his opinion, Judge Bazelon acknowledged that it was usually improper and unwise for judges to impose particular administrative procedures on an agency, saying such decisions were best left to the agency's discretion. Nevertheless, he recognized that an agency's choice of procedures inevitably influenced the substantive depth and quality of its decisions. Like Judge Wright, Bazelon was a proponent of administrative reform and frequently sought to open up agency decision making to a broader range of participants. One way to acccomplish that goal was for judges to require agencies to provide clearer and more detailed explanations of their actions. Although the courts might have been hesitant to require agencies to adopt particular procedures, they were not at all reluctant to pass judgment on the adequacy of the agency's decision record. According to Bazelon, it was the court's responsibility to "scrutinize the record as a whole to ensure that genuine opportunities to participate in a meaningful way were provided, and that the agency has taken a good, hard look at the major questions before it."[60] To the extent that the court did review an agency's procedures, its goal was to determine whether or not the agency had adequately "ventilated" the key issues.

The court also noted that NEPA required federal agencies to ensure that officials making the final decision were "informed of the full range of responsible opinion" on the environmental effects of an action in order to make an "informed choice." According to Bazelon, the AEC's decision to proceed by rulemaking did not relieve the agency of this responsibility, nor did it allow the AEC to rely on the intervenors to present the full range of scientific opinion. As it had in the *Calvert Cliffs* decision, the D.C. Circuit said the commission had an affirmative obligation to explore the issues in depth rather than wait for intervenors to take the initiative.[61]

Accordingly, Bazelon claimed that in order to determine whether the NRC had lived up to its statutory responsibilities, the court would have to examine the record to determine whether the commission's decision was based on a "real give and take" on the relevant issues. Bazelon added that "where only one side of a controversial issue is developed in any detail, the agency may abuse its discretion by deciding the issue on an inadequate record. A reviewing court must assure itself not only that a diversity of informed opinion was heard, but that it was genuinely considered."[62] Moreover, because judges were often incapable of making an informed analysis of scientific and technical issues such as those involved in this rulemaking, the court said it was dependent on the agency's expertise "as reflected in the statement of basis and purpose" to "distill the major issues which were ventilated and to articulate its reasoning with regard to each of them."[63] More specifically, Bazelon noted that "boilerplate generalities brushing aside detailed criticism on the basis of agency 'judgement' or 'expertise' avail nothing; what is required is a reasoned response, in which the agency points to particulars in the record which, when coupled with its reservoir of expertise, support its resolution of the controversy."[64]

According to the court, the commission failed to do this. What seemed to upset the court the most was that the commission offered very little in the way of details or scientific references in support of the rule. The court found that the "materials uncritically relied on by the Commission in promulgating this rule consist of extremely vague assurances by agency personnel that problems as yet unsolved will be solved."[65] That promise, said the court, was "an insufficient record to sustain" the rule, which it then set aside. As in the *Calvert Cliffs* case, the D.C. Circuit was clearly unhappy with the commission's apparent reluctance to provide good faith consideration to issues that threatened the licensing of nuclear reactors. The dilemma confronting the court, though, was how to require the agency to produce a more adequate record without prescribing specific procedural requirements as well.

Although Bazelon was hesitant to impose specific procedures on the NRC, he did offer some hints, noting that the commission had a variety of procedures available for its use in the rulemaking proceeding, including informal conferences, document discovery, advisory committees of outside experts, limited cross-examination, and literature surveys. Nevertheless, Bazelon stressed that the court would not dictate specific procedures to the commission, saying that whatever procedures the commission eventually adopted would have to generate a record that "fully developed" the factual issues. This requirement meant the commission would have to "identify and address information contrary to its own position, to articulate its reasoning, and to specify the evidence on which it relies."[66] Clearly, the court was willing to interpret its responsibilities broadly in an effort to force agencies to produce better decisions.

The D.C. Circuit's decision in the NRDC case was quite controversial and moved the joint committee to hold hearings to investigate the decision's effect on the licensing process. The commission and the nuclear industry were also quite upset with the ruling. In fact, the utilities involved in the case decided to appeal the ruling to the Supreme Court because they felt the decision established a precedent for the courts to revoke existing licenses. On appeal, the Supreme Court unanimously reversed the D.C. Circuit, accusing the lower court of excessive judicial activism, and even went so far as to characterize the reasoning of the lower court as "Kafkaesque."[67] In its decision, the Supreme Court ruled that the Administrative Procedures Act required only notice and comment procedures for informal rulemaking and said that the appeals court had erred in invalidating portions of the fuel cycle rule for lack of insufficient adjudicatory procedures.[68]

The decision in the *Vermont Yankee* case indicates that the Supreme Court was more willing than the D.C. Circuit to defer to the judgment of the commission when it came to administrative procedures. In fact, during the 1970s the Supreme Court consistently told district courts to refrain from second-guessing the commission's expertise.[69] As a result, judicial oversight of commission decision making became more relaxed after *Vermont Yankee*. Still, for most of the decade the trend had been toward increased judicial oversight of commission decision making, not less.

THE EFFECTS OF INCREASED OVERSIGHT

One of the most significant consequences of increased oversight by the courts was that the commission, and its staff, devoted greater attention to procedural rights in an attempt to ensure that its procedures were seen as fair and capable of generating a record that could withstand judicial scrutiny. Rather than run the risk of being overturned by a reviewing court, the commission would try to show that it had solicited and considered many points of view. This approach was clearly illustrated in a March 1971 opinion of one Atomic Safety and Licensing Board, which granted a late request by a local citizens' group to intervene in an operating license hearing. In explaining its actions, the board noted that it had "granted all requests for intervention including those which were technically untimely. . . . In doing so, the Board feels it acted consistently with the policies of the Atomic Energy Commission to encourage public participation, and *also with the clear trend of recent court decisions.*"[70]

In addition, the commission significantly revised its rules to allow greater public input into its decision-making process. In 1970, for example, the AEC changed its regulations to allow public disclosure of certain correspondence and reports between applicants and the regulatory staff. In 1973, the commission began to permit intervenors to meet informally with the regulatory staff and to attend presentations by the applicant and staff to the ACRS.[71] Later that same year the AEC announced plans to provide greater advance notice of its proposed rulemaking proceedings and to invite public comments before preparing the specifics of proposed rules. Furthermore, the commission adopted a new rule in 1977 that allowed parties in contested licensing proceedings to petition the commission for discretionary review of Atomic Safety and Licensing Appeal Board (ASLAB) decisions. The new rules also allowed parties to petition for a stay of all ASLAB decisions or actions pending commission review.[72] In 1978, the commission changed its rules to allow citizens to attend all meetings conducted by the technical staff as part of its review of applications for operating licenses or construction permits.[73] Some observers, however, believed these changes were more show than substance and were actually designed to extend procedural due process to the public "while not in any way changing the basic structure of the hearings to permit citizen group input to play an important role in the decision-making process."[74]

A second consequence of increased judicial oversight was a longer and more detailed review process that led, in turn, to more stringent environmental and safety standards. In an effort to satisfy its overseers, who were demanding more comprehensive and rigorous reviews, the commission upgraded the size and quality of its technical review staff. In order to carry out its new environmental review and reporting requirements under NEPA, for example, the commission expanded its environmental staff. In fact, the entire regulatory staff grew in size and sophistication throughout the late 1960s and 1970s. The larger, better, and more experienced regulatory staff began demanding more detailed information from utility applicants. Moreover, the commission was cognizant of the fact that the courts were more likely to overturn standards if the commission's decision-making process was procedurally deficient. As a result, the commission standardized its licensing review process in 1972.

Because nuclear technology was still relatively new, commission safety reviews in the 1960s had typically been rather informal, with the regulatory staff working closely with the applicant to resolve potential problems. At the time, the regulatory staff was working with only very general safety criteria and guidelines. In many instances, the staff knew very little about the design of the proposed reactor because the utility would not begin detailed design work until the construction permit was in hand. Because no two reactors were alike, the safety review process varied from reactor to reactor.[75] In the words of Clifford Beck, the commission's deputy director of regulation, early reactors were "evaluated and particular safety requirements specified more or less on a case by case basis with regulations, guides, and instructions setting forth mostly the principal areas of consideration."[76] Eventually, the commission recognized that it needed to bring some order to the process so the staff, and the applicant, would know what to expect.

As a result, the commission developed standard review plans for both safety and environmental analyses.[77] The standard review plans identified the information needed by the staff in performing their technical review of applications and suggested a format for its presentation. As a case in point, the standard review plans for safety analyses described in detail how the review was to be done and stated the criteria applied by the staff in assessing various safety systems. According to the commission, the purpose of the plans was to improve the quality and uniformity of staff reviews and to stabilize or formalize the licensing process. Perhaps most important, the commission also hoped that use of the standardized review format would provide a clearer basis for agency decisions, one that could stand up to judicial review.

The commission's shift toward more stringent safety standards also can be attributed to its desire to minimize political conflict. It has been suggested that the incentives facing agency administrators encourage them to adopt stringent standards rather than weak ones because stringent standards are less likely to provoke a response from either the public or the courts.[78] Because nuclear power was such a controversial issue in the 1970s, and because the D.C. Circuit was monitoring its actions so closely, the incentives facing the NRC may have been even more pronounced.

But it would be incorrect to attribute the commission's more stringent approach to regulation entirely to the political controversy over nuclear safety and the attendant increase in congressional and judicial oversight; other factors that predated the public debate also contributed.[79] For example, the commission's regulatory staff did grow in response to political pressures, but it also grew because of the increased regulatory workload facing the commission. Put simply, there were more applications for construction permits and operating licenses, so the regulatory staff had to grow to keep pace.[80] The larger, more experienced staff thus increased the commission's ability to conduct more detailed and demanding safety reviews. Moreover, by the early 1970s the staff were beginning to learn that some existing regulations were inadequate and failed to provide adequate margins of safety. As the staff reviewed more reactors and assessed existing standards, they uncovered problems that needed to be addressed and began to issue more specific safety criteria and regulations.[81]

In November 1970, for example, the regulatory staff established the practice of issuing "regulatory guides," which described the methods acceptable to the staff for implementing specific parts of the commission's regulations. In some instances, the regulatory guides described the techniques used by the staff in assessing certain problems. The regulatory guides also provided instructions to applicants concerning the information needed by the staff in their review. Although the guides were not formal regulations, they were usually treated as such by applicants.[82] The trend toward more rigorous regulation is illustrated by the steady increase in the number of regulatory guides issued by the staff, from 21 at the end of 1971 to 143 at the end of 1978. Several studies have shown that the imposition of more stringent regulatory requirements led to extensive design and construction changes as well as to more costly manufacturing, testing, and performance criteria for structural materials and components. Ironically, however, this approach helped undermine confidence in the agency's capabilities, because it seemed to be an admission that existing safety standards, and therefore existing reactors, were deficient. In other words, regulatory changes designed to enhance the long-term prospects for nuclear power conflicted with the short-term political and economic interests of the commission and the nuclear power industry.[83]

Finally, another factor contributing to the commission's increasingly tough regulatory standards was a dramatic increase in the size of nuclear reactors themselves. At the end of 1966 the largest reactor in operation was under three hundred megawatts, but by the end of the decade utilities were placing orders for plants two to three times larger. The problem was that larger, more powerful reactors posed more troublesome questions from a safety perspective. The fuel in larger reactors would overheat more quickly in the event of a failure in the plant's cooling system, and larger reactors contained higher levels of radioactivity. In short, larger reactors seemed to pose a greater risk to public health and safety, especially since utilities were pressuring the commission to approve reactors closer to population centers. Furthermore, by 1965 the ACRS had already concluded that containment structures, the standard means of protecting the public from radioactive releases, would not be as effective with the newer generation of larger reactors. Recognition of these facts forced the commission to shift its basic approach to safety. Previously, the AEC had relied upon a combination of remote siting and reactor containment; now it would place greater emphasis on accident prevention.[84] In discussing the effects of reactor location and size upon the commission's safety philosophy, Clifford Beck noted that "just to maintain the level of risk of individuals and to the population where it is now . . . would require improvement in the safety status of the facility."[85] This situation meant that the commission would have to pay much closer attention to reactor designs and safety systems to ensure that they would provide extra margins of safety.

INTEREST GROUPS AND THE NRC

Congressional lobbying is often the first priority of groups seeking to influence public policy because Congress attracts considerable media attention. This is particularly true of public interest groups that because of a chronic lack of resources are likely to pursue political strategies that promote the salience of their cause. But the policy process does not end in Congress; policies must still be implemented. Logically, then, public interest groups that seek to change the substance of public policies should also try to influence the bureaucracy. Many public interest groups, however, lack the financial, administrative, or technical resources to sustain any meaningful participation in the implementation phase. Industry groups, on the other hand, generally do not have to worry about either resources or maintaining the attention of their members; they can therefore devote their energies to both the legislative and administrative arenas.[86] As a result, industry groups have been able to maximize their influence over rulemaking because of their greater ability to monitor the process.

Given these facts, it should not be surprising to discover that the efforts of nuclear activists, Congress, and the courts to "remake" the regulatory process were not entirely successful. Although the ability of antinuclear groups to monitor Congress and the NRC was significantly enhanced, their access to the NRC's regulatory deliberations remained minimal. Conversely, industry groups, who had reorganized to improve their congressional lobbying capabilities, continued to enjoy privileged access to the regulatory process, where the NRC's standards and regulations were formulated.

In fact, one study of NRC–interest group relationships concluded that the active group constituency of the NRC was remarkably similar to that of the AEC, with the same groups having more frequent contact with the commission. Although national environmental groups and local citizens' groups tried to establish stable relationships with the commission, they were not nearly as successful as groups representing electric utilities and the reactor vendors. Among national groups, the most active in this regard were the Union of Concerned Scientists (UCS), Friends of the Earth, Natural Resources Defense Council (NRDC), Critical Mass, Sierra Club, and Public Interest Research Group (PIRG). Although these groups did become a factor in nuclear politics in the 1970s, their relationship with the NRC was largely limited to oversight, and they never rivaled the industry's influence with the commission.[87]

As in other policy areas, much of the explanation for this limited success can be traced to their lack of economic and technical resources. Although some groups such as the UCS, NRDC, and PIRG did acquire some technical expertise, they were fundamentally outmatched when it came to participating in rulemaking proceedings and deliberations over standards development, which placed a premium on technical knowledge and information. For example, in 1978 the NRDC had a staff of sixty-five and an annual budget of about $2.5 million, but only three of its scientific staff and 15 percent of its resources were devoted to NRC matters. Similarly, the UCS only had twelve staffers and a budget of $675,000 in 1978. Perhaps more important, its meager budget had actually increased fourfold from 1975 levels. Other groups opposed to nuclear power, such as Friends of the Earth and the Sierra Club, only allocated about 5 percent and 10 percent respectively of their resources to nuclear regulation. On the other hand, the typical interest group in the industry sector had seven times the financial resources and five times the human resources of the typical environmental group. The six environmental groups at least sporadically involved with NRC had total annual expenditures of $3.7 million and a staff of 109, while the three trade associations with regular NRC contact had combined resources of $29 million and a staff of 531. The industry figures do not include the Washington offices of either reactor vendors or major public utilities.[88] These figures suggest that antinuclear groups were not equally equipped to compete in the arena of regulatory politics.

This disparity was particularly true when it came to establishing relationships with the NRC staff, which remained relatively insulated from the demands of antinuclear groups. Interest groups have many reasons to establish relationships with regulatory staffers; informal staff contacts, in particular, can provide interested groups with valuable information on pending rules and regulations and may even allow groups to shape the regulatory agenda. A more telling indicator of regulatory influence, however, is the propensity of staffers to contact outside groups. In an effort to minimize technical mistakes, regulatory staffs routinely seek advice and information from interest groups, but they are more likely to solicit advice from sources they deem credible. It follows, then, that the NRC staff would be more likely to seek the advice of industry groups because of their greater technical expertise. Indeed, according to one student of the NRC, expert credibility was a major factor in establishing a working relationship with the NRC staff. As John Chubb has shown, this "resurrects group resources as a gatekeeper to organizational relationships. All things being equal, resources provide expertise, and expertise provides the possibility of privileged access."[89] In fact, only the Atomic Industrial Forum (AIF) and the Edison Electric Institute, two industry groups, maintained working relationships with the NRC staff. The AIF reported "daily contact" with the NRC staff, which initiated approximately half of the contacts. Despite their efforts, environmental groups were generally not contacted by the staff, with the exception of routine notifications of upcoming proceedings and public announcements, suggesting that the NRC, like the AEC before it, considered the industry groups to be more legitimate and valuable participants in the regulatory process.

National environmental groups, however, had greater success in establishing relationships with NRC commissioners, particularly after the election of Jimmy Carter. Several of the groups, including the Sierra Club and Friends of the Earth, were contacted by commissioners on an intermittent basis after 1977 for their views on policy matters. The commissioners, evidently, were responding to Carter's lukewarm attitude toward nuclear power and took the initiative to reach out to interests that had previously been excluded.[90] Still, most significant regulatory matters were handled by the staff or the licensing boards and not by the commissioners. In the final analysis, then, because of their shortage of resources and expertise antinuclear groups did not achieve equal access to or influence in the crucial early stages of rulemaking. On the other hand, sympathetic media coverage helped antinuclear groups keep the controversy in the public eye and enabled them to gain much greater access to Congress and the White House.

CONCLUSION

Through much of the 1950s and 1960s, the arena of nuclear policy was notable because it had so few access points; all roads led through the AEC and JCAE. This policy monopoly was supported by an overwhelmingly positive view of nuclear power. Shifting perceptions, however, helped critics of nuclear power transform the issue into a debate over public health and safety which, in turn, attracted the attention of many new governmental actors. I have argued here that the courts were among the first new actors to join the fray. As we have seen, the courts were receptive to the pleas of antinuclear activists and intervened to open up the AEC to greater and more meaningful citizen participation. Significant changes in commission licensing and rulemaking proceedings followed, and access to commission information and decision makers became far less exclusive than it had been at the beginning of the decade.

These changes were not simply the result of antinuclear groups demanding access to previously inaccessible forums. During the 1960s and 1970s, the federal courts had become similarly involved in a number of other policy areas dominated by subgovernments. The fall of many of these policy monopolies during the same period suggests that policy communities are not immune to broad social and political trends. At certain times, the American political system's structures of bias are radically altered. The public lobby era of the 1960s and 1970s was such a time. Different social groups mobilized; new institutions were created and older ones destroyed. Together, these changes worked against the operation of policy monopolies by rendering the political system more open and accessible to a wider range of interests. Many who had been excluded could now, for the first time, voice their demands with some chance of being heard. The federal courts played an important role in granting access to antinuclear groups. But fundamental policy shifts would require more than the courts could deliver. The AEC and the JCAE were on the defensive, to be sure, but they remained firmly in control of commercial nuclear policy. Other structural changes would be necessary before significant policy departures could be expected.

5
The Demise of the AEC

Knowledge will forever govern ignorance. And a people who mean to be their own governors must arm themselves with the power knowledge gives. A popular government, without popular information or the means of acquiring it, is but the prologue to a farce or tragedy.

—James Madison

During the 1970s venue changes within the executive and legislative branches buffeted the atomic subgovernment. The increasing importance of energy issues, the reorganization of committee jurisdictions within Congress, and the departure from government of many longtime supporters of nuclear power led to the demise of both the AEC and the JCAE, thereby allowing those seeking policy reform to press their demands in new venues. The factors leading to the demise of the AEC will be examined in this chapter; the institutional changes in Congress are the focus of the next chapter.

Beginning with NEPA's passage in 1969, new laws chipped away at the AEC's monopoly, granting other federal agencies some jurisdiction over commercial nuclear power. The rise of energy issues to prominence a few years later spurred a comprehensive effort to overhaul the federal government's energy apparatus and quickly led to the AEC's abolition, which deprived the nuclear industry of its primary ally in the executive branch. Its replacement, the Nuclear Regulatory Commission (NRC), could not be counted on to be quite as supportive. By the end of the decade, the number of access points to nuclear policy making had grown dramatically, creating valuable opportunities for groups that had previously been excluded. Critics of nuclear power were able to take advantage of those opportunities to gain a degree of success they had not been able to achieve in the insulated realm of subsystem politics.

THE END OF THE AEC MONOPOLY

Congress enacted several laws during the 1970s that contributed to the erosion of the AEC's exclusive jurisdiction over nuclear power plants. Some of the laws imposed new statutory hearing or reporting requirements on the commission, further contributing to the dissemination of information concerning its policies and programs. Many of these laws also granted citizens the right to sue administrative agencies for failing to perform certain nondiscretionary tasks.[1] In passing these laws, Congress was not only making information more widely available but it was challenging many agencies' sense of mission. The National Environmental Policy Act of 1969 (NEPA), for example, was intended to serve notice to administrators that they could no longer avoid consideration of environmental matters in agency decision making. In an effort to force administrators to adopt a comprehensive view of the consequences of their actions, section 102 of NEPA instructed administrators to ensure that environmental values be given "appropriate consideration" in decision making along with economic and technical concerns.[2] According to NEPA, the AEC would have to balance its traditional concern with licensing reactors against the new statutory obligation to protect the environment. The procedural requirements of section 102 were particularly important in this regard, as agencies were forced to prepare detailed environmental impact statements assessing, among other things, the environmental impact of the proposed action, alternatives to the action, and any irreversible and irretrievable commitment of resources that would be involved should the proposal be implemented. Certainly, one of the underlying motivations for the requirement to consider an alternative course of action would be to weaken the ability of organizations like the AEC to maintain a shared sense of mission, rendering the agency more accountable to the wishes of Congress. Finally, because the courts concluded that the section 102 procedures created "judicially enforceable" duties that were nondiscretionary, NEPA provided a new basis for judicial review of administrative action.

In the 1970s Congress also adopted several statutes that mandated the formal inclusion of other agencies in matters formerly under the exclusive jurisdiction of the commission. Laws affecting AEC jurisdiction were enacted during the following years:

Law	Year
Fish and Wildlife Coordination Act	1966
National Environmental Policy Act	1969
Water Quality Improvement Act	1970
Coastal Zone Management Act	1972
Federal Water Pollution Control Act	1972
Endangered Species Act	1973
Toxic Substances Control Act	1976
Clean Air Act	1977

It was during this period, for example, that the Fish and Wildlife Service, the Environmental Protection Agency (EPA), the Federal Energy Regulatory Commission, the Federal Emergency Management Administration, the Energy Research and Development Administration, and later the Department of Energy as well as many state governments inherited jurisdiction over some aspect of nuclear energy policy. Consequently, the number of agencies participating in nuclear energy matters proliferated. In addition, the statutory involvement of these new agencies meant that information about nuclear power would be more readily available. The Water Quality Improvement Act, for example, transferred to the EPA the responsibility for regulating thermal discharges from nuclear plants and gave the EPA the leading role in determining the type of cooling system to be used at power plants. Not only did the transfer involve another agency in nuclear energy policy, but it would later be an important factor in a number of siting controversies. After the EPA regional administrator set aside an earlier determination on the acceptability of the plant's cooling system, the NRC was forced to suspend the plant's construction permit pending further hearings and a revised cost-benefit analysis.

Similarly, section 122 of the Clean Air Act Amendments of 1977 made the EPA the responsible agency for regulating radioactive emissions, assuming jurisdiction from the commission.[3] According to the act, the EPA was required to determine within two years whether emissions of radioactive pollutants would cause or contribute to air pollution that could reasonably be anticipated to endanger public health. If the EPA determined that a pollutant was a threat to public health, the agency was to list each such pollutant under one of the act's three sections and promulgate national primary and secondary ambient air quality standards, new source performance standards, or hazardous air pollutant emission standards. In making such a determination, the EPA was directed to work with the commission. The amendments also gave states the authority to set air quality standards for radioactive materials. States were not only permitted to establish air quality standards more stringent than federal standards, but they could also issue their own standards in the absence of federal standards.[4]

During the 1970s many states also made efforts to stake a claim for themselves in the regulation of nuclear power. A number of them, for example, had assumed some responsibilities under the Agreement States Program, which was established pursuant to the Atomic Energy Act Amendments of 1959. The Agreement States Program authorized the AEC to transfer certain of its regulatory tasks to qualified states, but because these tasks were unrelated to the regulation of nuclear power plants, states were still relatively unimportant actors throughout the 1960s.[5] Moreover, because the Atomic Energy Act granted the AEC exclusive regulatory authority in the area of public health and safety, state efforts to regulate in these areas were routinely invalidated by the federal courts.[6] And yet, by the middle of the decade states had begun to play an increasingly important role in decisions involving nuclear power.

This change was accomplished primarily through comprehensive power plant siting laws, which were adopted by a significant number of states in response to the growing controversy over nuclear power.[7] Many of the siting laws gave the responsible state agency the authority to consider all of the relevant aspects of the proposed plant, including economic, environmental, and health factors. Due to the AEC monopoly on health and safety matters, however, those seeking to prevent the construction of nuclear plants began to focus their attention on questions of cost and the need for power, which have traditionally been within the purview of state and local decision-making bodies. The decision to focus on economic factors rather than on health and safety issues met with some success. By 1981 at least six states had enacted measures that, for reasons of cost, prohibited the construction of new reactors until the federal government had solved the high-level waste disposal problem.[8]

THE EARLY 1970s

The AEC's statutory mandate to develop, promote, and regulate nuclear power was a problem for the agency almost from the beginning. Supporters of nuclear power recognized quite early that the agency's multiple roles created a potential conflict of interest that threatened the public acceptance so crucial to the success of the nuclear enterprise. As early as 1957, the joint committee gave serious consideration to transferring the agency's developmental and regulatory responsibilities to two separate agencies, but the committee, citing the relative immaturity of nuclear technology as well as a shortage of scientific personnel that would make it difficult to adequately staff both agencies, decided such a move would be unwise.[9] The fledgling state of the nuclear industry made the joint committee's decision easier; at the time, a large-scale, competitive nuclear power industry was still a dream, and the handful of reactors that were operating were primarily experimental in nature. For the foreseeable future, then, the AEC would not have much to do in the way of regulation and could devote the bulk of its resources and energies to developing the technology. Nevertheless, it was commonly understood that the growth of the nuclear industry would inevitably lead to a corresponding increase in the commission's regulatory duties. At that point, the tension between the agency's multiple roles would have to be resolved. In the interim, the AEC would continue to develop, promote, and regulate the same industry.

Even though the commissioners were primarily concerned with encouraging the use of nuclear power, they recognized the importance of a credible regulatory apparatus in assuring public confidence in both the agency and the industry. As a result, the AEC took a number of steps over the years, including a seemingly endless series of internal reorganizations, to dispel perceptions that it was beset by a conflict of interest.[10] When only a handful of reactors were under review, the AEC could get by with small and inexperienced licensing and regulatory staffs.

But when utilities began to place orders for more—and bigger—reactors, the AEC had to bolster its staff just to keep pace. As an indication of the increase in the agency's workload, there were twenty-seven orders for reactors between 1953 and 1965. But utilities ordered twenty reactors in 1966 alone and followed that by ordering another thirty in 1967. By the end of 1973 a total of 151 reactors were subject to AEC review.[11] The surge in reactor orders meant that the AEC would have to place greater emphasis on its regulatory duties, which was reflected in a dramatic increase in the agency's staffing levels.

The licensing staff quadrupled between 1962 and 1967; in 1968 the AEC increased the number of inspectors by 50 percent.[12] Overall, the regulatory staff increased from approximately 350 in 1967 to just over 550 in 1971. Despite these increases, during the same period the average time needed for AEC review of an application for a construction permit doubled. With no end in sight to the upsurge in applications for construction permits or operating licenses, the AEC continued to add staff well into the 1970s. In 1970 the commission established an environmental staff group, which grew quite rapidly in the early part of the decade in response to the AEC's expanded environmental duties. In 1972 the AEC substantially increased the number of personnel in its Directorates of Licensing and Regulatory Standards. The commission also added regulatory staff in the area of reactor safety.[13]

Despite the many changes in staffing levels and internal organization, the AEC was unable to rid itself of charges of a conflict of interest. Charges by the UCS and Ralph Nader that the agency was suppressing vital safety information were reported widely in the national media.[14] Moreover, as the dispute among scientists was played out in public, opposition to nuclear power mounted. Public opinion surveys began to track sentiment on the nuclear issue and revealed a slow but steady increase in the number of citizens opposed to nuclear power. Citizens were becoming increasingly skeptical of the AEC's ability or inclination to monitor the nuclear industry.[15]

Largely as a result of the controversies over thermal pollution and radiation, by the early 1970s the AEC was clearly on the defensive, suffering from a deteriorating public image and an almost complete lack of credibility. Many believed that the agency, under the direction of its chairman of ten years, Glenn T. Seaborg, continued to act as a booster of nuclear power rather than an impartial regulator. Seaborg, who was credited with having "discovered" plutonium, was an unabashed advocate of nuclear power; his sheer enthusiasm for all things nuclear was often cited as a major factor in the success of the nuclear industry during the 1960s. Under Seaborg the AEC, as part of its public education programs, produced and distributed numerous films and pamphlets extolling the virtues of atomic energy. The AEC estimated that over 150 million Americans had seen their films, many of which had been coproduced by the Atomic Industrial Forum, the nuclear industry's trade association.[16] Seaborg was a "true believer," and he was proud of the agency's efforts in developing a new source of energy. In that sense, he was probably the perfect choice to spearhead the agency's drive in the mid-1960s to establish the commercial viability of light water reactors. But the same qualities that made him a perfect choice for that effort caused problems when the agency came under fire for minimizing environmental and safety concerns. Under Seaborg, the AEC seemed unable or unwilling to comprehend the extent of the developing controversy over nuclear power.

With Seaborg's term expiring in 1971, the Nixon administration had an opportunity to put its own stamp on the AEC. Nixon, who was a supporter of nuclear power, wanted to restore the agency's credibility so that it could get on with the business of licensing nuclear reactors and developing the next generation of reactors, the so-called "breeder reactors." Sensitive to the problems plaguing the AEC, Nixon sought an outsider to head the commission, someone who was not clearly identified with the agency or the controversies surrounding it. His choice to replace Seaborg as chair was James R. Schlesinger, who had been an assistant director of the Office of Management and Budget. Nixon filled another vacancy on the commission by appointing William O. Doub, who had served as chairman of the Maryland Public Service Commission. The appointments of Schlesinger and Doub were designed to restore public confidence in the agency. Neither man was perceived to have rigid views concerning the nuclear power controversy, and both seemed to go out of their way to acknowledge the need for changes in the commission's procedures and attitudes.

Schlesinger came to his new position with a number of objectives. On the one hand, he clearly sought to improve the agency's public image; he wanted to reestablish the AEC's reputation as a defender of the public interest and urged that the agency strengthen its regulatory capabilities and become more independent of the nuclear industry. On the other hand, Schlesinger also believed the AEC had a responsibility to the nuclear industry and to aid the commercialization of nuclear power by standardizing and streamlining the agency's licensing process.[17] To accomplish these goals, the AEC, according to Schlesinger, would have to adopt a new role, one that was more "neutral" and less sympathetic to the nuclear industry. In a widely publicized speech to a joint meeting of the Atomic Industrial Forum and the American Nuclear Society, Schlesinger told the industry representatives that although the AEC had once "fostered and protected the nuclear industry," it would no longer do so. He went on to say

> It is not the responsibility of the Atomic Energy Commission to solve industry's problems which may crop up in the course of commercial exploitation. That is industry's responsibility, to be settled among industry, the Congress, and the public. The AEC's role is a more limited one, primarily to perform as a referee serving the public interest. . . . The old ways were neater and more efficient, at least in a limited sense. But this is 1971. We are more crowded. There is a heightened public sensitivity on environmental issues—an insistence by the public that it be consulted. We shall all have to learn to operate

under these changed conditions. You will not only have to operate in the glare of publicity, you will have to take your case to the public. Do not expect us to do this for you.[18]

Under Schlesinger's leadership the AEC instituted a number of changes in its organization, procedures, and regulations. In its first major policy decision after Schlesinger became chair, the AEC announced that it would not appeal the decision of the D.C. Circuit in the *Calvert Cliffs* case. In announcing the decision, Schlesinger said the commission was trying to be "responsive to the concerns of conservation and environmental groups as well as other members of the public."[19] The same day the AEC convened a meeting of representatives from environmental groups and the nuclear industry to discuss new environmental regulations. One week later the commission announced the newly revised rules that were generally well-received by environmental groups.[20]

In another action designed to signal the AEC's new attitude, in November 1971 the AEC announced that the Atomic Safety and Licensing Appeal Boards (ASLAB) would be organizationally separated from the Atomic Safety and Licensing Boards (ASLB). Both the ASLAB and ASLB had been under the direction of the same chairperson, and the AEC wanted to make the appeal panel more independent. The commission had created the ASLAB in August 1969 to provide a mechanism for appeal of the decisions of its licensing boards in individual licensing cases. In February 1972, the AEC appointed four environmental specialists to the ASLB panel. In announcing the appointments, which were a direct result of the *Calvert Cliffs* decision, Schlesinger said that "this constitutes another important step in our effort to be responsive to the concern of many individuals and groups over the possible environmental impact of nuclear power plants."[21] As of September 1973, the ASLB panel had a total membership of seventy-two, including fifteen environmental specialists. Of that seventy-two, twenty were full-time and the rest part-time. Still, this change represented a significant increase, because a few years earlier the ASLB membership totaled twenty-five, with only five members serving full-time.

Also in 1972, the AEC began preparing its annual report to Congress in two volumes instead of one. This new practice was clearly motivated by the agency's desire to put some distance between its regulatory and developmental roles, because one volume discussed the developmental and operating functions under the jurisdiction of the general manager, while the second focused on the regulatory responsibilities under the director of regulation.

Despite Schlesinger's efforts to improve the AEC's public image, the changes he initiated did little to defuse the controversy over nuclear power. Observers of the AEC disagreed as to the significance of the changes; some believed the changes signaled a fundamental shift in the AEC's behavior, while others claimed they were more show than substance.[22] At times the AEC seemed to be moving in two directions at once, strengthening its regulatory staff and issuing new environmental and safety regulations while simultaneously proposing other measures that would streamline the licensing process by reducing the number of public hearings. The apparently contradictory nature of the AEC's actions in this period can be traced back to the incompatibility of its statutory goals. Schlesinger wanted to improve the agency's standing with its critics, but he believed he also had a responsibility to see that reactors were licensed. Given the distrust many opponents of nuclear power felt toward the commission, it is not surprising that some of the AEC's actions, such as its high-profile attempts to standardize its environmental and safety reviews, were perceived as being primarily responsive to the industry's complaints of licensing delays rather than to the worries of critics concerned with environmental and safety issues.

In any event, Schlesinger was not at the AEC long enough to convince the commission's critics that the agency had indeed had a change of heart. Less than two years after joining the AEC, Schlesinger had moved on and was succeeded as chair by Dixie Lee Ray, who had been trained as a marine biologist. Schlesinger's brief tenure as chair marked the beginning of a trend of frequent leadership changes at the commission and its successor agency, the Nuclear Regulatory Commission. In stark contrast to the previous decade, in which only one individual—Seaborg—had been chair, the commission would have no fewer than eight chairmen in the next eight years. The revolving leadership was a direct result of the escalating safety controversy, partisan changes in the White House and, as we will see, the accident at Three Mile Island. At the very least, such rapid turnover could be expected to create a certain amount of instability and uncertainty within the agency. It is also possible that the frequent changes would mean that the individuals serving as chair would be less likely to internalize the agency's norms or sense of mission and would therefore be less attached to the long-term maintenance of the agency.[23] Similarly, because new chairmen would not be easily identified with established positions or old policy battles within the agency, they would presumably be free to chart a more independent course for the agency, including initiating or lending their support to reform measures. Regulatory commissions are subject to a number of external pressures from presidents, Congress, the courts, and special interests that tend to limit their autonomy. In the case of the AEC, the dominant external influence had always been the joint committee, but as the scope of the conflict over nuclear power expanded during the 1970s, the JCAE found it was no longer the only one interested in the commission's actions. Certainly, one of Nixon's objectives in appointing an outsider to head the AEC was to establish a greater degree of presidential influence over the agency than had been possible when Seaborg was in charge. These altered conditions created an opportunity for AEC chairmen to resist JCAE pressures.

For example, Dixie Lee Ray's first significant decision as AEC chair was forcing through a controversial reorganization of the commission's staff in which the Division of Reactor Development and Technology, headed by Milton Shaw, was split into two separate divisions. The reorganization was interpreted as an attack not only on Shaw and his organization but on the prerogatives of the JCAE as well. Shaw was very popular with the JCAE, primarily because he, like many members of the committee, had been a strong proponent of the breeder reactor since assuming responsibility for the program in 1965. In 1962 the AEC decided to seek a more advanced reactor in an effort to bolster the future competitiveness of nuclear power. After a long dispute, the joint committee prevailed upon the AEC to select the fast breeder reactor for development. Responsibility for the breeder project fell to the Division of Reactor Development, which was responsible for both reactor development and safety research for the existing generation of light water reactors. According to many reports, during the 1960s the light water reactor safety research program was underfunded and neglected while Shaw's division pushed the development of the breeder reactor.[24] As an indication of the relative priorities of Shaw's research programs, after 1965 light water reactor safety research budgets declined in proportion to breeder development funds; the light water safety budget, which had been approximately 70 percent as large as the breeder budget in 1965, fell to 16 percent in 1974. As a percentage of total AEC expenditures, breeder research grew from about 1 percent in 1965 to 9 percent in 1974. Such figures led critics of Shaw to argue that the commission's safety research and development program was being minimized in favor of research and development on the breeder.[25]

The reorganization enacted by Ray established a Division of Reactor Research and Development and a Division of Reactor Safety Research. The Division of Reactor Safety Research was made responsible for AEC research on light water reactor safety. In announcing the move, Ray said the new setup would provide for "greater emphasis and effectiveness in our safety research programs." The underlying motive for the reorganization, however, seems to have been Ray's desire to put her own people in important positions within the agency. Safety research concerning the breeder remained with Shaw's Division of Reactor Research Development. Rather than consult the joint committee before making the move, as had been standard practice in the past, Ray instead sent the committee a letter on a Friday afternoon informing them that the reorganization had been enacted. Although many members of the joint committee were upset, there was little they could do. Much to the displeasure of the JCAE, Shaw announced his retirement shortly after the reorganization took place. Ray's actions in this instance reflected a desire to chart a more independent course for the commission.

Under Ray the AEC continued to adopt measures designed to restore the public's faith in the agency, but the measures were largely ineffective. If the agency's "reform" efforts accomplished anything at all, it was to spur calls for even greater change. No one seemed satisfied with the AEC. Opponents of nuclear power felt the agency was suppressing information that would prove that reactors were not as safe as the agency and the nuclear industry had claimed. The industry, on the other hand, argued that many of the agency's new procedures and regulations had added millions to the cost of building reactors and years to the licensing process. The agency continued to be plagued by charges that its ability and desire to regulate the nuclear industry were hampered by its statutory mandate to promote and develop the industry. By the fall of 1973, it was abundantly clear that the nuclear controversy was not going to fade away.

THE ENERGY REORGANIZATION ACT OF 1974

The primary goal of the Energy Reorganization Act of 1974 was reducing the nation's dependence on imported energy supplies. It was only in the later stages of the legislative process that the additional but secondary goal of enhancing reactor safety was added. A review of the legislative history clearly reveals that the legislation was not intended to be a rebuke of either the AEC or the nuclear power industry. Once that is understood, it is easier to explain the behavior of subsystem actors, who universally supported the legislation, even though it called for a significant restructuring of the nation's nuclear program. Recognizing the inevitability of the separation of the AEC's regulatory and developmental functions, members of the AEC, the JCAE, and the nuclear industry supported the legislation because they viewed it as an opportunity to emphasize the contribution nuclear power could make to solving the nation's energy problems. Hoping to enhance the prospects of nuclear power, subsystem members favored the proposal even though it meant sacrificing the AEC, whose responsibilities would be transferred to two new agencies—the Energy Research and Development Administration (ERDA) and the Nuclear Regulatory Commission (NRC).

In June 1973 President Nixon proposed legislation calling for a comprehensive reorganization of those parts of the executive branch responsible for energy and natural resources. In requesting the legislation, Nixon said the "acquisition, distribution, and consumption of energy resources have become increasingly complex and increasingly critical to the functioning of our economy and our society. But the organization of the Federal Government to meet its responsibilities for energy and other natural resource policies has not changed to meet the new demands."[26] Representatives Chet Holifield (D-Calif.) and Frank Horton (R-N.Y.), who had played an important role in shaping the administration proposal, introduced the legislation in the House. The bill was referred to the Subcommittee on Legislation and Military Operations of the House Committee on Government Operations, which was chaired by Holifield, a member of the JCAE since its inception and an ardent supporter of commercial nuclear power.[27] Showing that the bill had bipartisan support as well as the approval of the joint committee, among the cosponsors were the committee's chairman, Melvin Price (D-Ill.), and its ranking Republican, Craig Hosmer (R-Calif.).

Holifield's subcommittee held hearings on the bill in July and August, but the Arab oil embargo struck before the subcommittee had acted. In short order, energy became one of Nixon's top priorities. In a special message to Congress in January 1974, he said that "no single legislative area is more critical or more challenging to us as a people than the energy crisis." Nixon used the message to launch Project Independence, a sweeping proposal that advocated efforts to increase domestic energy supplies and national energy planning, saying that by the end of the decade it would "take us to a point where we are no longer dependent to any significant extent upon potentially insecure foreign supplies of energy." Accordingly, he urged Congress to move quickly and adopt his proposal for establishing ERDA. Nixon's energy message is also significant because it shows that the proposed legislation was not intended to be antinuclear. In fact, his message expressed confidence in nuclear power, saying that nuclear power was "an essential part of our program of achieving energy self-sufficiency" because it reduced the nation's dependence on imported fuels. Furthermore, Nixon urged that steps be taken to expedite the licensing and construction of nuclear plants.[28] Clearly, at least in Nixon's mind, the proposed reorganization of the AEC into two separate agencies was designed to enhance rather than reduce the contribution of nuclear power to the nation's energy supplies.

Just as clearly, subsystem members shared this assessment. Simply put, the reorganization as introduced was not a controversial piece of legislation. Political science conventional wisdom would lead us to expect that the AEC would have tried to defend its turf and oppose the proposed reorganization, but that was not the case. In fact, all of the members of the AEC at the time, including the chair, Dixie Lee Ray, supported the move. Why would the commissioners support the demise of their own agency? One plausible reason is that because they were all Nixon appointees, they were acting out of loyalty to the president. This explanation certainly seems to have been the case with Ray, upon whom Nixon relied for advice on numerous scientific and technical issues. Furthermore, Ray had only been on the job for a few months when Nixon announced his proposal, clearly an insufficient period to become committed to the agency or its mission. This lack of commitment, then, may explain her willingness to go along with a reorganization that threatened the agency's survival. Another reason Ray and the commissioners supported the proposal was because the House legislation would not have resulted in the loss of AEC jobs, even though the AEC itself would have been reorganized out of existence. More precisely, the AEC would not be abolished but instead would be renamed and would "continue to perform the licensing and related regulatory functions of the Chairman and the members of the Commission." No jobs would have been lost because the AEC commissioners, along with personnel in the licensing and regulatory units, would simply be working in a smaller agency with reduced responsibilities. The remaining AEC divisions—those involved in research and development—would have been transferred to ERDA and presumably would benefit from the additional research and development spending earmarked for the new agency. In other words, the various branches of the AEC would continue to exist, although in separate agencies.

Therefore, concerns about job cutbacks, normally an obstacle to proposed agency reorganization, were not a major factor.

Another reason subsystem members supported the bill was the general consensus that an expanded research and development effort was a necessary response to a dire situation. Although some members of the House were concerned that the new agency would be dominated by the AEC's research and development units and that as a result nuclear power would receive the bulk of the new agency's research money, the ERDA legislation sidestepped the potentially tricky question of which energy sources would be emphasized by offering something for everyone. The proposal called for increased research and development spending across the board, so that all of the various energy interests stood to gain from its passage. In describing ERDA's role in his subcommittee's hearings, Holifield said the new agency would "conduct a broad program of energy research and development, giving full attention and appropriate emphasis to all forms of energy research and development, not only nuclear."[29] The larger energy research and development pie is one reason why representatives of oil, coal, gas, and solar interests supported the bill.

Nuclear proponents also backed the AEC reorganization because they believed it would enhance the commercial prospects of the industry. First, a good portion of ERDA's personnel and programs would be devoted to nuclear power research, so there was little worry that the effort to develop nuclear power technology would suffer from the reorganization. Second, subsystem members had come to recognize that the AEC's dual mandate to develop and regulate commercial nuclear power was creating credibility problems for everyone involved. Critics were having a field day pointing out the apparent conflict of interest in having a single agency responsible for developing and regulating the same industry. The subsequent lack of public confidence in the AEC was seen as a major obstacle to the continued growth of the nuclear industry, which many insiders were expecting to reach one thousand plants by the year 2000. The reorganization seemed to offer a solution: divide the AEC into two agencies and the conflict of interest problem would disappear, thereby depriving nuclear opponents of one of their most potent rhetorical weapons. Chet Holifield made this point explicitly at an earlier set of joint committee hearings, saying that he would support reorganization of the AEC "if for no other reason than to allay this fallacious charge that there has been a conflict of interest, for no other reason than that, so that these perpetual complainers will no longer have that as a fallacious argument. . . . I will not have any more confidence in the independence of it as a result of that legal separation than I have in it right now. It has been independent, and I think it will be independent in the future. From the standpoint of public relations, I think I am perfectly willing to go along with it."[30] Similarly, AEC chair Ray seemed to suggest as much when she told a Senate committee that the reorganization should occur "not so much because a conflict of interest exists, but because the public thinks there is a conflict when both those who are responsible for development and promotion of a highly sophisticated technology and those who set the operating and licensing requirements report to the same individuals in the Commission."[31]

The nuclear industry supported the proposal for many of the same reasons, believing that the reorganization would actually serve to reduce criticism of nuclear power and pave the way for an expanded nuclear sector. John Simpson, president of Westinghouse Power Systems Company and also vice chairman of the Atomic Industrial Forum (AIF), the industry's trade association, testified in support of the reorganization, telling the subcommittee that the AIF believed "that the time for separating the Commission's regulatory and promotional functions is now at hand." He was quick to add, however, that the AIF's position was not intended as a criticism of the AEC but was instead a recognition of the fact that the commission "has been subjected to criticism for an organizational structure that is said to lend itself to a conflict of interest in nuclear plant licensing cases."[32] In his testimony before the Senate committee considering the companion measure to H.R. 11510, Simpson explained that the AEC's dual mandate to promote and regulate nuclear power had led to a "lack of confidence" in the agency. In his opinion, the proposed reorganization would give the nuclear program "increased credibility" leading to "more acceptance by those who have been protesting nuclear plants."[33] Simpson also used the opportunity to tell the House subcommittee that the reorganization provided an opportunity to speed up the licensing process and urged the subcommittee to consider amendments to that effect.[34]

Opponents of nuclear power supported the legislation for very different reasons, hoping that the division of the AEC's developmental and regulatory functions into two new agencies would result in better oversight of the nuclear industry. An independent regulatory agency, it was thought, would be better equipped to protect the health and safety of the public. This belief explains the apparently incongruous political alliance between pro- and antinuclear forces in a time of bitter and polarized debate over the future of nuclear power. Both opponents and supporters of nuclear power supported the reorganization proposal but for very different reasons.

In conclusion, members of the atomic subsystem did not oppose President Nixon's reorganization plan in the House because they did not see it as a threat to nuclear power. Rather, the hearings clearly show that they believed the reorganization would help nuclear power. A response to the energy crisis, the legislation was designed to help the nation achieve energy self-sufficiency, and it was clear that nuclear power was an important part of that design. The committee report to the House shows this to be the case, saying the bill was "designed to provide the organizational base for a well-managed, centrally-directed attack on energy problems in order to make this nation self-sufficient in clean energy for the decades ahead."[35] The report also said the reorganization of the AEC would reduce public criticism, place the regulation of nuclear power on a "sounder policy base and should enable the Commission to more effectively address the complicated, demanding tasks of licensing nuclear plants, materials, and activities."[36] As a further indication that the bill was not intended as a threat to nuclear power, the committee report also noted the "compelling evidence" for reducing licensing times for nuclear plants. Given these facts, it is not surprising that Holifield, one of nuclear power's strongest advocates, supported the bill so enthusiastically. Holifield steered the bill out of committee in just two weeks, with both the subcommittee and full committee voting unanimously to approve it. Floor debate on the bill was relatively uneventful; only a handful of amendments were offered, and they were soundly rejected. The full House approved the bill by a vote of 355 to 25, only four weeks after Holifield had introduced it. The speedy passage and lopsided vote were further indications that the proposal posed little threat to nuclear power interests.

Senate Action

The Senate version of the bill, S. 2744, was introduced by Abraham Ribicoff (D-Conn.) and was referred to his Subcommittee on Reorganization, Research, and International Organizations of the Committee of Government Operations. As introduced, the Senate bill was identical to H.R. 11510, the bill Holifield and Horton sponsored in the House. It is not surprising, then, that the early stages of Senate deliberations mirrored those in the House, with supporters stressing the need for expeditious action on energy research and development. Like Holifield, Ribicoff introduced the bill by saying it would "provide the organizational framework for the short- and long-range solutions to the energy crisis. It is an important step toward making our Nation self-sufficient in energy supply."[37] He began the subcommittee's hearings in a similar fashion, claiming that "the number one priority before this committee is how do we get this country moving as fast as possible in self-sufficiency in alternate sources of energy."[38]

Unlike Holifield, however, Ribicoff was neither a member of the joint committee nor a strong supporter of nuclear power. The referral of S. 2744 to Ribicoff's subcommittee proved to be a significant factor in determining the shape of the bill in the Senate, because Ribicoff was more receptive to efforts to amend the bill to ensure more effective regulation of the nuclear power industry. The subcommittee, for example, devoted a considerable amount of time during the hearings to the issue of nuclear materials safeguards. A number of senators, including Ribicoff, were concerned about the possible theft of nuclear materials by terrorists and wanted to establish stricter regulations to prevent the loss, theft, or sabotage of nuclear materials or facilities.[39] Ribicoff's subcommittee also heard testimony from a broader range of witnesses, including some who were critical of the proposed legislation because it did not go far enough in ensuring the safety of nuclear reactors. One of these witnesses, Daniel Ford of the Union of Concerned Scientists, criticized the House bill because it merely renamed the AEC without mandating any fundamental changes in agency personnel or behavior. Ford said the bill "takes the same people who have, in our judgement, performed quite badly and simply says to them that you are going to have continuing powers in this area."[40] With Ribicoff's subcommittee more receptive to the concerns of antinuclear forces, it is not surprising that his committee's version of the administration's energy reorganization proposal would differ from that of the House.

By the time the committee reported out the bill in June 1974, it contained a number of provisions not found in the House version. Both chambers considered energy self-sufficiency to be the primary goal of the legislation, but the committee report on S. 2744 also reflected the committee members' concern with nuclear safety.[41] When the full Senate began deliberations on the bill, Ribicoff said it addressed *two* of the nation's "urgent energy needs." One was the familiar need to "attain energy self-sufficiency," and the other was the need to upgrade the regulation of nuclear power, which he called "our most developed" and "most dangerous" source of energy. Ribicoff remarked that the separation of the AEC's regulatory functions from its developmental and promotional functions was a response to growing public criticism of a conflict of interest.[42] Unlike Holifield, who supported the reorganization because of its public relations appeal, Ribicoff believed that regulation of the nuclear power industry had genuinely suffered as a result of the AEC's dual mandate, saying that it was "clearly not in the public interest to continue this special relationship" now that the industry was becoming among the largest and most hazardous in the nation. He added that while the arrangement may have made sense at one time, it was now "difficult to determine in the organizational scheme of the AEC where the Commission ends and the industry begins."[43]

The two policy goals articulated by Ribicoff appear to be contradictory. On the one hand, the ERDA legislation was intended to move the nation toward energy independence, and a greater role for nuclear power was seen as an important part of that quest. But in calling for more stringent regulation of the nuclear power industry, on the other hand, the legislation would add to the time and cost of constructing nuclear reactors and slow the growth of the nuclear sector, thereby thwarting the goal of energy self-sufficiency. This tension reflected the ambivalence with which Congress was beginning to view nuclear power. Many members were concerned about the safety of nuclear plants but were unwilling to rule out nuclear power as an option because they saw it as a secure source of energy. Seen in this light, the two policy goals are not at all incompatible. Faced with demands for more energy and for greater safety and environmental protection at the nation's nuclear plants, Congress's response was to support both. If greater reliance were to be placed on nuclear energy, Congress would insist that it be safe. The result of this tension was a bill that was ambiguous enough to satisfy both pro- and antinuclear forces in the Senate.

The Senate bill differed from the House version in several important ways. First, the Senate bill clearly stated its intent that no energy technology should be given unwarranted priority, and it contained several provisions intended to en-sure that ERDA was not overwhelmed by the nuclear programs and personnel transferred from the AEC. Second, the Senate measure abolished the AEC rather than merely renaming it as called for in the House bill and transferred its licensing and regulatory functions to a new agency.

The committee bill also added measures designed to facilitate closer moni-toring of the nuclear industry. Section 205 of the committee bill required officers and employees of licensed nuclear facilities, or of companies supplying compo-nents to licensed facilities, to notify the commission of any defect that could cre-ate a safety hazard or of any failure to comply with the commission's regulations. Failure to report such defects or violations was subject to both civil and criminal penalties of up to $50,000 and one year in prison. Ribicoff said the provisions for civil or criminal penalties were patterned closely after sections of the Consumer Product Safety Act because the "unquestioned health and safety consideration implicit in the NSLC's need for information" was "as imperative" as the Con-sumer Product Safety Commission's need for such information.[44] Section 207 of the Senate bill required the Nuclear Safety and Licensing Commission to make quarterly reports to Congress on abnormal occurrences at nuclear plants and to notify the public within five days of learning about the incident.

The full Senate made only a few significant changes to the committee bill. It adopted an amendment by Senator Lee Metcalf (D-Mont.) requiring the regula-tory body to provide information, analyses, and technical assistance for witnesses and parties to any licensing or rulemaking proceeding. Metcalf, a critic of nuclear power, also proposed an amendment to the Freedom of Information Act to allow public disclosure of commercial information, trade secrets, and certain commis-sion records, including interagency memos or letters relating to safety.[45] The amendments were adopted by voice vote.

By far the most controversial amendment to S. 2744 was proposed by Senator Edward Kennedy (D-Mass.). The amendment, based in large part on a proposal drafted by Anthony Roisman, an attorney representing a number of intervenors in AEC licensing proceedings, authorized the new regulatory agency to reim-burse eligible parties in commission proceedings for the costs of participation, including "reasonable" attorney's fees. According to the amendment, the com-mission was to set a maximum amount allowed for each proceeding to encourage intervenors to consolidate their efforts. By encouraging intervenors to contest only "relevant issues," the amendment would not contribute to regulatory delay. The amount of assistance that would be available was to be based on the extent to which the party contributed to the development of facts, issues, and arguments relevant to the proceeding and upon the party's ability to pay their own expenses. Kennedy claimed that although citizen intervenors were an indispensable part of the commission's adversary process and had made a number of significant con-tributions to AEC proceedings in the past, inadequate resources prevented many such groups from intervening. According to Kennedy, the provision of funds to intervenors who had made "substantial contributions" was designed to ensure effective public participation in the commission's licensing and rulemaking proceedings and to promote nuclear regulation in the public interest. His amendment was supported by the American Bar Association, National Wildlife Fund, Environmental Defense Fund, Friends of the Earth, Natural Resources Defense Council, and Sierra Club.[46] Representatives of the nuclear industry, on the other hand, predicted that adoption of the financial assistance provisions would be "suicide for the civilian nuclear program."[47] A number of senators, including several leading members of the joint committee, objected to the amendment because they thought it would contribute to and even encourage delays in the licensing of nuclear plants.[48] The senators did not press their objections, however, and the amendment passed by a voice vote.

The Senate added several other minor amendments during the course of its deliberations on S. 2744. Reflecting the widespread support for the measure, the Senate passed the legislation on a voice vote on 15 August 1974. Because the Senate version contained provisions not found in H.R. 11510, a conference was scheduled for September.

Conference Committee Action

When the conference committee met in September, they had to reconcile some important differences in the two bills. The Senate bill, for example, seemed to place greater emphasis on nuclear safety and public participation in regulatory agency proceedings, which the House conferees, led by Chet Holifield, would be likely to oppose. In addition, the Senate version included provisions to prevent ERDA from being dominated by its nuclear energy personnel and programs. Despite these differences, the conference committee was able to reach an agreement as the conferees compromised on many of the differences in the two bills. The final agreement, however, more closely resembled the Senate version.

Both versions, for example, called for the creation of an Energy Research and Development Administration. The Senate, though, had added a number of provisions emphasizing nonnuclear research and energy conservation. The conference agreement on ERDA generally adopted the Senate's position, including the requirement that ERDA give "no unwarranted priority" to any one energy technology. The conference also accepted the Senate language requiring ERDA's top administrators to be energy generalists as well as the Senate provision establishing assistant adminstrators for energy conservation and environmental protection.

The conference agreement followed the Senate bill by abolishing the AEC rather than simply renaming it. Although all of the AEC's staff would be retained, the five AEC commissioners would have to be reappointed and confirmed by the Senate. The conferees called the new agency the Nuclear Regulatory Commission. They retained the Senate language requiring bipartisanship on the new commission but deleted the requirement that the commissioners possess certain technical qualifications. The conferees also dropped a Senate provision making the chairman the commission's chief administrative officer.

Similarly, the conference committee followed the Senate version by creating three coequal operating units within the new regulatory agency: the Office of Nuclear Reactor Regulation, the Office of Nuclear Material Safety and Safeguards, and the Office of Nuclear Regulatory Research. The Office of Nuclear Reactor Regulation would be responsible for licensing and related regulatory activities within the boundary of the reactor. The Office of Nuclear Material Safety and Safeguards would be concerned with materials and safeguards outside the reactor boundaries. According to the conferees, the Office of Nuclear Regulatory Research would be concerned with conducting and supporting research contributory to the needs of the other two. The conference report stated that this arrangement would provide the commission with "ample flexibility" in devising the most effective administrative arrangements within its own organization and at the same time give "due and proper emphasis" to protecting the public health and safety.[49]

The House conferees did succeed in modifying several provisions added by the Senate to facilitate closer monitoring of the nuclear power industry. For example, they accepted the Senate requirement that the commission report abnormal occurrences to the public, but they allowed the commission fifteen days to do so rather than five. Similarly, section 205 of the Senate version had established civil and criminal penalties for failure to report safety defects or noncompliance with commission rules. The conferees retained the reporting requirement but dropped the provision for criminal penalties.

In what was certainly the biggest victory for the House conferees, the conference committee deleted the provisions for technical and financial assistance to intervenors, even though members of the AEC and the nuclear industry had testified in favor of the provisions for technical assistance.[50] On the other hand, proponents of nuclear power strongly opposed the provisions for financial assistance, feeling they would only serve to encourage interventions and lead to further delays in the licensing process. Holifield explained his objections to the assistance provisions during the House's consideration of the conference agreement, saying that each of them "raised serious policy problems and carried the possibility of heavy administrative burdens and costs to the Commission as well as inordinate delays in administrative proceedings. As the Members well know, we have too many delays now in handling licensing applications for the construction and operation of nuclear plants. . . . We need to reduce, not add to, the delay factors, so that this nation can get on with the job of providing the energy so important to its welfare."[51] His remarks demonstrate not only his objections to these particular aspects of the Senate bill but also his strong commitment to nuclear power. Holifield, who was retiring at the end of the session, had often expressed an antipathy for those individuals and groups who had opposed nuclear plants, and he was not about to give his approval to legislation that would help them challenge construction permits or operating licenses.

In presenting the conference agreement to the Senate, Ribicoff said he regretted that the House conferees "refused to enter into any meaningful compromise" on the technical and financial assistance provisions. He added that the decision was not a rejection of the principle involved but rather a decision allowing the new commission or the courts to act while reserving the right for Congress to act at a future date. According to Ribicoff, giving in to the House was the only way to assure speedy passage of the legislation. Not everyone in the Senate, however, was so sanguine about the deletion. In fact, Senator Metcalf refused to sign the conference report in protest over the deletion of provisions for technical and financial assistance. According to Metcalf, the Senate had made it very clear that intervenors were an "indispensable part" of the adversary process and that they should be assisted by the commission in developing and preparing their case. Accordingly, the intent of the Senate in adding the assistance provisions was "to assure a balanced record before the Commission and to place the intervenor ... in at least a reasonably adequate position to make his case."[52]

Despite Metcalf's impassioned arguments, the Senate approved the conference report by voice vote on 10 October, one day after the House had approved it by a vote of 372 to 1. The bill was then sent to the White House where President Ford, who had labeled it his top priority energy measure, signed it on 11 October. The Atomic Energy Commission, which had managed the nation's atomic energy policy since 1946, was abolished on 19 January 1975.

CONCLUSION

The abolition of the AEC deprived the nuclear industry of a powerful patron and created a more complicated institutional framework for nuclear matters. Where there was once a small group of insiders restricting participation to program supporters, by the middle of the decade the range of governmental participants would be decidedly broader and less exclusive.[53] In addition to the Nuclear Regulatory Commission and ERDA, the courts, the EPA, the Fish and Wildlife Service, and state and local governments claimed jurisidiction. The AEC, for example, had not been very concerned with the environmental impacts of reactors, but the EPA and FWS were. More and more, licensing decisions were challenged in court, while state and local governments became involved through their siting and rate-making powers. For opponents of nuclear power, these multiple venues translated into new opportunities to shape nuclear decision making and to appeal unfavorable decisions to other, more receptive governmental actors. For these reasons, institutional shifts were a critical factor in the expansion of the conflict over nuclear power.

We have already noted that the 1970s were a time of fundamental changes in the principles, institutions, and processes of American politics. Many of these changes were designed to democratize government institutions, foster greater citizen participation, and facilitate substantive policy reforms. In the case of nuclear power, these reforms were cumulative and reinforcing; one established the conditions for the next. Newly mobilized interest groups demanded access to AEC decision making, which was granted by the federal courts. Under pressure from the courts and the public to open its doors, the commission made significant changes in its licensing and rulemaking proceedings. As more information became available, the AEC could no longer defend itself and was eventually abolished. Each successive venue change fanned the flames of conflict and contributed to the dismantling of the nuclear subgovernment; members found it increasingly difficult to maintain their influence within the more open political environment. In the following chapter, I examine shifts in congressional jurisdiction in order to show how they affected the politics of nuclear power.

6
Congressional Reorganization

We tend to think of the set of political values and institutions that we inherit, whether divine-right monarchy or liberal democracy, as eternal, immutable, and, above all, right. They are not. Political paradigms are, in fact, extraordinarily fragile creations.
—William Ophuls

Like the AEC, the Joint Committee on Atomic Energy came under attack in the 1970s for being overly protective of the nuclear power industry. The growing "wave of criticism" over nuclear power, coupled with the demise of the AEC, prompted increased scrutiny of the joint committee and fueled calls for its abolition as well. Just ten days after President Ford signed the Energy Reorganization Act of 1974 into law, a *New York Times* editorial contended that the joint committee had "grown almost as outmoded as the AEC, forcing an overconcentration and proprietary interest in nuclear energy at the expense of other . . . sources of power. This could be the logical moment for dismantling this legislative remnant of the early post-war era."[1] Over the next few years the once-invincible joint committee struggled to ward off challenges to its authority and to the nuclear program it had supported for so long. The joint committee would not win this battle, however, as it was eliminated by Congress in 1977.

The convergence of several factors led to its fall, including the dismantling of the AEC, the rise of environmental, safety, and energy issues to prominence, and the departure of many longtime JCAE members through retirements and electoral defeats. Jurisdictional shifts within Congress played a crucial role as well, altering the structure of bias in nuclear policy making by granting access to new actors demanding policy change. Some of these jurisdictional shifts were the product of the public lobby era reforms that swept through the American politi-

123

cal system in the 1960s and early 1970s, transforming the interest group environment, executive branch agencies, and courts. As a result, Congress became more open, individualistic, and decentralized and, like the others, more involved in administrative oversight. Indeed, greater attention to administrative decision making was a common thread linking the reforms across the various institutions.

In this chapter I examine how the "rules of the game" for nuclear policy making changed in Congress during the 1970s. We have already seen how the one-sided mobilization of interests that characterized the first twenty years of the atomic program changed in this period, but by themselves broader mobilizations are not enough to explain policy change. Institutional changes are also necessary, because institutions structure access to policy making. With the demise of the JCAE, longtime supporters lost control of the strategic junctures of policy making. Responsibility for nuclear policy was transferred to some two dozen subcommittees, some of which were sympathetic to the concerns voiced by antinuclear groups. For opponents of nuclear power, this decentralization reinforced previous venue changes and created additional access points to nuclear decision making. It also established opportunities to forge alliances with entrepreneurial members of Congress. As we will see, the new structural arrangements in Congress rendered the institution less exclusive and more permeable to outsiders but also made it more complicated. Although nuclear policy once had been shaped exclusively by the joint committee, it now seemed that everyone had some claim to nuclear oversight. With responsibility for nuclear policy dispersed so widely, it became increasingly difficult for Congress to resolve major policy issues.

Furthermore, Congress became increasingly ambivalent about nuclear power in the 1970s. This was partially the result of new actors entering the fray, but it was also due to changes in the policy environment. The Arab oil embargo thrust energy issues into the limelight and illustrated the nation's growing dependence on imported oil. Supporters of nuclear power saw this situation as an opportunity to emphasize the need for additional nuclear power plants. Hence, they urged Congress to rewrite the Atomic Energy Act in order to streamline the commission's licensing and regulatory procedures, claiming that overzealous regulation was standing in the way of energy self-sufficiency. Antinuclear forces resisted these efforts, arguing that there were still too many unanswered questions about nuclear reactors. They urged Congress to impose additional safety requirements on the nuclear industry and to force the commission to live up to its statutory mandate to protect the public health and safety. Faced with simultaneous demands for energy independence and reactor safety, members of Congress chose to pursue both. After the fall of the JCAE, Congress failed to articulate a consistent or overarching nuclear policy; instead, policy evolved in an incremental and sometimes contradictory manner.

CONGRESS AND ADMINISTRATIVE REFORMS

In the early 1970s the AEC was repeatedly attacked for suppressing information that was detrimental to the commercial prospects of the nuclear power industry.[2] All too often, the commission's reluctance to release certain documents or reports reinforced the perception that it was hiding something. This was so even though the AEC had established a public documents room in Washington as early as 1956, where it deposited for public review certain documents relevant to reactor permit and license applications. In most instances the information deposited by the commission consisted of records of license and permit applications, comments from interested parties on proposed regulations, and records of public licensing hearings. But many other documents, such as the mandatory safety analyses prepared by the regulatory staff and the Advisory Committee on Reactor Safeguards (ACRS), were unavailable because the commission considered them to be "internal documents" not subject to public review. Similarly, many test studies and reports conducted by the AEC or its national laboratories were also withheld by the commission.[3] Perhaps most important, transcripts of meetings between the applicant and regulatory staff as well as the records of commission meetings in which decisions were made on individual permit and license applications were frequently unavailable to the public. As opposition to nuclear power mounted, citizen groups complained that their inability to obtain relevant studies and documents from the AEC was impairing their ability to wage effective and timely interventions.

Concerned about abuses of administrative power by the Nixon administration, Congress in the 1970s began to retreat from its previous practice of drafting laws that provided administrative agencies with only very general policy guidance. Consequently, legislators enacted or amended several laws that required administrative agencies to open up their decision-making proceedings and files to greater public scrutiny. In this way, greater congressional oversight could ensure that policies and programs were not subverted by a hostile bureaucracy. The rationale underlying many of these laws was that public trust and confidence would be enhanced by a more open government and that greater openness would encourage broader participation in agency proceedings, more fruitful debate of agency policies, and increased agency accountability.[4] As might be expected, such measures were particularly prevalent in the years following Watergate. Although the laws facilitating the public's "right to know" were generally applicable to most federal agencies, they had a profound effect upon the commission, which was forced to alter its traditional means of doing business.

One of the laws intended to facilitate public participation in government was the Freedom of Information Act, which was passed by Congress in 1966 and then amended in 1974.[5] This law directed federal agencies to make certain agency documents, including final opinions and orders in adjudicatory proceedings, policy statements, and staff manuals, available for public inspection and copying.[6] By requiring agencies to make information more widely available, the Freedom of Information Act was designed to encourage the participation of public lobby groups in the administrative process. With greater access to agency files and records, such groups would be in a better position to monitor and evaluate the agency's decision-making process to ensure that its actions were sound. The law proved to be a valuable resource for critics of nuclear power, who were able to gain access for the first time to large amounts of previously unavailable information. Requests for commission records and documents under the act steadily increased throughout the decade, from forty-nine in 1975 to over five hundred in 1979.[7] One of the consequences of less exclusive information was that intervenors acquired a more sophisticated understanding of both nuclear technology and commission regulations, which in turn enhanced the credibility of their demands to be included in the policy-making process.

Many documents were not obtained without a fight, however, because the AEC (and later the NRC) frequently resisted Freedom of Information Act requests from antinuclear groups. The Union of Concerned Scientists, among others, obtained a number of documents only after filing or threatening to file suit against the commission.[8] The AEC released some important documents during the ECCS hearings in 1972, for example, only after being threatened with a Freedom of Information Act lawsuit by the intervenor groups. This instance was not an isolated one, because the commission's reluctance continued throughout the decade. As a case in point, to comply with the 1974 amendments to the act, the NRC amended its rules in February 1975 to provide that "final AEC records and documents . . . will be made available for inspection and copying."[9] There were, however, several disputes as to which commission records and documents should be considered "final." The UCS was frustrated on more than one occasion by the commission's refusal to release information because it was considered "pre-decisional" in nature.

During the 1970s Congress also passed several laws that required administrative agencies to open more of their proceedings to public review. In 1972, for example, Congress enacted the Federal Advisory Committee Act, which required that all federal advisory commmittees, including the Advisory Committee on Reactor Safeguards, announce their meetings and conduct at least part of them in public. The legislation reflected congressional concern that advisory committees often played a key role in influencing policy decisions.[10] The AEC initially resisted implementing the act, however, citing the need for confidential discussion in ACRS meetings. This was not the first time the commission had tried to prevent public scrutiny of the ACRS. Just one year earlier, for example, the commission had refused to allow ACRS members to testify in the controversial ECCS rulemaking hearings. Eventually the threat of legal action by the Union of Concerned Scientists, Ralph Nader, and the group Businessmen for the Public Interest, forced the AEC to relent and open ACRS meetings to the public and the press.[11] The ACRS was, however, allowed to keep certain meetings, and parts of others, out of the public eye by meeting in executive session. Still, the committee held its first open meetings in March 1973, and by the end of the year 57 of its 113 meetings had been open to the public.[12]

Although it is unclear what effect this new openness had on the committee's deliberations, one former ACRS chairman claims that it caused members of the AEC regulatory staff to be less forthright in their criticisms of utility applicants for fear of providing intervenors with potentially useful information. When ACRS meetings were closed to the public, the regulatory staff had freely expressed candid views on a variety of issues, including the ability or willingness of applicants to resolve certain safety concerns. However, with the advent of open meetings, they would only express those views in off-the-record conversations with ACRS members.[13]

The Federal Government in the Sunshine Act, passed by Congress in 1976, required all federal agencies with two or more presidential appointees to open all of their meetings to the public unless the subject matter was specifically exempted under the act's provisions. The exemptions were designed to permit closed discussion of certain issues including classified and proprietary information, personnel issues, and matters involved in pending litigation. After the law became effective in March 1977, the NRC opened the majority of its meetings to the public. Evidence suggests, however, that the NRC never fully embraced the act's goals and actually perceived it to be an obstacle to its daily operations. A 1984 study of the implementation of the Sunshine Act among eighteen federal agencies found that the NRC ranked at or near the bottom in several categories of compliance. According to the study, between 1977 and 1981, the NRC failed to provide adequate public notice of its meetings approximately half of the time and was twice reprimanded by the federal courts for illegally closing meetings in direct violation of the act.[14]

Other laws, such as the National Environmental Policy Act, imposed new statutory hearing and reporting requirements on the commission that in turn contributed to the transformation of nuclear politics by making information more widely available and by opening up the policy-making process to new agencies and groups. Several studies have suggested that subgovernments are most influential when information about their activities is limited—the paucity of information enables them to function for long periods without attracting the attention of outside interests. This was particularly true of the nuclear subgovernment, whose autonomy was largely dependent on its control of specialized information. But that autonomy was threatened when information about nuclear power became less exclusive. The laws passed by Congress enabled public lobby groups to gain access to the commission's files and proceedings, allowing them to obtain information that raised significant doubts about the safety of nuclear reactors and the effectiveness of the government's regulatory program.

In explaining the dynamics of conflict expansion, Schattschneider argued that "every increase or reduction in the number of participants affects the result."[15] This scenario was clearly the case with nuclear power. Because subsystem actors shared a common purpose, the spread of information, particularly negative information, threatened their influence. The visibility of the nuclear issue, together with the institutional and procedural changes enacted during the 1970s, led to an increase in the number of actors seeking to influence nuclear policy. With new laws granting access to more groups, the policy-making arena became more open and more crowded. Moreover, the introduction of new actors to the policy-making process meant that policymakers would have to consider a broader range of viewpoints, which in the end made it more difficult for subsystem members to frame the debate over nuclear power.

In addition to its affirmative steps to open up the commission's licensing and rulemaking proceedings, Congress also resisted repeated attempts by proponents of nuclear power to keep it closed. In practically every session of Congress during the decade, supporters of nuclear power introduced what they called "licensing reform" legislation. Although the proposals were in every instance jusitified as being motivated by the desire to achieve "more effective public participation in the licensing process" while avoiding "unnecessary licensing delay," in practice most of the measures would have severely curtailed public participation in the commission's proceedings. Many of the proposed "reform" measures would have established more stringent conditions for intervening in licensing proceedings, some would have eliminated mandatory public hearings, and others would have exempted the commission from the procedures of the Administrative Procedures Act.

An AEC bill introduced in 1972 is illustrative.[16] The bill, H.R. 13731, contained several provisions that would have discouraged or prohibited public participation at various points in the licensing process. According to the Atomic Energy Act, the commission was required to hold a mandatory adjudicatory-style public hearing prior to the issuance of a construction permit. A similar hearing would be convened at the operating license stage only if the license were contested. The AEC's proposal continued the existing practice with respect to the construction permit hearing but stipulated that a public hearing for an operating license would only be held if an intervenor could make a prima facie showing that a significant advance in technology had occurred after the construction permit had been issued, and that it would provide "substantial, additional protection to the public health and safety." In short, the AEC proposal required an intervenor to prove, as a condition of intervening, that a safety hazard existed, that the hazard could be substantially reduced by new technologies, and that the technologies were developed after the construction permit had been issued. Furthermore, any hearings eventually held at this stage would be legislative in nature and would not have to conform to provisions of the APA. Therefore, intervenors would have no rights of discovery or cross-examination. Finally, the commission proposal would have allowed the AEC to issue an operating license even before the hearing had been completed if it determined that an "urgent need for power" or some "other emergency situation" required it.

Similarly restrictive measures were introduced by pronuclear forces in every session of Congress in the 1970s.[17] Although nuclear supporters still held many key positions in Congress, they were unable to overcome the concerns many members were beginning to express about the potential hazards of nuclear reactors. As a result, none of the licensing reform measures were enacted. The failure of Congress to adopt any of these measures was testimony both to the body's desire to open up the commission's deliberations to greater public participation and to its growing ambivalence on the nuclear power issue. As we shall see, Congress in the 1970s was faced with simultaneous demands for enhanced reactor safety and energy self-sufficiency. Although Congress proved unwilling to forgo the nuclear option, it also was unwilling to curtail the public's "right" to participate in the commission's licensing or rulemaking proceedings.

CONGRESS AND NUCLEAR POWER

The story of the joint committee's demise was not one of steady and inevitable decline. On the contrary, during the first half of the decade the JCAE continued to be an influential force in nuclear policy making; Congress, as it had in the past, followed the committee's lead on most nuclear energy matters. In 1974, for example, the JCAE easily steered a ten-year extension of the Price-Anderson Act through Congress. Furthermore, the support of key joint committee members was, as we have already seen, an important factor in the passage of the Energy Reorganization Act of 1974. Interestingly, the course of the two bills was remarkably similar, with Congress granting final approval to the Price-Anderson extension less than two weeks before adopting the Energy Reorganization Act. The nearly simultaneous passage of both bills by overwhelming margins attests not only to the continued strength of the JCAE but also to its commitment to the nuclear program.

During the 1970s the joint committee supported a number of other legislative proposals to aid the nuclear industry. In 1972 utility representatives expressed concern that the environmental review procedures enacted by the AEC pursuant to the *Calvert Cliffs* case would delay the operation of some already constructed reactors and almost certainly result in serious energy shortages in certain regions of the country. At the time AEC regulations permitted utilities to test reactors at low-power levels on an interim basis without a completed environmental impact statement, but the Izaak Walton League challenged this practice in federal court, arguing that the agency's procedures violated provisions of NEPA. The D.C. Circuit Court agreed and ruled against the practice in what came to be known as the *Quad Cities* case.[18] Almost immediately the nuclear industry sought relief from the court's decision and asked the AEC and the JCAE to support legislation that would grant the commission the authority to issue temporary operating licenses pending the completion of environmental impact studies. Although the court's decision threatened to delay the issuance of operating licenses for only a few reactors, the nuclear industry lobbied hard for the amendment, saying it was needed to ensure adequate generating capacity in the Northeast and the South.

The bill, as proposed by the AEC, had three major provisions.[19] First, it would prohibit an applicant from undertaking any construction activities at the site prior to the issuance of a construction permit. The AEC had previously allowed applicants to engage in certain limited construction activities, such as site clearing and excavation, before a construction permit had been granted. Next, the bill contained a provision that would have made it more difficult for intervenors to obtain a hearing at the operating license stage. The proposed bill would have allowed the AEC to issue an operating license without holding a public hearing except in proceedings where intervenors made a prima facie showing that significant technological changes occurring after the most recent licensing action would provide "substantial additional protection to the public health and safety." The third provision specifically allowed the AEC to authorize interim operation of fully constructed plants prior to the completion of the environmental impact statement procedures set out in NEPA if there was an urgent need for the power. At the JCAE's urging, Congress passed an amended version of the AEC proposal containing only the provisions allowing the AEC to issue interim operating licenses.[20] As adopted, the amendment allowed the AEC to issue such temporary operating licenses for a period of up to six months before the commission completed its environmental impact study. The legislation also required that a public hearing be held before the temporary license was granted, saying that the hearings were to be conducted with such "expedited procedures as the Commission . . . may deem appropriate."[21] Despite the industry's dire predictions, energy shortages did not materialize, and the AEC issued only one temporary operating license before the provision expired in October 1973.

In another indication of both the joint committee's support of nuclear power and its influence within the legislature, Congress in 1975 approved a ten-year extension of the Price-Anderson Act. As already mentioned, Congress had passed a similar extension the year before, but President Ford refused to sign that bill because it contained a legislative veto provision. The JCAE had made passage of an extension to the Price-Anderson Act a top priority, even though the legislation was not set to expire until August 1977. The joint committee said the extension was necessary to help utilities avoid uncertainty and a slowdown in their lengthy planning process. Critics of the extension argued that the JCAE's desire to move on the legislation at such an early date was motivated by the impending retirement of five key members at the end of 1974: Senators George Aiken (R-Vt.), Wallace Bennett (R-Utah), Alan Bible (D-Nev.), and Representatives Chet Holifield and Craig Hosmer. Environmentalists urged the committee to postpone action until the results of the AEC's Reactor Safety Study, which became known as the Rasmussen report, were released. Some committee members agreed, but their efforts to postpone action were defeated by a vote of 8 to 3. The dissenting votes came from Manuel Lujan (R-N.Mex.), Teno Roncalio (D-Wyo.), and Joseph Montoya (D-N.Mex.), three of the JCAE's newest members. The committee approved the bill during what some members believed was the first open markup session in its history, an effort to dispel criticism that it was moving too hastily.

The bill that was reported out by the JCAE in June 1974 extended the Price-Anderson provisions for a ten-year period. The initial legislative proposal called for a twenty-year extension, but the joint committee decided a shorter renewal would be less controversial. The legislation proposed modifying the Price-Anderson Act by gradually phasing out the government's role in providing indemnity protection to license holders and by establishing a floating liability ceiling. As adopted, in the event of an accident exceeding the amount of available private insurance, the extension required all licensed plants to pay a deferred premium of between $2 million and $5 million per plant. When there were enough plants in operation, the liability ceiling would rise above the $560 million ceiling established in the original Price-Anderson legislation, thereby allowing the government to withdraw. In addition, the proposal would allow the liability ceiling to rise once the private insurance deferred premiums totaled $560 million. In a showdown on the House floor, the joint committee was able to defeat an amendment that would have limited the extension to two years.[22] In July 1974 the House approved the ten-year extension by a vote of 360 to 43.

The Senate approved its version of the legislation by a voice vote in August after reducing the extension to five years and prohibiting it from taking effect if Congress by concurrent resolution disapproved the extension after a review of the Reactor Safety Study. The conference committee reported the final version later that month, agreeing to the Senate amendments. The House adopted the conference report on 24 September by a vote of 376 to 10, while the Senate adopted the measure by voice vote one week later.[23] When President Ford vetoed the bill in October, opponents of nuclear power, who saw the measure as a blatant subsidy to the nuclear power industry, celebrated an apparent victory. With the legislative session drawing to a close, there would not be enough time for the joint committee to reintroduce the bill. Antinuclear forces were hopeful that the retirement of nuclear advocates such as Holifield and Hosmer would pave the way for a joint committee that would be more sympathetic to their concerns.

Any hopes they might have had with respect to the Price-Anderson Act were dashed in 1975 when the JCAE reintroduced the Price-Anderson extension. The new measure was virtually identical to the 1974 version, with two exceptions. The 1975 bill extended the Price-Anderson Act for ten years rather than five, and it omitted the legislative veto provision that caused Ford to disapprove of the earlier bill. The new bill, H.R. 8631, passed easily through both houses and was signed by the president.[24]

Although passage of the extension represented a major victory for the JCAE, there were indications that the committee was more vulnerable than in the past. For the first time, congressional opponents of nuclear power were able to engage the joint committee in a spirited debate on the floor of both chambers. In the House, the $560 million liability ceiling was the target of two amendments. One of them was offered by Representative Jonathan Bingham (D-N.Mex.), who was an outspoken critic of the nuclear program and the JCAE. Bingham's amendment would have eliminated the liability ceiling. Ironically, his position was enhanced by several AEC studies which had shown that property damages stemming from a large-scale nuclear accident could run into the billions of dollars. Despite general agreement that the $560 million ceiling was unrealistically low, the amendment was opposed by the JCAE, the administration, and the nuclear industry. In the face of intensive lobbying by JCAE members, the amendment was rejected by a vote of 217 to 176. A similar amendment was defeated in the Senate. Although the JCAE demonstrated its continued ability to get the necessary votes, the relatively narrow margin of its victory suggests that the committee could no longer expect to dictate nuclear policy to Congress.

Changing perceptions of nuclear power attracted the attention of many new actors. As the media and the public paid greater attention to energy matters, for example, so too did members of Congress, as the proliferation of committees and subcommittees with jurisdiction over energy policy attests. With responsibility for energy spread more widely throughout Congress, policy entrepreneurs like Bingham and Ribicoff were given greater incentives and opportunities to challenge the joint committee. The same is true of members interested in environmental policy or reactor safety.

Other unrelated congressional reforms likewise enhanced the ability of individual members to criticize existing policy, to claim jurisdiction over new issues, and to attract media attention. The growth of staff and the increasing devolution of authority to subcommittees and, therefore, subcommittee chairpersons transformed the circumstances in which Congress deliberated policy in the 1970s. Entrepreneurial members found that jurisdictional boundaries were no longer sacrosanct, and nuclear policy was no exception.

With these changes in its political environment, the JCAE found it more difficult to maintain its leadership role on nuclear issues. Other congressional working groups, most notably Ribicoff's Government Operations Subcommittee and the House Interior and Insular Affairs Subcommittee on Energy and the Environment, chipped away at the JCAE's exclusive jurisdiction over the NRC. The latter was particularly aggressive in challenging the JCAE. Under the leadership of its chairman, Morris Udall (D-Ariz.), the House Subcommittee on Energy and the Environment began holding NRC oversight hearings in July 1975. The following year the subcommittee convened hearings to consider a variety of other controversial topics, including the Reactor Safety Study, the NRC's proposal to license floating nuclear power plants, and public funding of intervenors in commission rulemaking proceedings.[25] The nuclear power issue had become so visible that the joint committee, although displeased with this obvious encroachment on its turf, was no longer capable of resisting.

In another indication of the joint committee's diminished influence, in 1976 the Senate rejected former JCAE staff director George Murphy for a position on the NRC despite intense lobbying from JCAE members. An obvious slap in the face for the joint committee, the Senate's decision was based primarily on the perception that the "business as usual" approach to nuclear regulation could no longer continue. The unraveling of the consensus on nuclear power also made it more difficult to expand existing programs or enact new policy initiatives. In 1976, for example, the JCAE made an unsuccessful effort to open up the uranium enrichment industry to private enterprise.[26]

The federal government developed the technology to enrich uranium during World War II, and it owned the three existing uranium enrichment plants in the United States. By 1974 these plants, which were operated by private companies under contract with the government, were operating at capacity, and it was estimated that the country would need to build additional plants to ensure an adequate supply of reactor fuel for domestic and foreign markets. The Ford administration, like the Nixon administration before it, wanted private industry to be allowed to build and operate all the additional enrichment capacity. In June 1975, Ford sent legislation to Congress to authorize the Energy Research and Development Administration (ERDA) to reach agreements with private companies that wanted to enter the business. The bill, known as the Nuclear Fuel Assurance Act, would have ended the government monopoly by giving ERDA the authority to provide technical assistance and the government-controlled technology to companies that wanted to build and operate enrichment facilities. The bill also gave ERDA the authority to acquire a private enrichment project and assume its liabilities if the firm could not bring the plant into operation. Moreover, ERDA was authorized to guarantee to domestic investors that the government would assume all of its assets and liabilities should their venture fail prior to the end of one year of commercial operation.

The joint committee unanimously reported an amended version in May 1976. The amended bill authorized ERDA to contract with private industry to produce enriched uranium, guaranteeing that the government-supplied technology would work. These contracts would be submitted to Congress, which would have sixty days to approve or disapprove the contract. The contracts could be executed only if Congress approved a favorable concurrent resolution. The legislation was controversial: many members of Congress were concerned that it would indirectly contribute to the proliferation of nuclear weapons, while others viewed it as a "giveaway" to the nuclear industry. The House passed its version in August 1976 by a 222 to 168 vote, but there were a number of very close votes on some key amendments. In the Senate, opponents of the measure managed to keep it off the floor until late in the session, when a motion to bring it up was rejected by a 33 to 30 vote.[27]

With support for nuclear power eroding, the joint committee was forced to shift its attention to the defense of existing policies and programs. Although the JCAE found it increasingly difficult to initiate policy action, it consistently succeeded in blocking measures that threatened the nation's commitment to nuclear power. In this respect, the JCAE remained a very influential force in Congress. As a case in point, it was the opposition of joint committee members that led the conference committee on the Energy Reorganization Act to delete the Senate's intervenor funding and technical assistance provisions. The joint committee also played a key role in defeating efforts to amend the Atomic Energy Act so that states would have a more significant role to play in establishing radiation standards. In another notable exercise of its veto powers, the JCAE effectively killed the various bills that sought to impose a moratorium on reactor operation and construction. One such measure, introduced as an amendment to the AEC's authorization legislation for FY 1975, was defeated on a voice vote after Chet Holifield accused its sponsors of being "doubting Thomases" seeking to "turn back the clock."[28]

ABOLISHING THE JOINT COMMITTEE

As John Chubb has noted, much of the political response to the energy crisis involved organizational change. Several executive branch agencies, including the AEC, were restructured, committee jurisdictions in Congress were redrawn, and there was a significant expansion in the number of interest groups in the policy-making arena. These organizational changes were so numerous that the traditional patterns of energy politics and policy making were fundamentally transformed.[29] Although it is true that the energy crisis prompted a shuffling of committee jurisdictions in the 1970s and that these changes had important ramifications for nuclear policy, it is also important to note that these events dovetailed with the much broader reform movement sweeping through Congress at the same time. Seeking to spread power more widely, an influx of new, more liberal members challenged the authority of committee chairs. This challenge resulted in an increase in the number and authority of subcommittees as well as an expansion in the size of individual and committee staffs. By the end of the decade, Congress was a more open institution populated by more independent legislators.[30] It was also a more fragmented and complex institution than ever before.

Although members of the joint committee supported the Energy Reorganization Act of 1974, most recognized that the changes mandated in the executive branch would inevitably result in a shuffling of committee jurisdictions in Congress. Similarly, because energy had become such a high-profile issue, the number of members of Congress seeking input to energy decisions increased dramatically, as did the number of committees and subcommittees with jurisdiction over some aspect of energy policy.

In one of the more important developments, the Democratic caucus appointed a special committee to study various means of reforming the House. Among the special committee's recommendations was a proposal to refine the jurisdictions of its standing committees. As part of this proposal, the committee urged the removal of legislative authority from all joint committees, including the JCAE. In opposing this particular measure, Chet Holifield indicated that members of the joint committee did recognize the need for some jurisdictional changes, but that he personally preferred reconstituting the joint committee as a broad-based committee on energy to parallel ERDA.[31] Although the House eventually adopted a weaker version of the committee's recommendations, it was unable to resolve many of the jurisdictional questions involving the energy and environmental committees and therefore deleted the provision affecting the JCAE.

Much of the JCAE's considerable weight in nuclear policy matters stemmed from the personal influence of its many longtime members, several of whom had served on the committee since its inception in 1946. In fact, the lengthy tenure of many joint committee members, such as Holifield, Hosmer, Price, Anderson, and Pastore, contributed significantly to the stability of nuclear policy and was a major factor in the committee's unwavering support of nuclear power. But during the 1970s, a combination of retirements and electoral defeats caused significant turnover on the joint committee, with thirteen of the committee's eighteen members in the 92d Congress departing by the beginning of the 95th. Representatives Wayne Aspinall (D-Colo.), Ed Edmonson (D-Okla.), William McCulloch (R-Ohio), and the influential Senator Clinton Anderson (D-N.Mex.) left at the end of 1972. Seven more members departed at the end of the 93d Congress: Senators Alan Bible (D-Nev.), George Aiken (R-Vt.), Wallace Bennett (R-Utah), Peter Dominick (R-Colo.), and Representatives Chet Holifield, Craig Hosmer, and Orval Hansen (R-Idaho).[32] John Pastore (D-R.I.), then the joint committee's senior senator as well as its chairman, retired at the end of 1976, as did Stuart Symington (D-Mo.). Three other Senate members, Joseph Montoya (D-N.Mex.), James L. Buckley (R-N.Y.), and John V. Tunney (D-Calif.), were defeated in the 1976 elections. The extensive turnover on the committee, especially the departure of longtime members such as Anderson, Pastore, Holifield, and Hosmer, deprived the nuclear program of some of its most influential and outspoken defenders.

With one-third of its members retiring or being defeated in the 1976 elections, the JCAE was suddenly vulnerable. According to some reports, many of the newer members of Congress elected in the aftermath of Watergate strongly believed the joint committee "had been too long and too much the uncritical proponent of nuclear power."[33] In fact, earlier in the session two of the committee's opponents, Jonathan Bingham and Clarence Long (D-Md.), had unsuccessfully introduced a proposal to abolish the JCAE.[34] Approximately one month after the November 1976 elections, Bingham tried again, proposing to the House Democratic Caucus that the House strip the JCAE of most of its legislative powers. On 8 December the caucus agreed. Bingham's proposal was included in a host of reforms accepted by the full House on 4 January 1977 when it was adopting the rules for the 95th Congress. But because the joint committee was created by statute in the Atomic Energy Act, it could only be abolished by amending that statute and not by the rules of either chamber. Therefore, the joint committee still formally existed after passage of the House resolution. But following adoption of the rule stripping the JCAE of its legislative powers, the House leadership voted not to fill its nine seats on the committee.

The Senate was expected to be a bigger obstacle to efforts to abolish the joint committee, but the departure of five senators after the 1976 elections made it easier to push for reform. The Senate, meanwhile, had appointed a special bipartisan committee to consider the possibility of revamping its own committee system. Chaired by Adlai Stevenson (D-Ill.), the group proposed the first major changes in the Senate's committee structure in over thirty years. Citing a desire to reduce demands on senators' time and workloads as well as the need to eliminate conflicting committee jurisdictions, the group recommended reducing the number of committees and subcommittees and limiting the committee assignments of individual senators. If adopted, the proposal was expected to reduce the number of subcommittees from 171 to 125. In addition, the group proposed that all joint committees be eliminated.[35]

The special committee defended its proposal by pointing out that senators in the 94th Congress served on an average of seventeen committees, subcommittees, and panels. As amended, the proposal limited the number of committee and subcommittee assignments to eight: individual senators would be allowed to serve on three subcommittees for each of their two major committee assignments and on two subcommittees on a minor committee. The proposal also called for limiting to three the number of committee and subcommittee chairmanships an individual senator could hold, of which only two could be on major committees.[36] As expected, there was opposition to the plan, especially from senators whose committees would be eliminated. Nevertheless, the plan was adopted, perhaps in part because by placing limits on the number of chairmanships any individual could hold, it ensured that more senators would have a chairmanship of their own.

By a vote of 89 to 1, the Senate approved the overhaul of its committee structure on 4 February 1977. The Senate Resolution (S. Res. 4), which included the abolition of the joint committee, divided the JCAE's responsibilities among three committees. Although the joint committee still officially existed, Senate Democrats, like the leadership of the House, declined to fill their five seats on the committee.[37] In March the Senate adopted S. 1153, which amended the Atomic Energy Act by formally abolishing the JCAE. The House passed an amended version of this bill by a voice vote on 5 August. The Senate cleared an identical measure that same day, bringing an end to the thirty-year reign of the JCAE and creating a dramatically new congressional environment for nuclear policy issues.[38]

THE NEW LEGISLATIVE FRAMEWORK

One of the more important consequences of the abolition of the joint committee was greater congressional oversight of the NRC. Prior to the demise of the JCAE, the commission had a very simple oversight structure and was one of the least frequently scrutinized federal agencies. During the 93d and 94th Congresses, for example, it ranked fourteenth out of seventeen in the frequency of oversight hearings. Furthermore, in that period the commission was the subject of only twenty-one hearings, while the average for all other regulatory agencies was sixty-two. But after the committee reforms were enacted in 1977, the volume of congressional oversight activity increased, and the number of oversight hearings more than doubled.[39] From FY 1977 through FY 1980, the total number of hearings involving the NRC steadily increased. In fiscal years 1977 and 1978, for example, the NRC was the subject of twenty-six and thirty-four hearings, respectively. The following year, which was punctuated by the accident at Three Mile Island (TMI), NRC personnel testified at forty-two hearings. In fact, there were twenty-four TMI-related hearings alone in the eighteen months following the accident.[40] For the NRC, the heightened scrutiny that resulted from the new legislative framework established a more complex political environment in which to operate.

Not only was there a quantitative increase in the amount of NRC oversight conducted after the dissolution of the joint committee, but there was a qualitative change as well stemming from the number of committees and subcommittees conducting that oversight. With the adoption of the committee reforms, the responsibilities of the JCAE were transferred to five standing committees in each chamber. In the House, primary jurisdiction over the regulation and oversight of the nuclear power industry was inherited by the Committee on Interior and Insular Affairs, chaired by Morris Udall. Critics of nuclear power were quite happy with this turn of events because Udall was considered to be an environmentalist and also because they believed it provided them with access to the policy process from the subcommittee stage—through Udall's Subcommittee on Energy and the Environment—for the very first time.[41] The Committee on Interstate and Foreign Commerce was charged with the regulation and oversight of nuclear production facilities, but through a broad interpretation of its authority, the committee often ventured into areas outside of its formal turf. The Armed Services Committee inherited jurisdiction over the military aspects of nuclear power, while questions concerning the export of nuclear technology were assigned to the International Relations Committee. Finally, the Committee on Science and Technology assumed responsibility for all nuclear research and development programs as well as oversight of ERDA.

In the Senate, the task of overseeing the regulation of the commercial nuclear power industry was handed over to a newly created Committee on the Environment and Public Works. Another new committee, the Committee on Energy and Natural Resources, was assigned jurisdiction for nuclear energy research and development programs. In addition, the Armed Services Committee assumed responsibility for nuclear issues involving the military, while the Committees on Foreign Relations and Governmental Affairs inherited the JCAE's jurisdiction for the international aspects of nuclear energy and nuclear export policy, respectively.

In addition to the committees that were formally granted jurisdiction over the NRC, a number of others eventually expressed an interest in the nuclear power issue. In the House, for example, the Appropriations, Judiciary, and Government Operations Committees all held hearings concerning NRC activities, as did the Appropriations and Commerce, Science, and Technology Committees in the Senate. In the years immediately following the reorganization, fourteen different standing committees held hearings involving the NRC. That number increased to eighteen in the aftermath of Three Mile Island. Including subcommittees, there were approximately two dozen congressional work groups claiming jurisdiction over some aspect of nuclear regulation. The numbers were even higher when all aspects of nuclear policy, including research and development, are considered. In the final analysis, the new committee structure created a more decentralized, more competitive, and infinitely more complicated policy-making process within Congress.

For critics of the NRC, the committee reorganization rendered Congress more permeable and created numerous opportunities to gain access to nuclear decision making. Indeed, efforts by antinuclear activists to remake nuclear policy would not have been possible in the absence of these important structural changes. Simply put, there was a veritable explosion in the number of legislators who could claim some authority over nuclear power. With the stranglehold of the joint committee broken and with responsibility for nuclear policy dispersed so widely, those seeking to initiate more aggressive regulation of the nuclear power industry were able to forge alliances with sympathetic and influential members of Congress. In some instances, representatives of antinuclear groups actually sought employment within Congress. In the late 1970s, for example, a lawyer who had formerly served as counsel for the UCS joined the staff of Senator Edward Kennedy. Kennedy, who was planning to challenge Jimmy Carter for his party's presidential nomination in 1980, was becoming increasingly vocal in his criticism of nuclear power and the NRC. Although lacking formal jurisdiction over nuclear power, Kennedy's Subcommittee on Health and Scientific Research was one of the first to hold hearings investigating the accident at Three Mile Island. One of the consequences of the proliferation of congressional working groups in the nuclear arena was to provide greater information and easier access to reform-minded interest groups.

In many instances, then, the relationship between nuclear activists and entrepreneurial members of Congress was mutually beneficial. Seeking to expand the conflict over nuclear power, it was clearly in the best interests of the activists to attract attention—and publicity—to their cause. One way to accomplish this goal was through congressional hearings sponsored by friendly legislators, such as Senator Kennedy. Many legislators were only too happy to oblige, seeing the growing controversy over nuclear power in general and reactor safety in particular as excellent opportunities to attract attention to themselves. As a result, some members of Congress chose to capitalize on the situation and became champions of the public interest, demanding that the NRC adopt more stringent regulations to ensure the safety of the public. It is important to note, however, that much of this behavior would not have been possible without the major reforms that were more or less simultaneously sweeping through Congress. The new committee assignments, together with the decentralization of power in Congress as manifested in the trend toward subcommittee government, greatly enhanced the incentive and ability of individual legislators to initiate new programs or reorient old ones. The net effect of the structural changes in Congress was to bolster the influence of those interests that were critical of nuclear power at the expense of those who were seeking to promote it. This tendency was particularly true in the House of Representatives, where public exposure and criticism of the NRC became commonplace.

Several committees and subcommittees in the House proved to be receptive to those seeking a more aggressive regulatory posture. As already noted, the Committee on Interior and Insular Affairs had long shown an interest in nuclear power and had even managed to carve out an oversight role for itself before the JCAE was abolished. With the demise of the JCAE, the Interior Committee inherited the primary responsibility for NRC authorizations and oversight as well as the oversight of nuclear power plants. Under Udall's leadership, the committee became a persistent critic of the NRC and the nuclear industry. As a case in point, in its report accompanying the NRC's FY 1979 authorization bill, the committee lamented the "frequent failure of the NRC to be frank and forthright in its relations with Congress." The committee added that "some of the Commissioners and staff continue to be imbued with the notion carried over from the Atomic Energy Commission era that there exists a duty to protect nuclear power from its critics rather than lay out all the facts, no matter how unpleasant they might be."[42]

For the most part, the Interior Committee flexed its muscles through the Subcommittee on Energy and the Environment, also chaired by Udall, which closely monitored the industry and the commission and held hearings on a variety of controversial issues during the latter part of the decade. At these hearings, industry representatives and NRC personnel experienced something unusual: tough questioning from subcommittee members, most notably Jonathan Bingham and Edward Markey. The Interior Committee also had a Subcommittee on Oversight and Special Investigations, which conducted investigations into several NRC programs including the commission's much criticized efforts to solve the nuclear waste disposal problem.

Several of the other House committees that inherited jurisdiction over NRC programs from the JCAE were sympathetic to concerns involving reactor safety and began to push for more effective regulation as well. The Committee on Interstate and Foreign Commerce had two subcommittees that regularly prodded the NRC to adopt a more aggressive regulatory posture. One, the Subcommittee on Energy and Power, was quite active in this regard, conducting hearings on NRC authorizations, a number of licensing reform proposals, and nuclear waste disposal and storage. The subcommittee Chair was John Dingell (D-Mich.), who had established a reputation as something of a skeptic with respect to nuclear power by challenging the AEC in the controversy over thermal pollution. John Moss (D-Calif.), an advocate of environmental concerns, chaired the Commerce Subcommittee on Oversight and Investigations. In addition, the Government Operations Subcommittee on Environment, Energy, and Natural Resources, which also played a key oversight role with respect to NRC programs, was headed during this same period by two liberal Democrats, Leo Ryan (D-Calif.) and Toby Moffett (D-Conn.).[43] Both were advocates of more rigorous regulation.

When the new committees assumed jurisdiction in the House, then, opponents of nuclear power were able to find allies who were willing, and able, to lend support to their cause. This situation is not intended to suggest, however, that supporters of nuclear power were completely left out in the cold. The Science and Technology Subcommittee on Energy Research and Production was chaired by Mike McCormack (D-Wash.), a former member of the JCAE and perhaps the most outspoken proponent of nuclear power in Congress. Although McCormack's subcommittee did not have jurisdiction over operating reactors, it was nonetheless able to play a key role in maintaining high levels of research support for more advanced reactor designs and nuclear waste disposal programs. The full House Science and Technology Committee also played a key role in repeatedly frustrating efforts by the Carter administration to kill off the controversial Clinch River Breeder demonstration project.[44] Pronuclear forces had another friend in Tom Bevill (D-Ala.), chair of the House Appropriations Subcommittee on Energy and Water Development, which had jurisdiction over the NRC's budget. In an effort to create pressure for expediting the NRC's licensing process, Bevill persuaded the NRC to prepare monthly reports detailing the estimated months of delay between reactor completion dates and estimated commission license approval dates. The purpose of these reports was to demonstrate that much of the "delay" was due to excessive NRC regulatory zeal and a drawn-out hearing process. Bevill later instructed the NRC to use the industry's construction schedule estimates, which were typically exceedingly optimistic, rather than the NRC staff's. The new calculations predictably fostered the impression that licensing delays were getting worse and were, in fact, a serious problem.[45]

On the whole, however, the new committee assignments in the House greatly enhanced the access and influence of antinuclear forces to the policy-making process. Much the same thing happened in the other chamber, although until Three Mile Island, Senate oversight tended to be sporadic and less critical than in the House. In part this difference was because responsibility for the regulation of nuclear plants was more centralized in the Senate, with the Environment and Public Works Committee in general and its Subcommittee on Nuclear Regulation in particular being the major actors. The chair of the full committee was Jennings Randolph, a West Virginia Democrat who was understandably protective of his state's very substantial coal interests. Although not overtly antinuclear, Randolph from time to time adopted positions inimical to the interests of the nuclear power industry. As a case in point, he opposed the Nuclear Siting and Licensing Act of 1978 because of the NRC's inability to find a satisfactory solution for the storage and disposal of high-level nuclear waste. Although the Environment and Public Works Committee was not as critical of the NRC as Udall's Interior Committee in the House, it was fairly active in maintaining pressure on the commission and the industry in an effort to reshape the nuclear regulatory regime.

One indication of this stance came in October 1977, when the committee voted to reject the nomination of Kent Hansen to the NRC. A Carter nominee, Hansen was opposed by environmentalists because of a perceived conflict of interest resulting from his previous work as a consultant to General Electric and Westinghouse, the two largest reactor vendors, and because he was seen as the personal choice of James Schlesinger, former AEC chair and then secretary of energy. The Department of Energy, and Schlesinger, were suspect in the eyes of many antinuclear activists because the agency had inherited the AEC's statutory authority for the promotion and development of nuclear technology.[46] In commenting on the committee's decision, Gary Hart (D-Colo.), chairman of the Subcommittee on Nuclear Regulation, said that "this movement of individuals back and forth between regulatory agencies and the industries they regulate has created a serious problem of public credibility."[47] The Subcommittee on Nuclear Regulation was generally more critical of nuclear power than the full committee, but its effectiveness was often questioned because of Hart's reputation for holding one-day hearings with little or no real oversight. Although this practice was certainly true in comparison with the Udall subcommittee in the House, the reality was that these one-day hearings did attract the attention of the press and the public to the nuclear safety issue and keep it in the headlines, which was something pronuclear forces would have preferred to avoid.

With respect to the other Senate committees that inherited responsibilities from the JCAE, the consequences appear to have been mixed. Some, like

Abraham Ribicoff's Committee on Governmental Affairs (previously Government Operations), investigated a range of regulatory issues and were generally sympathetic to the concerns of antinuclear activists. The committee held hearings in 1976, for example, on the question of whether dissenting staff views were given adequate consideration during NRC licensing reviews. For the most part, though, Ribicoff's committee was more concerned with questions involving the security of nuclear materials from sabotage and terrorism than it was with reactor safety per se. Other committees, such as the Committee on Energy and Natural Resources, focused on the broader question of energy research and development and tended to view nuclear power as one of several energy sources, albeit an important one. The Energy Committee appears to have been following the lead of its chairman, Henry Jackson (D-Wash.). Although Jackson was a former member of the joint committee, he also had become something of an expert on energy and environmental issues. As a result, his position on nuclear power was somewhat ambiguous—he supported its use but recognized that it was not the answer to the nation's energy woes. Jackson's desire was to craft a comprehensive national energy policy that utilized a diverse range of measures on both the supply and demand sides of the equation. In practical terms, this approach translated into greater research and development support for all energy sources, not just nuclear power.

THE CONGRESSIONAL RESPONSE TO THREE MILE ISLAND

As might be expected, a number of antinuclear measures were introduced in Congress after Three Mile Island (TMI). In the House, Edward Markey (D-Mass.) proposed two amendments to the NRC's fiscal year 1980 authorization legislation. One amendment, affecting a total of six reactors, would prohibit the NRC from issuing construction permits for a period of six months; the other would block the operation of newly licensed reactors until the government had developed a plan to respond to emergency situations such as Three Mile Island. Markey said his amendments had three goals: to send the NRC a clear signal that Congress wanted the agency to focus its efforts on ensuring the safety of those plants already holding operating licenses, as well as the ninety-four reactors then under construction; to force the NRC to resolve crucial safety issues at the construction permit stage; and to repair the commission's reputation, which had been badly damaged by Three Mile Island. Despite the opposition of chairman Udall, both amendments sailed through the Committee on Interior and Insular Affairs. Noting a "go-slow" feeling in Congress after TMI, Speaker of the House Tip O'Neill predicted that the full House would approve the Markey amendments later that session.[48] But before the amendments could reach the floor for a vote, they first would have to go through the Commerce Committee, which shared jurisdiction over NRC authorizations. In contrast to the Interior Committee, the Commerce Committee tended to be more hospitable to pronuclear arguments. In the interim, the utilities and reactor vendors had begun an intensive lobbying campaign in opposition to the amendments. Their efforts paid off in early June, when Commerce rejected the amendments by a vote of 24 to 18.

Markey reintroduced his construction moratorium amendment when the authorization bill came to a floor vote. During the debate, amendment supporters defended it as an opportunity for the NRC to focus on the safety of operating reactors rather than on the licensing of new ones. Opponents of the proposal argued, with some success, that it would only add to the nation's dependence on imported oil; in fact, Markey later estimated that this argument cost him at least twenty votes. Those votes would still not have been enough, as the amendment went down to defeat in November by a vote of 254 to 135. Although industry lobbying was crucial to the outcome, the vote was really a foregone conclusion after NRC chair Joseph Hendrie informed a House subcommittee several weeks earlier that legislation would be unnecessary because the commission was instituting a de facto licensing moratorium. According to Hendrie, the NRC planned to prohibit utilities from beginning construction or operation of any new plants for a period of at least six months and possibly for as long as two years. The one-sided vote demonstrated the nuclear industry's continued ability to win tough fights on the floor, prompting Mike McCormack, a former JCAE member and the leading supporter of nuclear power in the House, to claim that the vote was an indication of the body's "strong inclination to move forward aggressively in our nuclear energy program." Although McCormack's interpretation was unjustifiably optimistic, the vote was nevertheless an unmistakable sign that Congress was not about to slam the door on the nuclear option.[49]

In the Senate, meanwhile, the authorization bill was referred to the Environment and Public Works Committee, where Gary Hart, chair of the Subcommittee on Nuclear Regulation, also proposed an amendment calling for a six-month moratorium on the construction of new nuclear plants. As in the House, pronuclear forces were able to defeat the measure when it came to a floor vote later that summer.[50] The Senate also voted down a proposal that would have given each state a veto over storage of nuclear waste within its own borders. But the Senate did approve another Hart-sponsored amendment that required states to adopt federally approved emergency plans before the NRC could issue new operating licenses; furthermore, existing plants could be shut down by 1 June 1980 if emergency plans had not been approved. Critics of the measure, along with the nuclear power industry, tried to kill it on three separate occasions but were narrowly defeated each time by a bipartisan majority.[51] The combination of votes indicates that the Senate was eager to improve safety at operating reactors but was unwilling to rule out nuclear power as a potentially valuable source of electricity.

Congress also adopted legislation sponsored by Representative Jonathan

Bingham that required the commission to issue a report to Congress within 120 days describing how well each of the seventy-two reactors then in operation satisfied NRC safety requirements. The legislation also required the NRC to provide Congress with a list of all unresolved safety issues affecting reactors as well as a detailed schedule for their resolution.[52] In many respects, the Bingham amendment was merely the latest attempt by Congress to prod the NRC to take action on "generic" safety issues; the subject had been of concern to Congress since early 1976, when former NRC staffer Robert Pollard revealed that the NRC was investigating over two hundred generic issues.[53] So-called "generic" safety issues are problems that are common to many reactors; "unresolved safety issues," on the other hand, are those generic issues the NRC staff deemed most important from a safety perspective.[54]

According to commission rules, safety issues that have been labeled as "generic" do not have to be resolved before an operating license can be issued. Like the AEC before it, the NRC issued construction permits and operating licenses despite many unanswered questions. Indeed, most if not all licensed nuclear plants had been operating for years pending resolution of numerous safety issues. Typically, the regulatory staff would approve an operating license if the utility applicant agreed to meet certain conditions, including the adoption of interim measures that could assure adequate safety pending final resolution of the issue; the staff also would issue a license if it could "reasonably" expect the issue to be resolved before the plant began operation, or if the likelihood and consequences of an accident were small.[55]

Once the NRC classified an issue as generic, intervenors were prohibited from contesting it in individual licensing hearings. Although the commission usually promised to convene a single rulemaking proceeding on the issue that would be applicable to all affected plants, critics claimed that the practice of labeling an issue as generic was actually designed to remove it as an obstacle to the licensing of individual plants. After the accident at Three Mile Island, both the Kemeny Commission and the NRC Special Inquiry Group criticized the NRC's handling of generic issues, claiming that the commission used the practice as a "convenient way of postponing decision on a difficult question."[56] In the words of the Kemeny Commission, the NRC's failure to resolve generic issues illustrated that its "primary focus" was on licensing and that it paid "insufficient attention" to the "ongoing process of assuring nuclear safety."[57]

The NRC also was criticized for failing to resolve generic issues in a timely manner. The regulatory staff had been working on the problem since 1976, when it initiated a systematic review of the issues and ranked them according to their relative importance from the standpoint of public risk. As a result of their review, the staff compiled a list of over 350 generic issues deserving the highest priority. Worried about the potential safety implications, Congress amended the Atomic Energy Act in 1977 to require the NRC to develop a plan for identifying and analyzing unresolved generic issues and to take action to solve them. Congress also required the NRC to issue an annual report detailing the program's status. In its first such report, the NRC indicated that the number of unresolved problems had declined to 133; by the next year the number had been further reduced to 17.[58]

But according to the Union of Concerned Scientists, the claims of significant progress made in the NRC reports inaccurately represented the status of many generic safety issues and amounted to a deceptive "numbers game" that masked a very different reality. In practice, the dramatic reduction in the number of safety problems was not accomplished through an actual resolution of the problems but through creative bookkeeping techniques in which issues were lumped together or redefined. The NRC also adopted a rather unusual definition of "resolved" to pare down the number of generic safety issues on its list. In many instances, for example, issues were considered "resolved" when technical solutions had been developed but not installed in the affected plants; in other cases, problems were considered "resolved" when the staff accepted a conceptual solution to a problem even though the actual techniques or technologies for implementing that solution had not yet been developed or applied. Clearly, the NRC's definition of "resolved" did not reflect the common meaning of that word.[59]

The NRC's next report to Congress, issued in 1981 because it was delayed by the TMI accident, identified four new "unresolved safety issues." What the report did not reveal was that the investigation into the TMI accident uncovered far more than four new safety problems; the regulatory staff had actually identified 425 issues as candidates for classification as unresolved safety issues. However, the staff then put the items through a rigorous screening test that was done, according to the NRC itself, "without addressing the safety importance of the issue." Moreover, an issue did not pass the screening test if "definition of the issue requires long-term confirmatory or exploratory research."[60] Again, it seemed that the commission was going to extraordinary lengths to minimize the number of unresolved safety problems it reported to Congress.

This conclusion also was reached by the Kemeny Commission in its investigation into the accident at TMI, and it formed the basis of the panel's recommendation that Congress amend the Atomic Energy Act to require the NRC to set firm deadlines for resolving generic issues.[61] Congress failed to act, however, and a 1984 General Accounting Office study into the NRC's generic safety issue program found that the agency's generic issues program was plagued by chronic delays. The GAO reported that given the NRC's track record, it would take over ten years to eliminate the backlog of generic safety issues. The lengthy delays, said the GAO, were due to "management weaknesses" at the NRC, which lacked "sufficient management controls . . . to ensure resolution of issues and implementation of appropriate changes to affected nuclear plants and to NRC's regulatory procedures in a timely manner."[62]

NRC PERSONNEL AND BUDGET LEVELS

Congress can influence administrative policy making in a variety of ways, most notably through the appropriations process.[63] The appropriations process allows the relevant committees and subcommittees to establish an agency's overall budget and staffing levels, thereby allowing Congress to exercise a degree of control and oversight of agency actions. In this way, the appropriations process allows Congress to communicate its policy preferences to agency administrators. In addition, Congress can exercise considerable influence over an agency's ability to conduct certain tasks by adjusting appropriations for particular programs and activities. If Congress wants to discourage or curtail a certain program, it can either reduce the program's appropriations or place detailed restrictions on the use of appropriated funds. Conversely, Congress can encourage agencies to pursue certain programs by setting aside additional funds for that purpose. Similarly, when appropriations or staffing levels for agency programs and activities are increased (or cut) unequally, policy outcomes may be affected.[64] Therefore, a program-by-program examination of the NRC appropriations process in the 1970s may provide a mechanism for assessing congressional attitudes toward the commission and nuclear power. If there were any changes in congressional priorities, they should be reflected in the NRC's budget and staffing levels.

NRC appropriations steadily increased from $148 million in FY 1975 to $466 in FY 1981. Appropriations for all seven program areas increased as well. By far the largest program area was research, which accounted for nearly half of the agency's total budget during the entire period. Although the research program was responsible for a broad array of safety issues, there is considerable evidence that its agenda was driven by political rather than scientific concerns. For example, many NRC and ACRS personnel believed research priorities were established because of an issue's visibility and not because of its potential safety implications. As a case in point, it was argued that many significant safety problems were neglected because the NRC devoted nearly 60 percent of its research efforts to studying emergency core-cooling systems and loss of coolant accidents, two problems that had become highly visible and troublesome. There were also concerns that the NRC, like the AEC before it, was reluctant to conduct research that could raise doubts concerning either the adequacy of its own regulations or the safety of existing nuclear plants.[65]

Although there was an across-the-board increase in appropriations, there were significant shifts in each program's relative share of the NRC's total budget (see Table 6.1). The largest shift occurred in the materials safety and safeguards program, whose share increased by almost 6 percent. The increase was in response to the concerns of Senator Ribicoff's Governmental Affairs Committee, which held numerous hearings on the security of nuclear materials from the threat of sabotage or diversion. There were also significant shifts in appropriations for the three program areas most important from a regulatory perspective.

Table 6.1. NRC Budgets

	1975	1976	1977	1978	1979	1980	1981	Change 1975–81
Total (in millions)	$148	$222	$254	$288	$326	$396	$466	+$318
Licensing (%)	21.2	16.0	16.6	14.2	15.6	16.4	16.0	−5.2%
Standards and Development (%)	4.6	4.4	4.8	3.9	4.1	3.4	3.5	−1.1%
Inspection and Enforcement (%)	11.2	9.8	11.0	11.9	10.5	12.0	13.1	+1.9%
Material Safety and Safeguards (%)	2.5	5.8	8.3	8.3	8.6	7.2	8.3	+5.8%
Program Direction and Administration (%)	8.9	10.5	8.3	8.5	8.7	8.8	8.6	−0.3%
ACRS, Boards, and Legal (%)	5.1	4.4	4.0	4.2	4.1	4.2	4.2	−0.9%
Research (%)	46.5	49.1	47.0	49.0	48.4	48.0	46.3	−0.2%

Source: NRC annual reports.

The inspection and enforcement program's share of the budget increased by 1.9 percent, while the relative shares of the standards development and licensing programs decreased by 1.1 percent and 5.2 percent, respectively.

If one considers the tasks involved in these program areas, it is unclear what type of signals Congress was trying to send to the NRC. The inspection and enforcement program was responsible for monitoring and ensuring compliance with NRC regulations at all nuclear reactors. Therefore, by increasing appropriations for this program, Congress was ostensibly enhancing the NRC's ability to assure reactor safety. On the other hand, the program responsible for developing reactor design and safety regulations suffered a relative budget cut. In fact, the budget for the standards development program was consistently the smallest of all NRC activities. By cutting appropriations for an already meager standards development program, Congress was for all intents and purposes slowing the rate at which new safety standards could be promulgated. This action would have the effect of benefiting the nuclear industry, which frequently complained about the imposition of new, more stringent regulations. Finally, the licensing program was responsible for overseeing the application process for all construction permits and operating licenses. That the program's share of the agency's total budget had shrunk to 16 percent by FY 1981 could be interpreted to mean that Congress was not responding to the industry's desire to speed the licensing process.

But an examination of Congress's response to NRC appropriations requests does not support that conclusion. Indeed, it is clear that in some instances there were important policy differences between Congress and the NRC. With respect to licensing programs, Congress typically appropriated more money than the commission requested, suggesting that Congress really was interested in moving the licensing process along. Congress also allocated fewer resources to standards development than the NRC requested, again signaling its desire to shield the nuclear industry from rapidly changing regulatory demands. On the other hand, Congress was unwilling to let the NRC cut back on programs for inspection and enforcement and thus appropriated slightly more money than the NRC wanted.[66] These appropriations figures suggest that Congress was ambivalent about nuclear power. By setting aside additional funds for inspection and enforcement activities, Congress was demonstrating its concern that nuclear power be made safe. After all, a larger inspection and enforcement budget could result in more frequent and stringent inspections. But its decisions on the NRC's appropriations requests for licensing and standards development show that Congress also was interested in the continued licensing of nuclear plants.

The commission's staffing levels reveal similar trends. Like the NRC's budget, the total number of agency personnel increased dramatically throughout the decade, from just over 2,000 in FY 1975 to over 3,300 in FY 1981. Again, there were increases in all seven program areas, but they were not distributed equally; as a result, some programs fared better than others. Indeed, when each program's staffing levels are expressed as a percentage of the NRC's total employment, there were significant shifts among programs. During this period, for example, the percentage of NRC personnel employed in licensing activities declined by 7.4 percent, from 29 percent in FY 1975 to only 21.6 percent in FY 1981 (see Table 6.2). On the other hand, the most significant growth occurred in the material safety and safeguards and the inspection and enforcement programs, both of which more than doubled in size. The inspection and enforcement staff supplanted the licensing staff as the NRC's largest in 1978; it accounted for over 28 percent of the commission's total employment by FY 1981. As mentioned earlier, the dramatic growth in inspection and enforcement personnel reflected the commission's recognition of the need to monitor the steadily increasing numbers of reactors in operation. In fact, the NRC's creation in December 1975 of a Division of Operating Reactors was actually the culmination of a trend begun by the AEC, which had doubled the number of personnel assigned to operating reactors in its final year.[67] In enlarging its inspection and enforcement staff, the commission was responding to congressional and presidential pressure, most notably President Carter's frequent requests that the NRC place resident inspectors at all operating nuclear plants to better ensure compliance with safety requirements.

In many ways these numbers may be misleading because they only indicate congressional preferences as to spending and personnel, not how the NRC actually allocated them. Toward the latter part of the decade, in fact, several congressional committees expressed concern that the NRC was studiously ignoring congressional preferences. As a matter of fact, there is evidence that suggests that the NRC diverted resources and personnel from safety programs to licensing related activities in an effort to speed the licensing process. For example, spending

Table 6.2. NRC Personnel

	1975	1976	1977	1978	1979	1980	1981	Change 1975–81
Total	2006	2289	2499	2723	2691	3041	3336	+1330
Licensing (%)	29.0	26.0	24.6	22.4	22.6	21.4	21.6	−7.4%
Standards and Development (%)	5.6	5.7	6.0	5.6	4.8	4.7	4.8	−0.8%
Inspection and Enforcement (%)	20.9	22.1	23.6	26.3	26.9	27.9	28.3	+7.4%
Material Safety and Safeguards (%)	7.6	8.3	10.4	10.5	9.8	8.7	9.9	+2.3%
Program Direction and Administration (%)	22.3	23.4	21.6	21.4	21.3	23.6	22.3	0.0%
ACRS, Boards, and Legal (%)	9.9	9.4	8.8	8.4	9.0	8.7	8.2	−1.7%
Research (%)	4.7	5.1	5.0	5.4	5.7	5.0	4.9	+0.2%

Source: NRC annual reports.

on operating license reviews increased, while spending for operating reactors declined. Similarly, the NRC reassigned inspectors from operating reactors to those under construction to facilitate licensing; personnel were also shifted, on a temporary basis, from the research programs. One congressional report concluded that the NRC's actions caused numerous safety-related projects to fall behind schedule.[68] Although the "power of the purse" does provide Congress with leverage over an agency's actions, it is an imprecise tool, and agencies often retain significant discretion over the important decisions about resource allocation.

CONCLUSION

Decisions on the NRC's budget and personnel levels, licensing reform legislation, and Price-Anderson Act reflect congressional ambivalence toward nuclear power. Congress in the 1970s was inhospitable to decisive initiatives from either side, preferring to approach nuclear policy in an ad hoc manner. Still fearful of energy shortages, members of Congress were unwilling to close the door on the nuclear option, deeming it an essential short-term energy source, but at the same time they were unwilling to proceed with a full-scale nuclear program because of concerns about reactor safety. Congress was also ambivalent about citizen participation. On the one hand, it remained committed to protecting the rights of citizens to participate in the NRC's licensing proceedings and therefore resisted licensing reform proposals that would have resulted in fewer opportunities for citizen involvement. On the other hand, Congress was unwilling to fund an intervenor reimbursement program at the NRC, as it had done at other agencies.

Because nuclear power was so controversial in the 1970s, Congress was faced with some difficult questions. Which was more important: reactor safety or energy independence? The congressional solution was to duck the question and pursue both. Congress would increase funding for both reactor safety and licensing programs and also would insist on greater oversight of the NRC and the nuclear power industry. In this way, legislators could claim that they were doing everything possible to provide the nation with safe and secure energy supplies.

All policy-making systems have a structural bias, and as this chapter shows, there were dramatic changes in the structural bias of Congress in the 1970s. After the joint committee was abolished, Congress was far more accessible to interests seeking to reorient nuclear policy, and the range of views represented more accurately reflected the public debate raging around the issue. Furthermore, with responsibility for nuclear power dispersed so widely, it was no longer possible for one select committee of eighteen members of Congress to dictate nuclear policy. The multiple venues in Congress ensured that it would be more responsive to new policy ideas and that the politics of nuclear power in the latter half of the 1970s would be far less predictable than during the halcyon days of the joint committee.

The new bias in Congress reinforced, and magnified, similar changes in the court system, the administrative agencies, and the interest group environment. Critics were once excluded by the protective AEC and JCAE; by the decade's close, they could "venue shop" and choose the most receptive one. As we have seen, antinuclear groups were among the newly mobilized interests that demanded access to policy making in the 1960s. In opposing nuclear power, they claimed that the AEC, in its haste to license reactors, was neglecting its regulatory responsibilities and ignoring important safety questions. They also argued that the agency's decision-making procedures unfairly excluded them from policy deliberations. Seeking relief, they turned to the federal courts, who were sympathetic to their concerns about administrative politics. The courts, in turn, imposed new procedural obligations on the AEC, forcing it to open its deliberations to public participation and scrutiny. These actions were designed to counteract the influence of narrow interests in the administrative process and to improve the quality of agency decision making by forcing administrators to consider other perspectives. Once the AEC was forced to open up, program information became more accessible and it was harder for the agency to defend itself from attacks. Thoroughly discredited, the AEC was eventually abolished and replaced by two new agencies. The growing controversy over the AEC and nuclear power in turn subjected the joint committee to intense criticism, and it also was eliminated. By the end of the decade, access could be gained through the courts, numerous congressional subcommittees and federal agencies, and state and local governments; all proved to be more sympathetic than the AEC or JCAE had ever been.

That these changes in structural bias occurred simultaneously across institutions suggests a common source. The structural changes in Congress were, like the others, part of a larger effort to reshape regulatory politics. The same forces that dispersed power more widely in Congress also contributed to a more active judiciary, the mobilization of new groups, and the transformation of administrative politics. Congressional subcommittees, federal judges, and public lobby groups now would be actively involved in administrative oversight. This case indicates that institutions are connected and that structural changes can be cumulative and reinforcing.

The last few chapters have also shown that subgovernments are not as enduring or as immutable as once thought; they are based on positive policy images and institutions that discourage the participation of outsiders. If either one changes, subgovernments may crumble. Whenever actors can introduce new understandings of issues or shift jurisdiction to new institutions, they can upset a previously stable situation. Indeed, this interaction between changing images and venues, claim Baumgartner and Jones, is the cause of disequilibrium politics.[69] New policy images and venues can, they claim, lead to "dramatic and enduring shifts in policy outcomes."[70]

Changes in policy images and institutions can come from inside the subsystem or from exogenous factors. For example, the initial questions of reactor safety were raised by AEC scientists. Only later did safety issues capture the attention of antinuclear groups, the national press, and the general public and contribute to the increasingly negative preceptions of nuclear power. Other changes in image and institutions resulted from the rise to prominence of energy issues, subjecting all energy subsystems to heightened scrutiny. Clearly, subsystems are not immune from outside influences.

E. E. Schattschneider once wrote that "in politics as in everything else it makes a difference whose game we play. The rules of the game determine the requirements for success. Resources sufficient for success in one game may be wholly inadequate in another."[71] If that is the case, then those interests who can correctly identify which game is being played, or perhaps more important, can substitute one game for another, stand a better chance of winning. The dismantling of the AEC and the joint committee created a new game, and, as a result, the requirements for success changed. Technical expertise, deep pockets, and a commitment to nuclear power were no longer enough to ensure success in an environment that was suddenly crowded and highly visible. As the opponents of nuclear power knew, within the confines of the new game publicity and constant media attention also could be effective tools. It was a lesson the nuclear industry would have to learn in order to survive.

7

The Politics of Nuclear Power, 1975–80

I am continually amazed that the Nuclear Regulatory Commission gets smeared and burdened with problems, real or imagined, of the Atomic Energy Commission era. I find it ironic that the Commission, which is only a year old, seems to be in a position now of guilty until proven innocent.
—William A. Anders, NRC chairman, 1976

External stimuli can be delightful things for overcoming bureaucratic inertia.
—Victor Gilinsky, NRC commissioner, 1976

The institutional changes that characterized American politics in the 1970s dramatically altered the conditions in which nuclear policy was debated and formulated. The demise of the AEC and JCAE deprived the nuclear power industry of its most powerful advocates and spread responsibility for nuclear policy more widely throughout government. In short, the rules of the game had changed and created a very different structure of bias from what existed prior to the 1970s. In this chapter I will assess the initial effects of the new rules on nuclear politics and policy and address several questions. Was political activity any different in the new, more open era? Were there substantive shifts in the direction of nuclear policy? How did participants adapt to the new policy environment? And if the nuclear subgovernment collapsed, what, if anything, would emerge to replace it?

Greater presidential involvement is one of the new era's defining characteristics. We have seen that as is typical of most policy monopolies, presidents were generally uninterested and uninvolved in nuclear policy for most of the postwar period. Beginning with Richard Nixon, however, the conflict over nuclear power had become so intense that presidents could no longer ignore it. This is true even before Three Mile Island, which only heightened presidential scrutiny. Presidential involvement is significant because no other actors can rival their agenda-setting or gatekeeping powers. Interest group access, for example, is powerfully influenced by who controls the White House. The important question, then, is on which side of the debate would presidents intervene?

Another notable difference in the 1970s was the emergence of what Richard A. Harris calls "politicized management." More specifically, "politicized" means a growing awareness of government and its relevance to the activities of one's daily life, a rising concern about politics, and increased political participation and attempts to influence policymakers.[1] According to Harris, the institutional reforms of the public lobby era created a more open and complex decision-making environment that placed a premium on political and technical expertise. Public hearings and citizen suits were now prevalent in many areas of social regulation, and their proliferation forced business to become more actively involved in political affairs. Businesses that had once been comfortable operating in tight subgovernments had to deal with regulatory agencies, public lobbyists, and federal courts on a regular basis, and this repeated contact "politicized" management. Business thus had to find new ways of participating effectively in the changed environment. Many firms responded by establishing or upgrading corporate offices in Washington and by increasing the resources for political and regulatory analyses.[2] The nuclear power industry was no different.

THE INTEREST GROUP ARENA

The growth in the number of organized groups seeking access to the nuclear debate has already been noted. In addition to local citizen groups, national environmental organizations, and industry associations, a variety of groups interested in consumer, labor, and energy issues began to monitor the policy-making process, particularly in Congress. Among them were consumer groups such as Congress Watch and Energy Action, who were concerned about the rising cost of electricity generated by nuclear power plants. A number of oil companies, by virtue of their ownership of uranium supplies, also began to pay close attention to policy developments affecting the future of the nuclear power industry. As we have seen, some of this increase in interest group activity can be attributed to the many structural changes enacted during this period. More specifically, the dissolution of the AEC and JCAE enabled many of these groups, particularly those opposed to nuclear power, to gain access to the policy-making arena for the first time.

But it is important to note that these structural changes also prompted a reaction by those interests that traditionally had been active in nuclear policy making. Until the 1970s, the nuclear power industry was able to exercise its influence in the largely insulated and autonomous realm of subgovernment politics and thus had little need to engage in more visible and competitive forms of political activity. The demise of the AEC and JCAE, however, meant that the industry would have to adapt in order to participate effectively in the more complex and uncertain political environment. Accordingly, beginning shortly after passage of the Energy Reorganization Act of 1974, the nuclear power industry took a number of steps to organize and mobilize for political action. The objective of these initial efforts was to rehabilitate perceptions of nuclear power. Somewhat later, the industry would try to curtail public participation by closing some of the newly opened access points.

One of the industry's first actions was to launch intensive lobbying and public relations campaigns to shape (or reshape) perceptions of the nuclear issue. According to an internal 1974 memo from the president of the Atomic Industrial Forum (AIF), Carl Walske, to its board of directors, the AIF planned to increase its annual spending on such activities from $781,000 to $1.4 million. Walske's memo, which was leaked to the *New York Times,* outlined three reasons for the increased spending. First, the pending reorganization of the Atomic Energy Commission meant that instead of "countless A.E.C. features, speeches, media relations, booklets, films and background papers about the benefits of nuclear power there will soon be only a vacuum." Walske's words echoed those expressed by the NRC's first chairperson, William Anders, when he told the audience at the Edison Electric Institute's 1975 convention that since the abolition of the AEC, "a void had existed in Washington with respect to an advocate for nuclear power."[3]

The second reason was the declining influence of the joint committee. Walske lamented that "increasingly other committees—including those chaired by such critics as Senator Ribicoff—[were] staking a claim in nuclear power." To combat this situation would require a broader and more extensive effort by the AIF to lobby individual members of Congress. Finally, Walske believed the industry needed to take the offensive in presenting its case to the public. Recognizing that antinuclear forces had successfully widened the debate over nuclear power, Walske added that "the national media, with the middleman of the reporter and the editor, cannot be relied upon to publish a full and balanced account of nuclear power."[4] In addition to illustrating the industry's distrust of the media, this final comment also reveals that Walske shared the assumption held by most subsystem members that the controversy over nuclear power would fade away once the public understood the real "facts." In short, because the industry could no longer rely on the AEC and JCAE to make the case for nuclear power, and because the media was susceptible to sensational reporting and distortion, it would be up to the industry itself to communicate these "facts" to the public and government officials.

In 1975 the AIF, like so many other groups in the 1970s, moved its offices from New York to Washington to engage in greater advocacy. As part of its new public relations campaign, the forum began to ghostwrite and submit for publication pronuclear articles which claimed that nuclear power would reduce the nation's dependence on imported oil and hence move the nation farther down the path to energy self-sufficiency. The industry would rely on this line of reasoning again; in fact, after the Iranian revolution in 1979, industry representatives cited the "Ayatollah factor" as one of their strongest arguments in favor of the nuclear power option.[5]

The nuclear industry also took steps to reorganize its lobbying efforts. In 1975 the AIF changed its formal status from an educational organization to a trade association, allowing it more flexibility.[6] To handle its lobbying activities, the forum then established the American Nuclear Energy Council (ANEC), which was funded by contributions from approximately 125 firms engaged in the nuclear power industry. In an illustration of the continuing strength of the revolving door, Craig Hosmer, former ranking minority member of the JCAE, became the council's president. ANEC held weekly legislative workshops in Washington for lobbyists and industry representatives. The workshops provided an opportunity to discuss a variety of policy issues, such as the NRC budget, with congressional or executive branch staffers. The sessions also allowed participants to discuss and coordinate strategy on pending committee or floor action.[7] The weekly sessions sponsored by the council together with the forum's decision to relocate from New York gave the nuclear industry a formidable and full-time presence in the nation's capitol and allowed them to interact regularly with policymakers.

THE INDUSTRY RESPONSE TO THREE MILE ISLAND

As already noted, the industry decision to become more politically active coincided with the institutional reforms that were making nuclear policy making more complex and unpredictable.[8] Faced with a political environment that was becoming decidedly less supportive, the industry decided to take the offensive in efforts to convince the public and elected officials of the need for nuclear power. As a case in point, the Edison Electric Institute, an association of privately owned utilities and one of the leading industry groups, spent $3.5 million dollars in 1978 to increase public support for nuclear power. Even before the accident at Three Mile Island, the institute had planned to commit $5 million to a print advertising campaign for the same purpose.[9] The TMI accident served notice to the nuclear power industry that more intensive political action would be necessary. In the words of one industry representative, "Three Mile Island forced us to wake up and to catch up with other industries in our efforts to affect the political side of our business."[10]

To their credit, industry groups recognized that Three Mile Island demanded an immediate response which would send a clear signal that they took the accident seriously and were making every effort to prevent similar events in the future. Accordingly, shortly after TMI the Edison Electric Institute established the TMI Oversight Committee to study the accident. Within a few months, the committee, which had been granted broad powers by the industry groups, recommended numerous changes in reactor design and operating procedures to increase safety at nuclear plants. The committee then created another body, the

Nuclear Safety Analysis Center, and gave it a $3.5 million budget to continue the investigation into TMI with an eye toward determining if the accident had implications for other plants.

The TMI Oversight Committee also solicited $11 million in contributions from utilities to set up the Institute of Nuclear Power Operations (INPO), which, by some accounts, would be responsible for significant improvements in reactor safety. According to Lelan F. Sillin Jr., chairman of INPO's board of directors, "Our foremost objective is to make the process [of industry self-regulation through INPO] work and thus prevent the further intrusion of government and prescriptive regulation into our management."[11] Indeed, Joseph V. Rees has suggested that INPO has been more aggressive in pursuing safety improvements than the NRC, which allows the industry to regulate itself and frequently adopts INPO standards as its own. According to Rees, in 1987 INPO even worked behind the scenes to urge the NRC to shut down the troubled Peach Bottom plant in Pennsylvania.[12] If self-regulation through INPO is in fact the norm, one could legitimately wonder what purpose, if any, the NRC serves in this arrangement.

Industry groups also began to coordinate their activities in an attempt to maximize their political influence in Washington. Perhaps most important was the decision by the Atomic Industrial Forum and the Edison Electric Institute (EEI) to step up their already extensive contacts with the NRC staff to monitor TMI-related regulatory changes. The industry groups hoped that their relationship with the regulatory staff would give them some leverage in influencing new standards and safety requirements. Cooperation between the AIF and EEI was enhanced by the institute's decision to follow in the forum's footsteps and move its offices from New York to Washington. The institute's decision to relocate was an indication of the industry's commitment to its more overtly political role; in fact, in 1979 more than a dozen nuclear companies and utilities opened offices in the nation's capital. With much of the nuclear power industry now based in Washington, opportunities to share information and develop strategies increased. Like the American Nuclear Energy Council, the EEI held weekly meetings for the Washington-based representatives of nuclear utilities, industry lobbyists, and regulatory specialists. More specifically, the EEI held both legislative and regulatory work sessions; the former generally focused on political strategy, while the latter were more technical in nature, focusing on the details of standards and regulations.[13] In addition to the institute, the AIF also worked closely with the American Nuclear Energy Council in lobbying Congress and the White House. The council had an annual budget of $800,000 and six registered lobbyists, who were frequently dispatched to Capitol Hill to present the industry's position. The council also coordinated its actions with the American Public Power Association and the National Rural Electric Cooperative Association.

The industry also created the Committee on Energy Awareness (CEA) to handle its public relations functions, giving it a $1.6 million budget for the last half of 1979. In the words of Bill Perkins, the committee's director, "Three Mile Island was a public affairs disaster more than a substantive one, and the industry is looking for ways to cut our losses. We hope to have the kind of staff support that industry should have had all along."[14] The nuclear industry had compiled a wish list of over twenty programs it wanted the CEA to pursue, including private briefings for business and political leaders, roundtable discussions with the editorial staffs of newspapers, and outreach activities geared toward college students, labor leaders, senior citizens, and women's groups. The committee even organized strategy sessions for utility executives in states with pending antinuclear ballot initiatives. In November 1979 the CEA launched a $700,000 pronuclear advertising campaign, taking out full-page advertisements in the *New York Times, Los Angeles Times, Washington Post, Time, Business Week,* and *U.S. News and World Report.* Similarly, in the spring of 1980 the CEA ran pronuclear television commercials in nineteen markets in six states. The CEA hoped to convey four intertwined messages through its public relations activities: that the nuclear industry was making an all-out effort to improve reactor safety as a result of the lessons it had learned from TMI; that it was conscientiously seeking ways to minimize exposure to radiation and to solve the waste disposal issue; that nuclear power was an essential part of the nation's energy supplies; and that many individuals and the nation itself would suffer if nuclear power were abandoned as a source of energy.[15]

The CEA's top priority, however, was to shore up support for nuclear power among the business community. The nuclear industry was in dire economic straits even before the accident at TMI, and the accident only made matters worse. Seeking to reassure the financial community of nuclear power's economic viability, the CEA sent representatives to Wall Street in July, October, and November to speak to the New York Society of Security Analysts and to the Business Council. At these meetings, CEA representatives spoke of the need to retain the nuclear option, claiming that the only alternative was higher energy costs, rising unemployment, and continued dependence on imported oil.[16]

The industry's campaign to convince the American public of both the safety and importance of nuclear power did not let up. In February 1980 the Atomic Industrial Forum held a conference on "Nuclear Power and the Public," at which the Committee on Energy Awareness described a new political strategy and top priority: to reach those groups with a stake in adequate energy supplies in order to convince them that nuclear power was the key to the nation's energy woes. Because public opinion polls had shown that a plurality of women opposed nuclear power, the CEA sought to arrange meetings with the female editors of women's magazines and the lifestyles sections of newspapers. Specifically, the council wanted to point out the connection between cheap, plentiful energy, a growing economy, and women's search for equality. The council worked on similar appeals for senior citizens and minority communities. Finally, the CEA announced plans for an American Energy Week, which was designed to look like a grassroots pronuclear initiative but in reality was a product of the industry's own making.[17]

In the early months of 1979, industry lobbyists had geared most of their efforts on Capitol Hill toward persuading Congress to enact legislation addressing several of the industry's most pressing problems. Licensing reform again was high on the industry's list of legislative priorities, as were a variety of bills aimed at resolving the nagging problem of nuclear waste storage and disposal. But the accident at Three Mile Island reenergized opponents of nuclear power and forced the industry to postpone its proposed venue changes. Instead, the industry adopted a more defensive posture in Congress in order to contain TMI's political fallout. With the joint committee gone and its powers dispersed among so many committees, pronuclear forces no longer could be certain they would carry the day should Congress debate the nuclear power issue. Within days Congress began an extensive investigation of the accident that would last over one year and involve as many as eighteen committees. In announcing hearings shortly after TMI, House Interior and Insular Affairs chairman Morris Udall said, "The time has come for the country to get involved in the debate on the future of nuclear power." For an industry long accustomed to operating in the shadows of subgovernment politics, these were ominous words.

PRESIDENTIAL INTERVENTION

If low levels of presidential involvement are an indication of subgovernment dominance, then it should come as no surprise that the demise of the atomic subgovernment coincided with an increase in presidential interest in nuclear power issues.[18] In light of the unrivaled ability of presidents to set the policy agenda, presidential intervention becomes an especially important variable in explaining the expanding conflict over nuclear power. Until the early 1970s, presidents were almost uniformly inattentive to nonmilitary nuclear policy matters, preferring to leave most decisions in the hands of the atomic subgovernment. But the shock of the energy crisis and the widening controversy over reactor safety combined to make an issue that presidents no longer could choose to ignore. Richard Nixon became the first American president to devote considerable attention to nuclear affairs. As we have seen, Nixon was an advocate of nuclear power and his actions tended to promote the development and use of nuclear technology. His enthusiasm for nuclear power was expressed in several ways, including his proposals for an ambitious expansion in nuclear generating capacity as well as his repeated calls for licensing reform to expedite the construction and operation of nuclear plants.

Nixon's successor in the White House was also a proponent of nuclear power. Like Nixon, Gerald Ford envisioned a future in which nuclear power would contribute an ever larger share of the nation's energy needs. Accordingly, Ford consistently supported programs, such as the breeder reactor, that were highly valued by the nuclear industry. Despite Ford's brief tenure in office, fortuitous timing enabled his administration to play a vitally important role in shaping nuclear policy in the 1970s. The passage of the Energy Reorganization Act of 1974, which Ford had labeled his top legislative priority, gave him the opportunity to appoint all five commissioners to the newly established Nuclear Regulatory Commission.

Ford's NRC appointments were a clear indication that he did not want the new agency to depart radically from the policies of the now defunct AEC. Reflecting his desire that the new commission adopt a "business as usual" approach to regulation, all of the appointees were presumed to be supporters of nuclear power, and four of the five had previous ties with the AEC. For example, Ford's selection as the first chairman of the Nuclear Regulatory Commission was William A. Anders. A former astronaut, Anders had been an AEC commissioner since August 1973.[19] Also nominated to the NRC was Marcus Rowden, who at the time of his appointment was the AEC's general counsel. Rowden eventually became chair when Anders resigned in 1976. The third original member of the NRC was Edward A. Mason. At the time of his nomination, Mason was head of the Department of Nuclear Engineering at MIT, as well as a member of the ACRS. In fact, he had served as vice chairman of the ACRS in 1974. Ford's fourth nominee was Victor Gilinsky, who was then employed as head of the Rand Corporation's Physical Sciences Department. Prior to that he had served in a variety of positions at the AEC. As often happens, though, Gilinsky turned out to be more critical of the nuclear industry than Ford could have predicted. In fact, Gilinsky quickly won the respect of antinuclear activists for his willingness to question the decisions of the commission staff and even his fellow commissioners. He was reappointed to the commission by Jimmy Carter in July 1979. The fifth member of the new NRC, and the only one who had not previously been employed by the AEC, was Richard T. Kennedy. At the time of his nomination, Kennedy was the deputy assistant to the president for National Security Council planning.

Given the nature of these appointments, as well as Ford's public pronouncements on nuclear power, the Nuclear Regulatory Commission had very little reason to deviate from the patterns of regulatory behavior that had been established by the AEC. Ford's ability to influence nuclear policy, however, was mitigated somewhat by his brief time in office, by the very large Democratic majorities in both houses of Congress, and by the declining clout of the joint committee. Although the administration's policies were consistently pronuclear, they also were out of step with a Congress that was increasingly skeptical of nuclear power. For example, when Anders resigned in 1976, Ford nominated George Murphy, former executive director of the JCAE, to replace him. But in a vote that signaled defeat for both the JCAE and Ford, the Senate rejected Murphy.

The inauguration of Jimmy Carter as president sent shivers through the nuclear establishment. As a presidential candidate, Carter repeatedly had referred to nuclear power as an energy source of "last resort"; he also had endorsed an Oregon ballot initiative that proposed a moratorium on the construction of nuclear plants. The nuclear industry never forgot, or forgave, him for these transgressions; consequently, relations between the nuclear industry and the White House during Carter's term were characterized by distrust, even though there were significant differences between the campaign rhetoric of candidate Carter and the policies of President Carter. Although he was certainly more critical of nuclear power than either of his immediate predecessors, the policies Carter pursued once in office can best be described as ambiguous.

Throughout his term, Carter sent mixed signals on nuclear power. On the one hand, he opposed some programs that the nuclear industry deemed essential to its future success and survival. In a major address to Congress in April 1977, Carter unveiled his National Energy Plan, which spelled out his response to the energy crisis. In that address, Carter announced his opposition to advanced breeder technology and the commercial reprocessing of spent reactor fuel. He also urged the commmission to upgrade its safety standards and requested that the agency place resident inspectors at all reactors under construction and in operation. Finally, he called for greater energy conservation measures to "minimize the shift toward nuclear power" and repeated his belief that nuclear power was "a last resort."[20]

Carter's decision to halt work on both the Clinch River breeder and on commercial reprocessing was a major setback for the nuclear power industry, which believed that its long-term survival depended on being able to develop and use the breeder and reprocessing technologies to extend the supply of reactor fuel. The Carter administration, however, was more concerned that the spread of breeder and reprocessing technology throughout the world would enable more countries to divert plutonium from their commercial nuclear power programs to efforts to build nuclear weapons. Carter's decision to indefinitely postpone commercial reprocessing was in fact based on his desire to limit the global proliferation of nuclear weapons. This decision prompted intense lobbying by the nuclear industry and particularly by Westinghouse, which was planning to construct a mixed oxide fuel fabrication plant in South Carolina. Westinghouse, in fact, had hired former representative Orval Hansen as a lobbyist.[21]

Carter's proposal to cancel work at the Clinch River breeder demonstration project was even more controversial and sparked a fight that remained unresolved until well into the next decade. The Clinch River breeder was a demonstration project jointly financed by ERDA, the Tennessee Valley Authority, and a group of private utilities. Carter wanted to scrap the project because work was over budget and years behind schedule; in fact, the cost of the plant had approximately doubled from the initial projections of $700 million.[22] Seeking to mollify the industry and its supporters, Carter proposed that the money which would be saved by canceling Clinch River be used instead to develop alternative types of breeders that would be incapable of producing weapons-grade plutonium.[23]

Congressional supporters of Clinch River, with considerable help from the nuclear power industry, managed to thwart Carter's repeated efforts to terminate the project. The project's backers then secured funding for the project through a supplemental appropriations bill. They were forced to adopt this circuitous strategy because they lacked the votes to override a threatened veto of any appropriations bill that funded Clinch River. The underlying rationale for proceeding via a supplemental appropriations bill was that Carter would be unlikely to veto it because it also included funding for a number of projects that he supported.[24]

In an effort to work out a compromise on Clinch River, Carter held a meeting with industry representatives in June 1978. The meeting was attended by industry officials from the highest levels, including many chief executive officers from the four reactor vendors, the major nuclear utilities, the Edison Electric Institute, and the firms responsible for designing and building the Clinch River project. Carter offered the industry representatives a deal: in exchange for allowing him to remove the Clinch River breeder from the budget before the 1980 election, he promised to study and design a larger and more advanced breeder that could be built after the election. To sweeten the deal, Carter also offered to make a public statement strongly endorsing nuclear power. In making the offer, he stressed that he wanted to focus on a number of problems that he believed were more important for the industry's future success, particularly licensing reform and the disposal of high-level waste. The industry executives, however, did not believe Carter's promises and refused the deal, preferring to fight for Clinch River.[25]

Although many of Carter's policies antagonized the nuclear industry, his position was never entirely clear. During the same address to Congress in which he announced his breeder and reprocessing plans, Carter also called for increasing the number of nuclear plants, indicating that nuclear power was in fact something more than a "last resort." He also recommended changes in the NRC's licensing review process because he did not believe "it should take ten years to license a plant."[26] Accordingly, during the next two years Carter made NRC licensing reform one of his top energy priorities; somewhat ironically, this effort placed Carter in the position of championing one of the nuclear industry's favorite causes. He also pressured the Department of Energy, the NRC, and Congress to devise a solution to the nuclear waste problem, which was rapidly becoming one the most troubling problems confronting the nuclear industry.

In what was perceived as an effort by Carter to atone for his decisions on the breeder and reprocessing, the DOE announced in October 1977 that it was assuming legal responsibility for the disposal of high-level waste from nuclear plants. The nuclear waste issue had become a point of embarrassment for supporters of nuclear power. At the time, over two thousand metric tons of spent fuel were being temporarily stored at reactor sites, and according to government estimates, another one thousand metric tons would be added every year. Existing storage facilities were expected to reach capacity in the mid-1980s. Despite constant reassurances from government and industry officials, little progress had been made in resolving the problem. Moreover, antinuclear groups were discovering that the waste disposal issue was one of their most potent political and rhetorical weapons. The courts, for example, were very receptive to arguments urging consideration of the waste issue as an integral part of the licensing review process. Furthermore, nuclear activists had sought to block industry-backed licensing "reform" proposals by insisting that any such measures be contingent upon the resolution of the waste disposal problem. On one level, then, the DOE's decision to assume responsibility for finding a permanent solution to the waste problem was designed to quiet public concern over the waste issue and remove it as an obstacle to the future of the industry. But the DOE policy served another purpose as well: it relieved the nuclear industry, which was in dire straits financially, of the financial burden of finding their own solution. Although the policy amounted to another government subsidy masking the true cost of nuclear power, the industry's response was cautious. According to the Energy Department's plan, nuclear utilities would transport their spent fuel to a DOE collection center and pay a onetime storage fee. The industry liked the general idea but was concerned that the storage fees would be too high.[27]

Carter thus began his term by proposing an energy plan that antagonized both sides of the nuclear debate. He endorsed the use of present reactors while undermining the programs upon which the future plans of the nuclear industry were based. Given the apparently contradictory nature of his public remarks, it should come as no surprise that Carter's Energy Plan sparked confusion over his intentions. In fact, one congressional study remarked that the plan "provides only vague suggestions for increasing nuclear energy use and at the same time it virtually eliminates the long-term expectations of the industry."[28] Over time, however, Carter gradually came to believe that nuclear power was necessary for meeting the nation's short-term energy needs, and his position shifted to one of greater public support for light water reactors.

Although Carter was undeniably more sympathetic to the concerns of antinuclear forces than any other president, even going so far as to clear his NRC appointments with environmental groups before sending them to the Senate, his personnel decisions were nevertheless ambiguous. For example, critics of nuclear power finally were able to gain a hearing inside the White House. Gus Speth, a former National Resources Defense Council attorney who had been involved in several lawsuits against the AEC, had been appointed to the Council on Environmental Quality. Another reported critic of nuclear power, Katherine Schirmer, served as associate director of the domestic policy staff in the White House. Similarly, eight of the twenty-one participants in a Ford Foundation study that was critical of nuclear power, at least in the eyes of the Atomic Industrial Forum, became members of the Carter administration.[29] But Carter also appointed several prominent supporters of nuclear power to fill key positions within the administration. Perhaps most significant, he selected former AEC chairman James Schlesinger, widely perceived to be a supporter of nuclear power, to be the first

energy secretary. Despite the fact that Schlesinger was a Republican, Carter relied on him for advice on many energy-related matters, including nominations to
the NRC.

Consistent with his other actions, Carter's appointments to the NRC were a
curious mix that crossed partisan and ideological lines and thus defied easy characterization. Following Schlesinger's recommendation, Carter selected Joseph
Hendrie, a Republican, to be NRC chair in 1977. Like many of Ford's appointees,
Hendrie had previous ties to the AEC, having worked in the AEC's research
laboratories until 1973, when Schlesinger asked him to join the commission's Di-
rectorate of Licensing. Because of his connections with Schlesinger and the AEC,
Hendrie was assumed to be an advocate of nuclear power. So, too, was Carter's
second nominee, Kent Hansen, who was rejected by the Senate because of his
work as a consultant for General Electric and Westinghouse. Although the nominations of Hendrie and Hansen pleased the nuclear industry, opponents of nuclear power found solace in other nominees. One was Peter Bradford, who joined
the NRC in 1977. A Democrat, Bradford had previously served as an environmental adviser to the governor of Maine and had been a member of Maine's Public Utilities Commission for over six years. While on the state agency, Bradford
had helped initiate a number of environmental and consumer reforms. Furthermore, Carter's decision to reappoint Victor Gilinsky to a second five-year term in
1979 also pleased antinuclear forces.

Given the eclectic nature of these appointments, it seems possible that
Carter was trying to walk a tightrope on the issue by making sure that both sides
of the nuclear debate were represented on the commission. But in trying to please
everyone, Carter ended up pleasing no one. There were reports that the commission, which operated at less than full strength for almost a year after Hansen's
rejection, was internally divided and could provide no clear direction to the staff
on a variety of important issues. Although there were very few split votes, the
commissioners eventually drifted into two camps, with Hendrie and Kennedy in
one and Gilinsky and Bradford in the other. Hendrie and Kennedy were generally seen as more supportive of the nuclear industry, more concerned about possible delays in the commission's licensing process, and more willing to accept the
safety assurances of the NRC staff. Gilinsky and Bradford, on the other hand,
were more likely to call attention to potential safety problems and to allow full
public disclosure and debate over controversial matters. They tended to see themselves as "defenders of public health and safety" and believed the NRC should be
blind to any goals set elsewhere in the government for increasing the number of
nuclear plants.[30]

It was against this backdrop in 1978 that Carter appointed John Ahearne
to fill the vacancy on the commission. Because the NRC was so closely divided,
the nomination was subjected to intense scrutiny as a potential "swing" vote.
Ahearne, who had spent most of his career in the air force and the Pentagon,
had recently gone to work for Schlesinger in the Department of Energy. Despite

his relationship with Schlesinger, Ahearne was widely perceived as reasonable and open-minded on nuclear power and thus was acceptable to both industry supporters and opponents. During the course of his term, Ahearne proved to be the quintessential "swing" vote, siding at times with both sides of the nuclear debate. He later became the commission's fourth chairman in less than five years when Carter named him acting chair in the aftermath of Three Mile Island.

The expiration of commissioner Richard Kennedy's term in 1979 provided Carter with his final opportunity to determine the commission's personnel. As might be anticipated, the accident at Three Mile Island prompted criticism of the NRC's ability and inclination to regulate the nuclear industry. This criticism led Carter to promise he would name an "outsider" as the commission's next chairman. After a lengthy search that stretched well into 1980, an election year, Carter finally nominated Albert Carnesale, a professor of public policy at Harvard's Kennedy School of Government.[31] But Carnesale's nomination never came up for a vote because Senate Republicans, citing his concerns over the Clinch River breeder project, blocked the nomination. However, the real explanation for the Senate's failure to approve Carnesale can be traced to election-year partisan politics. Senate Republicans were heeding the request of their party's presidential nominee, Ronald Reagan, to defer action on important nominations until after the election. Reagan, who was an advocate of nuclear power, wanted to have the opportunity to select his own NRC chairman should he prevail in the election. He did, and Carnesale's nomination died.

Although most presidents lament their inability to control executive branch agencies, the use of their appointment and budgetary powers, as well as their unique ability to shape the nation's agenda, does give them significant leverage over agencies. At the very least, the exercise of these powers provides agency administrators with important signals or cues concerning the president's preferences on at least general policy issues. With respect to the NRC, the cues the agency received from President Ford were consistently promotional, and thus the agency had little reason to deviate from previous patterns of behavior. But what meaning could the commissioners attach to the signals conveyed by the Carter administration? At best, the signals were ambiguous; at worst, they were contradictory. As the debate over licensing reform shows, the problem was compounded by Congress, which also failed to establish a clear direction for nuclear policy.

LICENSING REFORM

Despite his less than enthusiastic support for nuclear power, Jimmy Carter consistently supported reform of the NRC's licensing process during his presidency. This position was truly ironic, because licensing reform was the top priority of the nuclear power industry, which never had a good relationship with the president. The industry, along with many others, saw licensing reform as essential to its future success. In fact, the industry hoped that a licensing reform bill would provide a much-needed legislative "endorsement" of nuclear power. Of primary concern to the industry was the ever-lengthening period needed to license and construct nuclear power plants. At the time, it took an average of two to three years for a utility to obtain a construction permit, while the construction phase itself had increased to almost eight years. Seeking to make the licensing process shorter and more predictable, proponents of licensing reform recommended changes that would eliminate "unnecessary duplication and delay," claiming that such changes could cut as much as five years from the time needed to license and build a nuclear plant. From the industry perspective, licensing reform would have the added benefit of curtailing public participation in policy making. Although industry representatives were skeptical, they reacted warmly to Carter's announcement in April 1977 that he would push for licensing reform.[32]

The responsibility for drafting the reform bill was given to the Department of Energy, which under Secretary Schlesinger was presumed to be supportive of nuclear power. At his confirmation hearings that August, Schlesinger stated that his agency hoped to be able to send a reform bill to Congress within one month. The DOE had hoped that by moving quickly it could produce an acceptable reform measure without encountering much resistance, but licensing reform was very controversial. Although everyone agreed that reform was necessary, no one could agree on precisely what needed reforming. As a result, the DOE bill was held up as a multitude of agencies and interests tried to reshape it. By the time the bill was introduced in Congress, it had been revised at least nine times.[33]

The Nuclear Siting and Licensing Act of 1978 was introduced in March 1978. Four different committees claimed jurisdiction and held hearings on the bill. In many respects, the bill that was finally introduced bore a striking resemblance to earlier licensing reform proposals.[34] Like the earlier bills, it included provisions for prior approval of plant sites and standardized designs, and it recommended the adoption of a "one-stop" licensing process that eliminated the requirement for a mandatory public hearing at the operating license stage. Instead, the commission would be authorized to issue a combined construction permit and operating license; hearings would only be held at the operating license stage if an intervenor could make a prima facie showing of the existence of a significant hazard to public health and safety. The reform bill contained other provisions aimed at limiting public involvement in the hearing process. These stipulations included measures to exempt the commission from provisions of the Administrative Procedures Act and to establish legislative-type hearings with no rights of discovery or cross-examination. As they had earlier in the decade, antinuclear activists opposed these measures, arguing that the nuclear industry was still too immature to be standardized and that mandatory adjudicatory hearings were necessary to allow intervenors to examine the important issues of reactor design and site suitability.[35] As these examples illustrate, battles over venue changes would continue to be one of the flash points in nuclear politics. Antinuclear groups would fight to maintain the access they had won earlier in the decade, while proponents would seek to restrict participation.

Although the Nuclear Siting and Licensing Act of 1978 was largely a rehash of earlier licensing reform proposals, there were two significant departures. First, it included provisions for intervenor funding. The intervenor funding measures were inserted by the White House in an attempt to win the support of environmentalists and antinuclear groups. The goal of the funding program was to facilitate the participation of public interest groups in the commission's licensing and rulemaking process to ensure that all interests were represented in the proceedings. But because of the commission's strong objections to the rest of the bill, the strategy did not work. Not only did the intervenor funding provisions fail to persuade antinuclear forces to support the reform measure, but they led the nuclear industry to oppose it as well. Although the industry liked most of the bill, it objected so strongly to the intervenor funding measures that it preferred no bill at all to the one on the table. The industry was concerned that the program would be used to enhance the views of antinuclear members of the commission. But because the assistance to be provided to intervenors was so slight, the industry's reaction must have been motivated by its perception that the intervenor funding measures amounted to no less than another restructuring of the administrative process, which if left unchallenged could threaten its dominance of the policy-making process.[36] In this sense, the controversy over intervenor funding was yet another attempt to control the future direction of regulatory policy by changing the rules of the game.

Although advocates of regulatory change succeeded in establishing intervenor funding programs at other regulatory commissions, such as the Federal Trade Commission, they faced a more difficult battle at the NRC. Like the AEC before it, the NRC had consistently resisted such proposals, arguing that they would almost certainly lead to lengthy delays in the licensing process. In 1975, for example, the commission convened a rulemaking to consider amending its rule to allow financial assistance to certain participants in licensing proceedings. But the agency terminated the rulemaking a year later without taking action, saying that a general program of intervenor assistance was unnecessary. That remained the position of the NRC until July 1980, when the NRC published amendments to its rules that established a one-year "pilot program" of procedural assistance to intervenors in contested proceedings for operating licenses. The commission's change of heart was apparently prompted by the investigation of its own special inquiry group into the accident at Three Mile Island, which urged the NRC to reimburse intervenors "who *contribute materially* to rulemaking or licensing efforts by pressing concerns that are not being urged by other parties."[37]

The second novel aspect of the 1978 reform bill was its recommendation for transferring the "need for power" and environmental impact issues to the states. This recommendation was an indication that the monopoly once exercised by the federal government was over; the conflict had expanded, and state and local governments were now significant participants in policy making. Both sides of the debate agreed the states could handle the new responsibilities, but antinuclear forces were wary because there were no guarantees of either intervenor funding or adjudicatory hearings in state-run proceedings.[38]

With only the DOE lobbying for its passage and with both pro- and antinuclear forces actively opposing it, the Nuclear Siting and Licensing Act of 1978 did not get very far. In fact, the bill never made it out of committee. The lack of political support was clearly one reason for its demise, but there were other reasons as well. Given public concern over reactor safety, proponents of licensing reform had an affirmative obligation to show that the proposed reforms would be in the public interest. They failed in this effort; indeed, the nature of the bill made it much easier for opponents to argue that the reforms actually would endanger public safety while also denying the public the opportunity to participate in the licensing process. Even under the best of circumstances, the reactor safety debate would have made it difficult to enact any reform measure. Neither the DOE nor the nuclear industry provided empirical evidence to support their claims that the NRC had "overregulated" or that any regulations that may have caused delay or increased construction costs were unnecessary from a safety perspective. Similarly, the bill's supporters failed to show how the NRC's licensing process was the cause of construction delays or that the proposed reforms actually would help reduce such delays.[39] One of the reasons they could not offer such proof was because the allegations were apparently not true. Studies conducted by several government agencies, including the General Accounting Office, the Congressional Budget Office, and the Congressional Research Service, showed that delays and increased costs were the result of other factors, such as the ratcheting of safety requirements, labor strikes, shortages of labor and equipment, and utilities' financial problems.[40] Even a study conducted by the NRC, which supported licensing reform, found that only a few cases of delay were attributable to the licensing process.[41] Proponents of licensing reform, in short, failed to convince either Congress or the American public that such reform was necessary.

Despite the lack of action on licensing reform in 1978, the nuclear industry was hopeful that Congress would give the issue more serious attention in the new year. But their hopes were dashed by the accident at Three Mile Island, which renewed concerns that reactors were unsafe and that the NRC was guilty of underregulating rather than overregulating. In spite of the political climate created by the TMI accident, President Carter continued his quest for a licensing reform bill. The administration bill, which was almost identical to the one drafted the previous year, prompted six members of the Senate Environment and Public Works Committee to write Carter asking him to withdraw the bill, which he did.

The failure of Congress to adopt a licensing reform bill in the 1970s was further testimony to the body's growing ambivalence on the nuclear issue. With the energy crisis looming at the top of the nation's policy agenda, members of Congress were unwilling to completely forgo the nuclear option and therefore refused to enact any legislation establishing a moratorium on reactor construction or operation. But faced with demands for greater reactor safety and environmental protection, members of Congress also were unwilling to curtail or eliminate any of the public's procedural rights to participate in the commission's licensing or rulemaking proceedings. Congress's solution to this dilemma was to hedge its bets: it would support increased nuclear research and development but insist that nuclear power be made safe.

THREE MILE ISLAND

At approximately 4:00 A.M. on 28 March 1979, there was a serious accident at the Three Mile Island nuclear facility near Harrisburg, Pennsylvania.[42] Although it would take months to reconstruct the events and circumstances that caused the accident, it was much easier to calculate the political damage to the nuclear power industry and the NRC. Put simply, the TMI accident renewed and deepened concerns about the safety of reactors, and in this section I examine the political response to that accident.

In early April President Carter appointed a blue-ribbon panel to investigate the accident at Three Mile Island. The President's Commission on the Accident at Three Mile Island, also known as the Kemeny Commission because its chairman was John G. Kemeny, president of Dartmouth College, issued its report in October.[43] The Kemeny Commission report was highly critical of the NRC and the nuclear industry and recommended major changes in the practices and attitudes of both. For example, the Kemeny Commission noted that the NRC had been split off from the AEC to separate its regulatory and promotional responsibilities, but the group found "evidence that some of the old promotional philosophy still influences the regulatory practices of the NRC." According to the commission, there was also evidence "that the NRC has sometimes erred on the side of the industry's convenience rather than carrying out its primary mission of assuring safety."[44]

Furthermore, the Kemeny group found serious inadequacies in both the NRC's licensing and its inspection and enforcement programs, which it traced to the NRC's "conviction" that nuclear power plants were sufficiently safe. The NRC was said to be "preoccupied with licensing" and insufficiently attentive to "the ongoing process of assuring nuclear safety." The NRC's reluctance to apply new safety standards to previously licensed plants was cited as evidence of the "old AEC attitude." In addition, the Kemeny Commission found that the NRC's vast body of regulations tended to focus the industry's attention rather narrowly on meeting regulations rather than on a "systematic concern for safety."[45] The NRC also was criticized for its "minimal" use of its statutory authority to impose fines on utilities for violations of safety regulations.[46]

After concluding that there was "no well-thought-out, integrated system for the assurance of nuclear safety within the NRC," the Kemeny Commission recommended a "total restructuring" of the agency. According to the commission, the NRC should be abolished and replaced by an independent agency within the executive branch, headed by a single administrator appointed from outside the NRC. This revamping presumably would bring "new blood" into the agency and result in the "change of attitudes that is vital" for the future of nuclear power.[47] The Kemeny Commission also unanimously urged that before issuing any new construction permits or operating licenses the NRC should, on a case-by-case basis, assess the need to introduce safety measures recommended in its report and in NRC and industry studies, review the competence of prospective licensees to manage the plant, and make licensing contingent upon federal of state and local emergency plans.[48]

The president's first public comments on the Kemeny report came in December. Although safety was his "top priority," Carter claimed that "we cannot shut the door on nuclear power for the United States," saying it was "critical if we are to free our country from its overdependence on unstable sources of high-priced foreign oil."[49] Although Carter issued a general endorsement of the commission's recommendations, he rejected some of the panel's most significant proposals, including the recommendation that the NRC be replaced by an independent executive branch agency headed by a single administrator. Carter's decision was undoubtedly influenced by opposition to the plan in Congress, particularly from those members whose committees had jurisdiction over the NRC.[50] Instead, Carter proposed to strengthen the NRC chair relative to the other commissioners and to increase the power of the executive director of operations relative to the program staff. According to Carter's proposal, the commission would retain responsibility for policy formulation, rulemaking, and adjudication, while the chairman would carry out all other commission functions and serve as the NRC's official spokesperson and chief executive officer.[51]

REGULATORY CHANGE AT THE NRC

During the 1970s, the Nuclear Regulatory Commission was one of the most controversial agencies in Washington. Never considered an impartial arbiter of the dispute over nuclear power, the NRC was generally viewed as either ineffectual by those at one end of the spectrum or too aggressive by those at the other. To those who favored strong regulation, NRC commissioners and staff were overly sympathetic to the demands of the nuclear power industry. The industry, on the other hand, claimed that excessive regulatory zeal by the NRC was the source of most of its problems. Consequently, the agency's actions were often the focus of bitter conflict.

The political reforms of the 1960s and 1970s helped transform some regulatory agencies, such as the Federal Trade Commission, into more activist agencies.

But the NRC never experienced this metamorphosis, even though it was established amid the broad developments in American politics that ushered in the public lobby era. Despite this lineage, the NRC was not a true product of that era nor did it ever fully embrace its values because the NRC was not really a new agency—it was merely a spin-off of the regulatory branch of the AEC. Although the Energy Reorganization Act succeeded in abolishing the Atomic Energy Commission, it never entirely displaced the commission's deeply entrenched belief in the value of nuclear power. Part of the explanation stems from the fact that the NRC was essentially a carryover from the AEC in terms of personnel, regulations, and attitudes. Four of the NRC's original commissioners had worked for the AEC, as had the overwhelming majority of NRC personnel. Similarly, most high-level positions, such as the executive director of operations, the director of the Office of Standards Development, the director of the Office of Public Affairs, the director of the Division of Operating Reactors, and the deputy executive legal director were occupied by former AEC employees.[52]

In addition, the NRC's first major policy action was to adopt all of the AEC's rules, regulations, and standards. By itself, the Energy Reorganization Act of 1974 could not dissolve the strong professional and institutional relationships linking former AEC personnel and the nuclear industry, nor could it eliminate the commission's well-defined sense of mission, a point not lost on the agency's critics.[53] Several years after the birth of the NRC, Morris Udall claimed that the commission was apparently unwilling to break from the AEC's promotional mindset, stating that "maybe it was a mistake to think we could make a new agency out of an old operation. They carried over the same people, the same files, the same outlook."[54] For the NRC, the criticism would only intensify, as it was attacked throughout the decade for being complacent and insufficiently aggressive in regulating the nuclear power industry.

Concerns over the attitudes of NRC personnel appear to have been well-founded. Surveys of elite attitudes toward nuclear power conducted in the early 1980s revealed the persistence of pronuclear beliefs among commission personnel. Members of the NRC staff, for example, were more likely than other elites, including members of Congress, to believe that the United States should proceed rapidly with the development of nuclear power. They were also more likely to maintain that engineering and technological concerns—rather than political or social ones—should be considered the primary factors in deliberations over nuclear power. These findings led the researchers conducting the survey to conclude that the NRC was a "bastion of support for nuclear power" and may in fact "represent an instance of regulatory capture."[55]

Even if the NRC had possessed the inclination to become an aggressive regulatory body, it was not equipped to do so. Until the mid-1970s, the commission's inspection and enforcement divisions were small and undernourished, reflecting the agency's long-term neglect of operating reactors. The shortage of qualified inspection personnel forced the agency to rely on the utility's own estimates of its compliance with NRC requirements. Typically, the inspections performed by inspection and enforcement personnel were limited to approximately 1 percent of the actual facility and less than 10 percent of the utility's quality assurance reports. In essence, the NRC was allowing the nuclear industry to police itself. In recognition of this fact, the NRC began to devote more resources and personnel to the inspection and enforcement program in the mid-1970s. This trend continued throughout the decade, as both Congress and President Carter urged the commission to upgrade the agency's inspection and enforcement capabilities. Despite these changes, the NRC's regulatory program, like that of the AEC before it, continued to emphasize the licensing of new reactors while neglecting the performance of reactors already on-line. The crucial tasks of standards development and safety research were also low priority items.

Furthermore, until the very end of the decade the NRC was reluctant to play the role of the enforcer, consistently stating that the primary objective of its enforcement program was corrective and not punitive.[56] That is, the NRC designed its enforcement program to ensure that items of noncompliance were corrected and to assure the nuclear industry that it would not be punished for detecting potential problems. In practice, the NRC generally did not take action against a licensee in situations that were identified by the licensee's own inspection program, provided the problem was not deemed "significant" and had been corrected; on the other hand, enforcement action was more likely where the problem was first discovered by NRC inspectors. Again, the incentive structure was designed to encourage the industry to improve its performance, not punish it. The severity of the action taken by the NRC was based on several factors, including the licensee's previous compliance record and the significance of the particular item of noncompliance. The commission's regulations provided the inspection and enforcement staff with considerable flexibility, establishing three levels of action. First, written notices of violation were provided for all items of noncompliance with NRC requirements. In general, notices of violation were issued for problems that did not pose severe risks to the public health and safety. If the notices were ineffective, the NRC could proceed to the second level of action, which were civil monetary penalties. These penalties, or fines, could be imposed on licensees who showed chronic, deliberate, or repetitive items of noncompliance. Licensees could also be fined for particularly significant first-time violations. Finally, there were cease and desist orders that provided for modification, suspension, or revocation of a license or permit.

For a variety of reasons, the NRC's enforcement program was not very effective. One reason was that the NRC's rules required the commission to bear the burden of proof in enforcement actions rather than the utility. Another reason was the commission's reputation as a paper tiger with respect to fines, which were not a very credible threat until the end of the decade. Traditionally, the commission had been reluctant to levy fines on utilities, preferring to use other, less punitive means of achieving compliance. Despite many instances of noncompliance with regulations, it was not until 1973 that the commission levied a fine on a utility. Although the number of fines increased as the decade wore on, the commission was handicapped by statutory limits on the size of the fines it was allowed to impose. According to the Atomic Energy Act, the maximum allowable penalties were $5,000 for a single violation of NRC regulations and $25,000 for all violations committed within a thirty-day period. Recognizing that these levels were unlikely to compel compliance, the NRC in 1978 asked Congress to make the enforcement threat more credible by increasing the size of the fines. Congress responded in June 1980 by giving the NRC the authority to impose fines as high as $100,000 for each violation of NRC rules, with no ceiling on the total fine for any thirty-day period.[57] With these new powers in hand, the NRC levied fines on over thirty utilities that year. Among the most significant were a $155,000 fine for Metropolitan Edison, the owner of Three Mile Island, for noncompliance items relating to the TMI accident; a $450,000 fine imposed on Consumers Power Company for operating its Palisades reactor for extended periods with its "containment integrity violated"; and a $100,000 fine for Babcock and Wilcox, the firm that supplied the reactor at Three Mile Island, for its failure to report information on potential safety problems that could have helped prevent or reduce the severity of the TMI accident.[58]

Another reason for the limited reform of the NRC was that neither Congress nor the White House provided the commission with a definitive mandate to guide its actions. In passing the Energy Reorganization Act of 1974, Congress directed the NRC to protect the public health and safety but offered no explicit instructions or guidance as to how the commission was to determine whether or not reactors were "safe." Moreover, despite recognition of the problems caused by the lack of statutory guidance, Congress made no serious efforts to clarify the issue, even ignoring pleas for help from the commission itself. In 1976, commissioner Victor Gilinsky told the joint committee that there "has never been an explicit quantitative standard set by the Congress or by the AEC, or by this Commission, and I think that we probably need to have one."[59] Similarly, in a 1978 interview with the *National Journal,* NRC chair Joseph Hendrie said that "the most important thing is to put the issue before the Congress so there will—explicitly and implicitly—be a national policy on nuclear matters."[60] But that was something legislators were unable—or unwilling—to do.

As we have seen, most members of Congress preferred to approach nuclear regulation in an ad hoc manner rather than enact any sweeping reform measures. The failure of Congress to produce a definitive nuclear policy in the 1970s was a reflection of how much nuclear politics had changed. With so many committees claiming jurisdiction, there were numerous opportunities for both supporters and opponents of nuclear power to find forums for their claims. Congressional decentralization undoubtedly created new access points, which enhanced the potential for some policy change, at least in the short term. And policy did become decidedly less supportive of nuclear power. But decentralization simultaneously limited the potential for large-scale policy change by increasing the number of legislative veto points. On the whole, congressional decentralization shielded the NRC from significant statutory change that might have induced broadscale regulatory reform.[61] Unable to move very far in either direction, Congress thus opted for a de facto nuclear policy endorsing the status quo: nuclear power would remain an option for the future, but greater attention would be devoted to assuring the safety of existing reactors.

Perhaps the most important factor explaining the NRC's failure to become an activist regulatory agency was its narrow jurisdiction. The commission, because it was responsible for regulating the actions of a single centralized industry dominated by a small group of large and powerful firms, operated in an environment that was ideally suited for regulatory capture. The tendency for regulatory capture, after all, is assumed to be most pronounced in agencies with narrow responsibilities. The scope of the NRC's authority thus rendered it more susceptible to capture than other regulatory agencies such as the Federal Trade Commission or the Environmental Protection Agency, which because of their broader statutory mandates were responsible for regulating a wider mix of industries and technologies. Furthermore, as a captive agency the NRC was sheltered from the vicissitudes of changing political tides and therefore was not infused with the attitudes or goals that transformed other regulatory agencies during the public lobby reform era.

When agencies are involved in significant political conflict, as the NRC was throughout the 1970s, they receive more attention from political officials.[62] But when the spotlight fades, as it inevitably does, agencies are left with a considerably smaller attentive public. This is particularly true of the more arcane and time-consuming implementation stages, which attract very little publicity. Nevertheless, regulatory agencies still need political support for their actions and credible information to establish effective regulations. The NRC was no different. But despite the efforts of antinuclear groups to become active and legitimate participants in developing rules and standards, the only interest that was consistently represented in these proceedings was the nuclear power industry, primarily as a result of the industry's greater economic and technical resources. Although the NRC staff had grown larger and more sophisticated in the 1970s, they were still heavily dependent upon reactor vendors and architect-engineers for technological data and reactor design information. Consequently, the staff would typically consult with industry sources before promulgating new regulations or revising old ones. After all, who would better know the consequences of a proposed regulation or standard than the affected industry? The danger, of course, was that in relying on the industry for so much information the staff was essentially allowing the industry to regulate itself.

It also seems that the resurgence of business influence in the regulatory process in the mid to late 1970s prevented the NRC from establishing its credentials as a regulatory watchdog. Just as public lobby groups were gaining access to policy making, the nuclear industry recognized that it could no longer rely on the AEC or JCAE to protect its interests and thus stepped up its political activities. In addition to more extensive lobbying efforts, the Atomic Industrial Forum, the Council on Energy Awareness, and the American Nuclear Energy Council worked to reshape the nuclear debate. It would take more than a public relations effort, however, to help the industry in the new regulatory environment.

THE CHANGING ECONOMICS OF NUCLEAR POWER

In the late 1960s the costs of producing electricity from coal and nuclear plants were comparable; nuclear plants were more expensive to build but had lower fuel and operating costs. By the early 1970s utilities were ordering roughly equal amounts of coal and nuclear capacity. Within a few years, though, the bottom fell out of the market, sparing no sector of the industry. Orders for new nuclear plants began to decline in 1974, and none would be placed after 1978. Furthermore, between 1974 and 1984 utilities canceled plans for over one hundred reactors, many of which were already under construction (see Table 7.1). Some of the abandoned reactors were more than 50 percent complete.[63]

The industry's economic woes were attributable to internal and external forces that caused construction and maintenance costs to skyrocket and utilities to scale back their plans to build additional nuclear generating capacity. Among the exogenous forces, none was more important than the OPEC oil embargo, which sparked sudden price hikes in fossil fuels and fundamentally transformed energy consumption patterns. Higher oil prices and the desire for secure energy sources might have been expected to make nuclear-generated electricity more attractive. Instead, fears of energy shortages and rising apprehension about American dependence on imported oil prompted Americans to use less energy, thus undercutting the need for new sources of electricity. Further reductions in electricity use resulted from the economic slowdown created in part by the higher energy prices and inflationary pressures characteristic of the period. With demand for electricity increasing at an average annual rate of 7 percent in the late 1960s, most utilities had planned to build additional generating capacity to meet anticipated future needs. After the energy crisis in 1973, however, the annual growth rate in the demand for electricity dropped to an all-time low of 0.55 percent before leveling off at approximately 2.5 percent for the rest of the decade.[64] The problem for utilities was that lower energy demand reduced their revenues and left many with excess generating capacity. Utilities responded by slashing their capital spending by 18 percent in the years from 1974–78.[65] Nuclear plants, because of their higher construction costs, were hit especially hard by these cutbacks.

The nuclear industry was also hurt by rapidly rising construction costs. Construction costs for all types of power plants increased between 1968 and 1977, but

Table 7.1. Market Collapse

Year	Reactors Ordered	Reactors Canceled
1970	14	0
1971	21	0
1972	38	7
1973	41	0
1974	28	8
1975	4	12
1976	3	1
1977	4	10
1978	2	14
1979	0	8
1980	0	12
1981	0	6
1982	0	18
1983	0	6
1984	0	6
1985	0	2
1986	0	2
1987	0	0
1988	0	3
1989	0	0

Source: Energy Information Administration, *Commercial Nuclear Power 1991: Prospects for the United States and the World* (Washington, D.C.: Government Printing Office, 1991), 105–10.

those for nuclear plants rose at twice the rate of coal plants and continued to increase into the next decade.[66] By almost any measure, nuclear plants became prohibitively expensive to build. Reactors coming on-line during the 1980s, for example, cost an average of $3,500 per kilowatt-hour (kWh) in 1983 dollars, compared with an average of $600 per kWh for the fifty-seven reactors completed before 1981.[67] The case of the Seabrook, New Hampshire, reactors is illustrative. In 1971, Public Service of New Hampshire announced plans to build two reactors at an estimated cost of $900 million. By the time Seabrook I was licensed in 1988, nine years behind schedule, its cost had ballooned to nearly $6 billion, the second reactor had been scrapped, and the utility had filed for bankruptcy.[68] Moreover, the Seabrook debacle was not unique. Cost overruns of 500 to 1,000 percent were common.[69]

A significant portion of the increased construction costs were attributable to new regulatory requirements that increased the amount of materials, labor, and time needed to build nuclear plants.[70] Although the nuclear industry argued that most of their problems, especially the rising construction costs, were the result of overly zealous NRC regulators, in reality the claim of excessive regulation is simply inaccurate and ignores other more compelling explanations. To support their arguments, industry sources pointed out that the number of new safety standards issued by the commission steadily increased, from 25 in 1972 to 167 in 1975.[71] To be sure, the NRC did take its regulatory responsibilities more seriously in this period, and the quest for greater safety did lead the AEC to impose new regulatory requirements, which certainly added to the cost of building nuclear plants. Contrary to industry claims, however, many of the new requirements were warranted; safety margins were not as large as the industry and the AEC had believed.

It also seems clear that earlier regulatory failures and industry mismanagement were responsible for some of the cost increases. As we have seen, the AEC neglected its regulatory duties for most of its history and devoted the bulk of its attention and resources to working with the private sector to develop and promote the new technology. Given this environment, the commission's small and inexperienced staff was understandably reluctant to impose tough standards because it did not want to kill off the very technology it was trying to commercialize. Moreover, the technology was so new that a certain amount of flexibility was needed to encourage innovation. In these early years, licensing reviews were typically informal and ad hoc, and the few safety standards issued by the regulatory staff were rather general. Applications for construction permits and operating licenses were often sketchy, and reactor designs were works in progress, with applicants providing detailed design information only after a construction permit had been issued. Although this process did facilitate reactor licensing in the short term, the case-by-case approach ultimately undermined the industry's long-term prospects.

In the mid-1960s there were very few operating reactors in the United States, with the largest producing 265 MWe of electricity. Despite little or no operating experience with even this handful of relatively small reactors, utilities began ordering large numbers of very powerful plants. It would soon become clear that most lacked the technical and managerial skills needed to build and operate such plants. Nevertheless, with the advent of the Great Bandwagon Market, there was a dramatic increase in both the number and size of plants being ordered. Average capacity jumped to 1,100 MWe by 1971. During this period of rapid scale-up, no two reactor designs were alike, so every application, and every application review, was unique. In addition, the larger plants were more complex and posed greater potential risks. This increase in the number and complexity of applications, along with the failure to standardize reactor designs, posed tremendous difficulties for the AEC's staff, which lacked the resources and experience to determine if the designs were adequate and if existing regulatory standards would assure public health and safety. The staff could not keep up, and licensing review times subsequently increased.

The AEC responded to the growing licensing workload by nearly doubling its staff and by developing standard review plans to formalize the review process. Staff increases, it should be noted, also stemmed from the more elaborate licensing and rulemaking proceedings established by the AEC in response to the demands of public interest groups and the courts. In the aftermath of the *Calvert Cliffs* and *NRDC* cases, for example, the AEC added environmental and safety specialists to its staff in an effort to satisfy the court's demands for more comprehensive and rigorous licensing reviews.[72] As the licensing and regulatory staffs became larger and more sophisticated, they adopted new environmental and safety reviews and demanded ever more detailed information from applicants. Furthermore, as the quality and quantity of reviews increased, the staff discovered that existing standards were often inadequate and began to impose more stringent safety and environmental requirements on both new and existing plants. Some of the new standards mandated extensive design and construction changes as well as more costly manufacturing, testing, and performance criteria for structural materials and components. In Chapter 3, for example, we saw that concerns over thermal pollution forced the owner of the Vermont Yankee reactor to redesign the plant and install cooling towers to dissipate the waste heat. In that case, as in many others, construction costs climbed as a result of design changes.

Other regulatory changes were a product of increased operating experience. Once a sufficient number of reactors actually came on-line in the 1970s, the commission and the industry had a chance to evaluate the sufficiency of existing standards, designs, and operating procedures. Over time, previously unanticipated equipment and design problems were discovered, and remedial steps were taken to correct them. A fire in the TVA-owned Browns Ferry plant in 1975, for example, nearly disabled the reactor and revealed a host of design, equipment, and training problems that compromised plant safety. The commission later issued new regulations calling for extensive and expensive changes to ensure that redundant safety systems could no longer be knocked out by fire. Somewhat later, the commission revised its seismic safety standards after the discovery of a fault beneath the Diablo Canyon facility. Plant owners were then required to install expensive structural reinforcements to pipes and supports to ensure that plant safety would not be jeopardized in the event of an earthquake. Finally, the accident at Three Mile Island sparked numerous recommendations from the NRC and the industry regarding reactor designs and operating procedures.

What these examples show is that many of the industry's economic wounds were either self-inflicted or were the result of regulatory failures by the AEC. If the industry and the AEC had not rushed to commercialize nuclear power before the technology was mature, much of the political controversy, licensing delays, and economic ills might have been avoided. A strong regulatory program might have detected potential problems early on, before reactors were built and even more important, before they started producing electricity. If such a program had been in place, costly design changes and construction stoppages would have been unnecessary. But that is not what happened. Instead, the discovery of unanticipated problems and reluctant admissions that some existing standards were insufficient undermined confidence in the agency and the industry and fed the growing safety controversy.

Cost increases could not have come at a worse time for the nuclear industry. Nuclear reactors are capital-intensive, and runaway costs increased the utilities' need for capital to build plants. Internal capital was scarce, however, because energy conservation measures had depressed utility revenues at the same time that state public utility commissions were becoming reluctant to approve rate increases. Indeed, public utility commissions (PUCs) were granting an average of only 60 percent of requested rate hikes, thereby forcing many utilities to seek external capital. By 1970, the utility industry was raising over half of its external financing through long-term bonds, offered at high interest rates.[73] Interest rates, it should be noted, were already quite high in the 1970s. Electric utilities once had been considered very safe investments, but the dramatic increases in the long-term debt of nuclear utilities typically hurt their credit ratings and stock prices.[74] In fact, by 1974, interest payments on power plant construction amounted to 25 percent of the plant's total cost.[75] With utilities borrowing so heavily, licensing and construction delays pushed construction costs even higher, increasing the need for capital.

The growing role of state public utility commissions illustrates the importance of new venues and actors. Critics of nuclear power joined forces with consumer advocates, who were concerned about rising energy costs, in opposing utility requests for rate increases. PUCS had previously attracted little attention, but rising energy prices politicized their decisions and thrust them into the spotlight. Some state regulators began to consider "need for power" issues, which forced utilities to undertake the costly process of demonstrating that additional capacity was needed and that the proposed plant was the best option for attaining it. Also controversial were utility requests to include the costs of construction work in progress in their rate base, and with costs escalating so rapidly, utilities were seeking very large rate increases. As noted above, PUCs disallowed many of the requests, forcing utilities to seek external capital. Indeed, the era was marked by billions of dollars in cost disallowances. As a case in point, the Long Island Lighting Company requested that the $4.7 billion cost of its Shoreham plant be included in its rate base, but New York's Public Service Commission disallowed $1.4 billion of the request, citing gross mismanagement. In 1987, the commission rejected the company's request for an $83 million rate hike. Similarly, the refusal of New Hampshire's public utility commission to grant an emergency rate increase to the owner of the Seabrook plant lead to the company's bankruptcy in 1988.[76] These disallowances introduced uncertainty to the planning and construction process, which put nuclear plants at a great disadvantage. Throughout the states, actors in these new venues played a crucial role in determining the future of nuclear power. Critics of nuclear power gained access through these multiple venues and thus influenced the economics of nuclear power.

In other states, PUCS enacted policies that hurt nuclear power. By the end of the 1980s, for example, ten states had adopted least-cost energy planning, which required utilities to meet energy demand by using the cheapest source available, whether it be coal, renewable energy, or conservation.[77] Faced with rapidly escalating costs, excess generating capacity, and a less than favorable economic environment, utilities were understandably reluctant to invest capital in new generating plants, especially nuclear reactors. Some opted for conservation programs; some built coal-burning plants; still others canceled reactor orders. By any standard, nuclear power limped into the 1980s as one moribund industry.

CONCLUSION

There were significant changes in nuclear politics and economics in the 1970s. The level of political activity surrounding the issue increased, as interest groups on both sides pressed their demands on policymakers and continued to battle over image and venues. Particularly important was the response of the nuclear industry, which in an effort to regain control of the debate launched a campaign to reshape perceptions of nuclear power. Faced with conflicting demands, a decentralized Congress refused to confront the question of safety directly, preferring to make incremental adjustments at the margins of nuclear policy. For its part, the NRC was embroiled in one controversy after another and could satisfy none of its overseers. In addition, the conflict over nuclear safety escalated to the highest levels of government as presidents began to play an active role in policy making. The federal monopoly continued to erode as well, as state and local governments became more involved through their powers to regulate land use and electricity rates. And all of this activity took place before Three Mile Island, which only reinforced preexisting trends. At the end of the decade, the politics of nuclear power bore few of the signs of subgovernment dominance. The one-sided mobilization of interests that characterized atomic energy's first twenty years had been replaced by two stable, well-defined coalitions organized for action, each seeking very different policy outcomes. The politics of nuclear power was now highly visible and rife with conflict.

As we have seen, policy change was promoted by powerful internal and external forces, including the rise of environmentalism, the energy crisis, the debate over reactor safety, the structural reforms of the public lobby era that sought to remake regulatory policy and build greater participation in government decision making, and the multiple new venues that gained jurisdiction over nuclear power. Together, these forces undermined the viability of the atomic subsystem, but they did not destroy it. To be sure, the policy-making arena was far more competitive than it had been in earlier years, and important structural changes had also expanded participation in the policy-making process. But the nuclear industry had not given up, and elected officials at the national level were unwilling to say "no" to nuclear power. Proponents of nuclear power instead turned their attention to keeping the nuclear option alive for another time. Furthermore, despite all the changes at the NRC, officials there continued to argue that nuclear plants were a safe and desirable source of energy. Given all of the tumultuous change, what prevented the NRC from changing as much as its critics would have liked?

There are several explanations, but none was more important than the NRC's narrow jurisdiction. Because the commission was responsible for overseeing one industry, it was an ideal candidate for capture. The NRC did not want to drive the industry out of business; to do so would risk its own survival. Second, although the NRC was created in 1975, it was not a public lobby era agency. Rather, it was essentially a spin-off from the AEC in terms of both personnel and attitudes. Old habits die hard. Relatedly, the issue-specific nature of this particular subgovernment inhibited reform. Nuclear power is a complex technical issue, which severely restricts the ability of nonexperts to participate and demand more dramatic policy change. It was hard enough for critics to suggest that reactors were not as safe as proponents claimed; it would be something else entirely to argue for the closure of existing plants or for a permanent moratorium on additional reactors. Next, the nuclear industry responded to its changing fortunes by aggressively resisting more stringent regulation from the NRC. The creation of the Institute of Nuclear Power Operations, for example, was intended to preempt the NRC by demonstrating that the industry could regulate itself. Finally, ambiguous signals from the White House and Congress left the agency with no clear mandate to guide its actions. Nuclear policy seemed hopelessly deadlocked, but the industry would soon have a friend in the White House.

8
Deregulation and Nuclear Power

Government is not the solution to our problems, government is the problem.
—Ronald Reagan

A central assertion of this study is that the case of nuclear power reflects major changes in the nation's social and political landscape. A number of analysts have argued that regulatory policy in the United States has evolved in distinct stages, each coinciding with a concerted political effort to redefine the role of the central government in regulating private enterprise. Furthermore, these stages have been characterized by qualitative shifts in ideas, institutions, and policies.[1] Harris and Milkis, for example, identify three distinctive regulatory periods or "regimes": the Progressive Era, the New Deal, and the public lobby era. Although each period was characterized by an expansion of federal regulatory power, each also had some unique traits. As a case in point, the New Deal was largely concerned with economic issues, while regulatory initiatives in the 1970s typically involved quality of life issues. Similarly, while the New Deal emphasized the delegation of authority to administrative agencies, the new social regulation reflected a distrust of bureaucratic power, preferring to rely instead on new institutional arrangements that involved Congress, the courts, and public lobby groups in the details of policy making. Reformers hoped the more permeable structure of bias would protect their policy victories from future political attacks.

By any measure, then, the elections of Ronald Reagan and George Bush posed serious questions about the durability of these reforms. Reagan came to office arguing that excessive federal regulation had harmed the nation's economy,

181

and he promised to provide regulatory relief, especially in the area of social regulation. In calling for a reduction of government intervention in the economy and a devolution of authority to the states, Reagan was seeking to reverse almost five decades of regulatory growth. Despite a more ambivalent stance at the beginning of his term, Bush eventually embraced his predecessor's antiregulatory posture.[2]

In this chapter I examine how deregulators fared in their efforts to redirect nuclear policy. As in the 1970s, procedural and institutional battles were again central to nuclear politics. Supporters of nuclear power tried to curtail public participation by closing off some of the venues that had previously allowed new actors to claim jurisdiction over nuclear power. These measures included proposals to reduce the number of public hearings and rule changes limiting access to commission information and proceedings. In an important exception to the policy of New Federalism, Presidents Reagan and Bush also supported efforts to limit the ability of state and local governments to regulate nuclear power. Conversely, antinuclear groups fought to protect the institutional reforms that had given them access to nuclear policy making, relying heavily on allies in Congress and on litigation.

The nuclear policy community of the 1980s, and the context in which it operated, was dramatically different from what had existed two decades earlier. The community was broader, more diverse, and more contentious. Most important, there were now *two* major coalitions espousing very different objectives. The pronuclear coalition consisted of reactor vendors and suppliers, nuclear utilities and construction firms, elected officials in some state and local governments, and the Department of Energy. With the elections of Reagan and Bush, the White House and the NRC moved solidly into the pronuclear coalition as well. The antinuclear coalition was composed of local citizen intervenor groups opposed to particular reactors, national environmental organizations such as the Sierra Club, safety groups including the Union of Concerned Scientists, and elected officials in Congress and in state and local governments. Rising electricity costs, concerns over emergency planning, and unresolved questions about nuclear waste disposal prompted consumer advocates, state utility commissions and planning boards, and large industrial users of electricity to join the antinuclear coalition.

NUCLEAR POWER AND STATUTORY REFORM

Presidential involvement was again a key factor in nuclear politics in the 1980s, but in a departure from the Carter years, Presidents Reagan and Bush strongly supported nuclear power. In a statement released shortly after taking office, for example, Ronald Reagan remarked that nuclear power was "one of the best potential sources of new electrical energy supplies in the coming decade."[3] President Bush's National Energy Strategy, conceived before the Iraqi invasion of Kuwait, envisioned doubling the number of nuclear plants by 2030. Throughout their tenures, Reagan and Bush tried with mixed success to resolve the nuclear industry's most pressing problems. Indeed, an inventory of White House actions in this period reads like a nuclear industry wish list: legislative proposals designed to resolve the high-level nuclear waste issue; use of the appointment power and executive orders to create a more favorable regulatory environment, facilitate the reform of reactor licensing procedures and ensure progress toward NRC certification of standardized reactor designs; and budgetary support for the DOE's research program on advanced reactors. Although the combination of statutory reform and executive action failed to immediately revive the nuclear industry, significant progress was made toward overcoming some of its biggest obstacles. By any standard, nuclear power's prospects were considerably brighter in 1992 than in 1980.

For most of the period, the accidents at Three Mile Island and Chernobyl precluded serious consideration of any changes in the Atomic Energy Act that might be perceived as easing safety standards. Unwilling to expend much political capital in a no-win situation, Reagan and Bush instead pursued their policy goals through executive orders, appointments, and budgetary policy rather than legislation. The preference for administrative measures is easily explained: most did not require congressional approval, an important consideration in a time of divided government.

There were, however, a few notable exceptions to this approach, and by the end of the decade a number of potentially significant statutory changes had been enacted. In 1988, for example, Congress overwhelmingly authorized a ten-year extension of the Price Anderson Act, increasing reactor operators' liability coverage from $700 million to approximately $7 billion.[4] The industry, joined by the White House and the DOE, argued that reauthorization was essential to its future and lobbied to limit its liability to $2 billion. Consumer and antinuclear groups, on the other hand, wanted to force the industry to bear all accident costs, but amendments designed to strengthen victim compensation and safety incentive provisions were easily defeated after President Reagan threatened a veto.[5] Under the new law, owners of commercial reactors are required to obtain the maximum amount of private insurance available, which then was about $160 million per reactor. If accident costs exceed the private insurance reserves, reactors could be assessed $63 million each, bringing the total liability coverage to $7 billion. If damages are even higher, the president would name a commission to study the need for additional compensation from the federal government, but Congress is not obligated to appropriate any money.

Congress also enacted legislation to resolve the nuclear waste issue, which had become one of the most intractable problems facing the nuclear power industry. Although the effort was ultimately unsuccessful and nuclear waste policy remains stalemated, the waste issue illustrates two important but conflicting traits of nuclear politics in the 1980s. First, there was continued strong support for nuclear power within the institutions of the national government, especially the

White House. One observer called the nuclear waste legislation enacted in the 1980s "a formal, legislative statement of the interests of the nuclear establishment" whose goal was to site and build a waste facility as soon as possible.[6] Second, state and local governments were active participants in policy making, and most actively resisted federal efforts to site nuclear waste repositories. The AEC had preempted state action until the 1970s, but the subsequent history of the nuclear waste program is characterized by intense conflict between federal, state, and local officials.[7] As a result of these disagreements, nuclear waste policy, like nuclear policy in general, has been plagued by cost overruns, missed deadlines, and intense political controversy.

The question of what to do with nuclear waste did not receive much attention in the early years of the atomic program. The AEC and others in the subgovernment were more concerned with the scientific challenges of harnessing the atom. Nuclear waste, in contrast, was generally assumed to be a less complex, essentially technical problem that would be easy to solve. For the technocrats in the AEC, it was merely a matter of learning how to isolate the waste, selecting the appropriate site for a storage facility, and choosing the best design for that facilty. Questions of public safety or environmental risks were not major concerns.[8] Additionally, with the first reactors just beginning to generate power, there was no pressing need for an immediate solution. Reflecting its low priority within the AEC, action on nuclear waste disposal was deferred indefinitely. This decision, like so many others in the program's early years, only made the problem worse, because the lack of an effective nuclear waste policy became one of the antinuclear movement's most potent arguments in the 1980s.[9]

Shortly after the accident at Three Mile Island, the states of Nevada, South Carolina, and Washington, where most low-level waste was stored, announced that they would no longer accept shipments of such waste from other states. Congress responded in 1980 by passing the Low-Level Radioactive Waste Act (LLRWA), which made states responsible for the disposal of their own low-level waste. Under the law, states were encouraged to form regional compacts, which would then select a single disposal site. If compacts could not agree on a site, each state would be responsible for its own waste.[10]

Although the LLRWA did provide a framework for the eventual resolution of the low-level waste problem, significant implementation problems ignited a national debate over nuclear waste. Because of fierce public opposition, the question of which states would host the repositories was particularly controversial. Very few states were willing to consider a disposal site within their own borders, and most, it turned out, did everything they could to ensure the selection of another state. Additionally, states that generated large amounts of waste, notably Texas and New York, were unwelcome in their regional compacts and were forced to go it alone. The ironic result of this game of "nuclear keep away" was a proliferation of low-level waste sites, all of which were bitterly contested.[11] Proponents of nuclear power had hoped the LLRWA would solve a problem, but its immediate effect was to multiply the number of disputes over nuclear waste, leading to a dramatic increase in publicity and public concern. By the middle of the decade, in fact, opinion surveys revealed that waste issues were near the top of public concerns about nuclear power.[12]

It was not until the 1970s that the commission made a serious effort to develop a comprehensive plan for the permanent storage of high-level nuclear waste. Initially, the AEC thought that spent reactor fuel would be reprocessed and used again as reactor fuel while the remaining waste would be permanently buried in remote locations. But the AEC had to abandon its first choice for a permanent geologic repository when studies revealed serious problems with the proposed site, an abandoned salt mine near Lyons, Kansas. When the problems were discovered, the state of Kansas objected to the project, and the AEC began the search for another site.

Responsibility for selecting a new site shifted to the Energy Research and Development Administration, and then to the Department of Energy when the AEC was abolished. The ERDA began its search for a high-level repository in 1976, and ultimately considered sites in thirty-six states. Despite the ERDA's informal offer to cooperate with the states and to abandon any project if it could not satisfy state concerns, many of the potential host states were worried about having no formal role in the selection process. In response, approximately two-thirds of the states enacted laws regulating some aspect of nuclear waste disposal, and by 1979 nineteen states actually had imposed bans or moratoria on repository siting.[13] Policy was stalemated, with much of the conflict centered on what role the public, including states and Indian tribes, would play in the siting process. Most sought guarantees that their interests would be represented; some even demanded a veto over the final decision. Against this backdrop, President Carter initiated an effort to formulate a high-level waste policy that included some formal role for the states in the repository siting process. Although Carter's nuclear waste policy task force did pave the way for congressional action, it was unable to resolve the issue of state participation. Rather than granting them a veto, the task force recommended "consultation and concurrence" with the states. Recognizing the need to legitimize the eventual decision, Carter also stressed the importance of full public disclosure and participation in the selection process.[14]

Meanwhile, Carter's 1977 decision to end commercial reprocessing meant that spent reactor fuel was piling up in cooling ponds at reactor sites around the nation. The cooling ponds, however, were not designed to store waste permanently, and most could hold no more than three years of spent fuel. Moreover, utilities could not expand their on-site storage capacity without state regulatory approval, which was by no means assured. By the late 1970s, with many utilities worried about running out of space and facing mounting on-site storage costs, the nuclear industry sought legislative relief, arguing that a federal commitment on high-level waste was essential to its future.

After several years of deliberation, Congress acted in 1982, adopting the Nuclear Waste Policy Act (NWPA).[15] The NWPA established detailed procedures and a schedule for the selection, construction, and operation of two permanent high-level waste repositories. Under the law, the DOE would conduct an intensive nationwide search for potential sites, which would be evaluated with a demanding set of technical criteria and guidelines, including environmental assessments. All of the studies and reports would be subject to review and comment through a public hearing process. The DOE was then to compile a list of potential sites from which the president would select two for further review and site characterization, one in the eastern United States and one in the west. The ambitious timetable required the president to designate the first site by 31 March 1987 and the second by 1 July 1989. The repositories would be licensed by the NRC.

In an effort to build public confidence into the selection process and promote acceptance of the final decision, Congress directed the DOE to work closely with the states. The NWPA authorized the Department of Energy to enter into binding, written agreements on screening and characterization studies with those states designated by the president as potential sites. The DOE would also provide money to the states to help them conduct their own site reviews and to hire independent consultants.[16] Finally, the law allowed the potential host state to veto its selection, but this veto could be overridden by a vote of both houses of Congress.

Other key provisions effectively shifted the legal and economic liabilities of waste disposal from the industry to the federal government. The DOE would begin accepting commercial waste in 1998, when the first repository was scheduled to open. To finance the repositories, the NWPA created the Nuclear Waste Fund, which levied a user fee of 0.1 cent per kWh on the consumers of electricity from the nation's nuclear plants.[17]

By all accounts, implementation of the Nuclear Waste Policy Act was a failure. Although the DOE met the act's 1983 deadline for issuing siting guidelines, virtually every other stage of the selection process was bitterly contested. All of the states considered as potential repository sites challenged that designation, with most arguing that the DOE was moving too quickly. In 1985 the DOE presented the president with a smaller list of three possible sites in the states of Texas, Washington, and Nevada. Officials from all three states and their congressional delegations protested, claiming that the DOE's technical analyses and site assessment procedures were seriously flawed. Each of the states, joined by numerous environmental and antinuclear groups, challenged the designation in court. The DOE's efforts to select a second repository site in the east were just as unsuccessful; none of the seven states identified as potential sites by the DOE were willing to accept the repository.[18] In 1986 a frustrated DOE announced that it was suspending its search for an eastern waste disposal site, which predictably upset the western states.

With the states in open rebellion, Congress tried to repair the damage by amending the NWPA. In December 1987, Congress rejected the multiple site search process established in the legislation and instead designated Yucca Mountain, Nevada, as the repository site. The search for a second site in the east was abandoned. Despite the profound policy shift, the changes never came up for a direct vote; instead, they were adopted in conference on a budget reconciliation measure, having been inserted into the bill by Senator Bennett Johnston (D-La.), a leading proponent of nuclear power. Although legislators from the other potential host states were understandably relieved with the passage of what came to be known as the "screw Nevada bill," officials from that state were livid. "It's nuclear rape," said Senator Richard Bryan.[19] Adding salt to the wound, Congress stipulated that to qualify for federal money to manage the job, Nevada had to relinquish its veto rights. These actions, as Michael Kraft suggests, gave Nevada little incentive to cooperate with federal officials and had a predictably negative effect on the state's relationship with the federal government.[20]

Over the next few years, officials from Nevada, joined by many national environmental groups including the National Resources Defense Council, the Sierra Club, and the Audobon Society, explored every conceivable means of blocking the facility. Concerned about the risks of repository construction and the adequacy of the Department of Energy's site characterization plans, the state denied DOE requests for the environmental permits necessary to begin site evaluation, temporarily stopping work on the project. Then, in 1989 the Nevada legislature passed a bill forbidding any government agency from storing high-level waste in the state, effectively vetoing the repository. When the DOE refused to consider the veto an official action under the NWPA, Nevada filed suit in federal court, prompting the DOE to countersue to have Nevada's action declared invalid. In 1990, the Ninth Circuit ruled in favor of the DOE; Nevada then appealed to the Supreme Court, which ultimately upheld the Ninth Circuit's decision.[21] Meanwhile, after two years of preliminary work and expenditures of nearly $500 million, the DOE announced in 1989 that it was abandoning the original repository plans because it lacked confidence in the technical quality of the proposal.[22]

The case of nuclear waste disposal demonstrates the increasingly decentralized nature of nuclear politics in the 1980s. The widespread search for suitable nuclear waste disposal sites touched many states and communities and brought multiple new actors, in the form of state and local governments, to the policymaking arena. Whatever their motivations, the new actors brought different perspectives and goals to the debate; indeed, most actively resisted federal efforts to site nuclear waste facilities. With states and local governments assuming a critical role in policy making, it is clear that the conflict over nuclear waste had expanded far beyond the confines of subgovernment politics.

At the same time, however, the nuclear waste issue illustrates that support for nuclear power within the federal government remained strong. With states impeding the siting of a high-level repository, the industry sought to shift the financial and legal risks of nuclear waste management to the federal government. The result was the Nuclear Waste Policy Act, which also assured that the final decision on repository siting would be made by the federal government, where industry influence was more pronounced, rather than by the states.[23] The consolidation of power at the national level was endorsed by the Reagan administration despite its avowed preference for devolving power to the states. Apparently, nuclear power was an exception to the policy of New Federalism.

Ironically, the federal government's efforts to aid nuclear utilities and their allies delayed the ultimate resolution of the waste problem. The ambitious timetable for repository siting and construction established by the NWPA, for example, may have jeopardized the quality of site evaluation studies and precluded meaningful state and public participation. As Michael Kraft notes, the short deadlines were dictated more by the utilities' need to quickly solve their on-site storage problems than by the requirements of scientific study or by the need to build public trust into the selection process.[24] A more flexible and realistic schedule, on the other hand, would have given the DOE more time to investigate potential sites and to consult with affected states and communities. Similarly, Congress could have authorized construction of a temporary storage facility, which would have met the utilities' need to move waste away from reactor sites while allowing further research into a permanent solution.[25] This approach would have added credibility to the site evaluation studies and might have led to greater public acceptance of siting decisions.[26] But in seeking an immediate fix, Congress sacrificed the public trust that is essential to hazardous facility siting.

Public confidence in the DOE's competence and impartiality was further undermined by the agency's technocratic approach to implementation. As its AEC roots might suggest, the Energy Department was an optimistic, problem-solving agency with a habit of consistently understating the potential risks of repository construction, a preference for working in secrecy, and an aversion to public participation. From the agency's perspective, repository siting was essentially a technical problem, a matter of finding the appropriate site and technology.[27] Lacking the requisite expertise, the public could not be expected to play a meaningful role in those activities. Accordingly, the DOE's efforts to involve the public consisted largely of "public education" programs designed to quell public concerns by exposing citizens to the "facts" about nuclear waste. Public opinion surveys suggest, however, that public opposition to nuclear waste facility siting resulted not from a paucity of information, as the DOE assumed, but from a distinct lack of trust in the source of the information.[28] Fewer than one in five urban Las Vegas residents, for example, believed the DOE to be "very trustworthy."[29] More generally, a 1982 report by the Office of Technology Assessment concluded that "the greatest single obstacle that a successful waste management program must overcome is the severe erosion of public confidence in the Federal government."[30] In the end, the absence of public trust in the DOE's ability to safely build and operate a high-level waste facility effectively ensured that state and local officials would withhold their cooperation, which was essential to program success.

A review of the Energy Department's actions also suggests that the agency, like the AEC before it, has failed to adapt to the more participatory era of regulatory politics set in motion during the public lobby era.[31] As we have seen, one of the trademarks of this new era is greater citizen participation in the details of policy making, including program implementation. This participation was encouraged, in part, by state and federal laws that afforded citizens numerous administrative and legal options for challenging agency decisions. The policy-making environment, in turn, has become denser and more complex, with a multitude of citizen groups and government officials from all levels clamoring to be heard. The difficulty of siting a nuclear waste facility in this environment is manifest.

REGULATORY OVERSIGHT IN THE REAGAN AND BUSH ADMINISTRATIONS

In many respects, the emphasis on administrative measures is a product of long-standing developments in American politics. The expansion of federal regulatory capabilities and commitments after the New Deal made administrative politics the focal point of government activity. With regulation affecting more and more areas of American life, the need for improved policy coordination and planning became apparent. This was of special concern to presidents who, despite public perceptions, face serious problems managing the large and disparate executive branch. Many presidents, in fact, have worried about the tendency of agencies to become "captured" by their constituent groups or congressional overseers. According to Terry Moe, the institutional fragmentation of American politics, the growing complexity of social problems, and the rising expectations for presidential performance gave presidents strong incentives to pursue their programs through unilateral executive action.[32] Consequently, decision-making authority has been systematically shifted from agencies to the White House, which is presumably more responsive to the president's programmatic goals. The result has been the emergence of the "administrative presidency," in which an increasingly centralized and politicized executive department strives to overcome the inertia inherent in the constitutional system of checks and balances.[33]

Concerns about the social, political, and economic consequences of government regulation in general, and the new social regulation in particular, developed in the mid-1970s. In the case of nuclear power, the industry had grown accustomed to self-regulation and complained about the economic burden of new safety rules. The NRC, even in its first days, proved to be sympathetic to the industry's pleas for regulatory relief. The NRC's behavior is not surprising, because regulatory agencies, particularly those that regulate only one industry, often are held responsible for the financial success of the regulated industry.[34] Recognizing this responsibility, agencies may be reluctant to impose costly regulations on that industry for fear that burdensome requirements will drive the industry out of business. This was the case with the NRC, as one of its internal reports shows. The report, noting the agency's reluctance to impose new safety requirements because of the industry's shaky status, claimed there was "an apparent management attitude that '[T]echnical [R]eviewers' should not raise new safety issues. . . . The nuclear steam suppliers are going broke (only four left) and T.R.'s shouldn't kill the industry."[35]

Another indication of the commission's desire to be more sensitive to the economic consequences of its regulations came in 1975 when the NRC announced that all proposed changes in existing requirements and practices for licensing that did not require direct commission action would have to be reviewed and approved by a special standing committee before taking effect. The new committee was known as the Regulatory Requirements Review Committee (RRRC). Composed of senior NRC officials, the RRRC was authorized to modify, defer, or reject any proposed regulatory changes that it found "unnecessary" or in need of further explanation or analysis.[36] In practice, the RRRC required demanding standards of evidence before approving new regulatory actions, in effect placing a very high burden of proof on proponents of new requirements, including those affecting reactor safety. In this way, the committee acted as a sort of bottleneck that slowed the rate at which new regulations were promulgated; the RRRC also was able to kill many proposed standards by sending them back to the staff for further analysis. The RRRC was the NRC's response to industry concerns about the unstable and unpredictable regulatory process.

As a further reflection of its sensitivity to the consequences of regulation on the nuclear industry, the commission changed its internal review procedures in 1975 to explicitly incorporate economic factors into its regulatory decision-making process. According to the NRC, this revision would be accomplished through "impact/value analysis," which was intended to be a "systematic assessment of the values and adverse impacts, including added costs to the public," that could be expected to result from proposed regulations.[37]

The commission was not undertaking these efforts in a vacuum. Both Presidents Ford and Carter were pushing other agencies to move in the same direction, urging a reduction in federal paperwork, closer agency review of the manner in which they made their rules, and greater responsiveness to the concerns of the industries being regulated. Carter expressed his sentiments to Congress in March 1977, saying, "We must look, industry by industry, at what effect regulation has—whether it protects the public interest or whether it simply blunts the healthy forces of competition, inflates prices, and discourages business innovation. Whenever it seems likely that the free market would better serve the public, we will eliminate government regulation."[38]

Although Presidents Ford and Carter took steps to control regulatory growth, they both believed that regulation, though flawed, was ultimately necessary and desirable. Ronald Reagan did not, as indicated by his preference for the term "regulatory relief" rather than the more common "regulatory reform."[39] Underlying Reagan's antipathy to command and control regulation was his conviction that it was too intrusive, unduly burdened business, and contributed to higher prices, higher unemployment, and lower productivity growth. In the case of nuclear power, Reagan claimed that it had "become entangled in a morass of regulations that do not enhance safety but that do cause extensive licensing delays and economic undertainty."[40] He thus recommended streamlining the NRC's licensing process as a means of expediting the construction and operation of nuclear plants. Moreover, Reagan was convinced that the institutional and procedural reforms of the public lobby era had allowed activists to seize control of regulatory politics. His election in 1980 therefore promised to raise regulatory reform to the forefront of the political agenda.[41]

As noted above, the Reagan administration relied on the president's executive powers to consolidate its control over rulemaking. The first step was the imposition of a sixty-day freeze on regulations adopted in the waning days of the Carter administration. Next, the budgets of most regulatory agencies were slashed, forcing significant reductions in staff and enforcement actions. The White House also carefully screened nominees and appointed only loyal conservatives who were sympathetic to its regulatory objectives.[42] In addition, Reagan issued executive orders establishing more centralized review procedures, with the Office of Management and Budget (OMB) playing the central role. Executive Order 12291, issued in February 1981, required all federal agencies, with the exception of the independent regulatory commissions, to assess the costs and benefits of each proposed major regulation and, to the extent permitted by law, to select the least costly option. After conducting their reviews, agencies would submit Regulatory Impact Analyses (RIAs) to the OMB for approval. In performing their RIAs, agencies were instructed to examine the costs and benefits of proposed rules and to consider a variety of regulatory and nonregulatory alternatives, including market-based approaches and even a "no regulation" alternative.[43] To further assert White House control, in 1985 Reagan issued Executive Order 12498, which required agencies to submit their yearly agendas to the OMB and to show that their proposed actions or programs were consistent with the administration's regulatory guidelines. Primary responsibility for this review rested with the conservative staff of OMB's Office of Information and Regulatory Affairs (OIRA).[44] Although these changes were controversial, the net effect was to make the OMB the crucial access point for those seeking to influence pending regulations. Furthermore, the administration's use of cost-benefit analysis effectively shifted the burden of proof to advocates of additional regulation, thereby slowing the issuance of new rules. In essence, as Harris and Milkis note, "the procedures governing regulation were transformed from an institutional setup that favored program advocates to one that benefited those who were avowedly hostile to regulatory initiatives."[45]

Reagan and Bush clearly found centralized regulatory review to be a tempting strategy. For those seeking fundamental and enduring policy shifts, however, it is often insufficent, especially during periods of divided government. As Harris and Milkis argue, executive action must be reinforced by similar changes in the statutory basis of regulation if it is to have lasting effect. Otherwise, "administrative victories may be subject to legal challenges in the short run and administrative reversals in the long run."[46] Moreover, centralized review works best when the policy has broad support among other key actors, and when the others are willing to delegate authority to the president and the executive agencies.[47]

That was clearly not the case during the Reagan and Bush years. On the contrary, most of the other key actors remained committed to effective regulation and were unwilling to defer to the executive. Of course, this phenomenon is not new; one of the consequences of divided government is that for much of the last two decades regulatory politics has been characterized by high levels of mistrust among the OMB, the regulatory agencies, the White House, and Congress. That mistrust explains why Congress has written so much substantive and procedural detail into regulatory statutes. Arguably, in times of divided government presidents have an even greater incentive to create centralized regulatory review mechanisms, because policy making through the bureaucracy is one of the few avenues of influence available to them.

NRC Appointments

Although most presidents lament their inability to control executive branch agencies, the use of their appointment powers provides them with important leverage over bureaucracies, enabling them to send administrators signals concerning their preferences on the overall direction of agency actions. Although all presidents recognize the importance of staffing the bureaucracy with loyal supporters, the Reagan administration raised this practice to a new level, carefully screening potential nominees to ensure that they shared the president's commitment to regulatory relief. The selection of loyal administrators was especially important at the independent regulatory commissions, like the NRC, which were exempted from the requirements of Executive Orders 12291 and 12498.

Upon taking office, Reagan tried to reorient the NRC by appointing commissioners who shared his aversion to regulation and his enthusiasm for nuclear power. Because the commission was closely divided on many issues, any change in the NRC's personnel could be significant. It would be several years, however, before his appointees would constitute a majority of the commission. In the interim, Reagan had to work with an NRC staffed largely by Carter appointees. Fortunately for the new president, he did have the opportunity to make several personnel decisions in his first months in office, including the chance to elevate commissioner Joseph Hendrie to acting NRC chair. Hendrie, it should be noted, previously had served as chairman, only to have President Carter replace him with John Ahearne after the accident at Three Mile Island. Because he was perceived as a proponent of nuclear power, Hendrie's resumption of the chairman-ship was widely interpreted as a sign of Reagan's interest in refocusing the com-mission's energies on the licensing of new reactors.

Reagan then turned his attention to filling the vacant chairmanship. His choice for the position was Nunzio Palladino, a strong proponent of nuclear power. Palladino had ties to both the nuclear power industry, having previously been employed by Westinghouse, one of the largest reactor manufacturers, and to the Atomic Energy Commission, where he worked as a reactor designer at one of the commission's national laboratories. Shortly after assuming his position, Pal-ladino said his priorities included eliminating "unnecessary" safety regulations and licensing delay.[48] To that effect, the new chair moved quickly to revamp the commission's decision-making process, instituting changes that effectively re-quired NRC staff to meet a higher burden of proof before proposing new safety regulations. Commission meetings emphasized measures to expedite licensing, while safety matters faded into the background. He also proposed several mea-sures limiting public access to commission records and meetings. Palladino's ten-ure would be a stormy one, moving from one controversy to another, many of them involving bitter confrontations with key members of Congress.

His efforts to redirect the commission were slowed, however, by Peter Brad-ford and Victor Gilinsky, two holdovers from the Carter administration. Both were persistent critics of commission policy under Palladino's leadership. Until Bradford stepped down in 1982, he took every opportunity to voice his concerns to sympathetic members of Congress. Shortly after leaving the commission, Bradford claimed that under Palladino the NRC had exhibited a pattern of in-terfering in licensing decisions "only on the side of the nuclear industry," and that this pattern had led to a "declining faith in the Commission's impartiality."[49]

Bradford's replacement was James Asseltine, an attorney with extensive ex-perience in nuclear regulation. Before joining the commission, Asseltine served as associate counsel for the Senate Committee on Environment and Public Works and as minority counsel for the Subcommittee on Nuclear Regulation. Be-fore that, he had served as a staff attorney in the NRC's legal office. Despite his lengthy "insider" résumé and the administration's careful screening procedures, Asseltine quickly proved his independence. Indeed, he was the only Reagan ap-pointee who consistently spoke out in favor of stringent safety regulations and against the numerous commission efforts to curtail public participation in agency decision making. When Gilinsky left the commission in 1984, he noted that the "deregulation process is going on through presidential appointment."[50] With Gilinsky's departure, Reagan had built a solid majority on the commission, and Asseltine was frequently the lone dissenter in numerous commission votes. When his term expired in 1987, twenty-one senators wrote to Reagan, unsuccessfully urging him to reappoint Asseltine to another term.

Another of Reagan's commissioners generated considerable controversy. Commissioner Thomas Roberts came under fire for a series of events in 1985 and

1987 in which he was suspected of breaching NRC confidentiality by, among other things, leaking an internal memo to a Louisiana utility being investigated for violating NRC safety regulations. All told, he was the subject of no fewer than five separate congressional investigations into allegations of improper activity. Roberts even went so far as to refuse to answer the questions of a key Senate subcommittee, invoking his Sixth Amendment right to counsel in criminal proceedings. Shortly thereafter, seven committee and subcommittee chairs requested his resignation in a letter to the president. Roberts refused to step down and served out the remainder of his term.[51]

Although centralized review was an essential part of President Bush's regulatory program, his NRC appointments did not exhibit any specific ideological agenda. As at other regulatory agencies, Bush sought individuals with political and administrative experience, not rabid ideologues philosophically opposed to regulation.[52] In addition, it was only in the third year of his presidency that Bush was able to put his stamp on the commission; until that point a majority of the NRC were Reagan appointees. Bush even elevated Carr, a Reagan appointee, to the chairmanship in 1989 after Zech left office. When Carr left in 1991, Bush nominated Ivan Selin as chair. Selin came to the NRC from the State Department, where he had served as undersecretary for management since 1989. A former business owner, Selin was known as a capable manager rather than an ideologue. From his perspective, the primary goal of regulation should be prevention rather than remediation.[53]

Budgetary Policy

In addition to the appointment process, President Reagan also used his budgetary powers to achieve his programmatic goals. Regulatory agencies had grown accustomed to uninterrupted growth in both appropriation and staffing levels, but the long-term trends were reversed in Reagan's first budget, which slashed overall spending for regulatory programs. The budget cuts were especially severe at those agencies responsible for the new social regulation and affected staffing levels at many of them. Whereas the total regulatory workforce increased by 168 percent from 1970–75, it declined by 16 percent in the first four years of the Reagan administration, with the largest reductions coming in 1981–82.

The Department of Energy's research and development budget suffered large cuts, reversing policies set in motion by the energy crisis. The budget cuts largely reflected Reagan's belief that "the Nation needs to let market forces work to encourage efficient energy production and use. The Federal Government should limit its role to such responsibilities as support for long term research and the strategic petroleum reserve."[54] Spending reductions were especially severe for most nonnuclear research and development programs. DOE spending for solar and renewable energy programs, for example, declined 94 percent between 1980 and 1990, while spending for energy conservation programs fell by 91 percent between 1981 and 1987.[55] With the exception of the termination of the breeder reactor program, the nuclear fission and fusion programs remained largely intact. Given Reagan's support for nuclear power and the Energy Department's roots in the AEC, this new set of priorities is not surprising, although it is inconsistent with a limited federal role and a reliance on market forces. Although funding for alternative energy sources dried up, the DOE heavily subsidized the industry's pet projects, including the development of a new generation of advanced reactors and research for smaller, simpler, and cheaper advanced light water reactor designs.[56] The trends in energy research and development spending in the 1980s suggest that the AEC's promotional mindset lived on in the DOE, which consistently supported nuclear research and development over alternative energy sources.

Only four regulatory agencies avoided staffing cuts.[57] The NRC was one of them, largely because the accident at Three Mile Island was still fresh in everyone's mind. By 1984, however, the NRC began to share the pain of budgetary cutbacks. Given Reagan's support for nuclear power and his desire to speed the licensing process, there were concerns that budget pressures would lead the NRC to divert resources away from its research and safety programs and toward its licensing activities. Indeed, this seems to be what happened. According to the commission's director of licensing, in 1984 the NRC was 20 percent over budget for licensing reviews and 13 percent under budget for operating reactor programs. The diversion pushed a number of safety-related programs behind schedule, including implementation of the TMI Action Plan and new requirements for fire protection, equipment qualification, and unresolved safety issues. Before leaving the commission later that year, Commissioner Gilinsky wrote to Palladino expressing concern that reactor safety had been jeopardized because reactor inspectors had been reassigned to licensing work in order to license plants more quickly.[58]

Budget problems also hindered the investigations and enforcement program, which had a backlog of 127 open cases in January 1988. About half of the cases were not being worked because of a lack of resources, according to Ben Hayes, the director of the Office of Investigations. At that time, the I&E staff had thirty-two investigators and over six thousand licensees. The budget cuts were not the only explanation for the slow pace of investigations. The NRC, like the AEC before it, was reluctant to investigate charges of wrongdoing because of its distaste for criminal prosecutions and its concern for the nuclear industry. An attorney who handled prosecutions for the NRC and other federal agencies testifed before the Senate that he knew "of no other regulatory or investigative agency where senior agency officials have taken as many bizarre and seemingly deliberate actions intended to hamper the investigation and prosecution of individuals and companies in the industry the agency regulates." He said that in contrast with the Securities and Exchange Commission, which believed that the more problems they uncovered, the more confidence the public would have in the agency and in the securities market, the "NRC will bend over backwards to avoid finding problems. They're concerned that bringing irregularities to light would adversely reflect on the industry, and, in turn, perhaps impair the future of nuclear power."[59]

In 1985, Commissioner Asseltine told Congress that the NRC's plans to cut back programs for reactor regulation and investigations and enforcement were unsound. The administration had requested that the NRC's budget be cut from $449.6 million to $429 million in FY 1986, and that the emphasis be shifted toward advanced reactor research and licensing.[60] That same month, Chairman Palladino told Representative Markey's subcommittee that the budget cuts would curtail the agency's research programs and reduce the number of safety inspections. An internal NRC memorandum, prepared by Victor Stello at the request of Commissioners Asseltine and Bernthal and released to the public by Markey, said the research cuts would prevent the NRC from completing a reassessment of the risk of severe accidents. Stello's memo claimed that "the program is now at the point where the most serious issues have been identified, but the ability to solve them has been reduced." He added that research cuts "are expected to have intermediate and long-term implications that will be detrimental to public health and safety."[61]

Despite Reagan's considerable success in reshaping agency budgets and personnel, additional steps would be needed to bring about more substantial changes in the commission's rules and regulations. According to Donald C. Winston of the Atomic Industrial Forum, Reagan's actions, while welcome, fell short of what was needed to revive the industry. "You could have a 'perfect' NRC," said Winston, "and you wouldn't solve the industry's problems. The real problem is economics."[62] It is to the commission's efforts to reduce the cost of regulation that we now turn.

ADMINISTRATIVE OVERSIGHT AND REGULATORY RELIEF

As chairman of the Nuclear Regulatory Commission, Palladino possessed administrative powers that gave him considerable influence over the agency's daily operations. Ironically, much of the chair's power was relatively new, stemming from a reorganization enacted by Jimmy Carter after Three Mile Island. Seeking to make the commission more responsive to presidential leadership, Carter strengthened the chair relative to the other commissioners.[63] Palladino used these new powers to reorient the commission and bring it into conformity with Reagan's regulatory goals.

Seeking to cut back on excessive regulations, Palladino enacted several measures that gave him greater control over the NRC's regulatory staff. Shortly after he assumed the chairmanship, the NRC established two internal working groups, both composed of senior NRC staff, to reform the commission's regulatory procedures. One of those groups, the Committee to Review Generic Requirements

(CRGR), was responsible for reviewing staff proposals for "generic" issues, which are unresolved safety problems that affect large groups of reactors. While the CRGR focused on generic issues, the Regulatory Reform Task Force (RRTF), established in November 1981, was given the broader mandate of overhauling the commission's overall regulatory process. Specifically, the task force was charged with developing legislative and administrative reforms to reduce licensing delays and "eliminate the slack" from the licensing process.[64] As a sign of its importance, the RRTF was housed next to Palladino's office. Both groups enacted changes that required the staff to meet more demanding standards of evidence to support new regulatory proposals, in effect placing a very high burden of proof on proponents of new requirements. Both groups were able to kill many proposed standards by sending them back to the staff for further analysis, frequently requesting estimates of the economic consequences of new regulations. In this way, the two groups acted as regulatory gatekeepers, slowing the rate at which new rules were promulgated.

Established in response to industry complaints that the NRC staff was overreacting to the TMI accident by imposing excessive regulatory requirements, the CRGR was charged with eliminating "unnecessary demands on licensees by ensuring that the need for a new requirement can be demonstrated by those proposing it."[65] Generic issues were a major point of contention in the licensing process in the 1970s and 1980s, with critics claiming that the NRC, in its desire to avoid licensing delays, used the generic label as a convenient mechanism for removing troublesome issues from individual licensing cases.[66] To address the problem, the CRGR subjected all proposed generic regulations to a multilayered review process. In evaluating proposed regulations, the CRGR sought assurances that the changes would be necessary for protecting public health and safety, were likely to result in "a net safety improvement," and were likely to have an impact on the public, the industry, and the government.[67] The CRGR frequently sent issues back to the regulatory staff for additional review and often mandated some form of cost-benefit analysis. Although Palladino believed the committee "sharpened the thinking in the agency on whether new staff proposals really had a good safety payoff," Commissioner Gilinsky claimed that it served as a "fairly undiscriminating bottleneck."[68] Supporting his contention, a 1983 internal NRC staff memorandum notes that "there has been a substantial reduction in the number of new generic requirements imposed on reactor licensees since the inception of CRGR. For instance, the staff had projected there would be 1,900 new operating reactor licensing actions generated in FY 1982, whereas the actual number was less than 900 actions. Most of this reduction was in the number of multi-plant actions and can, I believe, be attributed to the existence of CRGR."[69] In short, the CRGR, made it more difficult for the regulatory staff to propose new requirements.

Critics of the committee complained that it was almost completely insulated from public scrutiny, noting that only NRC staff and consultants could attend its meetings, that it allowed minimal access to files and other documents, and that it published only brief minutes of its meetings. The Union of Concerned Scientists argued that "the public cannot trust a decision-making process assessing the need for safety improvements to consider all relevant factors if it is not accessible to all parties in the debate."[70] Despite these complaints, in 1983 the NRC went even further in its efforts to limit access when it began withholding the minutes of CRGR meetings from the public until final resolution of the issue, claiming that until then the meetings were "predecisional" in nature and thus not subject to disclosure laws.[71] With such limited access, observers could not determine exactly how the committee had arrived at its decisions. In addition, the absence of a decisional record rendered judicial review problematic.

Like the CRGR, the Regulatory Reform Task Force functioned as an institutional means of impeding new regulatory requirements. This goal was typically accomplished by requiring the staff to incorporate a cost-benefit analysis into its decision making. The imposition of such tests was controversial, however, because the Atomic Energy Act expressly prohibited the consideration of cost in safety matters. By placing a greater emphasis on economic analysis, the task force thus fueled perceptions that the NRC was more interested in protecting the nuclear industry than in the health and safety of the public.

Nowhere was this conflict more apparent than in the case of *backfitting,* a term that refers to the imposition of new regulatory requirements on plants after they have been issued a construction permit or operating license. Backfits had long been the bane of the nuclear industry, prompting one industry spokesman in 1974 to call it "the most onerous of all licensing requirements plaguing the nuclear industry."[72] With the number of backfits increasing after Three Mile Island, the industry stepped up its demands for relief, claiming that NRC staff issued backfits without adequate justification. Despite being unable to offer Congress any examples of unnecessary backfits imposed by the regulatory staff, the commission ordered the Regulatory Reform Task Force to draft a new rule. In the course of its deliberations, the task force met with industry representatives to discuss the financial impacts of backfitting, which the industry claimed were substantial. Critics of nuclear power were not invited to the meeting, however, giving them little opportunity to influence the rule. Although similar private, off-the-record meetings had sparked great controversy at the Environmental Protection Agency and the Department of the Interior, this meeting, possibly because of its obscure and technical nature, attracted little attention from either Congress or the national media.

As a result, the new backfit rule, issued in September 1985, reflected many of the industry's concerns. It required the staff to automatically prepare a cost-benefit analysis when determining whether and how existing plants should be backfit to meet the Atomic Energy Act's standard of "adequate protection" for public health and safety, and it specified a number of highly restrictive standards the staff would have to follow in making the decision. In effect, the task force instructed the staff not to impose backfits unless they could conclusively demonstrate that the changes were absolutely necessary—and that the safety benefits clearly outweighed the costs. Commissioner Asseltine said "the emphasis in the rule on cost considerations, particularly when coupled with the high standard for imposing a new requirement, is likely to have a strong chilling effect on the staff's consideration and development of new safety requirements."[73]

The new rule was challenged in federal court by the Union of Concerned Scientists, which argued that the Atomic Energy Act prohibited the NRC from considering cost in backfit decisions. In announcing its decision two years later, the D.C. Circuit agreed and struck down the rule, saying the NRC had to disregard cost when deciding whether existing plants should be backfit to meet the Atomic Energy Act's standard for adequate protection.[74] This ruling was not the only time antinuclear activists successfully resisted the administration's deregulatory efforts in the courts. Indeed, the courts proved to be one of the more important institutional safeguards devised by the public lobby regime in the fight against regulatory relief at the NRC.[75]

Restricting Public Participation

Many in the Reagan administration were convinced that the procedures and institutions crafted by the public lobby regime, specifically those intended to facilitate openness and public participation, posed a serious threat to Reagan's programmatic goals. Therefore, if regulatory policy were to be redirected, the White House would have to devise new decision-making procedures that would allow it to regain control of the regulatory process. This goal could be accomplished by issuing new rules and regulations that reduced public access to agency deliberations; if public lobby groups had fewer opportunities to participate, they would be less likely to influence policy.

Before examining some of these measures in greater detail, it is important to note again the NRC's long history of antagonism toward public participation, based on the perception that most intervenor groups were merely seeking to delay the operation of reactors. This antagonism persisted despite the fact that in September 1983 the NRC told Congress that public hearings had never delayed the operation of a single reactor. Some of the hostility can be traced to the agency's long-standing support of nuclear power, but some also can be attributed to the background of commission members who because of their training and experience tended to be technological optimists, prompting Commissioner Asseltine, an attorney, to remark that "all too often the technical members of the commission have tended to view procedural questions with some degree of impatience, saying that these are impediments to making decisions and getting on with the job."[76]

As one might expect, proposals designed to restrict participation generated fears that a more exclusive policy-making arena would inevitably tilt toward the nuclear industry. In fact, many of the NRC's maneuvers prompted political and legal challenges by critics of nuclear power and their allies in Congress. The Union of Concerned Scientists, for example, filed a number of lawsuits challenging the commission's efforts to insulate its decision making, and several key congressional subcommittees stepped up their oversight seeking to limit the NRC's regulatory relief activities.

Although the commission had become more receptive to public participation in the late 1970s, it remained one of the more hostile federal agencies and had been reprimanded several times by the federal courts for illegally closing meetings in direct violation of the Government in the Sunshine Act.[77] One of those cases involved a successful Common Cause challenge of an NRC decision to exclude the public from budget meetings. The ruling by the D.C. Circuit Court came after the NRC ignored the orders of a district court judge to open the meetings; the NRC's subsequent refusal to release the meeting transcripts prompted the same judge to threaten commission members with jail terms.[78]

The commission's opposition to public involvement took many forms, ranging from rules designed to restrict participation in rulemaking proceedings to legislative initiatives reducing the number of public hearings in the licensing process. In 1981, for example, the NRC proposed limiting intervenors' right to discovery to fifty questions. Because most license application were thousands of pages, this change would have been a significant obstacle to groups contesting the license. Somewhat later, the Regulatory Reform Task Force recommended three key rule changes that effectively made it harder to contest a license. The White House and NRC were at first unwilling to push the new rules, which had broad support from the nuclear industry but were opposed by an alliance of states, local governments, and intervenor groups on the grounds that they would make it virtually impossible for parties to gain admittance to commission proceedings. Despite these objections, the rule changes were eventually adopted in 1989.[79]

The new rules required petitioners to file a list of contentions with the presiding officer, together with a statement of alleged facts or expert opinions supporting the contentions, and to identify all documents and expert opinions they would use during the hearing. Proponents of the rule changes argued that existing rules permitted too many meritless and hypothetical contentions, while critics claimed the rules were unduly burdensome. In particular, critics charged that the new rules required potential intervenors to present their entire evidentiary case *before* they had even been admitted to the licensing proceeding and *before* the NRC staff had released its own safety evaluation. Critics also noted that under the regulations utilities are not required to furnish all of the necessary documentation supporting the application at the time it is first submitted. Intervenors were nevertheless expected to prepare their case within thirty days of receiving notice of the hearing, an unrealistic task given that it typically took the NRC staff months to review all the technical data involved in applications for construction permits or operating licenses.

Second, the new rules imposed strict limits on the right to cross-examina-tion.[80] Intervenors have to file special requests with the licensing board, showing why the point cannot be made through direct testimony. In addition, the rules bar the board from considering any request for cross-examination unless it is accom-panied by a detailed cross-examination plan that contains a discussion of the key issues to be raised as well as a list of potential questions. Opponents criticized the new rules as jeopardizing safety in order to move NRC proceedings along, while others claimed they would produce better questions, less repetition, and shorter proceedings. The rules also require intervenors to submit the cross-examination plans to the board within fifteen days of receiving written testimony. This re-quirement was a tremendous burden to intervenor groups because, as we have seen, many of them had a difficult time finding legal and scientific assistance.[81]

Third, the new regulations limited discovery to those facts supportive of the NRC staff position; intervenors have no discovery rights to other information.[82] As already discussed, limited resources often force intervenors to rely on staff ex-pertise and information to uncover potential problems. Intervenors must there-fore be able to understand the staff's position in order to participate meaning-fully in agency proceedings. Under the new discovery rules, outside parties face a tremendous burden in gathering information, especially information that con-tradicts the staff. It is as if the nation's criminal courts granted defense attorneys full discovery rights to evidence that implicated their clients while denying them access to evidence that exonerated them. In addition to the obvious questions of fairness, the discovery rules also raise serious questions of accountability. How can the staff be held accountable for decisions if the public cannot gain access to all of the information underlying them?

Not all of the efforts to restrict participation were administrative in nature. In 1983, for example, the NRC asked Congress to amend the Atomic Energy Act for the purpose of establishing a one-step licensing process. Under the law, reac-tor licensing was a two-stage process. In the first stage, utilities would apply for a construction permit, and the commission would hold a mandatory public hearing to consider the application. When the plant was nearing completion, the utility would then apply for an operating license; hearings would be held at this stage only if the license were contested, which most were by this time. Because Three Mile Island was still a vivid memory, however, Congress did not give these licens-ing proposals serious consideration.

But that did not deter the NRC. The following year, the Regulatory Reform Task Force proposed similar licensing changes, arguing that they could be en-acted administratively and did not require amending either the Atomic Energy Act or the Administrative Procedures Act. One of the proposals would have eliminated the Atomic Safety and Licensing Appeal Boards (ASLAB) as some-what independent appeal tribunals, granting that function to the commission it-self. Although this measure may have reduced delays, it also threatened to under-mine the agency's ability to conduct thorough and credible safety reviews. This was not the first time the NRC tried to undercut its own technical review bodies. In 1981 the commission proposed changes that would have limited *sua sponte* review by the Atomic Safety and Licensing Boards. Although rarely used, this procedure allowed licensing boards to raise serious safety questions on their own or to pursue them when intervenors ran out of money. The proposal to abolish the ASLAB was finally enacted in 1990. In a potentially significant venue change, its duties would now be undertaken by the commission itself, which had been decidedly less receptive to the claims of intervenor groups. Although the change may streamline future licensing proceedings, it also deprives potential intervenors of an opportunity to contest unfavorable decisions.

In the same spirit, in April 1989 the commission unanimously approved new rules that dramatically streamlined the licensing process while providing fewer opportunities for meaningful public participation. The new rules authorized the NRC to certify standardized reactor designs, to issue early site permits, and to issue combined construction permit/operating licenses to utilities referencing a certified standard design and an early site permit. The rule change was clearly intended to revive the moribund nuclear industry and pave the way for new reactor orders before the decade's end.

Standardized Reactor Designs

Standardized reactor designs were a critical element of the industry's comeback plans. In its haste to commercialize nuclear energy, the atomic subgovernment made several mistakes that eventually crippled the industry. During the Great Bandwagon Market of the 1960s, for example, utilities submitted incomplete designs that the AEC, charged with developing and promoting nuclear power, typically approved. Consideration of many key issues was repeatedly postponed until later in the licensing process, when they would be more difficult and more expensive to correct. More important, the accumulation of unresolved issues fed perceptions that reactors were unsafe and undermined public confidence in nuclear energy and its regulators. Another crucial mistake was the failure to follow France's lead and develop one or two standard designs. Instead, American utilities, often with no nuclear experience, rushed to order larger and larger reactors. Because the technology was new and changed so quickly, no two American designs were alike, which posed enormous difficulties in verifying the safety of individual plants and identifying problems in transferring the safety lessons from one reactor to another. Somewhat belatedly, the NRC had begun encouraging the industry to develop a small number of standardized reactor designs, which the staff could then evaluate for safety. According to the NRC, standardization of design would enhance plant safety and reliability while requiring fewer resources in safety reviews. Design certification, in turn, was intended to encourage the use of standardized designs by utilities and to contribute to the early resolution of licensing issues.

According to the new rules, standardized designs may be preapproved by rulemaking. The rulemaking proceedings include opportunities for public notice and comment and for an informal hearing before an NRC licensing board. If the NRC decides a design is acceptable, it issues a design certification, which is effective for fifteen years and may be renewed. Once a design is certified, the NRC does not have to repeat the review when a utility files an application for one of those preapproved designs, thereby saving time and staff resources.[83]

Most of the parties who commented on the new rules agreed on the desirability of reactor standardization and the early resolution of licensing issues. There were serious disagreements, however, on how designs should be certified. The Union of Concerned Scientists argued that certification proceedings should be formal adjudications, with full discovery rights and oral cross-examination, rather than informal rulemakings. According to the UCS, certification rulemakings held in the absence of any plans to actually build a reactor at a particular site are unlikely to be subjected to careful public scrutiny, especially if they are held at NRC headquarters. Under those circumstances, very few citizens would have an incentive to participate in such a rulemaking. Industry groups and the DOE opposed formal hearings, citing the possibility of lengthy delays.[84]

The new rules also authorize the NRC to issue early site permits, which are valid for up to twenty years, and allow persons to apply for and receive site permits before applying for a construction permit or combined license.[85] This provision was designed to resolve important issues before construction begins and before large investments have been made, in stark contrast to prior practice. A site permit does not authorize construction, but it does establish design criteria for plant construction on the proposed site. Accordingly, applications for early site permit must contain important safety-related information as well as details of emergency plans and the relevant environmental reports. The NRC is required to hold a mandatory formal hearing before the issuance of early site permits.[86]

Part 52 of the NRC Rules of Practice also establishes a process by which an applicant may obtain a combined license, or more accurately a construction permit with a conditional operating license.[87] The commission requires an applicant to provide a much higher level of detail concerning the facility than was needed for a construction permit under the old rules. At this point, the NRC must also set forth the acceptance criteria for the proposed plant. Acceptance criteria are the tests, inspections, and analyses the NRC must conduct after construction to determine that the facility has been built and will operate in conformity with the terms of its license and with the Atomic Energy Act. Before issuing a combined license, the NRC must hold a formal hearing and must find that the proposed final design complies with the Atomic Energy Act and all NRC regulations. If, however, a combined license application references a certified design and an early site permit, all of the issues resolved in those earlier proceedings are out of bounds in the hearing. Members of the public thus cannot contest either the site or the reactor design at the combined license hearing, even though those proceedings may have taken place fifteen years earlier.

After construction is completed, and not less than 180 days before the date scheduled for initial fuel loading, the NRC shall publish a notice of intended operation. Any person whose interest may be affected by the plant may request a hearing on whether the plant as constructed complies with the acceptance criteria of the license. According to the rules, a request for a hearing shall show, "prima facie, that one or more of the acceptance criteria in the combined license have not been met and, as result, there is a good cause" to modify or prevent operation. If the NRC finds that the acceptance criteria have been met, the licensing analysis is concluded, and the plant is allowed to begin operating immediately. The preoperation hearing, if any, is limited to the subject of compliance with the acceptance criteria. Members of the public who want to question the adequacy of the criteria in light of new developments are not entitled to a preoperational hearing. Any events that transpire during construction, including accidents at similar plants, construction problems, or other issues that were not anticipated when the acceptance criteria were initially developed, cannot be raised. Instead, persons seeking to contest those issues may file a petition to modify the terms and conditions of the license under 10 C.F.R. 2.206. Under the new rules, the commission will consider the petition but need not hold a hearing on the request.

The new rules revise the licensing process in two ways. First, by combining a construction permit and an operating license, the NRC hears and decides more licensing issues earlier in the process. Adequacy of emergency plans, for example, would be considered at the combined license stage rather than after the plant has already been built. Second, the new rules alter the postconstruction hearing opportunity by requiring the NRC to hold a hearing upon request only with regard to issues concerning the conformity of the plant with the acceptance criteria.[88]

The new rules were challenged by the Nuclear Information and Resource Service, a public lobby group that had often been critical of the NRC. In discussing the new rules, Michael Mariotte, the group's executive director, said that "it seems to me that it is contradictory for the nuclear power industry and the NRC to acknowledge, on the one hand, that the key to their revival is increased public confidence, and on the other hand to be seeking to reduce the public's ability to participate in licensing decisions."[89] The group claimed that the rule changes violated the two-step licensing process established in the Atomic Energy Act. The D.C. Circuit Court agreed, ruling unanimously that the NRC must make a "postconstruction, pre-operation finding that a plant will operate in conformity" with the standards of the Atomic Energy Act. The court added that the NRC also must provide an opportunity for a public hearing to consider any significant new information that came to light after a plant's initial licensing.[90] The NRC appealed, however, and after a rehearing en banc, in 1992 the full Court of Appeals upheld the new rules.[91] In adopting the Energy Policy Act later that year, Congress amended the Atomic Energy Act to incorporate the rule changes, handing supporters of nuclear power an important victory in their long battle to alter the statutes governing reactor licensing. In the future, persons seeking to contest reactor licenses would have fewer opportunities to do so.

These were not the only examples, however, of NRC efforts to restrict participation. In April 1985 the commission voted to further reduce public access to commission meetings and to limit the availability of transcripts from closed meetings. The changes were proposed by Chairman Palladino, who argued that open meetings prevented the commissioners from engaging in frank and collegial discussions. The new rule was implemented immediately without advance notice or a public hearing on the matter. The NRC's action prompted Edward Markey, chairman of the House Subcommittee on Energy and the Environment, to say that the proposed changes reflected the NRC's "bunker mentality."[92]

The NRC exhibited the same traits when it voted in 1986 to change its rules to prohibit statements of dissent in letters to Congress, requiring the dissenting commissioners to mail their statements separately to Congress. The rule change, proposed by new chairman Lando Zech, was aimed directly at Commissioner Asselltine, who dissented in one-third to one-half of the commission's letters to Congress. Ironically, Asselltine believed that his views actually received greater attention in Congress because of the rule change.

In raising numerous obstacles to effective public participation, the NRC was seeking to transform its regulatory process. But the commission met with limited success, largely because public lobby groups like the Union of Concerned Scientists and their primary congressional allies, such as Markey and Ottinger, played key roles in resisting many of its initiatives. It did not help that many of the NRC's measures were perceived as heavy-handed and thus provoked considerable opposition.

Selective Enforcement of Regulations

A third approach to regulatory relief at the NRC involved changing or waiving regulations that threatened to close existing plants or to delay the licensing of new ones. In several cases where plants did not meet the regulations, the NRC simply changed the regulations to facilitate licensing. The commission's handling of the "operator qualification" regulation offers a good example. NRC regulations required applicants for reactor operator licenses at new plants to have "extensive actual operating experience at a comparable reactor."[93] But when the commission discovered in 1984 that the regulatory staff had interpreted this rule to allow experience on reactor simulators—not real reactors—to count as "actual" experience, they changed the rule. Henceforth, simulator experience would be acceptable. What was especially noteworthy about this rule change was that it occurred on the very same day the commission was to vote on the operating license for the Diablo Canyon plant, whose operators coincidentally had no actual operating experience. In addition, the commission decided that all licenses issued previously would be exempted from the new rule. Commissioner Gilinsky objected, arguing that a blanket exemption was essentially a rulemaking which, under the Administrative Procedures Act, would require the NRC to solicit and consider public comment. This stipulation was not met, and later that day the NRC issued Diablo Canyon a low-power license.[94]

The most notorious rule change involved the Seabrook and Shoreham nuclear plants, the most controversial reactors in the nation's history. After the accident at Three Mile Island revealed serious flaws in emergency and evacuation planning, the NRC issued new emergency planning regulations that required an emergency planning zone (EPZ) within a ten-mile radius of nuclear plants. The new rules also required state and local government approval of evacuation plans for all people living within the EPZ. No utility could receive an operating license until the Federal Emergency Management Administration (FEMA) approved the local evacuation plans. The problem facing the owners of the Shoreham and Seabrook plants was that state and county officials refused to prepare emergency plans, claiming that both reactors were located in areas that made evacuation impossible. Shoreham was located near New York City in heavily populated Long Island, while Seabrook was in a popular New Hampshire beach resort. According to NRC rules, then, the plants could not be licensed.

The new rules clearly gave state and local officials greater influence in nuclear decision making, and by 1983 the evacuation issue was becoming a major problem for the industry and the NRC. A Department of Energy study revealed that over 60 percent of the nation's reactors lacked formally approved evacuation plans and thus failed to meet the new requirements. In fact, the industry and the NRC feared that Seabrook and Shoreham would become models for opponents seeking to block nuclear plants. As we have seen, state and local officials were becoming increasingly critical of nuclear power, and the emergency planning regulations gave them a powerful new weapon to block reactor construction and licensing. Some utilities complained that local governments were using the evacuation issue to pressure utilities into paying a higher share of the plant's costs to the community. Proponents of nuclear power, including some members of Congress, urged the commission to find some way of issuing the licenses regardless of local participation.

As a result, the commission urged the regulatory staff to explore ways of shrinking the size of the emergency planning zone, thereby obviating the necessity for participation by some local governments. In the case of Seabrook, which was near the Massachusetts border, reducing the emergency planning zone would eliminate the need for approval from Massachusetts officials such as Governor Michael Dukakis, who opposed the plant. The NRC had established the ten-mile radius because earlier studies indicated that radiation levels dropped off sharply at that distance. The NRC was hoping new studies would show that the ten-mile radius was too conservative. But the NRC's research did not go as planned, leading Vic Stello, the NRC's executive director of operations, to inform the commission that the research could not support a reduction in the EPZ.[95] In the interim, the NRC revised its rules to allow a utility to proceed with low-power testing pending final approval of local evacuation plans. The Union of Concerned Scientists immediately filed suit against the NRC. As in a number of other instances, the UCS prevailed when the D.C. Circuit ruled that the NRC could not allow low-level testing until the evacuation plans had been tested and approved.[96]

Shortly thereafter, the staff proposed a new regulation that waived the requirement that state and local officials participate in evacuation plans. Instead, the commission would be allowed to issue an operating license if the plant's owners could demonstrate a "good faith effort" to gain local cooperation and had developed their own "reasonable" evacuation plans to compensate for the lack of cooperation by state and local officials. According to internal staff memos, the proposal was motivated by the frustration caused by local resistance to the licensing of completed plants. When he learned of the staff proposal, Representative Markey called it "unconstitutional and outrageous," saying the NRC was on the verge of declaring open warfare on state governments.[97]

Caught in the middle of a political firestorm, the NRC convened a long and contentious hearing on the proposed rule change in February 1987. A parade of public officials, including representatives of FEMA, attacked the proposal. New York governor Mario Cuomo called the new rule "absurd," adding that the commission appeared to be motivated by a "desire to protect commercial utility interests" rather than public health and safety. Ironically, he quoted from Ronald Reagan's 1984 letter to Republican House member William Carney in which Reagan said he did not favor overruling local concerns in licensing matters. This shows that, at least in the case of nuclear power, the administration would jettison its general policy of delegating regulatory authority to the states. Reagan's New Federalism apparently had limits. In the end, and despite all of the controversy, the commission voted to adopt the rule, allowing sixty days for public comment.[98]

At Markey's urging, the House Interior and Insular Affairs Committee held hearings on the proposal in April. During these hearings, the NRC's rationale for the rule change quickly became apparent. In defending its actions, the commission cited reasons of "equity and fairness," saying it would be wrong to allow a utility to invest billions of dollars only to permit late local opposition to prevent the plant's licensing. What was remarkable about this argument was that the commission had been arguing for years that evacuation planning was proper only after a plant had been built, and that cost would not be a factor in making the final decision on whether to issue an operating license. In fact, the commission had actively sought to prevent consideration of the evacuation issue at the construction permit stage of the licensing process. In effect, the commission's handling of this issue precluded consideration of whether any effective emergency plans could be developed until the plant had already been built and billions of dollars invested.[99]

Undeterred, the NRC later voted unanimously to adopt the new rule. Henceforth, utilities would be allowed to develop and test their own evacuation plans in the absence of plans offered by state and local governments. As one would expect with such a controversial regulation, it was challenged in court, this time by the Commmonwealth of Massachusetts. In this case, however, the NRC prevailed, as the Court of Appeals for the First Circuit upheld the new evacuation rule.[100]

Eventually, President Reagan intervened in the controversy by issuing an executive order in November 1988 that gave the federal government broad new authority to draft emergency evacuation plans. According to the order, FEMA would be allowed to draft emergency plans if state and local governments refused to participate. Although the decision had been made weeks earlier, its announcement was postponed until after the 1988 presidential election because the White House did not want to provide Michael Dukakis, the Democratic nominee, with a potentially helpful issue. Even the executive order was not enough to save the Shoreham plant, whose cost had now risen to $5.4 billion and threatened to plunge the plant's owners into bankruptcy. After extended negotiations, the Long Island Lighting Company (LILCO) agreed to sell the plant to the state of New York for one dollar and an annual 5 percent rate increase for ten years. The state would then dismantle the plant. In spite of the agreement, the NRC later voted unanimously to issue a full-power operating license to Shoreham. Observers noted that the NRC was trying to send a message to the industry and the public that it was not responsible for Shoreham's demise.

The Shoreham saga lingered on for another three years, at a cost to LILCO of $400,000 per day, awaiting NRC approval for state officials to rid the plant of radioactivity caused by low-power testing. In the interim, Iraq's invasion of Kuwait renewed fears of another energy crisis and prompted the Bush administration to consider ordering the NRC to block the plant's dismantling. In the eyes of White House chief of staff John Sununu, a fervent advocate of nuclear power, Shoreham was a "national asset" that should not be discarded. The NRC rejected the administration's pleas and cleared the way for Shoreham's demise by changing its license to "possession only," which allowed LILCO to transfer ownership to the state. The Justice Department then unsuccessfully sued the NRC to force a review of the environmental consequences of dismantling the reactor. When the NRC authorized decontamination in 1992, Shoreham became the first large-scale commerical plant to begin decommissioning. At an estimated cost of $1 billion, decommissioning would bring the plant's total cost to approximately $6.5 billion.[101]

Seabrook's fate, on the other hand, was quite different. Although its original owners had been forced into bankruptcy by the huge cost overruns, the plant eventually received its operating license in 1989 and has since operated without incident. The emergency planning issue vividly demonstrates the commitment to nuclear power on behalf of the NRC and the Reagan and Bush administrations, who did whatever they could to facilitate licensing of the two plants. When the NRC's own regulations threatened to delay the plants, they were simply changed or waived. When state and local opposition mounted, executive orders could pre-empt their authority, even if that meant contradicting the administration's own ideological preference for devolving power to state and local governments. The emergency planning issue also illustrates that unwavering presidential and NRC support, although important, is not decisive. Given the decentralized nature of nuclear policy making, at least some policy battles were waged in venues they could not control. State and local officials, for example, played a crucial role in the issue, and many resented the heavy-handed actions of the White House and the NRC to license the plants over their objections.

The emergency planning issue was not the only example of the NRC chang-ing a rule that threatened to close existing plants. In 1991 the NRC issued a rule allowing utilities to apply for twenty-year extensions of their operating licenses. Under the new rule, plants granted the extensions will be allowed to operate be-yond the forty years for which they were initially licensed.[102] The nuclear industry sought the rule change because the nation's reactor population was aging, and the licenses of a significant number of plants would expire within ten to fifteen years. By the year 2000, in fact, 62 of the nation's 109 reactors will be twenty years or older, and total nuclear generating capacity could begin to decrease as reactors reach the end of their initial operating licenses. Extending licenses is consider-ably less expensive than building new generating plants and thus offers utilities a cost-effective way of ensuring the adequacy of future generating capacity. It also guarantees, at least temporarily, the continued survival of the nuclear indus-try, which produces approximately one-fifth of the nation's electricity. Since no new reactor orders are expected in the near future, it is essential that existing reactors stay on-line to keep the nuclear option alive. Reactor vendors wor-ried that if current licenses were allowed to expire, any new generating capacity would almost certainly come from natural gas or coal, and that nuclear electric-ity would gradually become a less important component of the nation's total en-ergy mix.

The licensing extension rulemaking elicited nearly two hundred comments from interested parties. Recent events had suggested that reactor components were aging more rapidly than anticipated, and critics of the proposed rule argued that age-related degradation raised significant safety questions that must be evaluated before renewal licenses could be granted, especially because such is-sues had not been treated comprehensively in initial plant licensing proceedings. Of particular concern was the knowledge that over time, exposure to radia-tion embrittled reactor vessels. In the event of a loss of cooling accident, the emergency core-cooling system would deliver cold water to the reactor and the resulting stress could cause the reactor vessel to crack. The NRC agreed that age-related degradation was a critical new issue, and the extension rule afforded an opportunity for a formal public hearing to consider the adequacy of the utilities' proposals to address the problem. In reviewing renewal applications, however, the NRC will not require plants to meet the more demanding standards and criteria that apply to newer plants.

According to the NRC, existing plants have been inspected and reviewed many times since their initial licensing, providing reasonable assurance that continued operation will not endanger public health and safety.[103] The NRC did not acknowledge that many reactors could not satisfy the more rigorous standards and almost certainly would be forced to shut down. The new rule also stipulates that certain issues, such as the adequacy of current licensing criteria and the applicant's compliance history, are outside the scope of license renewal proceedings. Potential intervenors thus cannot contest a renewal application on the grounds that the license holder has a history of failing to operate the plant according to NRC regulations. As in other cases, public hearings will be allowed, but intervenors will be prevented from raising critical issues. The terms of the new rule suggest, in short, that the commission was more interested in extending the operating life of nuclear reactors than in protecting public health and safety.

CONCLUSIONS

Presidential involvement is a key element in nuclear politics, but even the strong support of the Reagan and Bush administrations could not bring about a fundamental shift in nuclear policy. To be sure, there were some significant accomplishments. By end of the decade, the nuclear industry had moved closer, via legislation or administrative action, to securing most of its goals: the creation of one-step licensing; new rules for license extensions and the certification of standardized reactor designs; reauthorization of the Price-Anderson Act; legislation addressing the nuclear waste issue; and federal subsidies for advanced reactor research. NRC rule changes, moreover, ensured that many of the venues used by antinuclear activists in the past would be harder to access in the future. Although these measures may someday yield results and facilitate the licensing of new reactors, they nevertheless fell short of what the beleaguered industry and its supporters had sought.

There were several reasons for the failure to deregulate in this area. First, proponents of deregulation were unable to offer convincing empirical or theoretical arguments for the changes they sought. Despite all of its rhetoric about licensing delays, for example, the NRC was unable to show that those delays were primarily the fault of intervenor groups; nor could the commission, when pressed by Congress, cite examples of the regulatory staff imposing unnecessary backfits. Deregulators thus failed to do what is required of those seeking fundamental change: convince people that there was something wrong with existing policy. In fact, Congress, the courts, and the public repeatedly expressed support for a strong regulatory presence. According to Eads and Fix, a successful regulatory review program must be perceived as fair, open, and driven by "neutrally applied principles."[104] Seen in this light, the private meetings with the nuclear industry, the rules restricting public participation, and the selective enforcement of regulations violated norms of open decision making and discredited the NRC. Moreover, the emphasis on regulatory costs at the expense of public safety struck many as inappropriate. As Derthick and Quirk have argued, it is more difficult to deregulate in environmental and health issues because they affect many people, are dramatic, and attract considerable media attention. These factors seriously limited Reagan and Bush's ability to pursue deregulatory initiatives.[105]

It is also clear that the procedural and institutional reforms crafted during the public lobby era played a crucial role in blocking deregulatory proposals. Frustrated by the inability of regulatory agencies and presidents to secure the public interest, public lobbyists set out to infuse administrative politics with the ideals of participatory democracy. The resulting changes enabled a cross-institutional partnership of congressional staff and subcommittees, the federal courts, public lobby groups, and state and local governments to assume a central role in administering regulatory policy. Because many of these reforms were created by law, they could not be overcome by executive action alone. Equally important, some of the changes allowed previously excluded interests, such as public lobby groups and state and local governments, to become fixtures in nuclear politics, possessing both the incentive and the means to protect their newfound influence. Acting as vigorous watchdogs, these new actors successfully resisted actions that threatened the relatively new regulatory status quo, frequently with the support of allies who controlled strategic junctures in the policy arena. Litigation, for example, was a particularly effective resource for antinuclear groups and the states, with the federal courts protecting their right to participate in regulatory decision making and blocking many of the NRC's deregulatory proposals. Sympathetic members of Congress, such as Ed Markey, were also formidable obstacles to regulatory relief, thanks to committee reorganizations that placed them at the top of the NRC's oversight subcommittees. Once one of the least scrutinized federal agencies, the NRC was soon being examined under a microscope, subjected to persistent criticisms that it was an "industry lapdog."[106]

That state and local governments played a crucial role in thwarting the Reagan/Bush initiatives is particularly ironic. Shifting authority from the federal government to the states after all was a key element of the Republican policy of New Federalism. States, it was argued, were more responsive, innovative, and efficient than the federal government and should therefore assume greater programmatic responsibilities. In the case of nuclear power, however, Presidents Reagan and Bush sought to bypass state and local governments and shift the final decisions on key matters to Congress, the Department of Energy, or the NRC, which have been more supportive of the nuclear industry. As I illustrate in this study, however, such efforts were ultimately unsuccessful. The federal monopoly on nuclear power is clearly over, and state and local governments are now active participants in reactor siting, emergency planning, rate regulation, and nuclear waste disposal. In fact, as state, county, and local officials have won more control over nuclear regulation, the resulting decentralization of political control hinders the ability of program supporters to engineer a political or economic recovery. According to Christian Joppke, this decentralization can explain why nuclear power remains stalled even though the national government is supportive and the national antinuclear movement has essentially disappeared.[107]

The net effect of the many procedural and institutional reforms enacted during the 1970s was to thwart deregulatory initiatives. Antinuclear groups were now part of the extended policy community and could use their positions to press for effective regulation of the nuclear industry. The same was true of state and local governments. The result was a form of policy stasis: critics of nuclear power were unable to convince policymakers to completely forgo the nuclear option, while proponents were unable to secure the statutory changes that might be needed to revive a moribund industry. Instead, nuclear regulation focused primarily on battles over those plants already in the licensing pipeline.

9

Nuclear Power in the 1990s and Beyond

Time will come when we know what happened here
Change will come in time and make it clear
We learn one thing if we learn at all
In the secret wars we call our lives
Anything can happen.

—Jackson Browne

There are currently 110 nuclear reactors operating in the United States, producing 21.1 percent of the nation's total utility-generated electricity. Six other units have valid construction permits, but work on all six has been canceled or postponed and it is unlikely that any of them will ever be built. Indeed, the last nuclear units under construction in the United States were abandoned in December 1994, when the Tennessee Valley Authority, citing escalating costs, canceled work on three reactors.[1] With half of today's plants reaching the end of their forty-year licenses in the decade between 2005 and 2015, it is quite possible that the high-water mark for nuclear power in the United States has come and gone.

This chapter begins with a discussion of the current status of nuclear power in the United States. Particular attention will be paid to the key issues confronting the industry in the 1990s, including trends in electricity usage, nuclear waste disposal, the recent shift to a deregulated and intensely competitive electric power market, and the policies of the Clinton White House. I argue that this combination of circumstances is unlikely to foster a favorable climate for a nuclear power revival. On the contrary, the current mix of economic and political conditions will likely lead to a continuation of the policy drift that has characterized nuclear politics for much of the last two decades. What distinguishes nuclear power in the 1990s, however, is that the issue no longer occupies a prominent place on either the systemic or governmental agendas. Although popular and elite understandings of nuclear power are still overwhelmingly negative, attention levels are quite low. About the only time the general public and most policymakers pay attention to the issue is in the context of the never-ending debates over nuclear waste and reactor safety. If these conditions persist—and they show no sign of changing in the near future—a rebirth of nuclear power is unlikely.

TRENDS IN ENERGY DEMAND

During nuclear power's heyday in the 1960s, electricity demand grew at an annual rate of 7 percent, nearly two times the rate of economic growth. Many utilities, expecting the high growth rates to continue, ordered additional generating capacity. The annual growth rate slowed dramatically in the 1970s, however, and has remained low ever since, averaging 2.9 percent in the period from 1983–93. As a result, for much of this period the United States had excess generating capacity. According to the Energy Information Administration, moreover, the annual growth rate for electricity demand is expected to be even lower in the years ahead, averaging between 0.8 percent and 1.4 percent until 2010. Lower economic growth rates and greater energy efficiency are primarily responsible for the reduced consumption.[2]

Before building any new generating capacity, the nation's utilities are expected to meet demand growth through the relicensing or repowering of existing plants, by importing power from Canada and Mexico, through demand-side management, or through purchases from cogeneration.[3] Even with these options, however, the Department of Energy projects that 450 new generating plants with a total of 135 gigawatts of capacity will be needed by 2010 to meet growing demand and to offset plant closures. Even this expansion is not expected to aid the nuclear power industry, however, because the DOE expects gas-fired or oil and gas–fired combined-cycle and combustion turbine technology to provide over 60 percent of any new generating capacity. These technologies, which have relatively low initial capital costs and are highly efficient and comparatively clean, are expected to have numerous advantages over nuclear power. In fact, it is estimated that by 2010, natural gas will supplant nuclear power as the nation's second largest source of electric power.[4] On the other hand, the DOE is projecting a 32 percent drop in nuclear-generated electricity by 2015 owing to the expected retirements of many existing reactors. It is always possible, of course, that reactor licenses may be extended beyond their forty-year terms, but it is also possible that utilities may opt to close reactors rather than undertake expensive modifications.

DEREGULATION IN THE ELECTRIC UTILITY MARKETS

The future of commercial nuclear power in the United States is also clouded by the dramatic changes currently under way in the electric power industry. Deregulation and increased competition unleashed by the Energy Policy Act of 1992 are transforming the industry, and it is not yet clear whether these developments will help or hurt nuclear power.[5] The 1992 law allows established utilities and independent power producers to compete freely in the wholesale power market and provides independent producers with greater access to utility-owned transmission lines. Provisions of the law amend the Public Utility Holding Company Act of 1935 (PUHCA) and thus curtail federal regulation of utility holding company structures that own wholesale generation facilities.[6] The new law allows utilities to operate independent wholesale plants outside their geographic territories and encourages independent producers to build and operate their own generating plants.

Although the effects of the new law are far from certain, the wholesale power market is becoming increasingly competitive as independent power producers and cogeneration have emerged as cheaper alternatives to utility-owned electric generation. In many states, when a need for new energy sources is identified, the competition among utility and nonutility producers is fierce, prompting utilities to reduce their costs in order to remain competitive. Indeed, some expect that competition will eventually force utilities to withdraw from the generation business and become strictly transmission and service providers.[7]

A growing number of state public utility commissions (PUC) also have taken steps to promote competition in their power markets. In an effort to prevent utilities from dominating the pool of power suppliers in the state, for example, California regulators have asked the state's utilities to divest themselves of half of their generation plants.[8] Some PUCs, concerned that traditional cost-based pricing does not provide utilities with sufficient incentives to reduce costs and provide electricity at the lowest possible rates, are now considering alternatives, such as price caps and retail wheeling. In essence, retail wheeling ends the local utility's monopoly and allows customers to choose their power suppliers just as they now choose their long-distance telephone carriers. Although California is leading the way, other states are taking similar steps to open their wholesale power markets to competition. In Michigan, for example, customers of the state's two largest utilities are now allowed to buy their power from other utilities or from nonutility sources, while several other states are considering plans to allow all of their residential and commercial customers to choose their power suppliers.[9]

At least in the short run, the newly competitive environment and the cost cutting it has induced have generated severe economic pressures for some utilities. The economic pressures are especially intense in New England, where utilities are heavily dependent on high-cost nuclear power. As a case in point, 60 percent of Northeast Utilities' power comes from nuclear plants—at double the average cost of power from the company's coal plants.[10] In other regions as well, it seems likely that nuclear utilities will come under increasing economic stress as they are forced to compete with lower cost electricity producers. It is expected,

for example, that many of the generating facilities operated by independent producers will be small to midsized and will rely on cheaper gas and coal technologies. According to Gary Miller, chief executive of Argon Consulting Group, high
operating and maintenance costs could lead to the retirement of ten to twenty
reactors in the next decade. Other analysts predict even more early retirements
because state regulators will be unwilling to allow utilities to charge ratepayers
for major repairs and shutdowns.[11]

With utilities struggling to cut costs, there are growing concerns about their
ability to maintain adequate reactor safety margins. In a departure from previous
practice, utilities are no longer exempting nuclear plants from cost-cutting measures. Northeast Utilities, for example, is $4 billion in debt and has announced
plans to reduce its workforce of three thousand nuclear employees by one-third
by the end of the century. According to the company, technical employees will be
shared among its nuclear plants and will not compromise safety. Others are not
so sure, citing the firm's troubled Millstone 3 and Connecticut Yankee plants,
which the NRC has threatened to close permanently unless the utility can prove
they are safe to operate. The utility is spending $15 million per month for replace-
ment power while the plants undergo repairs.[12] Then there is the case of the firm's
Maine Yankee plant. Co-owned by the Central Maine Power Company, the plant
was closed for most of 1995, and repairs and replacement costs reduced earnings
by 45 percent. The Union of Concerned Scientists claims that economic pressures
related to deregulation led the plant's owners to falsify test results in order to
conceal potential safety problems that would have kept the plant off-line for a
longer period.[13]

For its part, the NRC has expressed concern that deregulation is creating unprecedented economic pressures for nuclear utilities. Ivan Selin, NRC chair until 1995, said that although there was little evidence that reduced staffing at reactors had compromised safety, it certainly provided "an incentive to cut corners"
at expensive reactors. Selin added, "Utilities may be tempted to put off capital
investments that we consider necessary to maintain the equipment in top shape.
We have to be that much more alert about the safety implications." Accordingly,
noted Selin, the commission would begin considering whether financial pressures were straining the parent utility's resources and jeopardizing reactor
safety.[14]

On the other hand, it is conceivable that a restructured electric market could
open the door to new reactor orders. Some argue that the financing for a new generation of reactors most likely would come from independent power producers
rather than from utilities, because the independents would be able to base their
profits on revenues from the electricity produced and sold rather than on the
amount of capital invested in their plants.[15] Barring dramatic changes in the regulatory environment, however, it is hard to imagine any investors undertaking the
enormous financial risk of building a nuclear plant. It is much safer, and cheaper,
to build less controversial gas, coal, or solar facilities.

NUCLEAR WASTE

The failure to resolve the high-level nuclear waste issue continues to plague the industry's future as well. Although Congress in 1987 selected Yucca Mountain, Nevada, as the likely site for the nation's first high-level repository, the project is years behind schedule, billions over budget, and mired in political gridlock. In the words of Thomas P. Grumbly, DOE's assistant secretary for environmental management, "To even describe this as a coherent program right now is really a problem."[16] Despite having spent over $4 billion studying the site, the Department of Energy has been unable to determine whether the site would satisfy EPA guidelines, which require that high-level repositories isolate radioactivity for a period of ten thousand years, twice the span of recorded history. Indeed, given the many unknowns involving the risk of earthquakes, the movement of underground water, and the effects of high temperatures on the surrounding rock, many scientists are skeptical that the Yucca site will ever be proven safe. According to the most optimistic estimates, even if the site is found to be suitable, the earliest the facility could open would be 2010, twelve years after the Nuclear Waste Policy Act's 1998 deadline. Furthermore, even if the facility were built as planned, it still would be too small to hold the estimated 93,000 tons of spent fuel that will have built up by 2033.[17]

Opposition in Nevada has intensified in the wake of recent congressional attempts to accelerate the construction of the Yucca Mountain repository. Weary of the lack of progress, congressional Republicans introduced legislation that would require the DOE to begin construction of a repository at Yucca Mountain. In addition, the bill would allow Yucca to become an interim storage site even if the secretary of energy later determined that it should not be the permanent repository. As one might expect, the proposed legislation was the focus of intense debate, with Nevada officials claiming that this move was yet another attempt to force the state to accept the repository. In protest of the proposed measure, Nevada's two senators took the unusual step of filibustering the defense appropriations bill, holding it up for several weeks. The proposal did not become law, at least in part because of a threatened White House veto, but it did breathe new life into the nuclear waste controversy.[18]

Frustrated by the failure to site a permanent high-level repository, the nuclear power industry has argued that interim storage legislation is crucial to its survival. The industry's problem is that without a permanent repository spent reactor fuel continues to pile up at nuclear plants across the country, raising concerns about safety and cost. To date, the nation's nuclear plants have produced thirty thousand tons of spent fuel rods, most of which is stored on-site in cooling ponds. The ponds were not designed as permanent storage facilities, however, and most are too small to accommodate the quantities of waste being generated. When the pools fill up, as many have, they then are packed into steel casks and stored aboveground in concrete igloos. Most utilities need state regulatory approval in

order to expand their on-site storage facilities, and given the intense public opposition to nuclear waste facility siting, it is unlikely that many states will readily
approve such requests.[19] The more likely scenario is a proliferation of disputes
over nuclear waste, as state regulators are asked to approve the storage plans.

Indeed, there is considerable evidence that the states are as unhappy as the
nuclear industry with the failure to locate a permanent repository. Citing concerns with fairness and cost, both are seeking to force the DOE to take the waste
off their hands. Although consumers have paid nearly $12 billion into the Nuclear
Waste Fund, the opening of a repository is decades away. A number of states and
utilities have asked for the money back. Commenting on the situation, Michigan's attorney general said forcing consumers to pay for a site and not building
one was "nothing more than a high-level swindle . . . perpetrated by our own federal government."[20] In 1994, moreover, a group of energy authorities from twenty
states sued the DOE in federal court contending that the Nuclear Waste Policy
Act required the federal government to assume ownership of high-level nuclear
waste in 1998. Seeking to defer action, Energy Secretary Hazel O'Leary argued
that the law required the federal government to take possession of high-level
waste only after a permanent repository is completed. In ruling for the states, the
D.C. Circuit Court said the agency's arguments were inconsistent with the law,
but given the lack of either an interim or permanent storage facility, it is unclear
exactly how the DOE will be capable of resolving the issue. For the foreseeable
future, then, the nuclear waste issue will continue to dog the industry.

DECOMMISSIONING

In recent years the industry also has been plagued by the question of what to do
with nuclear plants once they reach the end of their useful lives. Over time, the
buildings and equipment in nuclear reactors become highly radioactive and thus
difficult to handle, transport, or store. As in the case of nuclear waste, early advocates of nuclear power opted to build first and ask the hard questions later, assuming that an acceptable solution eventually would be found. Instead, consideration of the decommissioning issue was postponed indefinitely because it was
either unglamorous or threatened to impede the commercialization of nuclear
power. In any event, the industry is now scrambling to find a solution; nine nuclear units have already been retired, and it is likely that numerous others will
close in the next decade.[21]

Nuclear Regulatory Commission rules require that plant owners decommis-
sion their facilities once they have been officially retired. Specifically, this requirement means all radioactive materials must be removed from the site and resid-
ual radioactivity must be reduced to a level permitting the site to be used for
any other purpose.[22] Utilities have three decommissioning options: they can dismantle the plant and decontaminate the site; they can "mothball" the plant for

several years until the level of radioactivity has diminished and then dismantle it; or they can entomb the plant in concrete and build a fence around it.[23]

Decommissioning poses several problems for the nuclear industry. First, utilities have very little experience dismantling nuclear reactors. The first commercial plant to begin decommissioning is Yankee Rowe 1 in Massachusetts, which was closed in 1992. As a result, the plant's owners are in uncharted waters and will have to learn as they go. Given the unique design of most U.S. reactors, it is unclear how much one utility can learn from the experiences of others. Second, decommissioning is expected to be very expensive, although cost estimates vary widely, in part because of the lack of experience. Managers of the Yankee Rowe plant have estimated that decommissioning will cost $370 million, which is almost ten times the reactor's original construction cost and double the original estimate.[24] Because the Yankee Rowe plant is relatively small (185 MW), it is likely that costs would be much higher for larger reactors. How utilities will pay for decommissioning is thus an important question.

The NRC and a number of state public utility commissions have recognized the potential expense and require utilities to establish funds to pay for decommissioning. Some states allow plant owners to cover the costs by raising their rates; others have prohibited that practice. For its part, the NRC requires utilities to set aside $105–135 million for decommissioning, but this figure is woefully inadequate given the cost of dismantling Yankee Rowe. The NRC also requires plant owners to prepare decommissioning plans, which include either their own cost estimates or a written certification that they have met the NRC's cost estimates. Although most utilities have had a difficult time complying with these requirements, the NRC has been reluctant to take enforcement action.[25]

NUCLEAR POWER AND THE CLINTON WHITE HOUSE

Until the Nixon administration, presidents played virtually no role in nuclear politics. With few exceptions, Presidents Truman, Eisenhower, Kennedy, and Johnson were mostly uninvolved in nuclear policy and left key decisions to the AEC and JCAE. This is consistent with subgovernment theories, which suggest that long periods of presidential inattention are crucial to maintaining the policy status quo. Because of their unrivaled ability to focus public attention on issues, however, presidential action can also be a key force in conflict expansion and policy change. In responding to concerns about reactor safety, Presidents Nixon and Carter, for example, helped redefine the nuclear issue and elevated it from the shadows of subgovernment politics. Presidents Reagan and Bush, by contrast, sought to roll back the scope of federal regulatory activity. Although there were few legislative victories, they did succeed in restricting access to the NRC and worked to ensure that the agency would be acutely sensitive to the nuclear industry's pleas for regulatory relief.

The election of Bill Clinton in 1992 thus raises a number of interesting questions for students of nuclear politics. As a Democrat, Clinton would presumably embrace a different regulatory philosophy and would be more receptive to the concerns of public lobby groups, including those opposed to nuclear power. Unlike his predecessors, Clinton generally has been more supportive of social regulation. The National Performance Review, for example, notes that regulation has "significantly improved our quality of life."[26] These sentiments are a far cry from the fundamental objections to federal action raised by antiregulatory forces in Republican administrations.

Indeed, Clinton's victory promised to end the debate over the legitimacy of federal regulation. In the words of Vice President Al Gore, "The argument is no longer pro-regulation or anti-regulation. The argument is about how we regulate."[27] Accordingly, the administration set out to transform the methods of regulatory decision making in order to create a more efficient, responsive, and accountable regulatory program. The Clinton White House has rejected the insulated and secretive practices characteristic of the Reagan and Bush years, and as a result, regulatory review is characterized by greater openness and opportunities for public participation. A wider range of viewpoints is now considered, and industry groups no longer have privileged access.

In other ways, however, President Clinton's approach to regulation is strikingly similar to that of Reagan and Bush. With few exceptions, the Clinton White House has not sought to expand significantly the regulatory commitments of the federal government. On the contrary, Clinton's State of the Union proclamation that "the era of big government is over" seemed to signal the triumph of Reagan's conservative, antiregulatory philosophy. Like his predecessors, Clinton recognizes that "command and control" regulation is often inefficient and has expressed a desire to create a more flexible, market-oriented approach that focuses more on results and less on narrow compliance with rules. Similarly, the administration's claim that its regulatory review proposals are designed to "lighten the load for regulated industries and make government regulations that are needed more cost-effective" could have been made by either Ronald Reagan or George Bush.[28]

For all its attention to improving regulatory procedures, however, the Clinton White House has yet to offer a clear picture of its regulatory goals. Whereas Reagan and Bush clearly sought to roll back regulatory programs, the Clinton administration vacillates between activism and retrenchment and often fails to provide agencies with clear signals about its intentions.[29] There is no overarching regulatory philosophy to guide agency decision making. In the words of one observer, "This is a centrist administration. They want win-win solutions. They want things that will make both sides happy or both sides equally unhappy."[30]

This appears to be the case with the NRC, which has received little attention from the Clinton White House. Outside of a 1992 pledge to "ensure safety," Bill Clinton has said little about either nuclear power or the commission. As we have

seen, a president's NRC appointments are often indicative of his general attitudes toward nuclear power. Jimmy Carter's ambivalence toward nuclear power
was reflected in his mixed bag of nominees, while Ronald Reagan's choices
were almost universally supportive of the nuclear industry. A review of Bill
Clinton's appointments, however, suggests that ideology has not been the guiding
principle in their selection; it also suggests that nuclear power has not been a priority issue.[31]

To begin with, the Clinton administration has been slow to fill openings on
the NRC. For most of Clinton's first term, the NRC has operated with two or
three vacancies; even today, the commission only has three members. As late as
mid-1995, three years into the term, the NRC only had two members, one of
whom was Kenneth C. Rogers, a holdover from the Reagan administration. Under these circumstances, agency staff could only guess what the administration
wanted them to do and settled into a holding pattern. Well into the Clinton presidency, the NRC is not noticeably different from the Reagan and Bush years.

For those Clinton has appointed to the NRC, diversity, experience, and prag-
matism rather than political philosophy appear to have been the primary selection criteria. After toying with the idea of renominating Ivan Selin, Clinton in
1995 chose Shirley Jackson as NRC chair. A black woman, Jackson had been a
physics professor at Rutgers University and also had spent sixteen years at AT&T
Bell Laboratories. Because Jackson has only been in office for a little over one
year, it is too early to gauge her impact on the commission. There is some evidence that the NRC is more open to outside scrutiny, and antinuclear groups are
cautiously optimistic. Clinton's only other successful nominee is Greta Dicus, a
former Arkansas health department official who was opposed by environmental
groups but supported by the nuclear industry. Clinton's other two nominations
were blocked by the nuclear industry and Senate Republicans. Robert Sussman,
former deputy administrator of the EPA and a law school friend of the president,
withdrew in early 1995 after his nomination languished in the Senate's Environment and Public Works Committee. The nomination of Dan Berkovitz, a former
aide to Senator Max Baucus, became stalled after eight of the nine Republicans
on the committee wrote to President Clinton urging him to withdraw the nomination because of concerns that Berkovitz would "impose burdensome regulations" on the industry.[32]

THE NRC IN THE 1990s

Although its status as an independent regulatory commission exempts the NRC
from most oversight measures, the agency's actions have been shaped by the National Performance Review. The NPR initiative, for example, has encouraged the
NRC to allow greater public participation in its rulemaking proceedings. In 1995,
participants in Atlanta, Chicago, and Philadelphia were linked with NRC officials

in Maryland in an experimental videoconference rulemaking session on fire protection. In addition, the NRC has created a web site and home page that disclose pending rulemakings and allow the public to comment on proposed rules. The comments, which can be viewed and responded to by any interested party, become part of the formal rulemaking record. This change is a step in the right direction, although it is unclear how much more access it provides average citizens.[33]

At the same time, however, there are troubling signs that the NRC continues to overlook potential safety problems at the nation's nuclear plants. In one instance, the NRC launched an investigation after an anonymous letter sent to the Union of Concerned Scientists alleged that the owner of the Maine Yankee plant knowingly used faulty data and manipulated computer simulations to hide potentially serious deficiencies in the plant's emergency core-cooling system. Specifically, it was alleged that Yankee Atomic, which was seeking NRC approval to operate at a higher power rating, used inaccurate data to create a computer simulation showing that the plant could operate safely at the higher power outputs. Because the NRC had previously granted two increases in power outputs based on the altered studies, critics charged that the situation illustrated the agency's cavalier approach to reactor safety. In particular, these events raise questions about how carefully the staff checks the documents that utilities submit when requesting license changes.[34]

Similarly, the NRC repeatedly has failed to address the problem of counterfeit and substandard parts despite the knowledge that such parts pose significant safety concerns. The issue first surfaced in the 1980s, when inspectors discovered that many plants were using parts that were either bogus or failed to meet safety standards. Congress held hearings on the matter in 1990, prompting Representative John Dingell to ask the General Accounting Office to investigate. The GAO reported that at least seventy-two plants were operating with counterfeit or substandard parts in their safety systems or had received such parts in their inventories. According to the GAO, if not corrected, "the problem would have a significant impact on safe plant operations." In its own study, the NRC found that twelve of thirteen utilities failed quality assurance examinations. Rather than take punitive action, the NRC decided the problem was so widespread that utilities needed time to weed out the bad parts. The commission dropped pending enforcement actions in 1990 against two utilities but promised Congress that new quality assurance inspections would begin in eighteen months. But they did not, and Congress was never told of the change. Complaints from We the People, Inc., an antinuclear group, prompted an investigation by the NRC's inspector general. According to the internal audit, the decision not to implement the inspection program had "serious safety implications." More significantly, the inspector general's report quotes an unnamed official in the Office of Investigations who claimed that when the counterfeit parts problem first came up, investigators were discouraged from pursuing the matter. As in numerous other cases over the years, the

NRC acted to protect the industry. If the problem is as widespread as the available evidence suggests, it could cost utilities hundreds of thousands of dollars per day to close reactors and replace the faulty parts.[35]

Finally, the NRC also has routinely failed to protect whistleblowers, a major source of safety information at nuclear plants. Despite federal guarantees of protection for whistleblowers, the NRC inspector general discovered that NRC officials were disclosing their identities to plant owners. Many of the employees, who thought their identities were confidential, faced harassment, and some were even threatened physically. Ann Harris, one of the whistleblowers, said, "I did ask the NRC to keep my name confidential and I thought I had that promise. I guess I'm the original dummy." To make matters worse, the NRC also failed to follow up on the whistleblower complaints to make sure that the safety problems were corrected. In this instance, the commission again placed the interests of the nuclear industry above its regulatory responsibilities.[36]

NUCLEAR RESEARCH AND DEVELOPMENT

Budgetary decisions provide presidents with another tool to shape policy. With respect to energy research and development, the Clinton White House has distinguished itself from prior administrations by being the first to propose deep cuts in funding for advanced reactor technology.[37] With the help of fiscal conservatives, who see many of the nuclear research programs as little more than corporate welfare, the White House has even eliminated some long-standing industry projects. Although these accomplishments are undoubtedly the result of the larger debate over balancing the budget, they also reflect the administration's policy preferences, because its budget requests have consistently sought increases for a variety of other energy programs, including solar, renewables, and conservation.[38] In singling out the nuclear program for cuts, the Clinton White House is clearly charting a different course for the nation's energy future, one that relies on greater efficiency and increased use of alternative energy sources and thus assumes little need for building new reactors.

Most of the Energy Department's civilian nuclear research and development programs have sustained significant cuts in the last three years. Overall spending for these programs has declined from $261 million in FY 1993 to $203 million in FY 1996, and Congress has appropriated one-third less for FY 1997. Budget cuts have forced the DOE to abandon work on two showcase programs for advanced reactor technology, which the White House argued were unnecessary and lacked any near-term commercial application. In the House, an unusual coalition of environmentalists and conservative Republicans joined forces to defund both the modular high-temperature gas-cooled reactor (HTGCR) and the advanced liquid metal reactor projects. Since the 1960s, the federal government had spent over $1 billion on the HTGCR project. In explaining the vote, Dana Rohrabacher (R-

Calif.), Chair of the House Subcommittee on Energy and the Environment, said, "Some of these nuclear research programs were nothing more than corporate and white-coat welfare."[39]

With the cancellations, the DOE will abandon its investigation of multiple technologies and will now focus its research and development efforts on a scaled-down program to design advanced versions of the current generation of light water reactors. Pursuant to the Energy Policy Act of 1992, the DOE has been working with reactor vendors and nuclear utilities to develop an improved light water reactor design, which could then serve as the basis for a series of standardized plants. Under the program, the DOE has provided considerable technical and financial assistance to companies seeking to develop such designs and also has paid for some research and engineering costs.[40] Although these projects were the nuclear industry's top priority, the recent reduction in DOE subsidies marks a profound shift in the level of support provided by the federal government. No longer can the industry count on unlimited and unquestioned research and development assistance.

THE CURRENT STATE OF NUCLEAR POLITICS AND POLICY

Policymakers continue to be ambivalent about commercial nuclear power. Although nuclear reactors provide a significant share of the nation's electricity, especially in certain regions, policymakers also worry about the problems of waste disposal and reactor safety. Reflecting this ambivalence, nuclear policy making has been marked by incrementalism, with policymakers unwilling, or unable, to stray far from the status quo. Barring another energy or environmental crisis, it is extremely unlikely that American utilities will soon begin building any additional nuclear plants. And in the absence of a severe accident, policymakers are equally unlikely to require the shutdown of existing reactors or to rule out the possibility of future contributions from nuclear power. In the interim, the range of acceptable policy options will continue to lie somewhere in between the two extremes.

This narrow range of alternatives reflects the power of American political culture and structures, which have a profound influence on policy debates. In the United States the prevailing political culture extols the virtues of individualism, private property, free enterprise, and limited government. The dominance of such values shapes the public agenda because it affects how people perceive policy issues. Policy proposals that fall outside prevailing values are effectively screened out of debate.[41] In the case of nuclear power, the strength of free market values means that certain policy options, such as a government takeover of the nuclear industry, never receive serious consideration. At the same time, Americans have grudgingly acknowledged that public power may sometimes be necessary to offset some of the undesirable consequences of unfettered capitalism. The desire to constrain corporate autonomy and assure a safer and more equitable society provides the rationale for government regulation of the private sector. Accordingly, the belief that corporations must be held accountable to society helps explain why efforts to deregulate the nuclear power industry do not go very far. Because of safety concerns, most Americans do not trust the industry to police itself. Taken together, these two contrasting views provide the parameters of recent debates over nuclear power.

The case of nuclear power is not unusual in this regard. Generally speaking, political arguments are bounded by widely shared ideas about which policies are legitimate and which are not. Because problem definition is contextual, political actors must try to frame issues in ways that are compatible with prevailing political values and governmental structures. In the United States, those actors seeking to privatize conflicts will stress those values—such as private property, individualism, and liberty—which can be used to justify minimal governmental involvement in business affairs or in matters of personal behavior. Those seeking to expand conflicts, on the other hand, will appeal to other values that, if accepted, can lead to greater governmental involvement. Advocates of civil rights for minorities and women, consumer protection, and environmental protection broadened their appeal by couching their arguments in terms of justice, equity, fairness, and citizen participation. In each instance, the strategy contributed to broader political engagements and policy change.

We have seen that widely accepted values condition policy debates. And yet nuclear power, like the interstate highway system and post-Sputnik education spending, was an exception to the norm of limited government.[42] Like these other policy areas, the deviation was defended on national security grounds, which was a compelling argument during the cold war era. Over time and with the breakup of the Soviet Union, that explanation became less compelling, and so advocates had a harder time sustaining the unusual government-business partnership. Increasingly, government support for nuclear energy research is seen as "corporate welfare" for undeserving special interests and not as a legitimate expenditure for national security.

Although public values certainly affect how issues are perceived, they can change over time. When this change occurs, certain actors and policy options are helped while others are hurt. In the case of nuclear power, shifts in public conceptions of the appropriate scope of government intervention in the private sector profoundly influenced policy making. As noted above, government-business relations in the United States reveal a fundamental tension between a long-standing aversion to centralized authority on the one hand and a fear of corporate autonomy on the other. Americans treasure free enterprise and the rights of private property, yet they worry about their effects on the democratic process. Over time, perceptions of the proper government-business relationship change, and depending on which set of values is dominant at any given time, certain problems and solutions are more or less likely to be acted upon.

During the public lobby era, many people became convinced that the general welfare was being sacrificed on the altar of free enterprise and insisted on measures designed to expand the federal government's regulatory responsibilities. Because they also were suspicious of big government, however, these activists insisted on opening up regulatory decision making to greater citizen participation. The power of government would be enhanced, but it would be controlled by the people themselves. Through their appeals to direct citizen involvement in the details of policy making, public lobby reformers avoided the fear of centralized governmental power. In the words of James Morone, "Redefining the issue of the moment into a question of enhancing democracy facilitates—indeed, it permits—the deployment of new kinds of public power in a polity biased against government action."[43] During the 1980s, however, the pendulum swung the other way, leading to calls for deregulation and privatization. Issues and programs that had previously been considered as appropriate exercises of public power were shifted to the private sector. In many locations, programs such as garbage collection, fire protection, and motor vehicle services were contracted out to private enterprise. With a resurgence of free market values, advocates of stricter regulation have a harder time framing or defining issues because most citizens will be predisposed toward smaller government.

Ironically, policy drift has been reinforced by the institutional and process reforms of the 1970s, which created a more permeable and crowded policy-making arena. Clearly, the politics of nuclear power is now less exclusive than it was in the halcyon days of the subgovernment, when only program supporters had meaningful access. And policy outcomes changed dramatically in the 1970s. But contemporary nuclear policy making is now more complex, and its many participants and venues make it virtually impossible to reconcile the conflicting interests. Both coalitions have the incentive, and often the ability, to resist the other's efforts to initiate policy change. As Irwin Bupp argues, the multitude of actors "can in large measure block each other's goals, frustrate each other's policies, and hence prevent the development of any coherent strategy in reactor licensing."[44] Under such conditions, dramatic policy breakthroughs are extremely unlikely.

As we have seen, the public lobby era reforms created a more fragmented and decentralized policy-making arena. As described by Stephen Skowronek, the American political system is now "thicker," with more organizations and agencies that are "firmly entrenched" and independent. Such systems are more permeable, to be sure, but they are also more prone to protracted conflict because policymakers, including presidents, have less freedom to maneuver and no one has the authority to impose a decision.[45] In fact, there are an almost infinite number of decision points. As a case in point, the devolution of power to multiple committees and subcommittees in Congress has increased regulatory oversight and made it harder for policy monopolies to operate, but it also has made it harder to forge the multiple majorities needed to enact legislation that could facilitate a policy breakthrough. Positive action now requires that none of the multiple federal agencies, congressional subcommittees, federal and state courts, and state and local planning boards disapprove of any proposed action. With so many institutional venues, decisions are rarely final, and actors have very little reason to accept defeat. On the contrary, they have strong incentives to keep fighting in the hope that they will eventually prevail in a more sympathetic policy venue. Parties unhappy with proposed rules, for example, now have numerous opportunities to appeal within the NRC and ultimately in the federal courts. Attaining policy "closure," as Christopher J. Bosso suggests, is exceedingly difficult in a system where actors are in a state of permanent mobilization.[46] The American political system, some say, now lacks the capacity to overcome stalemate and formulate good policy.

Some even go so far as to suggest that many of the changes enacted in this period have permanently transformed American politics. As a case in point, some suggest that actors who gained access during the public lobby era are now permanent players, firmly entrenched in their own secure institutional niches that enable them to fight for their policy goals.[47] In his discussion of pesticides policy, for example, Bosso claims that the political system "increasingly grants legitimacy to virtually any claim" and notes how certain interests show up "regularly and predictably" each time the issue comes up for discussion.[48] According to some accounts, the American political process is now so wide-open, so fragmented, and offers so many access points that it resembles the pluralist heaven in which all actors can get heard at some point in the process.

Are these claims of equal and permanent access accurate in the case of nuclear power? Although it cannot be denied that antinuclear activists gained greater access to the policy-making process during the 1970s, they were never able to rival the privileged position of the nuclear industry. To be sure, opponents had an easier time getting heard in Congress after the abolition of the joint committee. Except for a very brief period in the late 1970s, however, they were never able to obtain equal access to the NRC, especially at the highest levels. Antinuclear groups had their greatest successes in the decentralized implementation arenas, such as the courts and commission licensing boards, where the barriers to access were lower. For the most part, though, the decisions handed down by these venues involved individual reactors and did not establish general policy. And as the number of plants being licensed dwindled through the 1980s, there were fewer licensing hearings in which to participate. Consequently, opponents could intervene on a case-by-case basis, but they remained outsiders who were unable to gain stable access to the inner circles of policy formation. The nuclear industry, on the other hand, continued to be more influential in the crucial areas of rule-making and standard setting.[49]

These facts illustrate one of the flaws in the "interest group representation" analysis underlying many of the reform proposals of the 1970s. This analysis, according to Melnick, "assumes that when all major groups participate in policy-making, they confront each other directly, make compromises, and thus achieve balanced representation."[50] The problem, as Melnick points out, is that groups do not always confront one another directly in the policy-making process. In the case of nuclear power, antinuclear groups were much more successful at confronting their opponents in Congress, in the courts, and in the states. They were less effective at the commission, especially in the 1980s, when the Reagan administration pushed the agency back into the pronuclear coalition. As this case illustrates, nuclear policy making became more open in the 1970s, but it is hardly the level playing field many scholars find in other issue areas.

With respect to the question of permanent change, Jeffrey M. Berry and others have argued that fundamental changes in mobilization patterns and structural arrangements in the 1970s have "altered the nature of policymaking in Washington in ways that work against the operation of subgovernments."[51] Citing similar changes, Baumgartner and Jones speculate that it may be more difficult in the 1990s to maintain a subsystem independent of outside political influences because the American political system is more open and offers so many access points.[52] And Joppke suggests that a decentralization of political control undermined nuclear power in the 1970s and is likely to prevent a future revival of the industry.[53] The premise underlying each of these observations is that in this new American polity, subsystem demise is irreversible.

Suggestions that the current state of affairs is permanent are shortsighted. If the history of nuclear power has taught us anything, it is that institutions and policy are remarkably unstable over time. Just as regulatory institutions and processes changed in the 1970s, they could change once again, altering the mobilization of bias in ways that could aid nuclear power supporters. There are no guarantees that policy drift will continue forever. Of course, some of the inertia displayed in this case is because nuclear power is no longer a high profile issue. Many of the policymakers in Congress who were attracted to the issue in the late 1970s and early 1980s have either left government or, because the low attention levels have created different incentives, are now more interested in other issues. It was licensing conflicts over individual reactors that energized the antinuclear movement and propelled the issue to the agenda. But as the number of reactors in the licensing pipeline dwindled, the local citizen groups that formed the heart of the opposition have faded in importance. Many have disbanded. Similarly, national environmental organizations have moved on to other issues. With no reactors being licensed in recent years, levels of attention, and conflict, have thus been greatly reduced. There is now little reason for most policymakers, the media, or much of the general public to pay attention to nuclear power.

Yet policy change is possible. The low attention levels that now characterize nuclear politics will not endure forever. As in the past, public attention to the issue will be sporadic, and so nuclear power will at some point return to the agenda. The question is how it returns. If Baumgartner and Jones are correct, some combination of two things would have to happen for there to be serious policy shifts. First, popular and elite perceptions of nuclear power would have to change from negative to positive. Second, venue changes could create a more supportive policy environment for nuclear power and initiate new policy. With respect to the first factor, the most likely scenarios for such an image change are "spillovers" from related issues. Another energy crisis, renewed concerns about environmental problems, or some technological "solution" to the industry's intractable safety and waste problems could lead to a shift in perceptions of nuclear power. As noted earlier, the nuclear industry believes the "Ayatollah factor" and the threat to the nation's energy supplies are among its strongest arguments. A disruption of American oil supplies could renew fears of energy shortages and lead policymakers to reconsider nuclear power as a viable option. Alternatively, a string of abnormally warm years could once again raise global warming to agenda prominence and provide a boost to nonfossil energy sources. Nuclear power, of course, has its own environmental costs, most notably nuclear waste, which would have to be addressed before new reactor orders were placed. Finally, a scientific or technical breakthrough that promised a new generation of "inherently safe" reactors could assuage fears about nuclear power.

To date, there is little evidence to suggest that nuclear power is being viewed more positively. For all intents and purposes, the only time most people notice nuclear power today is when something bad happens at one of the nation's reactors. The overwhelming majority of stories in the popular press are negative, with reactor mishaps or disputes over waste disposal providing the typical context.[54] So long as the dominant perceptions of nuclear power remain so negative, policy breakthroughs are extremely unlikely because policymakers will lack any incentive to change course.

Venue changes played a key role in the transformation of the atomic monopoly, and theoretically they could lead to its eventual return. The pronuclear coalition could, for example, shift jurisdiction to sympathetic policymakers, or it could try to change the rules of the game in ways that make it harder for opponents to participate in policy making. In point of fact, the pronuclear coalition has had some success in following this path. As we have seen, Congress voted in 1992 to amend the Atomic Energy Act to provide for the issuance of a combined construction permit–operating license that would eliminate one of the two public licensing hearings.[55] This revision was a major victory for the nuclear industry, which had sought the change for decades, and it is potentially very important. The public hearings raised awareness of the issue and were thus an important part of the antinuclear coalition's efforts to expand the conflict. If any new reactors are ordered, the plant's opponents will have only one highly public opportunity to contest the license. In seeking to reduce the number of public hearings, the nuclear industry is again trying to privatize the conflict. In conjunction with rule changes limiting intervenors' rights of discovery, cross-examination, and appeal, the streamlined licensing proceedings are very different from those in place during the 1970s and present opponents of nuclear power with fewer opportunities to challenge reactors.

In addition, the Republican takeover of Congress is a potentially significant venue change. Although many conservative House members oppose federal research and development support for the industry, Republicans generally are far more supportive of nuclear power than are Democrats. They are also more hostile to federal regulation and to the forces that support it. We have seen that antinuclear groups relied on sympathetic staffers and members, such as Henry Waxman, Edward Markey, and John Dingell, who acted as gatekeepers allowing them access to nuclear policy making. With Republicans in the majority, antinuclear groups will find fewer sympathetic committee and subcommittee chairs and thus fewer access points to policy making. The industry may also have an easier time winning approval of its remaining policy goals, such as a speedup in the construction of a high-level waste repository. In pursuit of that goal, Republicans recently introduced legislation that would limit Nevada's ability to withhold the required permits or approvals to construct the facility. If successful, this attempt to preempt state authority could be a significant venue change because it would shift power back to the national government, where the industry has always had the upper hand. In short, today's Congress is quite different from that of the last twenty years, and if Republican control continues, it is conceivable that nuclear policy will again shift course.

SUBGOVERNMENTS, ISSUE NETWORKS, AND ADVOCACY COALITIONS

If the subgovernment approach no longer explains nuclear policy making, what does? Issue networks are said to be rather fluid, unstructured, and dynamic, but those terms do not describe contemporary nuclear politics. On the contrary, the nuclear policy community is rather structured, having evolved into two stable and well-defined coalitions. For this reason, nuclear politics is best explained by the advocacy coalition framework. As we saw in Chapter 3, both coalitions are organized around common belief systems. The pronuclear coalition, for example, consists of actors who are technological and scientific optimists, who believe that nuclear power will lead to greater economic growth and a higher standard of living, and who believe that experts should make policy decisions. Since these core beliefs tend to be stable over periods of a decade or more, so is coalition composition.[56] In this case, the two coalitions have been stable for nearly two decades. I have argued that the NRC shifted to a more neutral position during the wave of criticism in the 1970s but then tilted back to the pronuclear camp in the 1980s, when Ronald Reagan took office. This reinforces the claim that government agencies will tend to shift toward one coalition or another in response to exogenous events. In most instances, regulatory agencies serve multiple masters and thus seek to avoid extreme positions. The NRC's rhetoric has sought to portray the agency as an impartial regulator, but its actions over the last fifteen years indicate that it is supportive of nuclear power.

The level of conflict in a policy community, Sabatier and Jenkins-Smith note, varies depending on whether actors disagree on secondary or core beliefs.[57] The case of nuclear power supports that claim. In the program's first twenty years, conflict was essentially nonexistent, reflecting the wave of enthusiasm for nuclear power. The late 1960s and early 1970s, however, were marked by intense conflict as the two coalitions, seeking diametrically opposed policy outcomes, talked past each other. With nuclear power having fallen from the agenda, conflict over the last ten years has been intermittent.

This case also supports Sabatier and Jenkins-Smith's claim that coalitions use policy information in an advocacy fashion in order to further their policy goals.[58] Clearly, the spread of information was a crucial element of the antinuclear coalition's efforts to expand the scope of the conflict over nuclear power. Critics were able to use the information they obtained to highlight the environmental and safety costs of reactors, which helped them redefine the issue, enlarge their own coalition, and undermine the nuclear subgovernment. The pronuclear coalition, on the other hand, has sought to privatize the conflict by limiting access to policy making and program information.

In addition, each advocacy coalition has tried to manipulate the assignment of programs so that the government units they control have the most authority.[59] Institutions and decision processes clearly matter, which is why both sides have fought so hard to shape them. In the 1950s and 1960s, the AEC and JCAE had almost complete authority. In the 1970s, however, systemic changes in the structures of bias played a crucial role in the transformation of nuclear politics.

Finally, the advocacy coalition approach also recognizes that policy making often has a significant intergovernmental dimension.[60] Both coalitions include numerous actors from a variety of public and private institutions and from all levels of government. Many of the important battles over nuclear power were not waged in Washington but at the state and local levels. Local intervenor groups were important actors to be sure, but so were governors, state courts, state and county legislative bodies, and state utility commissions. Today, the most important battles are being waged over nuclear waste disposal, which involves actors from all levels of government.

ISSUE DEFINITION AND POLICY CHANGE

I have argued that the transformation of nuclear politics was caused by an expansion in the scope of conflict that pushed nuclear power to a prominent position near the top of the policy agenda. Changing perceptions of nuclear power were a crucial factor in the conflict's dramatic expansion. Initially defined as a matter of national security, growing concerns about the possible environmental and health consequences of reactors combined to make the issue more visible, leading more people to perceive that they had a stake in nuclear policy. The influx of new participants, and new perspectives, transformed the debate and shattered the consensus on nuclear power. The resulting conflict made the issue more visible, attracted the attention of more actors, and expanded the scope even further. By the middle of the 1970s, in fact, the nuclear power issue had been fundamentally redefined. As Bosso notes in his study of pesticides policy, "Subgovernment politics explodes into pluralist policymaking when enough people perceive their stakes in the issue and where the nature of the issue itself no longer is defined solely by the subgovernment."[61] As in the case of pesticides, loss of the ability to define the issue was probably the most critical factor causing the decline of the atomic subgovernment. Once the subgovernment lost the power to define the issue and establish the parameters of debate, it was dismantled.

This study supports the claim that battles over issue definition are often critical for understanding political conflicts and how they evolve over time. Issue definition, for example, can affect the scope of conflict over a given issue and thus lead to policy change. As Cobb and Elder note, if the original parties to a conflict can agree on a definition of the issue, it is likely that their dispute will remain narrow and the outcome will primarily be a function of the relative strength of the contestants. But if they cannot agree on a definition, perhaps because of fundamental differences over what the conflict involves, it is likely that the loser will try to communicate the conflict to others in the hope of enlisting their support. This can be done by changing the cleavage lines or by substituting one conflict for another.[62]

It also can be done by shifting attention to one aspect of a given problem rather than another. Baumgartner and Jones have argued that although policy issues have multiple aspects, policy debates rarely consider all aspects of an issue simultaneously. Typically, only some aspects of the issue are salient at any one time.[63] Consequently, the definition of the set of issues that come to be associated with a given policy is, in their view, probably the most important element in determining its outcome. In the case of nuclear power, experts played a critical role in the early stages of conflict expansion. It was the safety concerns raised by AEC scientists that gained the attention of outsiders and gave the technology's opponents credibility. Once this internal technical dispute came to the public's attention, the debate centered on nuclear power's environmental and safety consequences rather than on its utility as a source of electricity. Program advocates thus were forced to fight the battle on hostile terrain.

Issue definition is clearly an important part of the struggle to obtain political advantage. In an effort to restrict participation, actors try to define issues in narrow technical or procedural terms. Subsystem insiders, for example, sought to define the nuclear issue narrowly in order to minimize knowledge of their actions and thus restrict the scope of the conflict. To paraphrase Schattschneider, they wanted to keep the audience on the sidelines.[64] Conversely, those seeking to challenge the status quo tried to define issues broadly in order to attract the attention of others and thus change the balance of political forces. In this instance, critics of nuclear power won the battle over issue definition in large part by highlighting information warning of its potential environmental and health costs. As information became more widely available and stressed nuclear power's potential dangers, more actors demanded a role in policy making. Antinuclear activists also tried to connect the issue to broad social themes, such as participatory democracy, which were compelling and easily understood.[65] This linkage was made easier by the efforts of the AEC, JCAE, and nuclear industry to suppress information about reactor safety and restrict access to policy-making arenas. Such proposals only reinforced the perception that they were trying to hide something. The process of conflict expansion in this case appears typical, with the issue becoming more abstract and ambiguous over time, thereby attracting more people who believe they are potentially affected.[66]

POLICY COMMUNITIES AND BROAD POLITICAL TRENDS

The more or less simultaneous transformation of policy communities in nuclear power, pesticides, and agriculture, among others, suggests that they can be dramatically altered by events in other issue areas or by broader developments in the political environment. External events, for example, can redefine an issue and thrust it into prominence, leading to increased scrutiny of the community. As low-profile issues become more visible, awareness of the issue increases. In certain cases, policy change results. In this case, the Arab oil embargo forced public officials to undertake the first comprehensive examination of the nation's energy picture. All of the energy subsystems, including nuclear, were affected by the sudden shift in agenda status. Instead of being discussed in the near isolation characteristic of policy monopolies, policies were being debated in a more open and unpredictable environment. Fears of oil shortages might have been expected to boost the nuclear industry's prospects, but once energy became an issue of national concern it was pushed into open competition with other energy interests for government support. The point is not that the nuclear industry suddenly found itself on a level playing field with other energy groups but that the rules of the game had changed and the industry would have to learn to share the same field with other players. It might be more accurate to say that the game itself had changed; patterns of behavior that previously had been successful were no longer effective in the new, more crowded political arena.

One policy community can also be affected by changes in another. During the 1960s and 1970s, a number of "collective" issues such as civil rights, the environment, and consumer protection reached the governmental agenda. In the words of Walter Rosenbaum, "Once public awareness of collective problems is stimulated, a public mood is apparently created; public consciousness of yet other collective problems occurs while groups expand the scope of governmental agendas."[67] The antinuclear movement, for example, adopted many of the tactics and rhetorical symbols used by activists in other policy areas. Frustrated with conventional avenues of participation, they took to the streets in an effort to change policy. In fact, many of the largest post-Vietnam demonstrations concerned nuclear power. Rallies in Washington and New York drew crowds in the hundreds of thousands, while a demonstration in 1976 at New Hampshire's Seabrook reactor resulted in over 1,400 arrests.[68] As in other areas, in the later stages of conflict expansion, explicit appeals were made to broader values such as environmental protection, participatory democracy, and the common good.

Similarly, trends in regulatory policy also can affect the strength of policy monopolies. Changes in decision-making institutions and processes during the public lobby era, for example, modified the structures of bias and contributed to the dismantling of the atomic subgovernment. The passage of the National Environmental Policy Act, the Freedom of Information Act, and the Government in the Sunshine Act opened commission proceedings to outsiders. Additionally, expanded notions of standing enabled critics to challenge commission decisions in federal court, and litigation proved to be an effective tool in prying open the subsystem's deliberations. It would seem that during strong political movements to reform regulatory policy, policy communities can be reformed or even remade.[69]

During the 1980s, on the other hand, deregulatory pressures buffeted nuclear policy, undoing some of the procedural changes enacted in the previous decade. Deregulation did not go very far, however. As Derthick and Quirk have argued, the push for deregulation was more widely embraced at the economic regulatory agencies than at those charged with protecting public health and safety. Procompetitive deregulation had the support of both liberals and conservatives: liberals favored it because the call for lower prices and better service made it attractive as a proconsumer issue, while conservatives embraced it because of their commitment to free enterprise and limited government.[70] In contrast, much of the new "social" regulation enacted in the 1960s and 1970s enjoyed bipartisan support, at least in part because the public's commitment to health, environmental, and safety laws ran deep. Furthermore, the empirical evidence for deregulation in these areas was often ambiguous or weak, as it was in the case of nuclear power. Under these conditions, it became more difficult for advocates of regulatory relief to prove their claims that the industry was actually overregulated. As a result, agencies responsible for environmental and safety regulation, like the EPA and NRC, were somewhat insulated from the deregulatory movement that swept through Washington in the late 1970s and 1980s.

IS NUCLEAR POWER EXCEPTIONAL?

Although all policy monopolies are tied together by common interests, nowhere was this tendency more pronounced than in the case of nuclear power. In a remarkable departure from the norm of limited government, the nuclear power industry was created by the U.S. government, which then subsidized its growth both at home and abroad. Throughout the 1950s and 1960s, the AEC and the joint committee worked hand in hand with the private sector to remove the obstacles to the commercial success of the fledgling technology. In a very real sense, the history of commercial nuclear power reflects a partnership between government and business, and it was this sense of partnership that pervaded the policy community and contributed to its remarkable cohesion. This intimate, almost incestuous relationship also helps explain why the subgovernment was so powerful—it was impossible to distinguish the interests of the AEC and JCAE from the nuclear industry. Part of the reason policy change was not more extensive is that it is very difficult to remake an agency with jurisdiction over one industry, particularly if that industry was created and nurtured by the federal government. Indeed, given the unusual public-private partnership in this issue, it is surprising that policy outcomes changed as much as they did.

Other factors peculiar to this case explain why policy change was so limited. First, because the NRC was a carryover from the AEC, which was created in 1946, it was not a true product of the public lobby era; other agencies created in that era embraced its values more completely. The AEC's original mission was to develop, promote, *and* regulate nuclear power, and although the Energy Reorganization Act of 1974 replaced the AEC with the NRC, it was unable to completely displace the promotional mindset. Hence, despite significant changes in its political environment, the NRC never became an aggressive regulator. To be sure, in its first few years the NRC did tilt away from the pronuclear coalition, and regulation did become more stringent. In many instances, however, regulatory changes came belatedly and reluctantly, and only after they were forced upon the agency by citizen groups, presidents, Congress, or the courts. Moreover, the NRC never tilted so far that it became part of the antinuclear coalition, and in just a few years the agency would again become an advocate for nuclear power.

Policy drift since the mid-1970s also can be traced to the lack of elite convergence with respect to nuclear regulation. Nearly everyone agreed that some type of regulatory reform was needed, but they could not agree on precisely what needed reforming. Critics believed that reactors were unsafe and underregulated, while proponents argued that the nuclear industry was dying under the excessively heavy hand of the NRC. Perhaps most important, the commission never received any clear indication from either end of Pennsylvania Avenue as to the precise nature of its task. After the demise of the joint committee, Congress offered no clear directions to the agency. Meanwhile, signals from the White House were ambiguous in the Carter years, decidedly pronuclear after Reagan, and ambiguous again under Clinton.

The case of nuclear power is unusual in several other respects. Its definition as a highly technical national security issue exempted it from the decentralizing forces of American politics, including federalism. The need for specialized knowledge dramatically restricts participation, which means that subsystem politics is often normal for technoscience issues.[71] Here, the security classifications associated with the issue's national defense implications reinforced this tendency and excluded all but a relatively small number of actors from national government. Eventually, of course, nuclear power came to resemble other issues as the federal monopoly gave way to state and local government encroachment. Nevertheless, the most noteworthy aspect of nuclear power was not that state and local governments eventually became involved but that for so long they were not.

Federal-state relations in this case were unusual in another respect. At precisely the time that state and local governments were gaining more control over nuclear power, jurisdiction over a host of other issues that had been their responsibility was shifting to Washington. Indeed, during the 1960s the trend was toward centralized policy making, with the federal government assuming responsibility for more and more issues, including civil rights, poverty, housing, the environment, and consumer protection. In most of these issue areas, the process of conflict expansion was the mirror image of that in nuclear power: those seeking policy change enlarged the scope of conflict by nationalizing the debate and shifting power to Washington, which was more sympathetic to their goals. In the case of voting rights, for example, civil rights activists used registration drives and demonstrations to attract attention to their cause and enlist the support of the federal government. Progress came only after the Voting Rights Act abolished literacy tests and forced hostile state governments in the South to seek Justice Department approval of any changes in voting laws. Similarly, clean air advocates sought to nationalize the debate in an attempt to shift authority to Washington, where local industries had less influence. In nuclear power, on the other hand, policy change occurred when the conflict expanded to state and local governments, which were much less supportive of the nuclear industry.

The politics of nuclear power is also unusual in that its early stages were characterized by the minimal participation typically associated with technical and defense issues, while in the 1970s the issue manifested the polarization and intense conflict characteristic of debates over social policies such as abortion, gun control, and gay rights. Debates over these issues and others such as sexual harassment, drugs, and AIDS contain a significant moral dimension and are a product of competing notions of how individuals should live and behave.[72] A growing body of research suggests, in fact, that moral conflicts are at the heart of many contemporary social policy conflicts. Because the different sides in these policy disputes see the world differently, there is little agreement about the nature of social problems or their possible solutions. The issues are not easily compromised, which can and does lead to prolonged and acrimonious debates that often end up in the courts.[73]

The politics of nuclear power changed dramatically once a variety of social, political, and moral questions were introduced to the mix. At the height of the conflict, fundamentally different worldviews were evident in the positions of both sides. Supporters of nuclear power tended to be scientific optimists and problem solvers who believed that continued increases in the nation's energy supplies were essential to economic growth and improved living standards. Some even believed the debate over nuclear power was really a debate over the future of free enterprise and the American way of life, and it was commonly suggested that individuals and the nation would suffer if nuclear power were abandoned. Antinuclear activists, on the other hand, were less trusting of technology and technocrats. They argued that nuclear power was not simply a technical or engineering issue, and technical experts thus had no special authority to make policy decisions. As concerns about accountability and responsiveness in government became prominent in the later stages of the debate, they suggested that citizens should be allowed to participate meaningfully in decisions that affect their lives. As the issues became more abstract and normative in nature, the divisions between the two sides widened and the conflict became more intense. This chain of events is typical of many areas of social policy. Environmental issues, for example, initially revolve around some rather specific scientific or technical point but gradually evolve into a more heated debate between the virtues of public health and economic growth.

NUCLEAR POWER AND DEMOCRATIC PARTICIPATION

The purpose of this study was to investigate changes in the politics of nuclear power. I wanted to know why a policy that had been largely invisible for over two decades became the focus of a highly visible and contentious political debate. I also wanted to show how the dynamics of issue definition, conflict expansion, and venue shopping combined with broader trends in regulatory politics to create policy change in this important area of public policy. Undeniably, the once cozy and predictable world of nuclear policy making is decidedly less cozy and predictable today. But what are the normative implications of the policy-making arrangements that have evolved in this area? For example, is the current state of affairs an improvement in terms of democratic participation?

Many of the shifts in ideas, institutions, and policies that swept through the nuclear power policy community in the 1960s and 1970s were rooted in the democratic beliefs and principles that bind Americans together and periodically emerge to remake political practices and institutions. According to James Morone, at the heart of this reform tradition is a profound distrust of public power and a belief that direct citizen participation in politics can somehow create better citizens and produce better policies. The pursuit of direct democracy often leads reformers to redesign institutions and rules to facilitate the participation of previously excluded actors and conflicts.[74]

In a significant departure from earlier reform periods, however, the calls for change in the public lobby era issued not from political parties, which were increasingly viewed with distrust, but from public lobby groups. Although these groups were clearly concerned with substantive policy issues, they were also interested in the manner in which policy decisions were made. As we have seen, much of the reform strategy of the 1960s and 1970s was aimed at combating corporate privilege by opening up new channels of access within government and especially within the regulatory process. Public interest reformers believed that long-term policy change required fundamental changes in the policy-making process itself; therefore, to be successful, reformers would have to create stable access and influence within adminstrative agencies.[75] But how could this goal be accomplished? One way was to press for legislation that would grant the public, or their representatives, a meaningful role in the implementation of regulatory policy. As Michael McCann notes, such laws were a means of establishing a countervailing power to business interests, with an eye toward achieving a "civic balance" in regulatory proceedings.[76] In short, the reformer's solution was to expand access to governmental authority in an effort to make it more accountable to citizen action.

As a number of analysts have observed, this solution presented public interest activists with something of a dilemma: they resented and distrusted centralized power, but the reforms they pushed relied upon "big" government to check the arbitrary influence of "big" business.[77] More specifically, they urged a strengthening of regulatory institutions but insisted that these institutions be opened to direct citizen action. Reformers were clearly ambivalent about governmental authority—they feared its abuse but also believed it could be an agent of positive social change. In the words of McCann, reformers were seeking to redirect governmental power, not abolish it.[78]

But has it worked? Several studies suggest that these institutional changes may have had some unanticipated consequences. First, although the administrative process is certainly open to more voices than before, it falls well short of the ideal of direct democracy. Today, public participation in regulatory policy comes primarily in the form of organized groups debating policy in a language and setting that are inaccessible to most citizens. Grassroots participation is quite rare, as is informed and sustained public deliberation.

Second, the reforms may have undermined the public's ability to control regulatory policy. In his impressive study of popular participation in American politics, Morone contends that the institutional reforms designed to enhance direct democracy actually expanded the scope and authority of the state, especially its administrative capacity. According to Morone, "A great irony propels American political development: the search for more direct democracy builds up the bureaucracy."[79] More and more, decisions over regulatory policy are made in the agencies and the federal courts, two institutions that are relatively insulated from political pressures. With a decline in voter turnout and the advent of divided government, the traditional agents of popular control—elections and political parties—become less important in determining regulatory policy.[80] Groups seeking to influence policy thus focus their efforts on the less visible administrative and judicial arenas.

These are valid concerns, but it cannot be denied that policy making in nuclear power is decidedly more open and participatory today than during the 1950s. To be sure, average citizens rarely testify before congressional oversight committees or become actively involved in NRC rulemakings. As with most other technical and scientific issues, the specialized subject matter has and will continue to preclude mass involvement in policy formulation and implementation. Consequently, at the national level groups such as the Union of Concerned Scientists continue to act as surrogates for "the public" in these arenas. And yet, mass involvement in federal rulemaking proceedings may not be the most accurate measurement of the extent of citizen participation. Although gaining access to the institutions of national government was crucial, antinuclear activists were never able to rival the nuclear industry's influence there. On the other hand, they were received more favorably and met with much greater success at the state and local level. It is worth remembering that the earliest and most spirited opposition came from local citizen groups opposed to the construction and licensing of particular reactors. Although the licensing wars have largely ceased, the battles over decommissioning and nuclear waste disposal rage on, with state public utility commissions and local planning boards playing critical roles in their implementation. Opportunities for citizen participation are more pronounced at these subnational governments.

To be sure, the abundance of such forums may not be conducive to either informed public deliberation or to coordinated policy making. With a public that is averse to risks and increasingly skeptical of government, "not in my backyard"—ism is a significant problem that has the potential to disrupt and delay socially necessary projects. But however flawed, these arenas are broadly participatory. Today, the public *is* participating in nuclear policy making, just not in the way most political scientists think it should. There is no requirement or guarantee that when given the opportunity, citizens will participate effectively or intelligently. And just because citizen participation falls well short of most participatory ideals does not mean that policy is therefore unresponsive to public concerns. For better or worse, nuclear policy in the United States today accurately reflects public opinion. The American public does not want to build any new reactors, but neither does it want to forever close the door on nuclear power.

Schattschneider defined democracy as a "competitive political system in which competing leaders and organizations define the alternatives of public policy in such a way that the public can participate in the decision-making process."[81]

Because debates over policy alternatives are often highly specialized, access to policy formulation and implementation arenas is relatively restricted. In a large-scale democracy such as ours, opportunities for direct citizen participation are therefore assumed to be limited to voting in elections. But as this case demonstrates, there is often widespread public involvement in issue definition and agenda setting, which are also competitive political processes. The public may play a more active role than is commonly realized. Rather than passively waiting for policy alternatives to be presented to them by competing leaders, the public may actually participate in the definition of alternatives. In short, citizen participation in shaping the content of the agenda can help ensure that policy outcomes will be broadly responsive to public concerns.

Notes

CHAPTER 1. NUCLEAR POWER AND POLITICAL CHANGE

1. On the transformation of American politics, see Stephen Skowronek, *The Politics Presidents Make: Leadership from John Adams to George Bush* (Cambridge, Mass.: Harvard University Press, 1993), and James A. Morone, *The Democratic Wish: Popular Participation and the Limits of American Government* (New York: Basic Books, 1990). For illustrative examples of policy change, see Richard A. Harris and Sidney M. Milkis, *The Politics of Regulatory Change: A Tale of Two Agencies,* 2d ed. (New York: Oxford University Press, 1996); Christopher J. Bosso, *Pesticides and Politics: The Life Cycle of A Public Issue* (Pittsburgh: University of Pittsburgh Press, 1987); and John M. Hansen, *Gaining Access: Congress and the Farm Lobby, 1919–1981* (Chicago: University of Chicago Press, 1991).

2. See as examples Richard A. Harris and Sidney M. Milkis, eds., *Remaking American Politics* (Boulder, Colo.: Westview Press, 1989); Anthony King, ed., *The New American Political System* (Washington, D.C.: American Enterprise Institute, 1980); and John E. Chubb and Paul E. Peterson, eds., *The New Direction in American Politics* (Washington, D.C.: Brookings Institution, 1985).

3. For a sampling of opinion, see Robert Eden, "Dealing Democratic Honor Out: Reform and the Decline of Consensus Politics," and Stephen A. Salmore and Barbara G. Salmore, "Candidate-Centered Parties: Politics Without Intermediaries," both in *Remaking American Politics,* ed. Harris and Milkis.

4. James R. Temples, "The Politics of Nuclear Power: A Sub-Government in Transition," *Political Science Quarterly* 95, 2 (summer 1980): 239–60; Steven L. Del Sesto, *Science, Politics, and Controversy: Civilian Nuclear Power in the United States, 1946–1974* (Boulder, Colo.: Westview Press, 1979); John L. Campbell, *Collapse of an Industry: Nuclear Power and the Contradictions of U.S. Policy* (Ithaca, N.Y.: Cornell University Press, 1988); and Frank R. Baumgartner and Bryan D. Jones, *Agendas and Instability in American Politics* (Chicago: University of Chicago Press, 1993), especially chap. 4.

5. Harris and Milkis, *The Politics of Regulatory Change;* Marc Allen Eisner, *Regulatory Politics in Transition* (Baltimore: Johns Hopkins University Press, 1993); and Martha

Derthick and Paul Quirk, *The Politics of Deregulation* (Washington, D.C.: Brookings Institution, 1985).

6. Baumgartner and Jones, *Agendas and Instability,* 45.

7. Randall B. Ripley and Grace A. Franklin, *Congress, the Bureaucracy, and Public Policy,* 3d ed. (Homewood, Ill: Dorsey Press, 1984), 10; for a general discussion of subgovernments, see J. Leiper Freeman, *The Political Process: Executive Bureau—Legislative Committee Relations* (New York: Random House, 1955); Douglas Cater, *Power in Washington* (New York: Random House, 1964); and Emmette S. Redford, *Democracy in the Administrative State* (New York: Oxford University Press, 1969).

8. Ripley and Franklin, *Congress,* 23; see also Temples, "The Politics of Nuclear Power."

9. On the variable influence of subgovernments, see Jeffrey M. Berry, "Subgovernments, Issue Networks, and Political Conflict," in *Remaking American Politics,* ed. Harris and Milkis, 253-55. See also Tim R. Miller, "Recent Trends in Federal Water Resource Management: Are the Iron Triangles in Retreat?" *Policy Studies Review* 5 (1985): 395-412.

10. Harold P. Green and Alan P. Rosenthal, *Government of the Atom: The Integration of Powers* (New York: Atherton Press, 1963), 76.

11. Temples, "The Politics of Nuclear Power," 246.

12. For discussions of the regulatory process, see George J. Stigler, "The Theory of Economic Regulation," *Bell Journal of Economics and Management Science* 2, 1 (spring 1971): 3-21; Richard A. Posner, "Theories of Economic Regulation," *Bell Journal of Economics and Management Science* 5 (August 1975): 335-58; Mancur Olson, *The Logic of Collective Action* (Cambridge, Mass.: Harvard University Press, 1971); and Paul Quirk, *Industry Influence in Federal Regulatory Agencies* (Princeton, N.J.: Princeton University Press, 1981).

13. Baumgartner and Jones, *Agendas and Instability,* 83-90.

14. E. E. Schattschneider, *The Semi-Sovereign People: A Realist's View of Democracy in America* (Hinsdale, Ill.: Dryden Press, 1960), 2 (emphasis in original).

15. Ibid., 2, 7, 11, 38.

16. Bosso, *Pesticides and Politics,* 80.

17. Deborah A. Stone, "Causal Stories and the Formation of Policy Agendas," *Political Science Quarterly* 104:281-300; see also Bosso, *Pesticides and Politics,* 27-30, and Baumgartner and Jones, *Agendas and Instability,* 25-38.

18. Baumgartner and Jones, *Agendas and Instability,* 239.

19. Ibid., 30.

20. Bosso, *Pesticides and Politics,* 256; for an in-depth discussion of this issue, see especially 237-56.

21. Paul A. Sabatier and Hank C. Jenkins-Smith, *Policy Change and Learning: An Advocacy Coalition Approach* (Boulder, Colo.: Westview Press, 1993), 24, 45.

22. John W. Kingdon, *Agendas, Alternatives, and Public Policies* (Boston: Little, Brown, 1984), 100. For another view of agenda setting, see Roger W. Cobb and Charles D. Elder, *Participation in American Politics: The Dynamics of Agenda-Building* (Boston: Allyn and Bacon, 1972).

23. Schattschneider, *The Semi-Sovereign People,* 37 (emphasis in original).

24. Baumgartner and Jones, *Agendas and Instability,* 84.

25. Ibid., 192.

26. Ibid., 178.

27. Ibid., chap. 5.

28. Ibid., 89.

29. Ibid., 202.

30. Ibid., 89.

31. Schattschneider, *The Semi-Sovereign People,* 2.

32. Ibid., 16.

33. Ibid., 35.

34. See in particular Earl Latham, *The Group Basis of Politics* (Ithaca, N.Y.: Cornell University Press, 1952). For other views on the role of government, see Gabriel Almond, "The Return to the State," *American Political Science Review* 82 (September 1988): 853–74, and Theodore Lowi, *The End of Liberalism: The Second Republic of the United States,* 2d ed. (New York: W. W. Norton, 1979). See also the pluralist arguments of Robert A. Dahl, *A Preface to Democratic Theory* (Chicago: University of Chicago Press, 1956).

35. Schattschneider, *The Semi-Sovereign People,* 71, refers to this phenomenon as the "mobilization of bias."

36. Ibid., 48.

37. Walter A. Rosenbaum, *The Politics of Environmental Concern* (New York: Holt, Rinehart and Winston, 1977), 94, citing David B. Truman, *The Governmental Process* (New York: Alfred A. Knopf, 1951).

38. R. Shep Melnick, *Regulation and the Courts: The Case of the Clean Air Act* (Washington, D.C.: Brookings Institution, 1983), 295.

39. Bosso, *Pesticides and Politics,* 17.

40. For a general discussion of the stages of the policy-making process, see Charles O. Jones, *An Introduction to the Study of Public Policy,* 3d ed. (Monterey, Calif.: Brooks/Cole Publishing, 1984). On the relationship between policy-making arenas and nuclear policy, see Campbell, *Collapse of an Industry.*

41. Ripley and Franklin, *Congress,* 106.

42. On new directions in regulation, see W. Lilley and J. Miller, "The New Social Regulation," *Public Interest* 47 (1977): 49–62.

43. Anthony King, "The American Polity in the Late 1970s: Building Coalitions in the Sand," in *The New American Political System,* ed. King, 372–73.

44. On participatory changes in American politics in the 1960s and 1970s, see Samuel P. Huntington, *American Politics: The Promise of Disharmony* (Cambridge, Mass.: Harvard University Press, 1981); Samuel H. Beer, "In Search of a New Public Philosophy," in *The New American Political System,* ed. King; and Harris and Milkis, *Remaking American Politics.* Huntington, for example, describes the 1960s as a period of "creedal passion," which periodically overwhelms the incremental politics of pluralism. According to Huntington, these periods are "distinguished by widespread and intense moral indignation. Political passions are high, existing structures of authority are called into question, democratic and egalitarian impulses are renewed, and political change . . . occurs" (p. 91).

45. On the views of policy activists during this period, see Donald R. Brand, "Reformers of the 1960s and 1970s: Modern Antifederalists?" 37, and Sidney M. Milkis, "The Presidency, Policy Reform, and the Rise of Administrative Politics," 146, both in *Remaking American Politics,* ed. Harris and Milkis.

46. Seymour Martin Lipset and William Schneider, *The Confidence Gap: Business, Labor, and Government in the Public Mind,* 2d ed. (Baltimore: Johns Hopkins University Press, 1987).

47. Richard A. Harris, "Politicized Management: The Changing Face of Business in American Politics," in *Remaking American Politics,* ed. Harris and Milkis, 264.

48. W. Rosenbaum, *The Politics of Environmental Concern,* 101.

49. For a discussion of regulatory capture, see Marver H. Bernstein, *Regulating Business by Independent Commission* (Princeton, N.J.: Princeton University Press, 1955); Richard Noll, "The Economics and Politics of Regulation," *Virginia Law Review* 57 (September 1971): 1016–32; and Richard C. Leone, "Public Interest Advocacy and the Regulatory Process," *Annals of the American Academy of Political and Social Science* 400 (March 1972): 46–58.

50. W. Rosenbaum, *The Politics of Environmental Concern,* 101. See Richard A. Harris, "A Decade of Reform," in *Remaking American Politics,* ed. Harris and Milkis, 14.

51. See R. Shep Melnick, "The Courts, Congress, and Programmatic Rights," in *Remaking American Politics,* ed. Harris and Milkis, 203–4, and Richard B. Stewart, "The Reformation of American Administrative Law," *Harvard Law Review* 88 (June): 1669–1813.

52. For government-sponsored participatory measures, see Melnick, *Regulation and the Courts;* see also Mary G. Kweit and Robert W. Kweit, *Implementing Citizen Participation in a Bureaucratic Society: A Contingency Approach* (New York: Praeger, 1981).

53. PL 89-554, 80 Stat. 383.

54. See Melnick, *Regulation and the Courts,* especially chaps. 1 and 2.

55. Milkis, "The Presidency," in *Remaking American Politics,* ed. Harris and Milkis, 164–65.

56. Ibid.

57. Hugh Heclo, "Issue Networks and the Executive Establishment," in *The New American Political System,* ed. King, 88.

58. Ibid.

59. In the words of Jeffrey Berry, "No one argues that there are only issue networks or only subgovernments active in policymaking. Rather, the argument is over what is most typical and most descriptive of the political process" ("Subgovernments," in *Remaking American Politics,* ed. Harris and Milkis, 233–34).

60. Ibid., 256.

61. See William P. Browne, "Policy and Interests: Instability and Change in Classic Issue Subsystems," in *Interest Group Politics,* ed. Allan J. Ciglar and Burdett A. Loomis, 2d ed. (Washington, D.C.: Congressional Quarterly Press, 1986), and Miller, "Recent Trends."

62. Berry, "Subgovernments," in *Remaking American Politics,* ed. Harris and Milkis, 242.

63. Ibid.

64. Heclo, "Issue Networks," in *The New American Political System,* ed. King, 102.

65. Berry, "Subgovernments," in *Remaking American Politics,* ed. Harris and Milkis, 242.

66. Bosso, *Pesticides and Politics,* 245–46.

67. Ibid., 253.

68. Sabatier and Jenkins-Smith, *Policy Change and Learning,* 5.

69. Ibid., 6.

70. Ibid., 24.

71. Ibid., 27.

72. Ibid., 212.

73. Ibid., 26.

74. Ibid., 16.

75. Harris, "Politicized Management," in *Remaking American Politics,* ed. Harris and Milkis, 278.

76. Ibid., 279.

77. Ibid.

78. Baumgartner and Jones, *Agendas and Instability,* 6.

CHAPTER 2. SUBGOVERNMENT DOMINANCE, 1945–65

1. James R. Temples, "The Politics of Nuclear Power: A Sub-Government in Transition," *Political Science Quarterly* 95, 2 (summer 1980): 241; Bruce L. Welch, "Nuclear Energy on the Dole," *Nation,* 26 February 1977, 231, cited in Temples, 241.

2. George T. Mazuzan and J. Samuel Walker, *Controlling the Atom: The Beginnings of Nuclear Regulation, 1946–1962* (Los Angeles: University of California Press, 1984), 419.

3. Frank R. Baumgartner and Bryan D. Jones, *Agendas and Instability in American Politics* (Chicago: University of Chicago Press, 1993), 69–70.

4. For a discussion of the Manhattan Project, see Leslie R. Groves, *Now It Can Be Told: The Story of the Manhattan Project* (New York: Harper and Row, 1962).

5. See Corbin Allardice and Edward R. Trapnell, *The Atomic Energy Commission* (New York: Praeger, 1974), and Richard G. Hewlett and Francis Duncan, *A History of the Atomic Energy Commission, Vol. 2, Atomic Shield, 1947–1952* (University Park: Pennsylvania State University Press, 1969).

6. Atomic Energy Act of 1946 (PL 585, 60 Stat. 755-75, 42 U.S.C. 1801-19); Atomic Energy Act of 1954 (PL 83-703, 68 Stat. 919, 42 U.S.C. 2011-2282).

7. 42 U.S.C. 1802 (a)(1); 42 U.S.C. 1802 (a)(4).

8. Harold P. Green and Alan P. Rosenthal, *Government of the Atom: The Integration of Powers* (New York: Atherton Press, 1963), 76.

9. Ibid., 75.

10. 42 U.S.C. 1809 (a)(1–3); 42 U.S.C. 1805 (2); 42 U.S.C. 1804 (c)(1).

11. See Hewlett and Duncan, *Atomic Shield,* 18.

12. Ibid., 449.

13. 42 U.S.C. 1810 (a); 42 U.S.C. 1810 (b)(1); 42 U.S.C. 1810 (a)(1).

14. Lewis Strauss, *Men and Decisions* (New York: Doubleday, 1962), 225, 349.

15. David E. Lilienthal, *The Journals of David E. Lilienthal: The Atomic Energy Years 1945–1950,* Vol. 2 (New York: Harper and Row, 1964), 387 (20 July 1947).

16. 42 U.S.C. 1802 (b). For discussion of the General Advisory Committee, see Richard T. Sylves, *The Nuclear Oracles: A Political History of the General Advisory Committee of the Atomic Energy Commission, 1947–1977* (Ames: Iowa State University Press, 1987).

17. See, for example, W. Henry Lambright, *Governing Science and Technology* (New York: Oxford University Press, 1976).

18. For a discussion of JCAE-constituency relations, see Green and Rosenthal, *Government of the Atom,* 31–35.

19. 42 U.S.C. 1815 (b).

20. Green and Rosenthal, *Government of the Atom,* 28.

21. 42 U.S.C. 1815 (b), (e).

22. Green and Rosenthal, *Government of the Atom,* 266.

23. Green and Rosenthal, *Government of the Atom,* offer an interesting discussion of the JCAE's relationship with the AEC; see especially 266–71. For a more general discussion of committee-agency relationships, see J. Leiper Freeman, *The Political Process: Executive Bureau—Legislative Committee Relations* (New York: Random House, 1965), 120–26.

24. Green and Rosenthal, *Government of the Atom,* 27.

25. Ibid., 30 (emphasis in original), 66.

26. Lee C. Nehrt, *International Marketing of Nuclear Power Plants* (Bloomington: Indiana University Press, 1966), 27–28; cited in Steven L. Del Sesto, *Science, Politics, and Controversy: Civilian Nuclear Power in the United States, 1946–1974* (Boulder, Colo.: Westview Press, 1979). See also Del Sesto, *Science, Politics, and Controversy,* 77.

27. On the background of JCAE members, see Temples, "The Politics of Nuclear Power," and Green and Rosenthal, *Government of the Atom,* 199.

28. For a discussion of JCAE attitudes toward security, see Harry S. Hall, *Congressional Attitudes Toward Science and Scientists: A Study of Legislative Reactions to Atomic Energy and the Political Participation of Scientists* (New York: Arno Press, 1979).

29. *Congressional Record,* 81st Cong., 2d sess., 2 February 1950, 96, pts. 1 and 2:1343.

30. On the joint committee's sense of mission, see Green and Rosenthal, *Government of the Atom,* 45, 272–73.

31. Robert A. Dahl and Ralph S. Brown, *Domestic Control of Atomic Energy* (New York: Social Science Research Council, 1951), 10.

32. Cited in Green and Rosenthal, *Government of the Atom,* 63.

33. Ibid., 53.

34. Michio Kaku and Jennifer Trainer, eds., *Nuclear Power: Both Sides* (New York: W. W. Norton, 1982), 248.

35. See Ralph E. Lapp, *The New Priesthood: The Scientific Elite and the Uses of Power* (New York: Harper and Row, 1965), 4; Daniel Ford, *The Cult of the Atom: The Secret Papers of the Atomic Energy Commission* (New York: Simon and Schuster, 1982), 24; and Lewis Strauss, "Faith in the Atomic Future," *Reader's Digest* 67, 400 (August 1955): 17, cited in Ford, *Cult of the Atom,* 46. Admittedly, faith in science was not a product of the 1950s. See, for example, William Leiss, *The Domination of Nature* (New York: George Braziller, 1972), especially 3–97.

36. Lapp, *The New Priesthood,* 69.

37. See Glenn T. Seaborg and William R. Corliss, *Man and Atom: Building a New World Through Nuclear Technology* (New York: E. P. Dutton, 1971); cited in Ford, *Cult of the Atom,* 23.

38. Frank G. Dawson, *Nuclear Power: Development and Management of a Technology* (Seattle: University of Washington Press, 1976), 48.

39. Dahl and Brown, *Domestic Control of Atomic Energy,* 5.

40. Green and Rosenthal, *Government of the Atom,* 199.

41. For a similar account of the importance of information to a pesticides subgovernment, see Christopher J. Bosso, *Pesticides and Politics: The Life Cycle of a Public Issue* (Pittsburgh: University of Pittsburgh Press, 1987).

42. Dahl and Brown, *Domestic Control of Atomic Energy,* 8.

43. Quoted in Mazuzan and Walker, *Controlling the Atom,* 23.

44. Ibid.

45. "Nuclear Power for Industry," *London Times,* 23 October 1953; cited in Mark Hertsgaard, *Nuclear Inc.: The Men and Money Behind Nuclear Energy* (New York: Pantheon Books, 1983), 25.

46. For a discussion of U.S. foreign policy objectives, see Gerard H. Clarfield and William M. Wiecek, *Nuclear America: Military and Civilian Nuclear Power in the United States, 1940–1980* (New York: Harper and Row, 1984), 182.

47. See Irwin C. Bupp and Jean-Claude Derian, *Light Water: How the Nuclear Dream Dissolved* (New York: Basic Books, 1978), 19–20; Joseph A. Camilleri, *The State and Nuclear Power: Conflict and Change in the Western World* (Brighton, Sussex: Wheatsheaf Books, 1984), 38; and Clarfield and Wiecek, *Nuclear America,* 182–85.

48. For a detailed discussion of the Atoms for Peace proposal, see Clarfield and Wiecek, *Nuclear America,* 185.

49. Joint Committee on Atomic Energy, *Hearings on the Proposed Euratom Agreement and Legislation to Carry Out the Proposed Cooperative Program,* 85th Cong., 2d sess., 1958 (hereinafter called *Hearings on Euratom*); cited in Hertsgaard, *Nuclear Inc.,* 37.

50. Joint Committee on Atomic Energy, *Report of the Panel on the Peaceful Use of Atomic Energy,* 84th Cong., 2d sess., 1956, 95 (hereinafter called *Peaceful Use Hearings*).

51. Joint Committee on Atomic Energy, *Hearings on Atomic Power Development and Private Enterprise,* 83d Cong., 1st sess., 1953.

52. See Dawson, *Nuclear Power,* 5. See also Alfred D. Chandler, *The Visible Hand: The Managerial Revolution in American Business* (Cambridge, Mass.: Belknap Press, 1977).

53. 42 U.S.C. 1801 (a)—1946; 42 U.S.C. 2011 (b)—1954; 42 U.S.C. 2013 (d); 42 U.S.C. 2162 (a–e); 42 U.S.C. 2061 (a); 42 U.S.C. 2131–40; 42 U.S.C. 2181–90; 42 U.S.C. 31–33, 56.

54. *Congressional Record,* 83d Cong., 2d sess., 15 April 1954, 100, pts. 3–4:5236; cited in Mazuzan and Walker, *Controlling the Atom,* 29.

55. 42 U.S.C. 2151–60; for a discussion of these provisions, see Bennett Boskey, "Some Patent Aspects of Atomic Power Development," *Law and Contemporary Problems* 21 (winter 1956): 115.

56. The Dixon-Yates controversy was symptomatic of an intense ideological struggle within the AEC and between the AEC and JCAE over the issue of public power. Democratic members of the JCAE thought public power was the best way to develop nuclear's potential, so they favored government construction and operation of prototype demonstration plants. The AEC, on the other hand, favored private development. The commission's chair, Lewis Strauss, was an apostle of private power, which placed him in bitter conflict with Democrats on the JCAE. For a discussion of Dixon-Yates, see Aaron Wildavsky, *Dixon-Yates: A Study in Power Politics* (New Haven, Conn.: Yale University Press, 1962).

57. Lewis Strauss commented on the need for revising the 1946 act in his memoirs: "Our suggestions were designed to relax the Government monopoly and accelerate peacetime atomic power development by encouraging private partnership and participation" (*Men and Decisions,* 324).

58. See Clarfield and Wiecek, *Nuclear America,* 188–90.

59. 42 U.S.C. 2064. For this interpretation, see Dawson, *Nuclear Power,* 92.

60. 42 U.S.C. 2012.

61. Mazuzan and Walker, *Controlling the Atom,* 421.

62. See *Legislative History of the Atomic Energy Act of 1954,* comp. Madeleine W. Losee, 3 vols. (Washington, D.C.: U.S. Atomic Energy Commission, 1955).

63. 42 U.S.C. 2134.

64. Mazuzan and Walker, *Controlling the Atom,* 66.

65. Joint Committee on Atomic Energy, *Hearings on the Development, Growth, and State of the Atomic Energy Industry,* 84th Cong., 1st sess., 1955, 55–59 (hereinafter called *Atomic Energy Development Hearings*); cited in Mazuzan and Walker, *Controlling the Atom,* 69. Strauss quotation cited in Ford, *Cult of the Atom,* 52.

66. Atomic Energy Commission, commission meeting 1061, 30 March 1955.

67. For an in-depth discussion of AEC incentives to the nuclear industry, see William H. Berman and Lee M. Hydeman, *The Atomic Energy Commission and Regulating Nuclear Facilities* (Ann Arbor: University of Michigan Press, 1961).

68. Mazuzan and Walker, *Controlling the Atom,* 421.

69. 42 U.S.C. 2133 (b); 42 U.S.C. 2134 (b).

70. Mazuzan and Walker, *Controlling the Atom,* 70.

71. For a more detailed discussion of the JCAE's relationship with the House Appropriations Committee, see Green and Rosenthal, *Government of the Atom,* 168 ff.

72. 42 U.S.C. 2017.

73. See Green and Rosenthal, *Government of the Atom,* 83. In 1957, the JCAE gained additional control over the reactor program when a bill was passed giving it authorization power over all nonmilitary reactor projects. Total authorization power was obtained when section 261 was amended in 1963 in PL 88-72 (77 Stat. 84), Sec. 107, the AEC Fiscal Year 1964 Authorization Act.

74. See Robert W. Williams, "Labyrinth and Leviathan: Politics Versus the State in the Quest for American Nuclear Energy" (paper presented at the 1990 annual meeting of the American Political Science Association, San Francisco, 30 August–2 September).

75. Dawson, *Nuclear Power,* 93.

76. Irwin C. Bupp, "Priorities in the Nuclear Technology Program" (Ph.D. diss., Harvard University, 1971); cited in Desaix Myers, *The Nuclear Power Debate: Moral, Economic, Technical Issues* (New York: Praeger, 1977), 59.

77. See Mazuzuan and Walker, *Controlling the Atom,* for a detailed discussion of the various stages of the PRDP, especially 81–118.

78. Ibid., 418.

79. 42 U.S.C. 2077.

80. 42 U.S.C. 2073 (c); see also Berman and Hydeman, *Atomic Energy Commission,* 48.

81. For a discussion of the events leading up to the passage of the Price-Anderson amendments, see Mazuzan and Walker, *Controlling the Atom,* 93–121, 183–213.

82. JCAE, *Atomic Energy Development Hearings,* 252.

83. See Mazuzan and Walker, *Controlling the Atom,* 101–7.

84. Ibid., 107–8.

85. Ford, *Cult of the Atom,* 46.

86. Mazuzan and Walker, *Controlling the Atom,* 210.

87. Joint Committee on Atomic Energy, *Hearings on Government Indemnity and Reactor Safety,* 85th Cong., 1st sess., 1957, 146.

88. PL 85-256, 71 Stat. 576, (1957) Sec. 4. The $560 million ceiling is even more remarkable because an AEC report on the consequences of a reactor accident, requested by the JCAE before the Price-Anderson legislation was debated, estimated that there could be 3,400 fatalities and $7 billion in damages in a "worst case" accident (WASH-740, Theoretical Possibilities and Consequences of Major Accidents in Large Nuclear Power Plants,

March 1957). The AEC and the joint committee, eager to develop a nuclear program, downplayed these estimates and removed another obstacle to nuclear power. Congressional action regarding the Price-Anderson legislation reflects its commitment to promoting and developing nuclear power. John W. Johnson offers a discussion of the legal battles over the Price-Anderson bill in *Insuring Against Disaster: The Nuclear Industry on Trial* (Macon, Ga.: Mercer University Press, 1986).

89. Mazuzan and Walker, *Controlling the Atom,* 212.

90. Cited in Jim Falk, *Global Fission: The Battle over Nuclear Power* (New York: Oxford University Press, 1982), 118.

91. Joseph Bowring, *Federal Subsidies to Nuclear Power: Reactor Design and the Fuel Cycle* (Washington, D.C.: Department of Energy, 1981).

92. Joint Committee on Atomic Energy, *Improving the AEC Regulatory Process,* 87th Cong., 1st sess., 1961, Committee Print 2, 574; cited in Mazuzan and Walker, *Controlling the Atom,* 420. See also Del Sesto, *Science, Politics, and Controversy,* 77. As late as June 1961, two-thirds of all research and development and construction activities of the AEC's reactor program was still devoted to military applications.

93. Elizabeth Rolph, *Regulation of Nuclear Power: The Case of the Light Water Reactor* (Lexington, Mass.: Lexington Books, 1978), 32.

94. See James Q. Wilson, "The Politics of Regulation," in *The Politics of Regulation,* ed. Wilson (New York: Basic Books, 1980).

95. For a discussion of these changes in AEC regulations and licensing procedures, see Mazuzan and Walker, *Controlling the Atom,* 373–406.

96. Quoted in Myers, *The Nuclear Power Debate,* 41.

97. Paul Quirk, *Industry Influence in Federal Regulatory Agencies* (Princeton, N.J.: Princeton University Press, 1981), 12.

98. According to David Okrent, an ACRS member at the time, all of the light water reactors proposed to the AEC for construction permits until Dresden 2 in 1965 were generated without a set of safety criteria that the design was required to meet. On reactor siting criteria, see Okrent, *Nuclear Reactor Safety: On the History of the Regulatory Process* (Madison: University of Wisconsin Press, 1981), 214; see also Mazuzan and Walker, *Controlling the Atom,* 214–45.

99. Letter from Holifield to Kennedy, 13 February 1962, White House Central Files (FG 202, Atomic Energy Commission), Kennedy Papers; cited in Mazuzan and Walker, *Controlling the Atom,* 410.

100. U.S. Atomic Energy Commission, *Civilian Nuclear Power—A Report to the President,* reprinted in Joint Committee on Atomic Energy, *Nuclear Power Economics—1962 Through 1967,* 90th Cong., 2d sess., 1968, 92–253. See 122–23, 124–26, 134, 142–48; cited in Mazuzan and Walker, *Controlling the Atom,* 413–14.

101. Mazuzan and Walker, *Controlling the Atom,* 418.

102. E. E. Schattschneider, *The Semi-Sovereign People: A Realist's View of Democracy in America* (Hinsdale, Ill.: Dryden Press, 1960), 71.

103. Bupp and Derian, *Light Water,* 189.

104. Ibid.

105. See Martha Derthick and Paul Quirk, *The Politics of Deregulation* (Washington, D.C.: Brookings Institution, 1985).

106. Del Sesto, *Science, Politics, and Controversy,* 7.

CHAPTER 3. REDEFINING NUCLEAR POWER

1. Frank R. Baumgartner and Bryan D. Jones, *Agendas and Instability in American Politics* (Chicago: University of Chicago Press, 1993), 8.

2. Joseph A. Pika, "Interest Groups and the Executives: Presidential Intervention," in *Interest Group Politics,* ed. Allan J. Cigler and Burdett A. Loomis (Washington, D.C.: Congressional Quarterly Press, 1983), 304.

3. Christopher J. Bosso, *Pesticides and Politics: The Life Cycle of a Public Issue* (Pittsburgh: University of Pittsburgh Press, 1987), 256.

4. James Q. Wilson, *American Government: Institutions and Policies,* 2d ed. (Englewood Cliffs, N.J.: Prentice-Hall, 1982), 418–19.

5. John W. Kingdon, *Agendas, Alternatives, and Public Policies* (Boston: Little, Brown, 1984), 100. For another view of agenda setting, see Roger W. Cobb and Charles D. Elder, *Participation in American Politics: The Dynamics of Agenda-Building* (Boston: Allyn and Bacon, 1972).

6. E. E. Schattschneider, *The Semi-Sovereign People: A Realist's View of Democracy in America* (Hinsdale, Ill.: Dryden Press, 1960), 2.

7. Irwin C. Bupp and Jean-Claude Derian, *Light Water: How the Nuclear Dream Dissolved* (New York: Basic Books, 1978), 43.

8. Cited in Mark Hertsgaard, *Nuclear Inc.: The Men and Money Behind Nuclear Energy* (New York: Pantheon Books, 1983), 43.

9. For a detailed discussion of nuclear power economics, see Charles Komanoff, *Power Plant Cost Escalation: Nuclear and Coal Capital Costs, Regulation, and Economics* (New York: Van Nostrand Reinhold, 1981).

10. See the annual reports of the Atomic Energy Commission for information concerning the number of reactors on order, in operation, and under construction. For information on the market for nuclear plants in the 1960s, see Bupp and Derian, *Light Water;* see also Alfred A. Marcus et al., "Adapting to Rapid Change and Decline: Industry Influence on Nuclear Power Safety" (paper presented at the 1990 annual meeting of the American Political Science Association, San Francisco, 30 August–2 September).

11. See Frank G. Dawson, *Nuclear Power: Development and Management of a Technology* (Seattle: University of Washington Press, 1976), 22; Bupp and Derian, *Light Water,* 71–76.

12. Dawson, *Nuclear Power,* 22.

13. Bupp and Derian, *Light Water,* 76.

14. Ibid., 188.

15. Ibid., 189.

16. Gene Smith, "A Building Boom for Nuclear Power Plants," *New York Times,* 14 January 1973, sec. 3, p. 3.

17. See Christopher Flavin, "Nuclear Power: The Market Test," *Worldwatch Paper* 57 (Washington, D.C.: Worldwatch Institute, 1983); see also Komanoff, *Power Plant Cost Escalation.*

18. Walter A. Rosenbaum, *The Politics of Environmental Concern* (New York: Holt, Rinehart and Winston, 1977), 178–79.

19. Rachel Carson, *Silent Spring* (Greenwich, Conn.: Fawcett, 1962).

20. For a detailed discussion of the effect of environmental concerns upon the nuclear power issue, see J. Samuel Walker, "Nuclear Power and the Environment: The Atomic En-

ergy Commission and Thermal Pollution, 1965–1971," *Technology and Culture* 30, 4 (1989): 964–92; see also U.S. Atomic Energy Commission, *Nuclear Power and the Environment* (Rockville, Md.: Atomic Energy Commission Records, Nuclear Regulatory Commission, 1969).

21. There had been earlier opposition to some plants, but it was scattered. See John Holdren and Phillip Herrera, *Energy: A Crisis in Power* (San Francisco: Sierra Club, 1971). For example, a proposal by Southern California Edison to quintuple the capacity at its San Onofre facility was blocked by the state's Coastal Commission. According to an AEC spokesman, it was the first time a state agency had blocked a project after the AEC had issued a construction permit. The Coastal Commission ruled that the proposal would "deface some scenic cliffs, obstruct public access to a beach and damage marine life." It was the first instance in which permission to construct a plant had been denied purely on environmental grounds. The project had already been approved by the AEC and the California Public Utility Commission as well as by a regional panel of the Coastal Commission. The regional panel's decision was appealed to the statewide commission by an environmental coalition, including Friends of the Earth and the Center for Law in the Public Interest. See Gladwin Hall, "Nuclear Project Blocked by Coast Ecological Unit," *New York Times,* 7 December 1973, 46.

22. This discussion is largely indebted to Walker, *Nuclear Power and the Environment.*

23. See, for example, W. S. Davis, "Conditions for Coexistence of Aquatic Communities with the Expanding Nuclear Power Industry," *Nuclear Safety* 10, 4 (July/August 1969): 292–99; Stanley Auerbach, "Ecological Considerations in Siting Nuclear Power Plants: The Long-Term Biotic Effects Problem," *Nuclear Safety* 12, 1 (January/February 1971): 25–34; and Walker, *Nuclear Power and the Environment,* 970.

24. Walker, *Nuclear Power and the Environment,* 969–75.

25. On the notion of agency mission, see James Q. Wilson, *Bureaucracy: What Government Agencies Do and Why They Do It* (New York: Basic Books, 1989), 101.

26. Walker, *Nuclear Power and the Environment,* 978–79.

27. Ibid., 975–78.

28. House Subcommittee on Fisheries and Wildlife Conservation of the Committee on Merchant Marine and Fisheries, *Hearings on Miscellaneous Fisheries Legislation,* 89th Cong., 2d sess., 1966, 11273; cited in Walker, *Nuclear Power and the Environment,* 978.

29. Walker, *Nuclear Power and the Environment,* 981–82.

30. *New Hampshire v. AEC,* 706 F2d 170 (1969), cert. den. 395 U.S. 962 (1969).

31. Robert H. Boyle, "The Nukes Are in Hot Water," *Sports Illustrated,* 20 January 1969, 24–28; Walker, *Nuclear Power and the Environment,* 984.

32. Walker, *Nuclear Power and the Environment,* 987–89.

33. Elizabeth Rolph, *Regulation of Nuclear Power: The Case of the Light Water Reactor* (Lexington, Mass.: Lexington Books, 1978), 43–44.

34. See Steven Ebbin and Raphael Kasper, *Citizen Groups and the Nuclear Power Controversy: Uses of Scientific and Technological Information* (Cambridge, Mass.: MIT Press, 1974), 23.

35. *Northern States Power Co. v. State of Minnesota,* 405 U.S. 1035 (1972). Interestingly, the initial grounds for intervention among those opposed to this particular reactor was again thermal pollution. The concern with radiation emerged at a later date.

36. For a discussion of the AEC's weapons testing programs, see Howard Ball, *Justice Downwind: America's Testing Program in the 1950s* (New York: Oxford University Press,

1986); see also Special Subcommittee on Radiation of the Joint Committee on Atomic Energy, *Hearings on the Nature of Radioactive Fallout and Its Effects on Man,* 85th Cong., 1st sess., 27 May–7 June 1957.

37. See John W. Gofman and Arthur W. Tamplin, *Poisoned Power: The Case Against Nuclear Power Plants* (Emmaus, Pa.: Rodale Press, 1971); Ernest Sternglass, *Secret Fallout: Low-Level Radiation from Hiroshima to Three Mile Island* (New York: McGraw-Hill, 1981); and Richard Curtis and Elizabeth Hogan, *Perils of the Peaceful Atom: The Myth of Safe Nuclear Power Plants* (Garden City, N.Y.: Doubleday, 1969).

38. See *Nucleonics Week* for this debate.

39. A rem is a standard unit of radiation dosage. Frequently, dosage is measured in millirems for low-level radiation; one thousand millirems equal one rem.

40. J. Leiper Freeman, *The Political Process: Executive Bureau—Legislative Committee Relations* (New York: Random House, 1965), 61. Similarly, Bosso argues that "issues are not born big or small; they are made that way by actors seeking to keep out or bring in allies. Any a priori judgement about the 'size' of an issue is to ignore the dynamics inherent in issue expansion" (*Pesticides and Politics,* 259).

41. See Stanley M. Nealey, Barbara D. Melber, and William L. Rankin, *Public Opinion and Nuclear Energy* (Lexington, Mass.: Lexington Books, 1983).

42. For a discussion of images associated with nuclear power, see Spencer Weart, *Nuclear Fear: A History of Images* (Cambridge, Mass.: Harvard University Press, 1988).

43. Joel Primack and Frank von Hippel, *Advice and Dissent: Scientists in the Political Arena* (New York: Basic Books, 1974), 214.

44. See the series of articles by Robert Gillette, especially "Nuclear Reactor Safety: A Skeleton at the Feast?" *Science* 172 (28 May 1971): 918–19; "Nuclear Reactor Safety: At the AEC the Way of the Dissenter Is Hard," *Science* 176 (5 May 1972): 492–98; "Nuclear Safety (I): The Roots of Dissent," *Science* 177 (1 September 1972): 771–76; "Nuclear Safety (II): The Years of Delay," *Science* 177 (8 September 1972): 867–71; "Nuclear Safety (III): Critics Charge Conflicts of Interest," *Science* 177 (15 September 1972): 970–75; and "Nuclear Safety (IV): Barriers to Communication," *Science* 177 (22 September 1972): 1080–82.

45. See Gillette, "The Way of the Dissenter Is Hard," 493; see also Daniel Ford, *The Cult of the Atom: The Secret Papers of the Atomic Energy Commission* (New York: Simon and Schuster, 1982), 115–28.

46. For a discussion of the UCS and its meetings with AEC scientists, see Ford, *Cult of the Atom,* 111–15.

47. Gillette, "Nuclear Safety (III)," 970.

48. See, for example, William B. Cottrell, "ORNL Nuclear Safety Research and Development Program," in Annual Report (Oak Ridge, Tenn.: Oak Ridge National Laboratory, 1969), ORNL-4511.

49. Gillette, "Nuclear Safety (III)."

50. "AEC Experts Share Doubts over Reactor Safety," *New York Times,* 12 March 1972; see also the hearing transcripts, U.S. Atomic Energy Commission, *In the Matter of Interim Acceptance Criteria for Emergency Core-Cooling Systems for Light Water-Cooled Nuclear Power Plants,* AEC Docket RM 50-1, 5318.

51. *Weekly Energy Report,* 12 February 1973, 7.

52. Joint Committee on Atomic Energy, *Hearings of the Status of Nuclear Reactor Safety,* 93d Cong., 1st sess., 22 January 1973, pt. 2, vol. 1, phase III (hereinafter called *Nuclear Reactor Safety Hearings*).

53. Ibid., 13, 115, 333. These comments were made, respectively, by AEC chairperson James Schlesinger, JCAE member Mike McCormack, and AEC member William Doub.

54. Ibid., 23 January 1973, pt. 1, phases I and IIb, 27.

55. Ebbin and Kasper, *Citizen Groups*, 210; see also Joseph G. Morone and Edward J. Woodhouse, *The Demise of Nuclear Energy? Lessons for Democratic Control of Technology* (New Haven, Conn.: Yale University Press, 1989).

56. See John L. Campbell, *Collapse of an Industry: Nuclear Power and the Contradictions of U.S. Policy* (Ithaca, N.Y.: Cornell University Press, 1988).

57. See Rolph, *Regulation of Nuclear Power*, and David Okrent, *Nuclear Reactor Safety: On the History of the Regulatory Process* (Madison: University of Wisconsin Press, 1981).

58. For an in-depth discussion of the dynamics of this process, see Campbell, *Collapse of an Industry*, 58–63.

59. Dorothy Nelkin and Michael Pollak, *The Atom Besieged: Extraparliamentary Dissent in France and Germany* (Cambridge, Mass.: MIT Press, 1981), 21.

60. For a similar discussion on pesticides, see Bosso, *Pesticides and Politics*, 121.

61. David Burnham, "2,300 Scientists Petition U.S. to Reduce Construction of Nuclear Power Plants," *New York Times*, 7 August 1975, 4.

62. Edward Cowan, "Scientists, Citing Hazards, Urge Cuts in Reactor Operating Levels," *New York Times*, 7 February 1973, 18, and Cowan, "Atom Plant Perils Cited by Scientists," *New York Times*, 13 November 1974, 46.

63. Steven L. Del Sesto, *Science, Politics, and Controversy: Civilian Nuclear Power in the United States, 1946–1974* (Boulder, Colo.: Westview Press, 1979), 164.

64. David Burnham, "Power Reactors Face Safety Test," *New York Times*, 22 September 1974, 1.

65. Bridenbaugh had been with GE for twenty-three years. He was manager of performance evaluation and improvement and manager of Mark I containment, Nuclear Energy Division. With GE for sixteen years, Hubbard was manager of quality assurance in the Nuclear Energy Control and Instrumentation Department. Minor had also been with GE for sixteen years. He was the manager of advanced control and instrumentation in the Nuclear Energy Division. Their tenure and positions at GE made it difficult to portray them as irresponsible, but members of the JCAE tried to discredit them by attempting to tie them to religious cults.

66. Joint Committee on Atomic Energy, *Hearings on the Investigation of Charges Relating to Nuclear Reactor Safety*, 94th Cong., 2d sess., 23 February 1976, 133.

67. CBS News, *60 Minutes*, 8 February 1976.

68. David Burnham, "AEC Files Show Effort to Conceal Safety Perils," *New York Times*, 10 November 1974, 1; see also Ford, *Cult of the Atom*, and the Union of Concerned Scientists, *Safety Second: The NRC and America's Nuclear Power Plants* (Bloomington: Indiana University Press, 1987).

69. On the various roles played by public interest groups in this period, see Andrew S. McFarland, *Public Interest Lobbies: Decision Making on Energy* (Washington, D.C.: American Enterprise Institute for Public Policy Research, 1976), and Richard C. Leone, "Public Interest Advocacy and the Regulatory Process," *Annals of the American Academy of Political and Social Science* 400 (March 1972): 46–58.

70. McFarland, *Public Interest Lobbies*, 69; *Nuclear Reactor Safety Hearings*, 28 January 1973, pt. 2, vol. 1, phase III, 472–78.

71. Edward Cowan, "Shutdown of 20 Nuclear Plants as Threat to Life Asked in Suit," *New York Times,* 1 June 1973, 70.

72. In addition to Critical Mass, other Nader organizations eventually became involved in the fight against nuclear power. The Public Interest Research Group (PIRG), which was established in 1970, conducted research on the technical and procedural aspects of nuclear regulation and routinely provided its reports to intervenors in AEC proceedings.

73. John Walsh, "Opposition to Nuclear Power: Raising the Question at the Polls," *Science* 190 (5 December 1975): 964–66.

74. George B. Henderson II, "The Nuclear Choice: Are Health and Safety Issues Preempted?" *Boston College Environmental Affairs Law Review* 8 (1980): 821–72; Edward Berlin et al., "Power Plant Siting—An Overview of Legislation and Litigation," monograph no. 15, *Environment Reporter* 4 (22 June 1973); and L. B. Stone, "Power Plant Siting: A Challenge to the Legal Process," *Albany Law Review* 36 (fall 1971): 1–34.

75. Southern Interstate Nuclear Board, "Summary of New York Plant Siting Activities," in *Power Plant Siting in the United States* (Memphis: Southern Interstate Nuclear Board, 1974).

76. For a discussion of nuclear moratorium proposals, see Campbell, *Collapse of an Industry.* See also Gladwin Hill, "Nuclear Power Development Encounters Rising Resistance with Curbs Sought in a Number of States," *New York Times,* 29 July 1975, 15.

77. Luther J. Carter, "Nuclear Initiatives: Two Sides Disagree on Meaning of Defeat," *Science* 194 (19 November 1976): 811–12.

78. Baumgartner and Jones, *Agendas and Instability,* 176.

79. For a discussion of energy subsystems, see John E. Chubb, *Interest Groups and the Bureaucracy: The Politics of Energy* (Palo Alto, Calif.: Stanford University Press, 1983), 6.

80. Charles O. Jones, "American Politics and the Organization of Energy Decision Making," *Annual Review of Energy* 4 (1979): 105.

81. Christian Joppke, "Decentralization of Control in U.S. Nuclear Energy Policy," *Political Science Quarterly* 107 (winter 1993): 709–25.

82. See Emmette S. Redford, *Democracy in the Administrative State* (New York: Oxford University Press, 1969).

83. Joint Committee on Atomic Energy, *Hearings on Nuclear Powerplant Siting and Licensing: H.R. 11957, 12823, 13484, and S. 3179 (Bills Related to the Need for Review of and Improvements to the Process for Bringing Nuclear Powerplants on Line),* 93d Cong., 2d sess., 1974, vols. 1 and 2 (hereinafter called *H.R. 11957 Hearings*).

84. See also Ebbin and Kasper, *Citizen Groups,* 4.

85. Senate Committee on Interior and Insular Affairs, *Hearings on Environmental Constraints and the Generation of Nuclear Electric Power: The Aftermath of the Court Decision on Calvert Cliffs,* 92d Cong., 1st sess., 1971, pts. 1 and 2, 202 (hereinafter called *The Calvert Cliffs Hearings*).

86. For an in-depth discussion of problems facing intervenor groups, see Ebbin and Kasper, *Citizen Groups.*

87. See Harold P. Green, "Nuclear Power Licensing and Regulation," *Annals of the American Academy of Political and Social Science* 400 (March 1972): 116–28.

88. 10 C.F.R. 2.733.

89. Ibid.

90. 10 C.F.R. 2.714a.

91. Donald W. Stever, *Seabrook and the Nuclear Regulatory Commission: The Licensing of a Nuclear Power Plant* (Hanover, N.H.: University Press of New England, 1980), 83.

92. Letter to Arthur Murphy, 15 April 1972; quoted in Ebbin and Kasper, *Citizen Groups,* 160–61.

93. *The Calvert Cliffs Hearings,* 206.

94. Ebbin and Kasper, *Citizen Groups,* 246.

95. See Stever, *Seabrook,* for an example of how this worked in the case of the Seabrook, New Hampshire, reactor.

96. 10 C.F.R. 2.732.

97. Ebbin and Kasper, *Citizen Groups,* 235.

98. 10 C.F.R. 2, appendix A, pt. f, subpt. 1.

99. 10 C.F.R. 2.1046.

100. Ebbin and Kasper, *Citizen Groups,* 184.

101. *The Calvert Cliffs Hearings,* 206.

102. See Sidney M. Milkis, "The Presidency, Policy Reform, and the Rise of Administrative Politics," in *Remaking American Politics,* ed. Richard A. Harris and Sidney M. Milkis (Boulder, Colo.: Westview Press, 1989).

103. *H.R. 11957 Hearings,* 115.

104. For a discussion of participatory democracy, see Carole Pateman, *Participation and Democratic Theory* (New York: Cambridge University Press, 1970), 24–25; see also Del Sesto, *Science, Politics, and Controversy.*

105. *Nuclear Reactor Safety Hearings,* 28 January 1973, pt. 2, vol. 1, phases IIb and III, 204, 496.

106. Mary Sinclair, intervenor in ECCS, before the Michigan Public Service Commission; cited in Ebbin and Kasper, *Citizen Groups,* 189.

107. David E. Lilienthal, *Atomic Energy: A New Start* (New York: Harper and Row, 1980), 30; Ralph Nader's testimony, *Nuclear Reactor Safety Hearings,* 28 January 1973, pt. 2, vol. 1, phase III, 496.

108. Ebbin and Kasper, *Citizen Groups,* 224.

109. See Seymour Martin Lipset and William Schneider, *The Confidence Gap: Business, Labor, and Government in the Public Mind,* 2d ed. (Baltimore: Johns Hopkins University Press, 1987).

110. Ibid., 185.

111. Constance Ewing Cook, *Nuclear Power and Legal Advocacy: The Environmentalists and the Courts* (Lexington, Mass.: Lexington Books/D. C. Heath, 1980), 16.

112. These remarks were made in a speech, "An Analysis of the Current Energy Problem," 14 January 1971, Electrical World Conference for Utility Executives, Washington, D.C.

113. Quoted in Marver H. Bernstein, *Regulating Business by Independent Commission* (Princeton, N.J.: Princeton University Press, 1955), 121.

114. Bupp and Derian, *Light Water,* 11.

115. The phrase "dialogue of the deaf" was attributed to Claude Zangger, Switzerland's deputy energy director in the early 1970s; quoted in Jim Falk, *Global Fission: The Battle over Nuclear Power* (New York: Oxford University Press, 1982), 152.

116. Lilienthal, *New Start,* 28.

117. Hertsgaard, *Nuclear Inc.,* 180; U.S. Atomic Energy Commission, *The Annual Report of the Atomic Energy Commission—1970,* 2; Harold C. Brown Jr., "AEC Goes

Public—A Case History," *Nuclear Safety* 11, 5 (September/October 1970): 365–69; and William Mitchell, "Problems and Progress in Nuclear Facilities Licensing," *Nuclear Safety* 9, 3 (May/June 1968): 193–201.

118. *Nuclear Reactor Safety Hearings,* 27 September 1973, pt. 1, vol. 1, phase IIa, 333.

119. Del Sesto, *Science, Politics, and Controversy,* 182.

120. Bosso, *Pesticides and Politics,* passim.

121. Martha Derthick and Paul Quirk, *The Politics of Deregulation* (Washington, D.C.: Brookings Institution, 1985).

122. Baumgartner and Jones, *Agendas and Instability,* 36.

123. Ibid., 32.

CHAPTER 4. THE COURTS, LICENSING REFORM, AND VENUE SHOPPING

1. For a contrary view, see John E. Chubb, *Interest Groups and the Bureaucracy: The Politics of Energy* (Stanford, Calif.: Stanford University Press, 1983), 121–24.

2. Frank R. Baumgartner and Bryan D. Jones, *Agendas and Instability in American Politics* (Chicago: University of Chicago Press, 1993), 64.

3. Ibid., 69.

4. Ibid., 37.

5. Ibid., 64.

6. Ibid., 69.

7. As examples, see Richard A. Harris and Sidney M. Milkis, *The Politics of Regulatory Change: A Tale of Two Agencies,* 2d ed. (New York: Oxford University Press, 1996), and Marc Allen Eisner, *Regulatory Politics in Transition* (Baltimore: Johns Hopkins University Press, 1993).

8. W. Lilley and J. Miller, "The New Social Regulation," *Public Interest* 47 (1977): 49–62.

9. See Walter A. Rosenbaum, *Environmental Politics and Policy* (Washington, D.C.: Congressional Quarterly Books, 1985), 39, and Richard A. Harris, "A Decade of Reform," in *Remaking American Politics,* ed. Harris and Sidney M. Milkis (Boulder, Colo.: Westview Press, 1989), 16.

10. See Richard B. Stewart, "The Reformation of American Administrative Law," *Harvard Law Review* 88 (June 1975): 1669–1803, and R. Shep Melnick, *Regulation and the Courts: The Case of the Clean Air Act* (Washington, D.C.: Brookings Institution, 1983).

11. Constance Ewing Cook, *Nuclear Power and Legal Advocacy: The Environmentalists and the Courts* (Lexington, Mass.: Lexington Books/D.C. Heath, 1980), xvi.

12. The various remarks were made by Chet Holifield to the House Subcommittee on Legislation and Military Operations of the Committee on Government Operations, *Hearings on H.R. 9090: The Energy Research and Development Administration Act,* 93d Cong., 1st sess., 1973, 118–19; see also W. O. Doub, speaking to the Atomic Industrial Forum, San Francisco, 12 November 1973.

13. Melnick, *Regulation and the Courts,* 393.

14. Stewart, "Reformation," 1712.

15. See Melnick, *Regulation and the Courts,* 11; also see *Udall v. FPC,* 387 U.S. 428 (1967); *Environmental Defense Fund, Inc. v. Ruckelshaus,* 439 F2d 584 (1971); and *Moss v. C.A.B.,* 430 F2d 891 (D.C. Cir. 1970).

16. *Scenic Hudson Preservation Conference v. FPC,* 354 F2d 608, 620 (2d Cir. 1965).

17. 10 C.F.R. pt. 2, appendix A, sec. 2.

18. 10 C.F.R. pt. 2, appendix A, sec. 2b.

19. 10 C.F.R. 2.743.

20. 10 C.F.R. 2.760.

21. 10 C.F.R. pt. 2, subpt. H.

22. 10 C.F.R. 2.801; 10 C.F.R. 2.802; 10 C.F.R. 2.804; 10 C.F.R. 2.805; 10 C.F.R. 2.806.

23. *Environmental Defense Fund v. Hardin,* 325 F.Supp. 1401 (D.D.C. 1971).

24. According to Roger G. Noll, the more that an organization finds itself involved in conflictual regulatory proceedings, the more likely lawyers will dominate that organization. Agencies thus must develop complex procedures to resolve disputes, which in turn increases the demands for lawyers' skills at building and operating systems that resolve conflict in an equitable manner. Moreover, the more complex procedures adopted by agencies also give courts the impression that the agency has acted fairly in gathering information and in considering different points of view, thus increasing the likelihood that the agency will prevail in any appeal. Noll adds, however, that participation in a lawyer-dominated system creates problems of a selective representation of interests in the agency's decision-making process. Complex procedures tend to make participation more expensive, which may make it harder for some groups to be heard. The result is a slower, more costly process, but one that is more likely to address a range of political issues, not just technical concerns. See "Government Regulatory Behavior: A Multi-disciplinary Survey and Synthesis," in *Regulatory Policy and the Social Sciences,* ed. Roger G. Noll (Los Angeles: University of California Press, 1985), 31–48.

25. See Skelly Wright, "The Court and the Rulemaking Process: The Limits of Judicial Review," *Cornell Law Review* 59 (1974): 375.

26. See Paul Quirk, *Industry Influence in Federal Regulatory Agencies* (Princeton, N.J.: Princeton University Press, 1981), 11; also see Chubb, *Interest Groups and the Bureaucracy,* 94–112.

27. Chubb, *Interest Groups and the Bureaucracy,* 112.

28. In June 1977 the NRC formed a study group to recommend methods of improving the agency's licensing process. The group urged the commission to make more frequent use of rulemaking to resolve contested issues. The group's results were released in a 1978 report, "Preliminary Statement of General Policy for Rulemaking to Improve Nuclear Power Plant Licensing," NUREG-0499.

29. Steven Ebbin and Raphael Kasper, *Citizens Groups and the Nuclear Power Controversy: Uses of Scientific and Technological Information* (Cambridge, Mass.: MIT Press, 1974), 154.

30. *The Calvert Cliffs Hearings,* 205.

31. *Calvert Cliffs Coordinating Committee v. AEC,* 449 F2d 1109 (D.C. Cir. 1971).

32. *The Calvert Cliffs Hearings,* 205–6; Gus Speth, quoted in Claude Barfield, "Calvert Cliffs Decision Requires Agencies to Get Tough with Environmental Laws," *National Journal,* 18 September 1971, 1925. Speth was later appointed by Carter to the Council of Environmental Quality.

33. *State of New Hampshire v. AEC,* 406 F2d 170 (1st Cir., cert. denied, 395 U.S. 962, 1969).

34. *Calvert Cliffs Coordinating Committee v. AEC,* at 1122.

35. Id. at 1112 (emphasis in original).

36. Id. at 1111.

37. Id. at 1112, 1115.

38. Id. at 1113.

39. Id. at 1114.

40. 35 *Fed. Reg.* (4 December 1970): 18469; 10 C.F.R. 50, appendix D.

41. 10 C.F.R. 50, appendix D.

42. *Calvert Cliffs Coordinating Committee v. AEC,* at 1117.

43. Id. at 1117–18 (emphasis in original).

44. Id. at 1118.

45. Id. at 1119.

46. Id. at 1115.

47. Id. at 1122.

48. Id. at 1123.

49. 36 *Fed. Reg.* (9 September 1971): 18071; 10 C.F.R. 50, appendix D.

50. Barfield, "Calvert Cliffs Decision," 797–803.

51. Joint Committee on Atomic Energy, *Hearings on the Status of Nuclear Reactor Safety,* 93d Cong., 1st sess., 1973, pt. 1, vol. 1, phase IIa, 465.

52. 36 *Fed. Reg.* (1 December 1971): 22818.

53. U.S. Atomic Energy Commission, *The Annual Report of the Atomic Energy Commission—1973* (Washington, D.C.: Government Printing Office, 1974), 57.

54. *Izaak Walton League of America v. Schlesinger,* 3 E.R.C. 1453 (D.C. Cir. 1971); Richard D. Lyons, "Nuclear Reactor Delayed by Court," *New York Times,* 13 June 1975, 15; *York Committee for a Safe Environment v. NRC,* 527 F2d 812 (D.C. Cir. 1975).

55. In the other decision handed down on 21 July 1976, the D.C. Circuit ruled that the NRC had placed too stringent an evidentiary burden on groups seeking commission consideration of energy conservation issues in licensing proceedings for two Michigan reactors. The court also held that the ACRS report must be sufficiently explicit to inform the public of all matters of concern to the committee in regard to the application. As it had in the *NRDC* case decided the same day, the court also remanded the licensing proceeding to the commission to restrike the NEPA cost-benefit analysis so as to include an assessment of reprocessing and waste disposal issues. See *Nelson Aeschliman v. NRC,* 547 F2d 622 (D.C. Cir. 1976).

56. *Natural Resources Defense Council v. NRC,* 547 F2d 633 (D.C. Cir. 1976).

57. Joint Committee on Atomic Energy, *Hearings on the Extent and Significance of the Impact on Reactor Licensing of Recent Court Decisions,* 94th Cong., 2d sess., 1976, 4.

58. *Vermont Yankee Nuclear Power Corporation v. NRDC* and *Consumers Power Company v. Aeschliman,* 435 U.S. 519 (1978).

59. See Antonin Scalia, "Vermont Yankee: The APA, the DC Circuit, and the Supreme Court," *Supreme Court Review* (1978): 371.

60. *Natural Resources Defense Council v. NRC,* 547 F2d 633 (D.C. Cir. 1976) at 644.

61. Id. at 645.

62. Id. at 645–46.

63. Id. at 646.

64. Id.

65. Id. at 653.

66. Id. at 654.

67. See *Vermont Yankee Nuclear Power Corporation v. NRDC* and *Consumers Power Company v. Aeschliman,* 435 U.S. 519, 1978. For a discussion of the Supreme Court decision,

see Scalia, "Vermont Yankee"; Richard B. Stewart, "Vermont Yankee and the Evolution of Administrative Procedure," *Harvard Law Review* 91 (1978): 1805-22; James F. Raymond, "A Vermont Yankee in King Burger's Court: Constraints on Judicial Review Under NEPA," *Boston College Environmental Affairs Law Review* 7 (1979): 629-64; and Clark Byse, "Vermont Yankee and the Evolution of Administrative Procedure," *Harvard Law Review* 91 (1978): 1823-32.

68. With respect to the *Aeschliman* case, the Supreme Court also reversed, holding that the sufficiency of an environmental impact statement was to be judged from the perspective of the time when it was written and that energy conservation was not an obvious alternative to nuclear plants in 1972.

69. See Lettie McSpadden Wenner, "The Courts and Environmental Policy," in *Environmental Politics and Policies: Theories and Evidence,* ed. James P. Lester (Durham, N.C.: Duke University Press, 1989), 243-45.

70. Quoted in Ebbin and Kasper, *Citizen Groups,* 71 (emphasis added).

71. AEC Press Release R-139, 6 April 1973; AEC Press Release R-67, 2 February 1973.

72. 10 CFR 2.786

73. U.S. Nuclear Regulatory Commission, *The Annual Report of the Nuclear Regulatory Commission—1978* (Washington, D.C.: Government Printing Office, 1978), 217.

74. Ebbin and Kasper, *Citizen Groups,* 143.

75. See David Okrent, *Nuclear Reactor Safety: On the History of the Regulatory Process* (Madison: University of Wisconsin Press, 1981).

76. Joint Committee on Atomic Energy, *Hearings on Licensing and Regulation of Nuclear Reactors,* 90th Cong. 1st sess., 1967.

77. The standard review plans were formally known as "Standard Format and Content for Safety Analysis Reports of Nuclear Power Reactors."

78. Melnick, *Regulation and the Courts,* 280.

79. For different interpretations of the factors leading to increased regulation see Irwin C. Bupp and Jean-Claude Derian, *Light Water: How the Nuclear Dream Dissolved* (New York: Basic Books, 1978); John L. Campbell, *Collapse of an Industry: Nuclear Power and the Contradictions of U.S. Policy* (Ithaca, N.Y.: Cornell University Press, 1988); Charles Komanoff, *Power Plant Cost Escalation: Nuclear and Coal Capital Costs, Regulation, and Economics* (New York: Van Nostrand Reinhold, 1981); Joseph G. Morone and Edward J. Woodhouse, *The Demise of Nuclear Energy? Lessons for Democratic Control of Technology* (New Haven, Conn.: Yale University Press, 1989); and Elizabeth Rolph, *Regulation of Nuclear Power: The Case of the Light Water Reactor* (Lexington, Mass.: Lexington Books, 1978).

80. Charles Komanoff, *Power Plant Cost Escalation,* traces much of the increased regulatory stringency to an expansion in the size of the nuclear sector; see especially chaps. 1 and 2.

81. The commission emphasized licensing reviews and standards rather than operating experience. In fact, the commission had no systematic program to review operating experience until the accident at Three Mile Island. There was no office to monitor the reports of operating reactors, to evaluate the safety implications of commonly reported operating problems, or to oversee that corrective action had taken place.

82. In preparing regulatory guides, the staff often delegated the work of writing the guide to industry committees. In many instances, the standards recommended by the industry reflected the current state of industry practice. Because the staff would often adopt

the industry standards in the regulatory guides, the industry was, in effect, writing the rules that governed its own behavior.

83. Daniel Ford, *The Cult of the Atom: The Secret Papers of the Atomic Energy Commission* (New York: Simon and Schuster, 1982), 195.

84. See Morone and Woodhouse, *Demise of Nuclear Energy,* 71–89; Rolph, *Regulation of Nuclear Power;* and Okrent, *Nuclear Reactor Safety.*

85. Clifford K. Beck, "Current Trends and Perspectives in Reactor Location and Safety Requirements," *Nuclear Safety* 8, 1 (fall 1966): 14.

86. See Chubb, *Interest Groups and the Bureaucracy,* 44.

87. Ibid., 100.

88. Ibid., 101–3.

89. Ibid., 107–8.

90. Ibid., 108.

CHAPTER 5. THE DEMISE OF THE AEC

1. The reporting requirements of NEPA and other laws, in conjunction with grants of standing to sue, transformed administrative politics. These mechanisms, designed to limit agency discretion, imposed new procedural obligations on agencies and forced them to consider additional viewpoints at each stage of decision making. They also expanded the information available to potential critics and greatly facilitated their access to rulemaking proceedings. Litigation, as we have seen, was an important element in the expansion of the nuclear conflict.

2. On the effects of NEPA, see Frederick R. Anderson, *NEPA in the Courts: A Legal Analysis of the National Environmental Policy Act* (Baltimore: Resources for the Future, 1973), and Richard N. L. Andrews, *Environmental Policy and Administrative Change* (Lexington, Mass.: Lexington Books, 1976).

3. 42 U.S.C.A. 7422.

4. U.S. Nuclear Regulatory Commission, *The Annual Report of the Nuclear Regulatory Commission—1977* (Washington, D.C.: Government Printing Office, 1977), 9.

5. PL 86-373, 73 Stat. 688, 42 U.S.C. 2021.

6. See *Northern States Power Co. v. State of Minnesota,* 447 F2d 1143 (8th Cir. 1971), in which Minnesota was prohibited from establishing radiation emissions standards that were more stringent than the AEC's. For a discussion of the preemption issue, see George B. Henderson II, "The Nuclear Choice: Are Health and Safety Issues Preempted?" *Boston College Environmental Affairs Law Review* 8 (1980): 821–72.

7. According to Henderson, twenty-four states had enacted such laws by 1977; see "The Nuclear Choice," 822.

8. The courts proved more sympathetic to objections to nuclear power based on economic considerations than to those based on safety. In 1983, the Supreme Court upheld a California law that placed a moratorium on the construction of new reactors until the high-level waste disposal problem was resolved. The state claimed that the measure was designed to prevent the state from bearing the financial burden of funding nuclear plants that might later be closed because of inadequate waste disposal facilities. The Court agreed, saying the moratorium was economic in nature and therefore unrelated to protec-

tion against radiation, which was reserved to the commission under the Atomic Energy Act. States, according to the Court, "retain their traditional responsibility in the field of regulating electrical utilities for determining questions of need, reliability, cost, and other related state concerns." See *Pacific Gas and Electric Co. v. Energy Resources Conservation and Development Commission*, 461 U.S. 190, 205 (1983).

9. George T. Mazuzan and J. Samuel Walker offer an interesting discussion of the joint committee's decision to leave the AEC intact in *Controlling the Atom: The Beginnings of Nuclear Regulation, 1946–1962* (Los Angeles: University of California Press, 1984); see especially 183–213.

10. Ibid., 373.

11. Testimony of L. Manning Muntzing, AEC director of regulation, to the Joint Committee on Atomic Energy, *Hearings on Nuclear Powerplant Siting and Licensing: H.R. 11957, 12823, 13484, and S. 3179 (Bills Related to the Need for Review of and Improvements to the Process for Bringing Nuclear Powerplants on Line)*, 93d Cong., 2d sess., 1974, vols. 1 and 2, 350.

12. Elizabeth Rolph, *Regulation of Nuclear Power: The Case of the Light Water Reactor* (Lexington, Mass.: Lexington Books, 1978), 29; see also U.S. Atomic Energy Commission, *The Annual Report of the Atomic Energy Commission—1968* (Washington, D.C.: Government Printing Office, 1968), 108.

13. Rolph, *Regulation of Nuclear Power*, 65.

14. See Edward Cowan, "Scientists, Citing Hazards, Urge Cut in Reactor Operating Levels," *New York Times*, 7 February 1973, and Cowan, "A-Plant Hearings Termed Charade," *New York Times*, 26 March 1974.

15. For a survey of public opinion on nuclear power throughout this period, see Stanley M. Nealey, Barbara D. Melber, and William L. Rankin, *Public Opinion and Nuclear Energy* (Lexington, Mass.: Lexington Books, 1983).

16. AEC Press Release S-18-170, 25 May 1970, 5.

17. For a discussion of Schlesinger's goals, see Rolph, *Regulation of Nuclear Power*, and Irwin C. Bupp and Jean-Claude Derian, *Light Water: How the Nuclear Dream Dissolved* (New York: Basic Books, 1978).

18. Speech to the Atomic Industrial Forum–American Nuclear Society Annual Meeting, Harbour, Florida, 20 October 1971, 3–4.

19. AEC press release O-147, 27 August 1971.

20. See Claude Barfield, "Calvert Cliffs Decision Requires Agencies to Get Tough with Environmental Laws," *National Journal*, 18 September 1971, 1925–33.

21. AEC Press Release P-31, 4 February 1972, 1.

22. For a discussion of Schlesinger's tenure, see Rolph, *Regulation of Nuclear Power*.

23. For a general discussion of the relationship between the tenure of agency chairpersons and their commitment to the agency's norms, see Martha Derthick and Paul Quirk, *The Politics of Deregulation* (Washington, D.C.: Brookings Institution, 1985), 90–95.

24. On the controversy over Shaw's treatment of safety research, see Robert Gillette, "Nuclear Reactor Safety: A Skeleton at the Feast?" *Science* 172 (28 May 1971): 918–19.

25. John W. Finney, "New A.E.C. Chairman Moves Against Dominance of Congressional Joint Panel," *New York Times*, 22 May 1973, 17.

26. Presidential address to the U.S. Congress, 29 June 1973.

27. For a sympathetic account of Holifield's role in atomic energy affairs, see

Richard W. Dyke, *Mr. Atomic Energy: Congressman Chet Holifield and Atomic Energy Affairs, 1945–1974* (New York: Greenwood Press, 1989).

28. Presidential message to Congress, 23 January 1973.

29. House Subcommittee on Legislation and Military Operations of the Committee on Government Operations, *Hearings on H.R. 11510: The Energy Reorganization Act of 1973,* 93d Cong., 1st sess., 27–29 November 1973, 31, 32 (hereinafter called *H.R. 11510 Hearings*).

30. *Nuclear Reactor Safety Hearings,* pt. 1, vol. 1, phases I and IIa, 331.

31. Senate Committee on Government Operations, *Hearings on S. 2135: The Administration's Proposal to Establish a Department of Energy and Natural Resources, and ERDA,* 93d Cong., 1st sess., 31 July, 1 August, and 13 September 1973, 137 (hereinafter called *S. 2135 Hearings*).

32. *H.R. 11510 Hearings,* 57–58.

33. Senate Subcommittee on Reorganization, Research, and International Organizations of the Committee on Government Operations, *Hearings on S. 2744: The Energy Reorganization Act of 1973,* 93d Cong., 1st sess., 1973, 145 (hereinafter called *S. 2744 Hearings*).

34. *H.R. 11510 Hearings,* 58.

35. House Committee on Government Operations, *The Energy Reorganization Act of 1973,* 93d Cong., 1st sess., 7 December 1973, H. Rept. 93-707.

36. Ibid.

37. *Congressional Record,* 93d Cong., 1st sess., 27 November 1973, 119, 38078.

38. Senate Subcommittee on Reorganization, Research, and International Organizations of the Committee on Government Operations, *Hearings on S. 2135: The Administration's Proposal to Establish a Department of Energy and Natural Resources and an Energy Research and Development Administration; and S. 2744, to Establish an Energy Research and Development Administration and a Nuclear Safety and Licensing Commission,* 93d Cong., 2d sess., 26–27 February, 12–13 March 1974, 100.

39. *Congressional Record,* 93d Cong., 2d sess., 28 May 1974, 120, 16416–17.

40. *S. 2744 Hearings,* 229.

41. Senate Committee on Government Operations, *The Energy Reorganization Act of 1974,* 93d Cong., 2d sess., 1974, S. Rept. 93-980.

42. *Congressional Record,* 93d Cong., 2d sess., 13 August 1974, 120, 28128.

43. Ibid., 28129.

44. Ibid., 28135.

45. *Congressional Record,* 93d Cong., 2d sess., 15 August 1974, 120, 28591.

46. Ibid., 28607.

47. The words are those of Carl Horn, president of Duke Power, to the Joint Committee on Atomic Energy, *Hearings on Nuclear Powerplant Siting and Licensing,* 727.

48. *Congressional Record,* 93d Cong., 2d sess., 15 August 1974, 120, 28610.

49. House, *Conference Report on H.R. 11510, the Energy Reorganization Act of 1974,* 93d Cong., 2d sess., 1974, H. Rept. 93-1445.

50. See Joint Committee on Atomic Energy, *Hearings on Nuclear Powerplant Siting and Licensing.*

51. *Congressional Record,* 93d Cong., 2d sess., 9 October 1974, 120, 34755.

52. Ibid., 34856.

53. For a similar analysis of pesticides, see Christopher J. Bosso, *Pesticides and Politics: The Life Cycle of a Public Issue* (Pittsburgh: University of Pittsburgh Press, 1987), 189–90.

CHAPTER 6. CONGRESSIONAL REORGANIZATION

1. Editorial, *New York Times,* 21 October 1974, 32.

2. See Robert Gillette, "Nuclear Reactor Safety: A Skeleton at the Feast?" *Science* 172 (28 May 1971): 918-19.

3. See Daniel Ford, *The Cult of the Atom: The Secret Papers of the Atomic Energy Commission* (New York: Simon and Schuster, 1982).

4. See David Welborn, William Lyons, and Larry Thomas, *Implementation and Effects of the Federal Government in the Sunshine Act* (Washington, D.C.: Administrative Conference of the United States, 1984).

5. PL 89-554, 80 Stat. 383.

6. 5 U.S.C. 552a.

7. See U.S. Nuclear Regulatory Commission, *The Annual Report of the Nuclear Regulatory Commission—1976* (Washington, D.C.: Government Printing Office, 1976), 17, and *The Annual Report of the Nuclear Regulatory Commission—1979* (Washington, D.C.: Government Printing Office, 1979), 246.

8. See *Union of Concerned Scientists v. NRC* (D. D.C. no. 76-0370). The suit sought to compel disclosure of all notes and memoranda submitted by staff members to the AEC's director of regulation. The NRC claimed that the documents fell within exemption 5 of the Freedom of Information Act (FOIA). The court upheld the NRC on sixty of seventy-seven documents; *Natural Resources Defense Council v. NRC* (D. D.C. no. 76-0592). The NRDC sought all documents prepared by the commission and its staff in developing the 14 November 1975 *Federal Register* notice on the mixed-oxide fuel rulemaking. The commission had denied the request after determining they were intraagency documents that were exempt from disclosure according to commission rules. The court upheld the NRC on sixty of eighty documents; *John Abbotts et al. v. NRC* (D. D.C. no. 77-624). Abbotts and the NRDC challenged the NRC decision to withhold safeguards documents; *Applegate v. NRC* (D. D.C. no. 82-1829, 24 May 1983). The district court said that "evidence was uncovered in the record suggesting that despite the existence of carefully drafted official NRC FOIA policies and procedures, the personnel assigned to implement FOIA in OIA executed those rules in a manner designed to thwart the release of responsive materials. These procedures appeared to include the removal of documents from agency files, taking documents home, and the use of carefully worded oral inquiries designed to avoid identification of documents. . . . It is disturbing to this Court that unbeknownst to agency management, an office in the NRC was able to design a filing and oral search system which could frustrate the clear and express purposes of FOIA. The assertion of an exemption is one thing, avoidance borders on dishonesty."

9. The NRC's rules for complying with the Freedom of Information Act can be found in 10 C.F.R. 2.790a.

10. PL 92-463, 86 Stat. 770. For a discussion of the Federal Advisory Committee Act, see Joel Primack and Frank von Hippel, *Advice and Dissent: Scientists in the Political Arena* (New York: Basic Books, 1974), 35.

11. Steven Ebbin and Raphael Kasper, *Citizen Groups and the Nuclear Power Controversy: Uses of Scientific and Technological Information* (Cambridge, Mass.: MIT Press, 1974), 27.

12. U.S. Atomic Energy Commission, *The Annual Report of the Atomic Energy Commission—1973* (Washington, D.C.: Government Printing Office, 1973), 20.

13. Interview with William Stratton, former ACRS member, 13 March 1991.

14. See Welborn, Lyons, and Thomas, *Sunshine Act.*

15. E. E. Schattschneider, *The Semi-Sovereign People: A Realist's View of Democracy in America* (Hinsdale, Ill.: Dryden Press, 1960), 2.

16. See Joint Committee on Atomic Energy, *Hearings on H.R. 13731 and H.R. 13732 to Amend the Atomic Energy Act of 1954 Regarding the Licensing of Nuclear Facilities,* 92d Cong., 2d sess., 1972, pt. 1 (hereinafter called *H.R. 13731 Hearings*).

17. See also *H.R. 11957 Hearings;* Joint Committee on Atomic Energy, *Hearings on S. 1717 and H.R. 7002: Proposed Nuclear Siting and Licensing Legislation,* 94th Cong., 1st sess., 1975; House Subcommittee on Energy and the Environment of the Committee on Interior and Insular Affairs, *Hearings on the Nuclear Siting and Licensing Act of 1978,* 95th Cong., 2d sess., 1978.

18. See *Izaak Walton League et al. v. Schlesinger et al.* (D. D.C. no. 2207-71, 13 December 1971).

19. See *H.R. 13731 Hearings,* pt. 1.

20. PL 92-307, 86 Stat. 191.

21. 42 U.S.C. 2242 and 42 U.S.C. 2242 (a).

22. The vote on the measure was 267 to 138. See *Congress and the Nation* (Washington, D.C.: Congressional Quarterly Press, 1977), 4: 248.

23. Ibid., 225–26.

24. PL 94-197, 89 Stat. 1111–15.

25. See U.S. Nuclear Regulatory Commission, *The Annual Report of the Nuclear Regulatory Commission—1976,* 202–3.

26. Uranium-235, the fuel used in light water reactors, must be enriched to make a fission reaction possible. Uranium-235 constitutes only 0.7 percent of raw uranium.

27. *Congress and the Nation,* 4: 272.

28. A number of moratorium bills were introduced during the 93d Congress. In the Senate, Mike Gravel (D-Alaska) introduced S. 1217, which called for a gradual phasing out of the construction, operation, and export of nuclear plants by January 1980. In the House, three identical bills were introduced by Jerome Waldie (D-Calif.), Hamilton Fish Jr. (R-N.Y.), and Carleton King (R-N.Y.). The bills called for a five-year moratorium on the construction of new plants until the Office of Technology Assessment had completed a study of reactor safety.

29. John E. Chubb, *Interest Groups and the Bureaucracy: The Politics of Energy* (Palo Alto, Calif.: Stanford University Press, 1983), 68.

30. For a more general discussion of changes in Congress, see Thomas E. Mann and Norman Ornstein, eds., *The New Congress* (Washington, D.C.: American Enterprise Institute, 1981); see also Lawrence C. Dodd and Bruce I. Oppenheimer eds., *Congress Reconsidered,* 3d ed. (Washington, D.C.: Congressional Quarterly Press, 1985).

31. *Congressional Record,* 93d Cong., 2d sess., 4 June 1974, 120, 17583.

32. Hosmer went on to direct the American Nuclear Energy Council, an industry group that lobbied Congress on nuclear issues. Hosmer's post-Congress employment was further testimony to the continued strength of the revolving door that had long characterized the atomic subgovernment.

33. John Walsh, "Congress: House Redistributes Jurisdiction over Energy," *Science* 195 (11 February 1977): 562.

34. John Walsh, "Congress: Election Impacts Atomic Energy, Science Committees," *Science* 194 (19 November 1976): 812.

35. Michael J. Malbin, "You Can Please Some of the Senators Some of the Time," *National Journal*, 15 January 1977, 106.

36. "The Shape of the Senate Committees . . . After the Long Battle over Reform," *National Journal*, 12 February 1977, 258.

37. "For the Staff of the Joint Atomic Energy Committee, It's Time to Fold the Tent," *National Journal*, 12 March 1977, 398.

38. For a discussion of these events, see *Congress and the Nation*, vol. 5, 462, and Walsh, "Congress: Election Impacts Atomic Energy," 812–14.

39. Chubb, *Interest Groups and the Bureaucracy*, 115.

40. See U.S. Nuclear Regulatory Commission, *The Annual Report of the Nuclear Regulatory Commission—1975, 1976, 1977, 1978, 1979, 1980*.

41. *Congress and the Nation*, 5: 462.

42. Quoted in Dick Kirtschen, "The Curious Goings-On at the Nuclear Regulatory Commission," *National Journal*, 25 May 1978, 839. Udall continued this type of criticism into the next decade, saying in 1985 that NRC personnel were "good, honest, dedicated, to-be-nuclear-is-to-be-for-America kind of guys" (*New York Times*, 1 January 1985).

43. See for example, House Committee on Government Operations, *Licensing Speedup, Safety Delay: NRC Oversight*, 97th Cong., 1st sess., 20 October 1981, H. Rept. 97-277.

44. See *National Journal*, 22 April 1978, 649.

45. See Union of Concerned Scientists, *Safety Second: A Critical Evaluation of the NRC's First Decade* (Cambridge, Mass.: Union of Concerned Scientists, 1987), 83–86.

46. The Department of Energy was established by Congress in August 1977 pursuant to a request by President Carter. It was created by consolidating ERDA, the Federal Energy Administration, the Federal Power Commission, and programs from five other federal agencies (Commerce, Defense, Housing and Urban Development, Interior, and Transportation). See the Department of Energy Reorganization Act of 1977, PL 95-91, 91 Stat. 577.

47. Quoted in William J. Lanouette, "The Revolving Door—It's Tricky to Try to Stop It," *National Journal*, 19 November 1977, 1796; see also "Senate Panel Nixes Two Carter Nominees," *National Journal*, 11 October 1977, 1658.

48. David Burnham, "House Panel Votes Limits on A-Plants," *New York Times*, 10 May 1979, 20.

49. William J. Lanouette, "Under Scrutiny by a Divided Government, the Nuclear Industry Tries to Unite," *National Journal*, 12 January 1980, 45.

50. *Congressional Quarterly Weekly Reports*, "Senate Bill Would Close Nuclear Plants in States Without Emergency Plans," 21 July 1979, 1441–42.

51. Ibid.

52. David Burnham, "Freeze on Building of Nuclear Plants Rejected by House," *New York Times*, 30 November 1979, 1; Joint Committee on Atomic Energy, *Hearings on the Investigation of Charges Relating to Nuclear Safety*, 94th Cong., 2d sess., 1976, vols. 1 and 2.

53. The NRC formally defined an "unresolved safety issue" as any "matter affecting a number of nuclear power plants that poses important questions concerning the adequacy of existing safety requirements for which a final resolution has not yet been developed and that involves conditions not likely to be acceptable over the lifetime of the plants affected."

54. See U.S. Nuclear Regulatory Commission, *Identification of Unresolved Safety Issues Relating to Nuclear Power Plants—A Report to Congress* (Washington, D.C.: Government Printing Office, January 1979), NUREG-0510.

55. U.S. Nuclear Regulatory Commission, *The Annual Report of the Nuclear Regulatory Commission—1978,* 20.

56. John G. Kemeny et al., *Report of the President's Commission on the Accident at Three Mile Island* (Washington, D.C.: Government Printing Office, October 1979), 20.

57. Ibid.

58. See U.S. Nuclear Regulatory Commission, *Program for the Resolution of Generic Issues Related to Nuclear Power Plants* (Washington, D.C.: Government Printing Office, January 1978), NUREG-0410, and *Identification of Unresolved Safety Issues,* NUREG-0510.

59. See Union of Concerned Scientists, *Safety Second,* 19–24.

60. See U.S. Nuclear Regulatory Commission, *Identification of New Unresolved Safety Issues Relating to Nuclear Power Plants* (Washington, D.C.: Government Printing Office, March 1981), NUREG-0705, 4–5.

61. Kemeny et al., *Report of the President's Commission,* 65.

62. U.S. General Accounting Office, *Management Weaknesses Affect Nuclear Regulatory Commission Efforts to Address Safety Issues Common to Nuclear Power Plants* (Washington, D.C.: Government Printing Office, September 1984), GAO/RCED-84-149, 28–29.

63. For an in-depth discussion of the use of the appropriations process to influence agency action, see Richard Fenno, *Power of the Purse: Appropriations Politics in Congress* (Boston: Little, Brown, 1966).

64. See Barry Weingast, "Congress, Regulation, and the Decline of Nuclear Power," *Public Policy* 28 (spring 1980): 244–45.

65. William C. Wood, *Nuclear Safety: Risks and Regulation* (Washington, D.C.: American Enterprise Institute, 1983).

66. On the appropriations process and the commission, see Weingast, "Decline of Nuclear Power" 246–53.

67. Testimony of Ben C. Rusche, director of the Office of Nuclear Reactor Regulation, *Hearings on the Investigation of Charges Relating to Nuclear Safety,* 322.

68. House Committee on Government Operations, *Licensing Speedup,* H. Rept. 97-277, 37–43; see also Union of Concerned Scientists, *Safety Second,* 63–75.

69. Frank R. Baumgartner and Bryan D. Jones, *Agendas and Instability in American Politics* (Chicago: University of Chicago Press, 1993), 14–21.

70. Ibid., 14.

71. Schattschneider, *The Semi-Sovereign People,* 48.

CHAPTER 7. THE POLITICS OF NUCLEAR POWER, 1975–80

1. Richard A. Harris, "Politicized Management: The Changing Face of Business in American Politics," in *Remaking American Politics,* ed. Richard A. Harris and Sidney M. Milkis (Boulder, Colo.: Westview Press, 1989), 262.

2. Ibid., 269.

3. Reginald Stuart, "Ford to Increase Efforts to Back Nuclear Power," *New York Times,* 5 June 1975, 51.

4. David Burnham, "Atomic Industry To Promote Views," *New York Times,* 17 January 1975, 34.

5. Reginald Stuart, "Nuclear Power Campaign Is On," *New York Times,* 26 May 1975, 21; see William J. Lanouette, "Under Scrutiny by a Divided Government, the Nuclear Industry Tries to Unite," *National Journal,* 12 January 1980, 46.

6. Stuart, "Nuclear Power Campaign," 21.

7. William J. Lanouette, "Off the Hill and Off the Record, Lobbyist Clubs Dine on Gourmet Tips," *National Journal,* 10 April 1982, 630–34.

8. Lanouette, "Under Scrutiny," 44–48.

9. *Congressional Quarterly Weekly Reports,* "Three Mile Reactor Accident Clouds Future of Industry," 7 April 1979, 630.

10. Lanouette, "Under Scrutiny," 44.

11. Lelan F. Sillin Jr., speech delivered at INPO CEO conference, Atlanta, 22 September 1983; cited in Joseph V. Rees, *Hostages of Each Other: The Transformation of Nuclear Safety Since Three Mile Island* (Chicago: University of Chicago Press, 1994), 44.

12. Rees, *Hostages of Each Other,* 115.

13. Lanouette, "Off the Hill," 630–34.

14. Lanouette, "Under Scrutiny," 44.

15. Mark Hertsgaard, *Nuclear Inc.: The Men and Money Behind Nuclear Energy* (New York: Pantheon Books, 1983), 187.

16. Ibid., 188.

17. Ibid., 199–200.

18. See Randall B. Ripley and Grace A. Franklin, *Congress, the Bureaucracy, and Public Policy,* 3d ed. (Homewood, Ill.: Dorsey Press, 1984).

19. Anders resigned from the NRC in 1976; he later joined General Electric in 1977 as head of its nuclear division. Anders's actions were not atypical and demonstrate the continued flow of personnel between the AEC/NRC and the nuclear power industry. Evidence supporting the existence of the revolving door was provided by a Common Cause study which found that nearly 72 percent of the NRC's 429 most senior personnel had been employed by private enterprise in the energy field, with 90 percent of them coming from firms holding licenses, permits, or contracts with the commission. There are also numerous examples of individuals who at one time or another worked for either the AEC, the NRC, and the nuclear industry. Perhaps the ultimate nuclear insider was James T. Ramey who during the course of his career served as the AEC's assistant general counsel, the executive staff director of the joint committee, an AEC commissioner, and a JCAE consultant. Upon leaving the government, Ramey went to work as a consultant for Stone and Webster, one of the leading firms involved in the construction of nuclear plants. A partial list of some of the other individuals who passed through the revolving door reads like a veritable AEC/NRC "Who's Who." Included in the list are former commissioners William O. Doub, Marcus Rowden, and Joseph Hendrie, as well as former staffers Ben C. Rusche, the NRC's first director of the Office of Nuclear Reactor Regulation; Thomas F. Engelhardt, the NRC's deputy executive legal director; Robert Hollingsworth, the AEC's general manager from 1964–74; L. Manning Muntzing, the AEC's director of regulation in the early 1970s; Howard Larson, who left the NRC's Division of Materials and Fuel Cycle

Facility Licensing to become vice president of the Atomic Industrial Forum; and Robert Minogue, director of the AEC's Office of Standards Development.

20. Dick Kirtschen, "Nuclear Licensing Reform—A Bomb About to Explode," *National Journal,* 7 January 1978, 13–15.

21. Dick Kirtschen, "Nuclear Lobbying—It's Not as Simple as 'Us Against Them,' " *National Journal,* 18 February 1978, 261–64.

22. By the time the project was finally canceled in 1984, the cost estimate had risen to between $4 billion and $8 billion.

23. Hertsgaard, *Nuclear Inc.,* 87.

24. "House Votes To Start Clinch River Plant," *National Journal,* 24 September 1977, 1506. See Robert J. Samuelson, "Pulling the Plug on Plutonium," *National Journal,* 30 July 1977, 1182; see also *Congress and the Nation* (Washington, D.C.: Congressional Quarterly Press, 1977), 4:261.

25. See Hertsgaard, *Nuclear Inc.,* 90–94; *Mother Jones,* June 1979; industry representatives included Robert Kirby, chairman of Westinghouse; Walter Dance, vice chairman of the board for General Electric; Arthur Santry Jr., president of Combustion Engineering; George Zipf, president of Babcock and Wilcox; James J. O'Connor, Commonwealth Edison; William Lee, Duke Power; Sherwood Smith, Carolina Power and Light; William Kuhns, chairman of the board, General Public Utilities; William McCollum Jr., president of Edison Electric Institute; Harry Reinsch, president of Bechtel Power; William Allen, president of Stone and Webster, the construction firm for Clinch River; Kenneth Roe, president of Burns and Roe, the architect-engineer for Clinch River; and Willard Rockwell, chairman of the board of Rockwell International.

26. Richard Corrigan, Dick Kirtschen, and Robert J. Samuelson, "Jimmy Carter's Energy Crusade," *National Journal,* 30 April 1977, 656–72.

27. William D. Metz, "Nuclear Licensing: Promised Reform Miffs All Sides of Nuclear Debate," *Science* 198 (11 November 1977): 590–93. Congress followed up in 1982 with the Nuclear Waste Act, which effectively solved the spent fuel and reprocessing problems facing the utilities. The law allowed utilities to store spent fuel in on-site storage pools until permanent disposal sites were ready.

28. Cited in Kirtschen, "Nuclear Lobbying," 263.

29. Ibid.

30. Quoted in Dick Kirtschen, "The Curious Goings-On at the Nuclear Regulatory Commission," *National Journal,* 25 May 1978, 839.

31. Carnesale was not Carter's first choice. The position was offered to several others who turned it down, including former Washington governor Daniel Evans, former EPA administrator William Ruckelshaus, and former EPA deputy administrator John Quarles.

32. Kirtschen, "Nuclear Licensing Reform."

33. Ibid.

34. H.R. 11704, S. 2775; see also Chapter 4.

35. Dick Kirtschen, "Administration Acts to Keep Nuclear Option Alive," *National Journal,* 25 March 1978, 484.

36. Richard A. Harris and Sidney M. Milkis, *The Politics of Regulatory Change: A Tale of Two Agencies,* 2d ed. (New York: Oxford University Press, 1996).

37. U.S. Nuclear Regulatory Commission, *Three Mile Island: A Report to the Commissioners and to the Public,* prepared by Mitchell Rogovin et al. (Washington, D.C.: Government Printing Office, January 1980), NUREG/CR-1250, 142–43 (emphasis in original).

38. See Metz, "Nuclear Licensing: Promised Reform."

39. Marshall R. Goodman and Frederic P. Andes, "The Politics of Regulatory Reform and the Future Direction of Nuclear Energy Policy," *Policy Studies Review* 5, 1 (August 1985): 111-21.

40. See "Reducing Nuclear Powerplant Leadtimes: Many Obstacles Remain," Report to the Congress by the Comptroller General of the United States, March 1977; Congressional Research Service, "The Role of Licensing in Nuclear Power Plant Construction Times," by Carl E. Behrens, analyst for the Environment and Natural Resources Policy Division, 20 October 1977; see also House Committee on Government Operations, *Licensing Speedup, Safety Delay: NRC Oversight,* 97th Cong., 1st sess., 20 October 1981, H. Rept. 97-277.

41. U.S. Nuclear Regulatory Commission, *Nuclear Power Plant Licensing: Opportunities for Improvement* (Washington, D.C.: Government Printing Office, June 1977), NUREG-0292.

42. John G. Kemeny et al., *Report of the President's Commission on the Accident at Three Mile Island* (Washington, D.C.: Government Printing Office, October 1979).

43. Ibid.

44. Ibid., 19.

45. Ibid., 20.

46. Ibid.

47. Ibid., 22.

48. Ibid., 22, 24.

49. See Ann Pelham, "Carter Urges New Nuclear Plant Licensing," *Congressional Quarterly Weekly Reports,* 15 December 1979, 2845.

50. Ibid.

51. The President's Reorganization Plan no. 1 of 1980 cleared Congress in June and became effective 1 October 1980.

52. In order, the individuals were Lee V. Gossick, Robert Minogue, Victor Stello Jr., John A. Harris, and Thomas Engelhardt.

53. Walter A. Rosenbaum, *Environmental Politics and Policy,* 2d ed. (Washington, D.C.: Congressional Quarterly Press, 1991), 241.

54. Quoted in Kirtschen, "Curious Goings-On," 843.

55. Robert L. Cohen and S. Robert Lichter, "Nuclear Power: The Decision-Makers Speak," *Regulation* 7, 2 (March/April 1983): 37.

56. See U.S. Nuclear Regulatory Commission, *The Annual Report of the Nuclear Regulatory Commission—1976, 1977, 1978, 1979, 1980* (Washington, D.C.: Government Printing Office, 1976-80).

57. PL 96-295, 94 Stat. 780.

58. U.S. Nuclear Regulatory Commission, *The Annual Report of the Nuclear Regulatory Commission—1980,* 148-52.

59. Testimony at the Joint Committee on Atomic Energy, *Hearings on the Investigation of Charges Relating to Nuclear Reactor Safety,* 94th Cong., 2d sess., 1976, vols. 1 and 2.

60. Kirtschen, "Nuclear Licensing Reform," 15.

61. See Harris and Milkis, *The Politics of Regulatory Change,* on the Federal Trade Commission, chap. 5.

62. See Martha Derthick and Paul Quirk, *The Politics of Deregulation* (Washington, D.C.: Brookings Institution, 1985), for example, on telecommunications policy and the FCC.

63. John L. Campbell, *Collapse of an Industry: Nuclear Power and the Contradictions of U.S. Policy* (Ithaca, N.Y.: Cornell University Press, 1988), 3.

64. Edison Electrical Institute Statistical Yearbook of the Electric Utility Industry for 1977 (New York: Edison Electrical Institute, 1978), 18; see also Constance Ewing Cook, *Nuclear Power and Legal Advocacy: The Environmentalists and the Courts* (Lexington, Mass.: Lexington Books/D.C. Heath, 1980), 2.

65. Gene Smith, "Nation's Utilities Cut Back on Construction Plans by 18%," *New York Times*, 12 October 1974, 1.

66. See Charles Komanoff, *Power Plant Cost Escalation: Nuclear and Coal Capital Costs, Regulation, and Economics* (New York: Van Nostrand Reinhold, 1981).

67. Christian Joppke, "Decentralization of Control in U.S. Nuclear Energy Policy," *Political Science Quarterly* 107 (winter 1992–93): 709–25.

68. William Sweet, "Seabrook, the Clams, and the Commission," *Bulletin of the Atomic Scientist* 34 (October 1978): 53–54.

69. Walter Rosenbaum, *Environmental Politics and Policy*, 2d ed. (Washington, D.C.: Congressional Quarterly Press, 1991), 250.

70. See Komanoff, *Power Plant Cost Escalation*, passim.

71. House Committee on Appropriations, *Hearings on the Public Works for Water and Power Development and Atomic Energy Commission Appropriations*, 94th Cong., 1st sess., 1975.

72. See Chapter 4 for a more detailed discussion of these two cases.

73. Campbell, *Collapse of an Industry*, 96–100.

74. Frank R. Baumgartner and Bryan D. Jones, *Agendas and Instability in American Politics* (Chicago: University of Chicago Press, 1993), 76–79, and Campbell, *Collapse of an Industry*, 99.

75. Campbell, *Collapse of an Industry*, 96–100.

76. Joppke, "Decentralization of Control," 719; see also Kinsey Wilson, "Lights Out for Shoreham," *Bulletin of the Atomic Scientist* 48 (June 1992): 40–46.

77. Joppke, "Decentralization of Control," 720.

CHAPTER 8. DEREGULATION AND NUCLEAR POWER

1. For a discussion of regulatory regimes, see Richard A. Harris and Sidney M. Milkis, *The Politics of Regulatory Change: A Tale of Two Agencies*, 2d ed. (New York: Oxford University Press, 1996); Marc Allen Eisner, *Regulatory Politics in Transition* (Baltimore: Johns Hopkins University Press, 1993); and Thomas K. McCraw, ed., *Regulation in Perspective: Historical Essays* (Cambridge, Mass.: Harvard University Press, 1981).

2. Harris and Milkis, *The Politics of Regulatory Change*, chap. 7.

3. White House Office of the Press Secretary, "Statement by the President," 10 October 1981, 1; cited in Susan J. Tolchin and Martin Tolchin, *Dismantling America: The Rush to Deregulate* (New York: Oxford University Press, 1983), 210.

4. Price-Anderson Act Amendments of 1988 (PL 100-408, 102 Stat. 1066–85).

5. *Congress and the Nation, 1985–1988* (Washington, D.C.: Congressional Quarterly Press, 1990), 7: 480–83.

6. Bruce B. Clary, "The Enactment of the Nuclear Waste Policy Act of 1982: A Multiple Perspectives Explanation," *Policy Studies Review* 10 (winter 1991–92): 96.

7. Luther J. Carter, *Nuclear Imperatives and the Public Trust* (Washington, D.C.: Resources for the Future, 1987), chaps. 4–5; see also Edward J. Woodhouse, "The Politics of Nuclear Waste Management," in *Too Hot to Handle? Social and Policy Issues in the Management of Radioactive Waste,* ed. Charles A. Walker, Leroy C. Gould, and Woodhouse (New Haven, Conn.: Yale University Press, 1983), 151–83.

8. T. Greenwood, "Nuclear Waste Management in the United States," in *The Politics of Nuclear Waste,* ed. E. W. Colglazier Jr. (New York: Pergamon Press, 1982), 7.

9. There are actually several categories of nuclear waste, each of which emits varying levels of radioactivity and poses different disposal problems. High-level wastes include spent reactor fuel and liquids from reprocessed nuclear fuels; these wastes are highly radioactive and are dangerous for very long periods. Plutonium, for example, has a half-life of twenty-four thousand years, which means it would have to be isolated for a period longer than the span of recorded history. Deep burial in remote locations is presumed to be the preferred disposal method. Less radioactive are low-level wastes, which include materials such as tools, equipment, and clothing from hospitals and commercial reactors.

10. Low Level Radioactive Waste Act (PL 96-573, 94 Stat. 3347–49).

11. Walter Rosenbaum, *Environmental Politics and Policy,* 2d ed. (Washington, D.C.: Congressional Quarterly Press, 1991), 253.

12. Christian Joppke, "Decentralization of Control in U.S. Nuclear Energy Policy," *Political Science Quarterly* 107 (winter 1991–92): 721; Edward L. Gershey et al., *Low Level Radioactive Waste* (New York: Van Nostrand Reinhold, 1990); Michael E. Kraft, "Evaluating Technology Through Public Participation: The Nuclear Waste Disposal Controversy," in *Technology Politics,* ed. Kraft and Norman J. Vig (Durham, N.C.: Duke University Press, 1988).

13. Michael E. Kraft, "Public and State Responses to High-Level Nuclear Waste Disposal: Learning from Policy Failure," *Policy Studies Review* 10 (winter 1991–92): 153.

14. Ibid.

15. Nuclear Waste Policy Act (PL 97-425, 96 Stat. 2201–63).

16. Kraft, "Public and State Responses," 155.

17. Clary, "Nuclear Waste Policy Act," 94.

18. *Congressional Quarterly Weekly Reports,* "Nuclear Waste: An Issue That Won't Stay Buried," 14 March 1987, 451–56.

19. Curt Suplee, "A Nuclear Problem Keeps Growing," *Washington Post,* 31 December 1995, 1.

20. Kraft, "Public and State Responses," 161.

21. Matthew L. Wald, "U.S. Will Start Over on Planning for Nevada Nuclear Waste Dump," *New York Times,* 29 November 1989, 1.

22. Rosenbaum, *Environmental Politics and Policy,* 254.

23. Clary, "Nuclear Waste Policy Act," 96–101.

24. Kraft, "Public and State Responses," 163.

25. The NWPA prohibited licensing of a monitored retreivable storage facility (MRS) until a license was granted for a permanent repository. Supporters argued that an MRS facility could offer a temporary solution to the waste problem, buying time to allow further research and consensus-building. Critics have suggested, however, that such a facility would remove the incentive to build a high-level repository. In effect, they contend that a "temporary" MRS would become the de facto permanent repository.

26. William Lyons, Michael R. Fitzgerald, and Amy McCabe, "Public Opinion and Hazardous Waste," *Forum for Applied Research and Policy* 2 (fall 1987): 89–97.

27. Gerald Jacob, *Site Unseen: The Politics of Siting a Nuclear Waste Repository* (Pittsburgh: University of Pittsburgh Press, 1990).

28. Michael E. Kraft and Bruce B. Clary, "Public Testimony in Nuclear Waste Repository Hearings: A Content Analysis," in *Nuclear Waste: Citizens View Repository Siting*, ed. Riley E. Dunlap, Kraft, and E. A. Rosa (Durham, N.C.: Duke University Press, 1992).

29. K. David Pijawka and Alvin H. Mushkatel, "Public Opposition to Siting of the High-Level Nuclear Waste Repository: The Importance of Trust," *Policy Studies Review* 10 (winter 1991–92): 180–94.

30. U.S. Office of Technology Assessment, *Managing Commercial High-Level Radioactive Wastes* (Washington, D.C.: Government Printing Office, 1982), 31.

31. Kraft, "Public and State Responses," 158.

32. Terry M. Moe, "The Politicized Presidency," in *The New Direction in American Politics*, ed. John E. Chubb and Paul E. Peterson (Washington, D.C.: Brookings Institution, 1985), 239.

33. Richard Nathan, *The Administrative Presidency* (New York: John Wiley and Sons, 1983).

34. See Paul Quirk, *Industry Influence in Federal Regulatory Agencies* (Princeton, N.J.: Princeton University Press, 1981), 12.

35. Report from Raymond Scholl, NRC staff member, in the McTiernan Report, 189; cited in Daniel Ford, *Meltdown: The Secret Papers of the Atomic Energy Commission* (New York: Simon and Schuster, 1986), 224.

36. U.S. Nuclear Regulatory Commission, *The Annual Report of the Nuclear Regulatory Commission—1975* (Washington, D.C.: Government Printing Office, 1975), 8.

37. Ibid., 7.

38. Richard E. Cohen, "Carter Has Landed Running on Regulatory Reform Issues," *National Journal* 9, 16 (16 April 1977): 892.

39. Tolchin and Tolchin, *Dismantling America*, 58.

40. White House Office of the Press Secretary, "Statement by the President," 10 October 1981, 1; cited in Tolchin and Tolchin, *Dismantling America*, 210.

41. *Public Papers of the Presidents of the United States: Ronald Reagan* (Washington, D.C.: Government Printing Office, 1982), 18 February 1981, 113. For more on the Reagan program, see George Eads and Michael Fix, eds., *The Reagan Regulatory Strategy: An Assessment* (Washington, D.C.: Urban Institute, 1984), and Christopher DeMuth, "Strategy for Regulatory Reform," *Regulation* (March/April 1984): 25–29.

42. Eads and Fix, *The Reagan Regulatory Strategy*, 4–6.

43. Executive Order 12291, 46 Fed. Reg. (17 February 1981): 13193.

44. Executive Order 12498, 50 Fed. Reg. (4 January 1985): 1036.

45. Harris and Milkis, *The Politics of Regulatory Change*, 106.

46. Ibid., 133.

47. Ibid., 138. For information on regulatory review in the Bush administration, see Robert J. Duffy, "Divided Government and Institutional Combat: The Case of the Quayle Council on Competitiveness," *Polity* 23 (spring 1996): 379–99, and Charles H. Tiefer, *The Semi-Sovereign Presidency: The Bush Administration's Strategy for Governing Without Congress* (Boulder, Colo.: Westview Press, 1994), especially chap. 4.

48. U.S. Nuclear Regulatory Commission, *The Annual Report of the Nuclear Regulatory Commission—1982*, 1.

49. Peter Bradford, speech before the Environmental Defense Fund Associates, New York, 7 October 1982.

50. "Nuclear Panel Member Sworn in After Bypassing Senate Hearings," *New York Times,* 6 July 1984, 10.

51. Reagan's other NRC appointments proved to be reliable supporters of the administration's regulatory goals as well. Most of the others, Frederick Bernthal, Kenneth M. Carr, Kenneth Rogers, and Lando Zech Jr., had ties to either the AEC or the nuclear industry. Zech, who became chair after Palladino's departure in 1986, was a former navy admiral with experience in the nuclear navy. In 1984, Reagan took the relatively unusual step of making a recess appointment, allowing Zech to hold the position until the end of 1985 without going through the regular appointment process. Bernthal had been an aide to Senator Howard Baker; his staff responsibilities had included managing the fight to keep the controversial Clinch River breeder project alive. Rogers, who later was reappointed to a second term by George Bush, had been a director of Public Service Electric and Gas, a utility that owned three nuclear plants. *New York Times,* 22 April 1987, 1; *Congressional Quarterly Weekly Reports,* 20 June 1987, 1334.

52. Harris and Milkis, *The Politics of Regulatory Change,* 283–86.

53. When Lando Zech left the NRC in 1989, President Bush elevated Kenneth Carr to the chairmanship. To fill the opening left by Zech's departure, Bush nominated Forrest Remick, who had thirty-four years of nuclear power experience, including considerable time as a judge on the ASLB and ACRS. Later that year, Bush filled another opening by nominating E. Gail dePlanque, who had worked for years in DOE's Environmental Measurement Lab.

54. Office of Management and Budget, *Budget of the United States Government, Fiscal Year 1984* (Washington, D.C.: Government Printing Office, 1983), 5–33.

55. Michael E. Kraft and Norman J. Vig, "Environmental Policy from the Seventies to the Nineties: Continuity and Change," in *Environmental Policy in the 1990s,* 1st ed., ed. Vig and Kraft (Washington, D.C.: Congressional Quarterly Press, 1990), 20.

56. Office of Management and Budget, *Budget of the United States Government, Fiscal Year 1997* (Washington, D.C.: Government Printing Office, 1996), 51–55.

57. Murray Weidenbaum, "Regulatory Reform Under the Reagan Administration," in *The Reagan Regulatory Strategy: An Assessment,* ed. George Eads and Michael Fix (Washington, D.C.: Urban Institute, 1984).

58. House Committee on Government Operations, *Licensing Speedup, Safety Delay: NRC Oversight,* 97th Cong., 1st sess., 20 October 1981, H. Rept. 97-277, 37–43.

59. Matthew L. Wald, "Nuclear Agency Said to Lag in Seeking Out Crime," *New York Times,* 31 January 1988, A30.

60. Mark Crawford, "Congress Rearranges NRC's Priorities," *Science* 228 (17 May 1985): 830–31.

61. Matthew L. Wald, "Cuts in Research Funds Seen Imperilling Nuclear Safety Study," *New York Times,* 17 November 1986, 16.

62. Robert D. Hershey Jr., "Few Changes Expected Soon in Nuclear Agency's Policies," *New York Times,* 11 August 1981, 4.

63. President's Reorganization Plan no. 1 of 1980.

64. Nunzio Palladino, memorandum of 17 November 1981.

65. U.S. Nuclear Regulatory Commission, "Charter of Committee to Review Regulatory Requirements," 17 November 1981.

66. Commission rules stipulated that once an issue was labeled "generic," it no longer could be contested in individual licensing cases.

67. U.S. Nuclear Regulatory Commission, *The Annual Report of the Nuclear Regulatory Commission—1986,* 3.

68. House Subcommittee on Energy and the Environment of the Committee on Interior and Insular Affairs, *NRC Budget Request for Fiscal Years 1984 and 1985,* 98th Cong., 1st sess., 1983, 6; cited in Union of Concerned Scientists, *Safety Second: The NRC and America's Nuclear Power Plants* (Bloomington: Indiana University Press, 1987), 47.

69. Cited in Union of Concerned Scientists, *Safety Second: The NRC,* 49.

70. Ibid., 47.

71. Ibid., 46–47.

72. Joint Committee on Atomic Energy, *Hearings on the Status of Nuclear Reactor Safety,* 93d Cong., 1st sess., 1973, pt. 1, phases I and IIa, 339.

73. Union of Concerned Scientists, *Safety Second: The NRC,* 39–41.

74. *Union of Concerned Scientists v. Nuclear Regulatory Commission,* 824 F2d 108 (D.C. Cir. 1987).

75. Harris and Milkis, *The Politics of Regulatory Change,* 263.

76. Matthew L. Wald, "Retiring U.S. Official Assails Nuclear Plant Safety," *New York Times,* 7 June 1987, 32. See also Steven Ebbin and Raphael Kasper, *Citizen Groups and the Nuclear Power Controversy: Uses of Scientific and Technological Information* (Cambridge, Mass.: MIT Press, 1974), and Max Paglin and Edgar Shor, "Regulatory Agency Responses to the Development of Public Administration," *Public Administration Review* (March/April 1977): 140–48.

77. David Welborn, William Lyons, and Larry Thomas, *Implementation and Effects of the Federal Government in the Sunshine Act* (Washington, D.C.: Administrative Conference of the United States, 1984), 3–5.

78. *Common Cause et al. v. United States Nuclear Regulatory Commission,* 674 F2d 921 (D.C. Cir. 1982).

79. 10 C.F.R. 2.714.

80. 10 C.F.R. 2.743.

81. Union of Concerned Scientists, *Safety Second: The NRC,* 93–95.

82. 10 C.F.R. 2.720.

83. 10 C.F.R. 50, appendix O.

84. 54 *Fed. Reg.* (18 April 1989): 15372.

85. 10 C.F.R. 52.17–52.33.

86. 10 C.F.R. 52.51.

87. 10 C.F.R. 52.97.

88. House Subcommittee on Energy and Power of the Committee on Energy and Commerce, *Hearings on National Energy Strategy, Part 2,* 102d Cong., 1st sess., 1991, 841.

89. House Subcommittee on Energy and the Environment of the Committee on Interior and Insular Affairs, *Hearings on the National Energy Strategy,* 102d Cong., 1st sess., 1991, 136.

90. *Nuclear Information and Resource Service et al. v. United States Nuclear Regulatory Commission,* 918 F2d 189 (D.C. Cir. 1990).

91. *Nuclear Information and Resource Service v. United States Nuclear Regulatory Commission*, 969 F2d 1169 (D.C. Cir. 1992).

92. Mark Crawford, "NRC Tries to Reduce Public Access," 228 *Science* (10 May 1985): 679.

93. 10 C.F.R. 55.28.

94. Union of Concerned Scientists, *Safety Second: The NRC*, 114–17.

95. *Orange County Register*, 7 December 1986, 18–19.

96. *Union of Concerned Scientists v. United States Nuclear Regulatory Commission*, 735 F2d 1437 (D.C. Cir. 1984).

97. Ben A. Franklin, "U.S. May Seek End to Local Vetoing of Nuclear Plants," *New York Times*, 6 February 1987, 1; *New York Times*, 7 February 1987, 50.

98. Ben A. Franklin, "Officials Deride Proposal on Nuclear Evacuations," *New York Times*, 25 February 1987, 14.

99. Ben A. Franklin, "Proposal Assailed on Atomic Permit," *New York Times*, 29 April 1987, 26.

100. *Commonwealth of Massachusetts v. United States Nuclear Regulatory Commission*, 856 F2d 378 (D.C. Cir. 1988).

101. Kinsey Wilson, "Lights Out for Shoreham," *Bulletin of the Atomic Scientist* 48 (June 1992), 43; see also Sarah Lyall, "U.S. Is Suing to Salvage Shoreham," *New York Times*, 12 July 1991, B1.

102. 10 C.F.R. 54.29–54.31.

103. 56 *Fed. Reg.* (13 December 1991): 64945.

104. The failure to achieve significant statutory reform was, in the eyes of many critics, the signal failure of the administration's deregulatory program. See Eads and Fix, *The Reagan Regulatory Strategy*, 142–50, and Harris and Milkis, *The Politics of Regulatory Change*, 133–39.

105. See Martha Derthick and Paul Quirk, *The Politics of Deregulation* (Washington, D.C.: Brookings Institution, 1985).

106. Ben A. Franklin, "Nuclear Agency Rebuts Charge It Sacrificed Safety," *New York Times*, 15 October 1987, 24.

107. Joppke, "Decentralization of Control," 711.

CHAPTER 9. NUCLEAR POWER IN THE 1990s AND BEYOND

1. Figures for the current status of nuclear power are from the Energy Information Administration, *Monthly Energy Review* (October 1996): 103. The TVA decided to abandon the reactors even though construction was nearly complete. To that point, TVA had spent $6.3 billion, but it was estimated to cost another $1.8 billion to finish the plants; "End of a Nuclear Generation," *New York Times*, 15 December 1994.

2. Energy Information Administration, *Monthly Energy Review* (April 1996), 26.

3. Ibid., 29.

4. In 1993, coal plants produced 53 percent of the nation's electricity. It is expected that coal-fired plants will continue to be the primary source of power through 2010; Energy Information Administration, *Monthly Energy Review* (April 1996), 29.

5. Energy Policy Act of 1992 (PL 102-486, 106 Stat. 2776).

6. For a discussion of the Public Utility Holding Company Act, see Duane A. Siler,

"Reforming the U.S. Electric Industry: A Leap in the Dark," in *U.S. Energy Imperatives for the 1990s*, ed. Donald L. Guertin, W. Kenneth Davis, and John E. Gray (New York: University Press of America, 1992), 199–214.

7. Agis Salpuka, "Pacific Gas and Electric to Sell Four Power Plants," *New York Times*, 23 October 1996, D4.

8. Ibid.

9. The California law mandates that some customers be allowed to purchase power from the cheapest source, regardless of the location, by 1998. All customers will be allowed to choose their supplier by 2002. For a discussion of the law, see Energy Information Administration, *Monthly Energy Review* (April 1996), 27.

10. Ross Kerber, "Nuclear Industry Faces Charges of Cutting Corners," *Wall Street Journal*, 1 February 1996, B4.

11. Ibid.

12. Ross Kerber, "NRC May Close Two Plants Owned by Northeast Utilities, Citing Safety," *Wall Street Journal*, 11 March 1996, A16.

13. Kerber, "Nuclear Industry," B4.

14. Matthew Wald, "Regulator Fears That Economics Could Lead A-Plants to Scrimp," *New York Times*, 9 September 1994, A19.

15. Mason Willrich, "Restructuring the U.S. Electric Supply Industry," in *U.S. Energy Imperatives for the 1990s*, ed. Guertin, Davis, and Gray, 181–98.

16. Curt Suplee, "A Nuclear Problem Keeps Growing," *Washington Post*, 31 December 1995, 1.

17. Ibid.

18. Lori Nitschke, "Panel Speeds Construction of Yucca Waste Site," *Congressional Quarterly Weekly Reports*, 16 March 1996, 684.

19. Suplee, "Nuclear Problem," 1.

20. Ibid.

21. Energy Information Administration, *Monthly Energy Review* (April 1996): 107.

22. U.S. General Accounting Office, "Nuclear Regulation: NRC'S Decommissioning Procedures and Criteria Need to be Strengthened" (Washington, D.C.: Government Printing Office, May 1989), GAO/RCED-89-119, 2–3.

23. David H. Davis, *Energy Politics*, 4th ed. (New York: St. Martin's Press, 1993), 232.

24. *New York Times*, "Officials Raise by $123 Million Estimate of Dismantling Reactor," 4 November 1994, A24.

25. Walter A. Rosenbaum, *Environmental Politics and Policy*, 2d ed. (Washington, D.C.: Congressional Quarterly Press, 1991), 255–56.

26. Al Gore, *Improving Regulatory Systems: Accompanying Report of the National Performance Review* (Washington, D.C. Government Printing Office, 1993), 7.

27. Stephen Barr, "White House Shifts Role in Rule-Making," *Washington Post*, 1 October 1993, 12.

28. Ibid.

29. Richard A. Harris and Sidney M. Milkis, *The Politics of Regulatory Change: A Tale of Two Agencies*, 2d ed. (New York: Oxford University Press, 1996), 356.

30. Viveca Novak, "The New Regulators," 25 *National Journal*, 17 July 1993, 1802.

31. Shirley Anne Warshaw, *The Domestic Presidency: Policy Making in the White House* (Boston: Allyn and Bacon, 1997), 179–89.

32. Donald Southerland, "Equation for Success: A Life of Struggle Takes D.C.'s Shirley

Jackson to NRC's Helm," *Washington Post,* 4 May 1995, B10; Al Kamen, "In the Loop," *Washington Post,* 22 September 1995, A17; Al Kamen, "In the Loop," *Washington Post,* 22 February 1995, A7; Al Kamen, "In the Loop," *Washington Post,* 26 May 1995, A25.

33. Under the leadership of Vice President Gore, the NPR seeks to improve the efficiency and effectiveness of the federal government. See Matthew Wald, "Nuclear Agency to Use Internet to Receive Ideas for New Rules," *New York Times,* 24 November 1995, A30, and Wald, "Agency Tests New Kind of Hearing," *New York Times,* 15 January 1996, D2.

34. According to some reports, the utility deliberately timed its request for a power increase to arrive at the NRC between Thanksgiving and Christmas, when the agency's "staff is least vigilant." See Peter Spotts, "Federal Probe of Maine Nuclear Plant," *Christian Science Monitor,* 12 December 1995, A4.

35. John Dillin, "U.S. Audit Flags Gaps in Nation's Nuclear Safety," *Christian Science Monitor,* 8 August 1994, A1.

36. John Dillin, "Whistle Blowers on Safety Risks Betrayed by Nuclear Agency," *Christian Science Monitor,* 29 July 1994, A1.

37. The Department of Energy estimates that taxpayers spent $24 billion on research and development for nuclear reactors in the years from 1948 to 1992. Adjusted to 1993 dollars, the figure is $50 billion. The total does not include subsidies for regulating the industry, Price-Anderson, fuel preparation, or waste disposal. See Jon Healey, "Budget-Cutting Blaze Could End Quest for Perfect Reactor," *Congressional Quarterly Weekly Reports,* 29 May 1993, 1350-55.

38. During the Clinton administration, there has been strong support for solar and renewable energy research and development. In the budget for FY 1994, spending on solar and renewable energy increased $97 million and increased another $50 million in FY 1995.

39. Ralph Vastabidian, "Falling Federal Support Dims Nuclear Industry's Future," *Los Angeles Times,* 29 December 1995, A24. Under the most recent budget, the HTGCR project will be closed out in FY 1997, while final shutdown of the liquid metal program is expected in FY 1998.

40. Energy Policy Act of 1992 (PL 102-486, 106 Stat. 2776). The law authorized an ambitious research and development program to commercialize advanced reactor technologies that would be safer and more efficient than the present generation of light water reactors. Under the act, the energy secretary was to prepare a five-year plan to commercialize these designs, establishing 1996 as the target date for approving a standardized design for an advanced light water reactor. That was also the target date for researching other advanced technologies, including the HTGCR, to determine whether the government should select one for a demonstration project. DOE was directed to solicit preliminary engineering proposals for the advanced technology demonstration project and report to Congress in 1998 whether a full-scale prototype should be built.

41. David A. Rochefort and Roger W. Cobb, "Problem Definition: An Emerging Perspective," in *The Politics of Problem Definition: Shaping the Policy Agenda,* ed. Rochefort and Cobb (Lawrence: University Press of Kansas, 1994), 5-7; Christopher J. Bosso, "The Contextual Bases of Problem Definition," in *The Politics of Problem Definition,* Rochefort and Cobb, 183. For another persective, see James A. Morone, *The Democratic Wish: Popular Participation and the Limits of American Government* (New York: Basic Books, 1990), especially chap. 1.

42. Bosso, "Contextual Bases," 185.

43. Morone, *The Democratic Wish,* 8.

44. Irwin C. Bupp, "Nuclear Power: The Promise Melts Away," in *Energy Future: Report of the Energy Project at the Harvard Business School,* ed. Robert Stobaugh and Daniel Yergin (New York: Random House, 1983), 162.

45. Stephen Skowronek, *The Politics Presidents Make: Leadership from John Adams to George Bush* (Cambridge, Mass.: Harvard University Press, 1993), 55.

46. Christopher J. Bosso, *Pesticides and Politics: The Life Cycle of a Public Issue* (Pittsburgh: University of Pittsburgh Press, 1987), 246–63.

47. Harris and Milkis, *The Politics of Regulatory Change,* 364; William P. Browne, "Organized Interests and Their Issue Niches: A Search for Pluralism in a Policy Domain," *Journal of Politics* 52 (May 1990): 477–509; Elaine B. Sharp, "Paradoxes of National Antidrug Policymaking," in *The Politics of Problem Definition,* ed. Rochefort and Cobb, 110–13.

48. Bosso, *Pesticides and Politics,* 244–46.

49. John L. Campbell, *Collapse of an Industry: Nuclear Power and the Contradictions of U.S. Policy* (Ithaca, N.Y.: Cornell University Press, 1988), 78ff.

50. R. Shep Melnick, *Regulation and the Courts: The Case of the Clean Air Act* (Washington, D.C.: Brookings Institution, 1983), 366.

51. Jeffrey M. Berry, "Subgovernments, Issue Networks, and Political Conflict," in *Remaking American Politics,* ed. Richard A. Harris and Sidney M. Milkis (Boulder, Colo.: Westview Press, 1989), 239.

52. Frank R. Baumgartner and Bryan D. Jones, *Agendas and Instability in American Politics* (Chicago: University of Chicago Press, 1993), 215.

53. Christian Joppke, "Decentralization of Control in U.S. Nuclear Energy Policy," *Political Science Quarterly* 107 (winter 1992–93): 711.

54. In an effort to gauge media coverage, I attempted to replicate Baumgartner and Jones's methodology of counting and coding articles in the *Reader's Guide to Periodical Literature for the Years 1987-94* (see pp. 255–63 in their book). Following their guidelines, I simply counted the number of articles on civilian nuclear power per year and then tried to determine whether each article was positive or negative in tone. A story on the environmental benefits of nuclear power was considered to be "positive," while those on accidents were considered "negative." Two findings stand out. First, media interest in nuclear power over this period is quite low and has declined over time. In each of the last five years, for example, the total number of nuclear power articles has not exceeded fifty. In comparison, during the 1970s the number of articles routinely averaged well over a hundred per year. Second, the overwhelming majority of stories are still quite negative. Over the entire period, negative stories outnumber positive by a ratio of six to one. In some years, there were only a handful of positive stories. Clearly, the nuclear power industry has a long way to go in rehabilitating its product's image.

55. PL 102-486, 106 Stat. 2944, 3120.

56. Paul A. Sabatier and Hank C. Jenkins-Smith, *Policy Change and Learning: An Advocacy Coalition Approach* (Boulder, Colo.: Westview Press, 1993), 24–26.

57. Ibid., 19.

58. Ibid., 45.

59. Ibid., 23.

60. Ibid., 16.

61. Bosso, *Pesticides and Politics,* 256.

62. Roger W. Cobb and Charles D. Elder, *Participation in American Politics: The Dynamics of Agenda-Building* (Boston: Allyn and Bacon, 1972), 51.

63. Frank R. Baumgartner and Bryan D. Jones, "Attention, Boundary Effects, and Large-Scale Policy Change in Air Transportation Policy," in *The Politics of Problem Definition*, ed. Rochefort and Cobb, 51.

64. E. E. Schattschneider, *The Semi-Sovereign People: A Realist's View of Democracy in America* (Hinsdale, Ill.: Dryden Press, 1960).

65. Rochefort and Cobb, *The Politics of Problem Definition*, 5.

66. Cobb and Elder, *Participation in American Politics*, 115.

67. Walter A. Rosenbaum, *The Politics of Environmental Concern* (New York: Holt, Rinehart and Winston, 1977), 61.

68. Antinuclear protests are discussed in Jim Falk, *Global Fission: The Battle over Nuclear Power* (New York: Oxford University Press, 1982).

69. Harris and Milkis, *The Politics of Regulatory Change*, 221–24.

70. Martha Derthick and Paul Quirk, *The Politics of Deregulation* (Washington, D.C.: Brookings Institution, 1985), 51–52.

71. See W. Henry Lambright, *Governing Science and Technology* (New York: Oxford University Press, 1976).

72. As examples, see Ellen Frankel Paul, "Sexual Harassment: A Defining Moment and Its Repercussions," in *The Politics of Problem Definition*, ed. Rochefort and Cobb; in the same volume, see David A. Rochefort and Roger W. Cobb, "Instrumental Versus Expressive Definitions of AIDS Policymaking," and Elaine B. Sharp, "Paradoxes of National Antidrug Policymaking."

73. Raymond Tatalovich and Byron W. Daynes, "Introduction," in *Social Regulatory Policy*, ed. Tatalovich and Daynes (Boulder, Colo.: Westview Press, 1988), 2.

74. Morone, *The Democratic Wish*, 12.

75. Rosenbaum, *The Politics of Environmental Concern*, 103.

76. Michael W. McCann, *Taking Reform Seriously: Perspectives on Public Interest Liberalism* (Ithaca, N.Y.: Cornell University Press, 1986), 58.

77. See McCann, *Taking Reform Seriously;* see also Sidney M. Milkis, "The Presidency, Policy Reform, and the Rise of Administrative Politics," in *Remaking American Politics*, ed. Richard A. Harris and Milkis (Boulder, Colo.: Westview Press, 1989).

78. McCann, *Taking Reform Seriously*, 98.

79. Morone, *The Democratic Wish*, 1.

80. Benjamin Ginsberg and Martin Shefter, *Politics By Other Means: The Declining Importance of Elections in America* (New York: Basic Books, 1990).

81. Schattschneider, *The Semi-Sovereign People*, 141.

Bibliography

SECONDARY SOURCES

Allardice, Corbin, and Edward R. Trapnell. 1974. *The Atomic Energy Commission.* New York: Praeger.

Allen, James. 1952. *Atomic Imperialism: The State, Monopoly, and the Bomb.* New York: International Publishers.

Allen, Wendy. 1977. *Nuclear Reactors for Generating Electricity: U.S. Development from 1946–1963.* Santa Monica, Calif.: Rand.

Almond, Gabriel A. 1988. The Return to the State. *American Political Science Review* 82 (September): 853–74.

Anderson, Fredrick R. 1973. *NEPA in the Courts: A Legal Analysis of the National Environmental Policy Act.* Baltimore: Resources for the Future.

Andrews, Richard N. L. 1976. *Environmental Policy and Administrative Change.* Lexington, Mass.: Lexington Books.

Auerbach, Carl A. 1972. Pluralism and the Administrative Process. *The Annals of the American Academy of Political and Social Science* 400 (March): 1–13.

Auerbach, Stanley. 1971. Ecological Considerations in Siting Nuclear Power Plants: The Long-Term Biotic Effects Problem. *Nuclear Safety* 12, 1 (January/February): 25–34.

Ball, Howard. 1986. *Justice Downwind: America's Testing Program in the 1950s.* New York: Oxford University Press.

Barkenbus, Jack. 1984. Nuclear Power and Government Structure: The Divergent Paths of the United States and France. *Social Science Quarterly* 65, 1 (March).

Baumgartner, Frank R., and Bryan D. Jones. 1993. *Agendas and Instability in American Politics.* Chicago: University of Chicago Press.

Bauser, Michael A. 1975. The Development of Rulemaking Within the AEC: The NRC's Valuable Legacy. *Administrative Law Review* 27 (spring): 165–84.

Beck, Clifford K. 1966. Current Trends and Perspectives in Reactor Location and Safety Requirements. *Nuclear Safety* 8, 1 (fall): 12–16.

Beer, Samuel H. 1980. In Search of a New Public Philosophy. In *The New American Political System,* ed. Anthony King. Washington, D.C.: American Enterprise Institute.

Berman, William H., and Lee M. Hydeman. 1961. *The Atomic Energy Commission and Regulating Nuclear Facilities.* Ann Arbor: University of Michigan Press.

Bernstein, Marver H. 1955. *Regulating Business by Independent Commission.* Princeton, N.J.: Princeton University Press.

———. 1972. Independent Regulatory Agencies: A Perspective on Their Reform. *Annals of the American Academy of Political and Social Science* 400 (March): 14–26.

Berry, Jeffrey M. 1978. *Lobbying for the People.* Princeton, N.J.: Princeton University Press.

———. 1984. *The Interest Group Society.* Boston: Little, Brown.

———. 1989. Subgovernments, Issue Networks, and Political Conflict. In *Remaking American Politics,* ed. Richard A. Harris and Sidney M. Milkis. Boulder, Colo.: Westview Press.

Boorstin, Daniel. 1953. *The Genius of American Politics.* Chicago: University of Chicago Press.

Boskey, Bennett. 1956. Some Patent Aspects of Atomic Power Development. *Law and Contemporary Problems* 21 (Winter): 113–31.

Bosso, Christopher J. 1987. *Pesticides and Politics: The Life Cycle of a Public Issue.* Pittsburgh: University of Pittsburgh Press.

———. 1994. The Contextual Bases of Problem Definition. In *The Politics of Problem Definition: Shaping the Public Agenda,* ed. David A. Rochefort and Roger W. Cobb. Lawrence: University Press of Kansas.

Bowring, Joseph. 1981. *Federal Subsidies to Nuclear Power: Reactor Design and the Fuel Cycle.* Washington, D.C.: Department of Energy.

Brand, Donald R. 1989. Reformers of the 1960s and 1970s: Modern Antifederalists? In *Remaking American Politics,* ed. Richard A. Harris and Sidney M. Milkis. Boulder, Colo.: Westview Press.

Breyer, Stephen. 1978. Vermont Yankee and the Court's Role in the Nuclear Energy Controversy. *Harvard Law Review* 91:1833–45.

———. 1982. *Regulation and Its Reform.* Cambridge, Mass.: Harvard University Press.

Browne, William P. 1988. *Private Interests, Public Policy, and American Agriculture.* Lawrence: University Press of Kansas.

———. 1995. *Cultivating Congress: Constituents, Issues and Interests in Agricultural Policymaking.* Lawrence: University Press of Kansas.

Bupp, Irwin C. 1971. Priorities in the Nuclear Technology Program. Ph.D. diss., Harvard University.

———. 1983. Nuclear Power: The Promise Melts Away. In *Energy Future: Report of the Energy Project at the Harvard Business School,* ed. Robert Stobaugh and Daniel Yergin. New York: Random House.

Bupp, Irwin C., and Jean-Claude Derian. 1978. *Light Water: How the Nuclear Dream Dissolved.* New York: Basic Books.

Burnham, Walter Dean. 1982. *The Current Crisis in American Politics.* New York: Oxford University Press.

Byse, Clark. 1978. Vermont Yankee and the Evolution of Administrative Procedure. *Harvard Law Review* 91:1823–32.

Caldwell, Lynton K. 1972. Environmental Quality as an Administrative Problem. *Annals of the American Academy of Political and Social Science* 400 (March): 103–15.

Camilleri, Joseph A. 1984. *The State and Nuclear Power: Conflict and Change in the Western World.* Brighton, Sussex: Wheatsheaf Books.

Campbell, John L. 1988. *Collapse of an Industry: Nuclear Power and the Contradictions of U.S. Policy.* Ithaca, N.Y.: Cornell University Press.

Carter, Luther C. 1976. Nuclear Initiatives: Two Sides Disagree on Meaning of Defeat. *Science* 194 (19 November): 811–12.

Carter, Luther J. 1987. *Nuclear Imperatives and the Public Trust.* Washington, D.C.: Resources for the Future.

Cary, William L. 1967. *Politics and Regulatory Agencies.* New York: McGraw-Hill.

Cater, Douglas. 1964. *Power in Washington.* New York: Random House.

Chandler, Alfred D. 1977. *The Visible Hand: The Managerial Revolution in American Business.* Cambridge, Mass.: Belknap Press.

Checkoway, Barry, and Jon Van Til. 1978. What Do We Know About Citizen Participation? A Selective Review of Research. In *Citizen Participation in America,* ed. Stuart Langton. Lexington, Mass.: Lexington Books.

Chong, Dennis. 1991. *Collective Action and the Civil Rights Movement.* Chicago: University of Chicago Press.

Chubb, John E. 1983. *Interest Groups and the Bureaucracy: The Politics of Energy.* Stanford, Calif.: Stanford University Press.

Chubb, John E., and Paul E. Peterson, eds. 1985. *The New Direction in American Politics.* Washington, D.C.: Brookings Institution.

Clarfield, Gerard H., and William M. Wiecek. 1984. *Nuclear America: Military and Civilian Nuclear Power in the United States, 1940–1980.* New York: Harper and Row.

Clary, Bruce B. 1991. The Enactment of the Nuclear Waste Policy Act of 1982: A Multiple Perspectives Explanation. *Policy Studies Review* 10.

Cobb, Roger W., and Charles D. Elder. 1972. *Participation in American Politics: The Dynamics of Agenda-Building.* Boston: Allyn and Bacon.

Cohen, David. 1978. The Public-Interest Movement and Citizen Participation. In *Citizen Participation in America,* ed. Stuart Langton. Lexington, Mass.: Lexington Books.

Cohen, Linda. 1979. Innovation and Atomic Energy: Nuclear Power Regulation, 1966–Present. *Law and Contemporary Problems* 43 (winter/spring): 67–97.

Cohen, Robert L., and S. Robert Lichter. 1983. Nuclear Power: The Decision-Makers Speak. *Regulation* 7, 2 (March/April): 32–37.

Cook, Constance Ewing. 1980. *Nuclear Power and Legal Advocacy: The Environmentalists and the Courts.* Lexington, Mass.: Lexington Books/D.C. Heath.

Curtis, Richard, and Elizabeth Hogan. 1969. *Perils of the Peaceful Atom: The Myth of Safe Nuclear Power Plants.* Garden City, N.Y.: Doubleday.

Dahl, Robert A. 1953. Atomic Energy and the Democratic Process. In *The Annals of the American Academy of Political and Social Science: The Impact of Atomic Energy,* ed. Robert A. Dahl. Philadelphia: American Academy of Political and Social Science.

———. 1956. *A Preface to Democratic Theory.* Chicago: University of Chicago Press.

Dahl, Robert A., and Ralph S. Brown. 1951. *Domestic Control of Atomic Energy.* New York: Social Science Research Council.

Davis, David H. 1993. *Energy Politics.* 4th ed. New York: St. Martin's Press.

Davis, Joyce P. 1972. Taming the Technological Tyger. *Fordham Urban Law Journal* 1, 1 (summer): 19–47.

Dawson, Frank G. 1976. *Nuclear Power: Development and Management of a Technology.* Seattle: University of Washington Press.

Dean, Gordon. 1959. *Report on the Atom.* New York: Alfred A. Knopf.

Dellinger, David. 1982. The Antinuclear Movement. In *Nuclear Power: Both Sides,* ed. Michio Kaku and Jennifer Trainer. New York: W. W. Norton.

Del Sesto, Steven L. 1979. *Science, Politics, and Controversy: Civilian Nuclear Power in the United States, 1946–1974.* Boulder, Colo.: Westview Press.

———. 1980. Conflicting Ideologies of Nuclear Power: Congressional Testimony on Nuclear Reactor Safety. *Public Policy* 28 (winter): 39–70.

Derthick, Martha, and Paul Quirk. 1985. *The Politics of Deregulation.* Washington, D.C.: Brookings Institution.

Dodd, Lawrence C., and Bruce I. Oppenheimer, eds. 1985. *Congress Reconsidered.* 3d ed. Washington, D.C.: Congressional Quarterly Press.

Doub, W. O. 1974. Federal Energy Regulation: Toward a Better Way. *American Bar Association Journal* 60 (August): 920–23.

Downey, Gary. 1986. Risk in Culture: The American Conflict over Nuclear Power. *Cultural Anthropology* 1, 4 (November): 388–412.

Downs, Anthony. 1972. Up and Down with Ecology—The "Issue-Attention Cycle." *Public Interest* 28 (summer): 38–50.

Dunlap, Riley E., and Marvin E. Olsen. 1984. Hard-Path Versus Soft-Path Advocates: A Study of Energy Activists. *Policy Studies Journal* 13, 2 (December): 413–28.

Dyke, Richard W. 1989. *Mr. Atomic Energy: Congressman Chet Holifield and Atomic Energy Affairs, 1945–1974.* New York: Greenwood Press.

Eads, George, and Richard R. Nelson. 1971. Governmental Support of Advanced Civilian Technology: Power Reactors and the Supersonic Transport. *Public Policy* 19, 3 (summer): 405–27.

Ebbin, Steven, and Raphael Kasper. 1974. *Citizen Groups and the Nuclear Power Controversy: Uses of Scientific and Technological Information.* Cambridge, Mass.: MIT Press.

Eden, Robert. 1989. Dealing Democratic Honor Out: Reform and the Decline of Consensus Politics. In *Remaking American Politics,* ed. Richard A. Harris and Sidney M. Milkis. Boulder, Colo.: Westview Press.

Edwards, Katherine B. 1980. NRC Regulations. *Texas Law Review* 58:355–91.

Eisner, Marc Allen. 1993. *Regulatory Politics in Transition.* Baltimore: Johns Hopkins University Press.

Elliott, Dave et al. 1978. *The Politics of Nuclear Power.* London: Pluto Press.

Evans, Nigel, and Chris Hope. 1984. *Nuclear Power: Futures, Costs, and Benefits.* New York: Cambridge University Press.

Faich, Ronald G., and Richard P. Gale. 1971. The Environmental Movement: From Recreation to Politics. *Pacific Sociological Review* 14, 3 (July): 270–87.

Falk, Jim. 1982. *Global Fission: The Battle over Nuclear Power.* New York: Oxford University Press.

Fenn, Scott. 1981. *The Nuclear Power Debate: Issues and Choices.* New York: Praeger.

Flavin, Christopher. 1983. Nuclear Power: The Market Test. In *Worldwatch Paper* 57. Washington, D.C.: Worldwatch Institute.

———. 1987. Reassessing Nuclear Power: The Fallout from Chernobyl. In *Worldwatch Paper* 75. Washington, D.C.: Worldwatch Institute.

Ford, Daniel. 1982. *The Cult of the Atom: The Secret Papers of the Atomic Energy Commission.* New York: Simon and Schuster. Revised and updated as *Meltdown: The Secret Papers of the Atomic Energy Commission.* 1986. New York: Simon and Schuster.

Freeman, J. Leiper. 1955. *The Political Process: Executive Bureau—Legislative Committee Relations.* New York: Random House.

Freudenberg, William, and Rodney Baxter. 1985. Nuclear Reactions: Public Attitudes and Policies Toward Nuclear Power. *Policy Studies Review* 5, 1 (August): 96–110.

Garvey, Gerald. 1977. *Nuclear Power and Social Planning.* Lexington, Mass.: Lexington Books.

Gershey, Edward L., Robert C. Klein, Esmerelda Party, and Amy Wilkerson. 1990. *Low Level Radioactive Waste.* New York: Van Nostrand Reinhold.

Gillette, Robert. 1971. Nuclear Reactor Safety: A Skeleton at the Feast? *Science* 172 (28 May): 918–19.

———. 1972a. Nuclear Reactor Safety: At the AEC the Way of the Dissenter Is Hard. *Science* 176 (5 May): 492–98.

———. 1972b. Nuclear Safety (I): The Roots of Dissent. *Science* 177 (1 September): 771–76.

———. 1972c. Nuclear Safety (II): The Years of Delay. *Science* 177 (8 September): 867–71.

———. 1972d. Nuclear Safety (III): Critics Charge Conflicts of Interest. *Science* 177 (15 September): 970–75.

———. 1972e. Nuclear Safety (IV): Barriers to Communication. *Science* 177 (22 September): 1080–82.

Glick, Henry R. 1992. *The Right to Die: Policy Innovation and Its Consequences.* New York: Columbia University Press.

Gofman, John W. 1982. George Orwell Understated the Case. In *Nuclear Power: Both Sides,* ed. Michio Kaku and Jennifer Trainer. New York: W. W. Norton.

Gofman, John W., and Arthur R. Tamplin. 1971. *Poisoned Power: The Case Against Nuclear Power Plants.* Emmaus, Pa.: Rodale Press.

Golay, Michael. 1980. How Prometheus Came to Be Bound: Nuclear Regulation in America. *Technology Review* 83:29–39.

Goodman, Marshall R., and Frederic P. Andes. 1985. The Politics of Regulatory Reform and the Future Direction of Nuclear Energy Policy. *Policy Studies Review* 5, 1 (August): 111–21.

Green, Harold P. 1956. Information Control and Atomic Power Development. *Law and Contemporary Problems* 21 (winter): 91–112.

———. 1964. Nuclear Technology and the Fabric of Government. *George Washington Law Review* 33 (October): 121–61.

———. 1972. Nuclear Power Licensing and Regulation. *Annals of the American Academy of Political and Social Science* 400 (March): 116–28.

———. 1973. Nuclear Power: Risk, Liability, and Indemnity. *Michigan Law Review* 71:485.

Green, Harold P., and Alan P. Rosenthal. 1963. *Government of the Atom: The Integration of Powers.* New York: Atherton Press.

Groves, Leslie R. 1962. *Now It Can Be Told: The Story of the Manhattan Project.* New York: Harper and Row.

Hall, Harry S. 1979. *Congressional Attitudes Toward Science and Scientists: A Study of Legislative Reactions to Atomic Energy and the Political Participation of Scientists.* New York: Arno Press.

Hansen, John M. 1991. *Gaining Access: Congress and the Farm Lobby, 1919–1981.* Chicago: University of Chicago Press.

Harris, Richard A. 1989. A Decade of Reform. In *Remaking American Politics,* ed. Richard A. Harris and Sidney M. Milkis. Boulder, Colo.: Westview Press.

————. 1989. Politicized Management: The Changing Face of Business in American Politics. In *Remaking American Politics,* ed. Richard A. Harris and Sidney M. Milkis. Boulder, Colo.: Westview Press.

Harris, Richard A. and Sidney M. Milkis. 1996. *The Politics of Regulatory Change: A Tale of Two Agencies.* 2d ed. New York: Oxford University Press.

Hartz, Louis. 1955. *The Liberal Tradition in America: An Interpretation of American Thought Since the Revolution.* New York: Harcourt, Brace.

Hatch, Michael T. 1986. *Politics and Nuclear Power: Energy Policy in Western Europe.* Lexington: University Press of Kentucky.

Hayes, Denis. 1977. *Rays of Hope: The Transition to a Post-Petroleum World.* New York: W. W. Norton.

Hays, Samuel P. 1987. *Beauty, Health, and Permanence: Environmental Politics in the United States, 1955–1985.* New York: Cambridge University Press.

Heclo, Hugh. 1980. Issue Networks and the Executive Establishment. In *The New American Political System,* ed. Anthony King. Washington, D.C.: American Enterprise Institute.

————. 1989. The Emerging Regime. In *Remaking American Politics,* ed. Richard A. Harris and Sidney M. Milkis. Boulder, Colo.: Westview Press.

Henderson, George B., II. 1980. The Nuclear Choice: Are Health and Safety Issues Preempted? *Boston College Environmental Affairs Law Review* 8:821–72.

Hertsgaard, Mark. 1983. *Nuclear Inc.: The Men and Money Behind Nuclear Energy.* New York: Pantheon Books.

Hewlett, Richard G., and Oscar E. Anderson. 1962. *A History of the Atomic Energy Commission, Vol. 1, The New World, 1939–1946.* University Park: Pennsylvania State University Press.

Hewlett, Richard G., and Francis Duncan. 1969. *A History of the Atomic Energy Commission, Vol. 2, Atomic Shield, 1947–1952.* University Park: Pennsylvania State University Press.

Holdren, John, and Phillip Herrera. 1971. *Energy: A Crisis in Power.* San Francisco: Sierra Club.

Huntington, Samuel P. 1981. *American Politics: The Promise of Disharmony.* Cambridge, Mass.: Harvard University Press.

Jacob, Gerald. 1990. *Site Unseen: The Politics of Siting a Nuclear Waste Repository.* Pittsburgh: University of Pittsburgh Press.

Jaffe, Louis L. 1954. The Effective Limits of the Administrative Process: A Reevaluation. *Harvard Law Review* 67:1105–35.

Johnson, John W. 1986. *Insuring Against Disaster: The Nuclear Industry on Trial.* Macon, Ga.: Mercer University Press.

Jones, Charles O. 1979. American Politics and the Organization of Energy Decision Making. *Annual Review of Energy* 4:99–110.

————. 1984. *An Introduction to the Study of Public Policy.* 3d ed. Monterey, Calif.: Brooks/Cole.

Joppke, Christian. 1991. Decentralization of Control in U.S. Nuclear Energy Policy. *Political Science Quarterly* 107:709–25.

Jungk, Robert. 1978. *The Nuclear State.* Trans. by Eric Mosbacher. London: John Calder.

Kaku, Michio, and Jennifer Trainer, eds. 1982. *Nuclear Power: Both Sides.* New York: W. W. Norton.

Kaufman, Herbert. 1969. Administrative Decentralization and Political Power. *Public Administration Review* 29 (January/February): 3-15.

King, Anthony. 1980. The American Polity in the Late 1970s: Building Coalitions in the Sand. In *The New American Political System,* ed. Anthony King. Washington, D.C.: American Enterprise Institute.

Kingdon, John W. 1984. *Agendas, Alternatives, and Public Policies.* Boston: Little, Brown.

Klema, Ernest D., and Robert L. West. 1977. *Public Regulation of Site Selection for Nuclear Power Plants: Present Procedures and Reform Proposals—An Annotated Bibliography.* Washington, D.C.: Resources for the Future.

Kohlmeier, Louis M. Jr. 1969. *The Regulators: Watchdog Agencies and the Public Interest.* New York: Harper and Row.

Komanoff, Charles. 1981. *Power Plant Cost Escalation: Nuclear and Coal Capital Costs, Regulation, and Economics.* New York: Van Nostrand Reinhold.

Kraft, Michael E. 1974. Ecological Politics and American Government: A Review Essay. In *Environmental Politics,* ed. Stuart S. Nagel. New York: Praeger.

———. 1988. Evaluating Technology Through Public Participation: The Nuclear Waste Disposal Controversy. In *Technology Politics,* ed. Michael E. Kraft and Norman J. Vig. Durham, N.C.: Duke University Press.

———. 1991. Public and State Responses to High-Level Nuclear Waste Disposal: Learning from Policy Failure. *Policy Studies Review* 10.

Kraft, Michael E., and Bruce B. Clary. 1992. Public Testimony in Nuclear Waste Repository Hearings: A Content Analysis. In *Nuclear Waste: Citizens View Repository Siting,* ed. Riley E. Dunlap, Michael E. Kraft, and E. A. Rosa. Durham, N.C.: Duke University Press.

Kweit, Mary G., and Robert W. Kweit. 1981. *Implementing Citizen Participation in a Bureaucratic Society: A Contingency Approach.* New York: Praeger.

Ladd, Anthony E., Thomas C. Hood, and Kent D. Van Liere. 1983. Ideological Themes in the Antinuclear Movement: Consensus and Diversity. *Sociological Inquiry* 53, 2/3 (spring): 252-72.

Lambright, W. Henry. 1976. *Governing Science and Technology.* New York: Oxford University Press.

Langton, Stuart. 1978. Citizen Participation in America: Current Reflections on the State of the Art. In *Citizen Participation in America,* ed. Stuart Langton. Lexington, Mass.: Lexington Books.

———. 1978. What Is Citizen Participation? In *Citizen Participation in America,* ed. Stuart Langton. Lexington, Mass.: Lexington Books.

Lapp, Ralph E. 1965. *The New Priesthood: The Scientific Elite and the Uses of Power.* New York: Harper and Row.

Latham, Earl. 1952. *The Group Basis of Politics.* Ithaca, N.Y.: Cornell University Press.

Leiss, William. 1972. *The Domination of Nature.* New York: George Braziller.

Leone, Richard C. 1972. Public Interest Advocacy and the Regulatory Process. *Annals of the American Academy of Political and Social Science* 400 (March): 46-58.

Lewis, Richard S. 1972. *The Nuclear-Power Rebellion: Citizens vs. the Atomic Industrial Establishment.* New York: Viking Press.

Lilienthal, David E. 1947. We Must Grasp the Facts About the Atom. *New York Times Magazine,* 4 May, 7.

———. 1964. *The Journals of David E. Lilienthal: The Atomic Energy Years 1945–1950, Vol. 2.* New York: Harper and Row.

———. 1980. *Atomic Energy: A New Start.* New York: Harper and Row.

Lilley, W., and J. Miller. 1977. The New Social Regulation. *Public Interest* 47:49–62.

Lindblom, Charles E. 1965. *The Intelligence of Democracy: Decision Making Through Mutual Adjustment.* New York: Free Press.

———. 1968. *The Policy-Making Process.* Englewood Cliffs, N.J.: Prentice-Hall.

Lipschutz, Ronnie. 1980. *Radioactive Waste: Politics, Technology, and Risk.* Cambridge, Mass.: Ballinger.

Lipset, Seymour Martin, and William Schneider. 1987. *The Confidence Gap: Business, Labor, and Government in the Public Mind.* 2d ed. Baltimore: Johns Hopkins University Press.

Losee, Madeline W., comp. 1955. *Legislative History of the Atomic Energy Act of 1954.* 3 vols. Washington, D.C.: U.S. Atomic Energy Commission.

Lovins, Amory B. 1974. World Energy Strategies: The Case for Long-Term Planning, Part II. *Bulletin of the Atomic Scientist* (June): 38–50.

Lovins, Amory B., and L. Hunter Lovins. 1980. *Energy/War: Breaking the Nuclear Link.* San Francisco: Friends of the Earth.

———. 1982. Soft Energy Paths. In *Nuclear Power: Both Sides,* ed. Michio Kaku and Jennifer Trainer. New York: W. W. Norton.

Lowi, Theodore. 1979. *The End of Liberalism: The Second Republic of the United States.* 2d ed. New York: W. W. Norton.

Lyons, William, Michael R. Fitzgerald, and Amy McCabe. 1987. Public Opinion and Hazardous Waste. *Forum for Applied Research and Policy* 2 (fall): 89–97.

MacAvoy, Paul W., ed. 1970. *The Crisis of the Regulatory Commissions: An Introduction to a Current Issue of Public Policy.* New York: W. W. Norton.

Macpherson, C. B. 1972. Democratic Theory: Ontology and Technology. In *Philosophy and Technology,* ed. Carl Mitcham and Robert MacKey. New York: Free Press.

Mann, Dean E. 1986. Democratic Politics and Environmental Policy. In *Controversies in Environmental Policy,* ed. Sheldon Kamieniecki, Robert O'Brien, and Michael Clarke. Albany: State University Press of New York.

Mann, Thomas E., and Norman Ornstein, eds. 1981. *The New Congress.* Washington, D.C.: American Enterprise Institute.

Marcus, Alfred A. et al. Adapting to Rapid Change and Decline: Industry Influence on Nuclear Power Safety. Paper presented at the 1990 annual meeting of the American Political Science Association, San Francisco, 30 August–2 September 1990.

Mayhew, David R. 1974. *Congress: The Electoral Connection.* New Haven, Conn.: Yale University Press.

Mazuzan, George T., and J. Samuel Walker. 1984. *Controlling the Atom: The Beginnings of Nuclear Regulation, 1946–1962.* Los Angeles: University of California Press.

McCann, Michael W. 1986. *Taking Reform Seriously: Perspectives on Public Interest Liberalism.* Ithaca, N.Y.: Cornell University Press.

McConnell, Grant. 1966. *Private Power and American Democracy.* New York: Vintage Books.

McFarland, Andrew S. 1976. *Public Interest Lobbies: Decision Making on Energy.* Washington, D.C.: American Enterprise Institute for Public Policy Research.

Meehan, Richard L. 1984. *The Atom and the Fault: Experts, Earthquakes, and Nuclear Power.* Cambridge, Mass.: MIT Press.

Melnick, R. Shep. 1983. *Regulation and the Courts: The Case of the Clean Air Act.* Washington, D.C.: Brookings Institution.

————. 1989. The Courts, Congress, and Programmatic Rights. In *Remaking American Politics,* ed. Richard A. Harris and Sidney M. Milkis. Boulder, Colo.: Westview Press.

Metzger, H. Peter. 1972. *The Atomic Establishment.* New York: Simon and Schuster.

Milkis, Sidney M. 1989. The Presidency, Policy Reform, and the Rise of Administrative Politics. In *Remaking American Politics,* ed. Richard A. Harris and Sidney M. Milkis. Boulder, Colo.: Westview Press.

Miller, Tim R. 1985. Recent Trends in Federal Water Resource Management: Are the Iron Triangles in Retreat? *Policy Studies Review* 5:395–412.

Mitchell, Robert. 1981. From Elite Quarrel to Mass Movement. *Society* 18, 5 (July/August): 76–84.

Moe, Terry M. 1985. The Politicized Presidency. In *The New Direction in American Politics,* ed. John E. Chubb and Paul E. Peterson. Washington, D.C.: Brookings Institution.

Morone, James A. 1990. *The Democratic Wish: Popular Participation and the Limits of American Government.* New York: Basic Books.

Morone, Joseph G., and Edward J. Woodhouse. 1989. *The Demise of Nuclear Energy? Lessons for Democratic Control of Technology.* New Haven, Conn.: Yale University Press.

Murphy, Arthur W. 1972. The National Environmental Policy Act and the Licensing Process: Environmentalist Magna Carta or Agency Coup de Grace? *Columbia Law Review* 72, 6 (October): 963–1007.

Myers, Desaix. 1977. *The Nuclear Power Debate: Moral, Economic, Technical Issues.* New York: Praeger.

Nadel, Mark V. 1971. *The Politics of Consumer Protection.* Indianapolis: Bobbs-Merrill.

Nader, Ralph, and John Abbotts. 1977. *The Menace of Atomic Energy.* New York: W. W. Norton.

Nader, Ralph, and Richard Pollack. 1982. The Industry's Worst Enemy. In *Nuclear Power: Both Sides,* ed. Michio Kaku and Jennifer Trainer. New York: W. W. Norton.

Nagel, Stuart S., ed. 1974. *Environmental Politics.* New York: Praeger.

Nathan, Richard. 1983. *The Administrative Presidency.* New York: John Wiley and Sons.

Nau, Henry. 1974. *National Politics and International Technology: Nuclear Reactor Development in Western Europe.* Baltimore: Johns Hopkins University Press.

Nealey, Stanley M., Barbara D. Melber, and William L. Rankin. 1983. *Public Opinion and Nuclear Energy.* Lexington, Mass.: Lexington Books.

Nehrt, Lee C. 1966. *International Marketing of Nuclear Power Plants.* Bloomington: Indiana University Press.

Nelkin, Dorothy, and Susan Fallows. 1978. Evolution of the Nuclear Debate: The Role of Public Participation. *Annual Review of Energy* 3:275–312.

Nelkin, Dorothy, and Michael Pollak. 1977. The Politics of Participation and the Nuclear Debate in Sweden, the Netherlands, and Austria. *Public Policy* 25, 3 (summer): 333–57.

————. 1981. *The Atom Beseiged: Extraparliamentary Dissent in France and Germany.* Cambridge, Mass.: MIT Press.

Newman, James R., and Byron S. Miller. 1948. *The Control of Atomic Energy: A Study of Its Social, Economic, and Political Implications.* New York: McGraw-Hill.

Nivola, Pietro S. 1986. *The Politics of Energy Conservation.* Washington, D.C.: Brookings Institution.

Noll, Richard. 1971. The Economics and Politics of Regulation. *Virginia Law Review* 57 (September): 1016–32.

Northrop, Robert M. 1956. The Changing Role of the Atomic Energy Commission in Atomic Power Development. *Law and Contemporary Problems* 21 (winter): 14–37.

Nuclear Energy Policy Study Group. 1977. *Nuclear Power Issues and Choices: Report of the Nuclear Energy Policy Study Group.* Cambridge, Mass.: Ballinger.

Nuse, James D., comp. 1965. *Legislative History of the Atomic Energy Act of 1946.* 3 vols. Washington D.C.: U.S. Atomic Energy Commission.

Okrent, David. 1981. *Nuclear Reactor Safety: On the History of the Regulatory Process.* Madison: University of Wisconsin Press.

Olson, Mancur. 1971. *The Logic of Collective Action.* Cambridge, Mass.: Harvard University Press.

Ophuls, William. 1977. *Ecology and the Politics of Scarcity.* San Francisco: W. H. Freeman.

Oppenheimer, Bruce. 1980. Policy Effects of U.S. House Reform: Decentralization and the Capacity to Resolve Energy Issues. *Legislative Studies Quarterly* 5:5–31.

Pateman, Carole. 1970. *Participation and Democratic Theory.* New York: Cambridge University Press.

Patterson, Samuel C. 1980. The Semi-Sovereign Congress. In *The New American Political System,* ed. Anthony King. Washington, D.C.: American Enterprise Institute.

Pertschuk, Michael. 1982. *Revolt Against Regulation: The Rise and Pause of the Consumer Movement.* Los Angeles: University of California Press.

Pika, Joseph A. 1983. Interest Groups and the Executive: Presidential Intervention. In *Interest Group Politics,* ed. Allan J. Cigler and Burdett A. Loomis. Washington, D.C.: Congressional Quarterly Press.

Pollock, Cynthia. 1986. Decommissioning: Nuclear Power's Missing Link. *Worldwatch Paper* 69. Washington, D.C.: Worldwatch Institute.

Posner, Richard A. 1975. Theories of Economic Regulation. *Bell Journal of Economics and Management Science* 5 (August): 335–58.

Price, Jerome. 1982. *The Antinuclear Movement.* Boston: Twayne.

Primack, Joel, and Frank von Hippel. 1974. *Advice and Dissent: Scientists in the Political Arena.* New York: Basic Books.

Pringle, Peter, and James Spigelman. 1981. *The Nuclear Barons.* New York: Holt, Rinehart, and Winston.

Quirk, Paul. 1981. *Industry Influence in Federal Regulatory Agencies.* Princeton, N.J.: Princeton University Press.

Raffaele, Joseph Antonio. 1978. *The Management of Technology: Change in a Society of Organized Advocacies.* Washington, D.C.: University Press of America.

Raymond, James F. 1979. A Vermont Yankee in King Burger's Court: Constraints on Judicial Review Under NEPA. *Boston College Environmental Affairs Law Review* 7:629–64.

Redford, Emmette S. 1969. *Democracy in the Administrative State.* New York: Oxford University Press.

Rees, Joseph V. 1994. *Hostages of Each Other: The Transformation of Nuclear Safety Since Three Mile Island.* Chicago: University of Chicago Press.

Ripley, Randall B., and Grace A. Franklin. 1984. *Congress, the Bureaucracy, and Public Policy.* 3d ed. Homewood, Ill.: Dorsey Press.

Rochefort, David A., and Roger W. Cobb. 1994. Problem-Definition: An Emerging Perspective. In *The Politics of Problem Definition: Shaping the Policy Agenda,* ed. David A. Rochefort and Roger W. Cobb. Lawrence: University Press of Kansas.

Rolph, Elizabeth. 1978. *Regulation of Nuclear Power: The Case of the Light Water Reactor.* Lexington, Mass.: Lexington Books.

Rosenbaum, Nelson M. 1978. Citizen Participation and Democratic Theory. In *Citizen Participation in America,* ed. Stuart Langton. Lexington, Mass.: Lexington Books.

Rosenbaum, Walter A. 1974. The End of Illusion: NEPA and the Limits of Judicial Review. In *Environmental Politics,* ed. Stuart S. Nagel. New York: Praeger.

———. 1977. *The Politics of Environmental Concern.* New York: Holt, Rinehart and Winston.

———. 1978. Public Involvement as Reform and Ritual: The Development of Federal Participation Programs. In *Citizen Participation in America,* ed. Stuart Langton. Lexington, Mass.: Lexington Books.

———. 1991. *Environmental Politics and Policy.* 2d ed. Washington, D.C.: Congressional Quarterly Press.

Rothman, Stanley, and S. Robert Lichter. 1982. The Nuclear Energy Debate: Scientists, the Media, and the Public. *Public Opinion* 5:47–52.

———. 1987. Elite Ideology and Risk Perception in Nuclear Energy Policy. *American Political Science Review* 81, 2 (June): 383–404.

Sabatier, Paul A., and Hank C. Jenkins-Smith. 1993. *Policy Change and Learning: An Advocacy Coalition Approach.* Boulder, Colo.: Westview Press.

Scalia, Antonin. 1978. Vermont Yankee: The APA, the DC Circuit, and the Supreme Court. *Supreme Court Review* 1978: 345–409.

Schattschneider, E. E. 1960. *The Semi-Sovereign People: A Realist's View of Democracy in America.* Hinsdale, Ill.: Dryden Press.

Schlozman, Kay L., and John T. Tierney. 1986. *Organized Interests and American Democracy.* New York: Harper and Row.

Seaborg, Glenn T., and William R. Corliss. 1971. *Man and Atom: Building a New World Through Nuclear Technology.* New York: E. P. Dutton.

Sharp, Elaine B. 1994. Paradoxes of National Antidrug Policymaking. In *The Politics of Problem Definition: Shaping the Policy Agenda,* ed. David A. Rochefort and Roger W. Cobb. Lawrence: University Press of Kansas.

Shrader-Frechette, K. S. 1980. *Nuclear Power and Public Policy.* Boston: D. Reidel.

Siler, Duane A. 1992. Reforming the U.S. Electric Industry: A Leap in the Dark. In *U.S. Energy Imperatives for the 1990s,* ed. Donald L. Guertin, W. Kenneth Davis, and John E. Gray. New York: University Press of America.

Sive, David. 1970. Some Thoughts of an Environmental Lawyer in the Wilderness of Administrative Law. *Columbia Law Review* 70:612–51.

Skowronek, Stephen. 1982. *Building a New American State: The Expansion of National Administrative Capacities, 1877–1920.* New York: Cambridge University Press.

Spitzer, R. 1987. Promoting Policy Theory: Revising the Arenas of Power. *Policy Studies Journal* 15, 4:675–89.

Sprout, Harold, and Margaret Sprout. 1978. *The Context of Environmental Politics: Unfinished Business for America's Third Century.* Lexington: University Press of Kentucky.

Sternglass, Ernest. 1981. *Secret Fallout: Low-Level Radiation from Hiroshima to Three Mile Island.* New York: McGraw-Hill.

Stever, Donald W. 1980. *Seabrook and the Nuclear Regulatory Commission: The Licensing of a Nuclear Power Plant.* Hanover, N.H.: University Press of New England.

Stewart, Richard B. 1975. The Reformation of American Administrative Law. *Harvard Law Review* 88 (June): 1669–813.

———. 1978. Vermont Yankee and the Evolution of Administrative Procedure. *Harvard Law Review* 91:1805–45.

Stigler, George J. 1971. The Theory of Economic Regulation. *Bell Journal of Economics and Management Science* 2, 1 (spring): 3–21.

Stobaugh, Robert, and Daniel Yergin, eds. 1983. *Energy Future: Report of the Energy Project at the Harvard Business School.* New York: Random House.

Stoler, Peter. 1985. *Decline and Fail: The Ailing Nuclear Power Industry.* New York: Dodd, Mead.

Strauss, Lewis. 1955. Faith in the the Atomic Future. *Reader's Digest* 67, 400 (August): 17–21.

———. 1962. *Men and Decisions.* New York: Doubleday.

Sylves, Richard T. 1987. *The Nuclear Oracles: A Political History of the General Advisory Committee of the Atomic Energy Commission, 1947–1977.* Ames: Iowa State University Press.

Tatalovich, Raymond, and Byron W. Daynes. 1988. *Social Regulatory Policy.* Boulder, Colo.: Westview Press.

Taylor, Serge. 1984. *Making Bureaucracies Think: The Environmental Impact Statement Strategy of Administrative Reform.* Stanford, Calif.: Stanford University Press.

Temples, James R. 1980. The Politics of Nuclear Power: A Sub-Government in Transition. *Political Science Quarterly* 95, 2 (summer): 239–60.

Thomas, Morgan. 1956. *Atomic Energy and Congress.* Ann Arbor: University of Michigan Press.

———. 1956. Democratic Control of Atomic Power Development. *Law and Contemporary Problems* 21 (winter): 38–59.

Truman, David B. 1951. *The Governmental Process.* New York: Alfred A. Knopf.

Union of Concerned Scientists. 1977. *The Risks of Nuclear Power Reactors: A Review of the NRC Reactor Safety Study WASH-1400 (NUREG-75/014).* Cambridge, Mass.: Union of Concerned Scientists.

———. 1987. *Safety Second: The NRC and America's Nuclear Power Plants.* Michelle Adato, principal author, with James MacKenzie, Robert Pollard, and Ellyn Weiss. Bloomington: Indiana University Press.

Vogel, David. 1980. The Public Interest Movement and the American Reform Tradition. *Political Science Quarterly* 95 (winter): 607–27.

Walker, J. Samuel. 1989. Nuclear Power and the Environment: The Atomic Energy Commission and Thermal Pollution, 1965–1971. *Technology and Culture* 30, 4 (October): 964–92.

Walsh, John. 1975. Opposition to Nuclear Power: Raising the Question at the Polls. *Science* 190 (5 December): 964–66.

———. 1976. Congress: Election Impacts Atomic Energy, Science Committees. *Science* 194 (19 November): 812–14.

———. 1977. Congress: House Redistributes Jurisdiction over Energy. *Science* 195 (11 February): 562–63.

Warshaw, Shirley Anne. 1997. *The Domestic Presidency: Policy Making in the White House.* Boston: Allyn and Bacon.

Weart, Spencer. 1988. *Nuclear Fear: A History of Images.* Cambridge, Mass.: Harvard University Press.

Webb, Richard E. 1976. *The Accident Hazards of Nuclear Power Plants.* Amherst, Mass.: University of Massachusetts Press.

Webber, David J. 1982. Is Nuclear Power Just Another Environmental Issue? An Analysis of California Voters. *Environment and Behavior* 14, 1 (January): 72–83.

Weinberg, Alvin. 1971. The Moral Imperatives of Nuclear Energy. *Nuclear News* 14 (December): 33.

Weinberg, Alvin et al. 1985. *The Second Nuclear Era: A New Start for Nuclear Power.* New York: Praeger.

Weingast, Barry. 1980. Congress, Regulation, and the Decline of Nuclear Power. *Public Policy* 28 (spring): 231–55.

Welborn, David, William Lyons, and Larry Thomas. 1984. *Implementation and Effects of the Federal Government in the Sunshine Act.* Washington, D.C.: Administrative Conference of the United States.

Wenk, Edmund. 1979. *Margins for Survival: Overcoming Political Limits in Steering Technology.* New York: Pergamon Press.

Wenner, Lettie McSpadden. 1989. The Courts and Environmental Policy. In *Environmental Politics and Policy: Theories and Evidence,* ed. James P. Lester. Durham, N.C.: Duke University Press.

Wildavsky, Aaron. 1962. *Dixon-Yates: A Study in Power Politics.* New Haven, Conn.: Yale University Press.

Williams, Robert C., and Philip L. Cantelon, eds. 1985. *The Americam Atom: A Documentary History of Nuclear Policies from the Discovery of Fission to the Present, 1939–1984.* Philadelphia: University of Pennsylvania Press.

Wilson, James Q. 1989. *Bureaucracy: What Government Agencies Do and Why They Do It.* New York: Basic Books.

Wilson, James Q., ed. 1980. *The Politics of Regulation.* New York: Basic Books.

Winner, Langdon. 1986. *The Whale and the Reactor.* Chicago: University of Chicago Press.

Wood, William C. 1983. *Nuclear Safety: Risks and Regulation.* Washington, D.C.: American Enterprise Institute.

Woodhouse, Edward J. 1983. The Politics of Nuclear Waste Management. In *Too Hot to Handle? Social and Policy Issues in the Management of Radioactive Waste,* ed. Charles A. Walker, Leroy C. Gould, and Edward J. Woodhouse. New Haven, Conn.: Yale University Press.

Wright, Skelly. 1974. The Court and the Rulemaking Process: The Limits of Judicial Review. *Cornell Law Review* 59:375–97.

Zimmerman, Joseph. 1988. Regulating Atomic Energy in the American Federal System. *Publius* 18 (summer): 51–66.

Zwerdling, Joseph. 1972. The Role and Function of Federal Hearing Examiners. *Annals of the American Academy of Political and Social Science* 400 (March): 27–35.

PRIMARY SOURCES

Atomic Energy Commission

U.S. Atomic Energy Commission. 1962. *Civilian Nuclear Power—A Report to the President.*
    Reprinted in U.S. Congress. Joint Committee on Atomic Energy. 1968. *Nuclear Power
    Economies—1962 Through 1967.* 90th Cong., 2d sess., 92–253.
U.S. Atomic Energy Commission. 1968–73. *The Annual Report of the Atomic Energy Com-
    mission.*
U.S. Atomic Energy Commission. 1969. *Nuclear Power and the Environment.* Rockville,
    Md.: Atomic Energy Commission Records, Nuclear Regulatory Commission.
U.S. Atomic Energy Commission. 1974. *Environmental Survey of Uranium Fuel Cycle.*
    WASH-1248. Washington, D.C.: Government Printing Office, April.
U.S. Atomic Energy Commission. *In the Matter of Interim Acceptance Criteria for Emer-
    gency Core-Cooling Systems for Light Water-Cooled Nuclear Power Plants.* Atomic En-
    ergy Commission Docket RM 50-1, 5318.

Congress

U.S. Congress. House. Committee on Merchant Marine and Fisheries. Subcommittee on
    Fisheries and Wildlife Conservation. 1966. *Hearings on Miscellaneous Fisheries Legis-
    lation.* 89th Cong., 2d sess.
U.S. Congress. House. Committee on Government Operations. Subcommittee on Legisla-
    tion and Military Operations. 1973. *Hearings on H.R. 9090: The Energy Research and
    Development Administration Act.* 93d Cong., 1st sess.
U.S. Congress. House. Committee on Government Operations. Subcommittee on Legisla-
    tion and Military Operations. 1973. *Hearings on H.R. 11510: The Energy Reorganiza-
    tion Act of 1973.* 93d Cong., 1st sess.
U.S. Congress. House. Committee on Government Operations. 1973. *The Energy Reorgani-
    zation Act of 1973.* 93d Cong., 1st sess. H. Rept. 93-707.
U.S. Congress. House. 1974. *Conference Report on H.R. 11510, the Energy Reorganization
    Act of 1974.* 93d Cong., 2d sess. H. Rept. 93-1445.
U.S. Congress. House. Committee on Appropriations. 1975. *Hearings on the Public Works
    for Water and Power Development and Atomic Energy Commission Appropriations.*
    94th Cong., 1st sess.
U.S. Congress. House. Committee on Interior and Insular Affairs. Subcommittee on En-
    ergy and the Environment. 1975. *Oversight Hearings on Nuclear Energy—Overview of
    the Major Issues.* 94th Cong., 1st sess.
U.S. Congress. House. Committee on Interior and Insular Affairs. Subcommittee on En-
    ergy and the Environment. 1978. *Hearings on the Nuclear Siting and Licensing Act of
    1978.* 95th Cong., 2d sess.
U.S. Congress. House. Committee on Interior and Insular Affairs. Subcommittee on En-
    ergy and the Environment. 1979. *Oversight Hearings.* 96th Cong., 1st sess.
U.S. Congress. House. Committee on Government Operations. 1981. *Licensing Speedup,
    Safety Delay: NRC Oversight.* 97th Cong., 1st sess. H. Rept. 97-277.
U.S. Congress. House. Committee on Energy and Commerce. Subcommittee on Energy

Conservation and Power. 1983. *Hearings on NRC Licensing Reform.* 98th Cong., 1st sess.

U.S. Congress. House. Committee on Interior and Insular Affairs. Subcommittee on Energy and Environment. 1984. *Hearings on the Licensing Process at the Shoreham Nuclear Power Plant.* 98th Cong., 2d sess.

U.S. Congress. House. Commerce Committee. Subcommittee on General Oversight and Investigations. 1987. *NRC Coziness with Industry: An Investigative Report.* 100th Cong., 1st sess.

U.S. Congress. House. Committee on Interior and Insular Affairs. Subcommittee on Energy and the Environment. 1988. *Hearings on Nuclear Regulatory Commission Reorganization Legislation.* 100th Cong., 2d sess.

U.S. Congress. House. Committee on Energy and Commerce. Subcommittee on Energy and Power. 1991. *Hearings on National Energy Strategy, Part 2.* 102d Cong., 1st sess.

U.S. Congress. House. Committee on Interior and Insular Affairs. Subcommittee on Energy and the Environment. 1991. *Hearings on the National Energy Strategy.* 102d Cong., 1st sess.

U.S. Congress. Joint Committee on Atomic Energy. 1949. *Hearings Investigating the U.S. Atomic Energy Project.* 81st Cong., 1st sess.

U.S. Congress. Joint Committee on Atomic Energy. 1951. *The Development and Control of Atomic Energy.* 82d Cong., 1st sess.

U.S. Congress. Joint Committee on Atomic Energy. 1952. *Atomic Power and Private Enterprise.* 82d Cong., 2d sess., Committee Print.

U.S. Congress. Joint Committee on Atomic Energy. 1953. *Hearings on Atomic Power Development and Private Enterprise.* 83d Cong., 1st sess.

U.S. Congress. Joint Committee on Atomic Energy. 1954. *Amending the Atomic Energy Act of 1946: Report to Accompany S. 3690.* 83d Cong., 2d sess., S. Rept. 1699.

U.S. Congress. Joint Committee on Atomic Energy. 1954. *Hearings on S. 3323 and H.R. 8862 to Amend the Atomic Energy Act of 1946.* 83d Cong., 2d sess.

U.S. Congress. Joint Committee on Atomic Energy. 1955. *Hearings on the Development, Growth, and State of the Atomic Energy Industry.* 84th Cong., 1st sess.

U.S. Congress. Joint Committee on Atomic Energy. 1956. *Hearings on Government Indemnity for Private Licensees and AEC Contractors Against Reactor Hazards.* 84th Cong., 2d sess.

U.S. Congress. Joint Committee on Atomic Energy. 1956. *Hearings on Proposed Legislation for Accelerating the Civilian Reactor Program.* 84th Cong., 2d sess.

U.S. Congress. Joint Committee on Atomic Energy. 1956. *Report of the Panel on the Peaceful Use of Atomic Energy.* 84th Cong., 2d sess.

U.S. Congress. Joint Committee on Atomic Energy. 1957 Special Subcommittee on Radiation. *Hearings on the Nature of Radioactive Fallout and Its Effects on Man.* 85th Cong., 1st sess.

U.S. Congress. Joint Committee on Atomic Energy. 1957. *Hearings on Government Indemnity and Reactor Safety.* 85th Cong., 1st sess.

U.S. Congress. Joint Commitee on Atomic Energy. 1957. *A Study of AEC Procedures and Organization in the Licensing of Reactor Facilities.* 85th Cong., 1st sess.

U.S. Congress. Joint Committee on Atomic Energy. 1958. *Hearings on the Proposed Euratom Agreement and Legislation to Carry Out the Proposed Cooperative Program.* 85th Cong., 2d sess.

U.S. Congress. Joint Committee on Atomic Energy. 1961. *Improving the AEC Regulatory Process.* 87th Cong., 1st sess., Committee Print.

U.S. Congress. Joint Committee on Atomic Energy. 1968. *Nuclear Power Economics—1962 Through 1967.* 90th Cong., 2d sess.

U.S. Congress. Joint Committee on Atomic Energy. 1969. *Hearings on the Environmental Effects of Producing Electric Power.* 91st Cong., 1st sess.

U.S. Congress. Joint Committee on Atomic Energy. 1972. *Hearings on H.R. 13731 and H.R. 13732 to Amend the Atomic Energy Act of 1954 Regarding the Licensing of Nuclear Facilities.* 92d Cong., 2d sess. Pt. 1.

U.S. Congress. Joint Committee on Atomic Energy. 1973. *Hearings on the Status of Nuclear Reactor Safety.* 93d Cong., 1st sess. Pt. 1, vol. 1, phases I and IIa; pt. 2, vol. 1, phases IIb and III; pt. 2, vol. 2.

U.S. Congress. Joint Committee on Atomic Energy. 1974. *Hearings on Nuclear Powerplant Siting and Licensing: H.R. 11957, 12823, 13484, and S. 3179 (Bills Related to the Need for Review of and Improvements to the Process for Bringing Nuclear Powerplants on Line).* 93d Cong., 2d sess. Vols. 1 and 2.

U.S. Congress. Joint Committee on Atomic Energy. 1975. *Hearings on Browns Ferry Nuclear Plant Fire.* 94th Cong., 1st sess.

U.S. Congress. Joint Committee on Atomic Energy. 1975. *Hearings on H.R. 8631 to Amend and Extend the Price-Anderson Act.* 94th Cong., 1st sess.

U.S. Congress. Joint Committee on Atomic Energy. 1975. *Hearings on S. 1717 and H.R. 7002: Proposed Nuclear Powerplant Siting and Licensing Legislation.* 94th Cong., 1st sess.

U.S. Congress. Joint Committee on Atomic Energy. 1976. *Hearings on the Extent and Significance of the Impact on Reactor Licensing of Recent Court Decisions.* 94th Cong., 2d sess.

U.S. Congress. Joint Committee on Atomic Energy. 1976. *Hearings on the Investigation of Charges Relating to Nuclear Reactor Safety.* 94th Cong., 2d sess. Vols. 1 and 2.

U.S. Congress. Senate. Committee on Public Works. Subcommittee on Air and Water Pollution. 1968. *Hearings on Thermal Pollution—1968.* 90th Cong., 2d sess.

U.S. Congress. Senate. Committee on Interior and Insular Affairs. 1971. *Hearings on Environmental Constraints and the Generation of Nuclear Electric Power: The Aftermath of the Court Decision on Calvert Cliffs.* 92d Cong., 1st sess. Pts. 1 and 2.

U.S. Congress. Senate. Committee on Interior and Insular Affairs. 1972. *Hearings on Interim Nuclear Licensing.* 92d Cong., 2d sess.

U.S. Congress. Senate. Committee on Government Operations. 1973. *Hearings on S. 2135: The Administration's Proposal to Establish a Department of Energy and Natural Resources, and ERDA.* 93d Cong., 1st sess.

U.S. Congress. Senate. Committee on Government Operations. Subcommittee on Reorganization, Research, and International Organizations. 1973. *Hearings on S. 2744: The Energy Reorganization Act of 1973.* 93d Cong., 1st sess.

U.S. Congress. Senate. Committee on Government Operations. Subcommittee on Reorganization, Research, and International Organizations. 1974. *Hearings on S. 2135: The Administration's Proposal to Establish a Department of Energy and Natural Resources and an Energy Research and Development Administration; and S. 2744, to Establish an Energy Research and Development Administration and a Nuclear Safety and Licensing Commission.* 93d Cong., 2d sess.

U.S. Congress. Senate. Committee on Government Operations. 1974. *The Energy Reorganization Act of 1974.* 93d Cong., 2d sess. S. Rept 93-980.

U.S. Congress. Senate. Committee on the Environment and Public Works. Subcommittee on Nuclear Regulation. 1978. *Hearings on Nuclear Siting and Licensing Act of 1978.* 95th Cong., 2d sess.

U.S. Congress. Senate. Committee on the Environment and Public Works. Subcommittee on Nuclear Regulation. 1983. *Hearings on Nuclear Licensing and Regulatory Reform.* 98th Cong., 1st sess.

Department of Energy and Nuclear Regulatory Commission Documents

U.S. Department of Energy. Energy Information Administration. 1991. *Commercial Nuclear Power 1991: Prospects for the United States and the World.* Washington, D.C.: Government Printing Office.

U.S. Nuclear Regulatory Commission. 1975–95. *The Annual Report of the Nuclear Regulatory Commission.* Washington, D.C.: Government Printing Office.

U.S. Nuclear Regulatory Commission. 1975. *Reactor Safety Study—An Assessment of Accident Risks at U.S. Commercial Nuclear Power Plants.* WASH-1400, NUREG-75/014. Washington, D.C.: Government Printing Office, October.

U.S. Nuclear Regulatory Commission. 1976. *Final Generic Environmental Impact Statement on the Use of Recycled Plutonium in Mixed Oxide Fuel in Light Water-Cooled Reactors.* NUREG-0002. Washington, D.C.: Office of Nuclear Safety and Safeguards, August.

U.S. Nuclear Regulatory Commission. 1976. *Supplement to WASH-1248: Reprocessing and Waste Management.* NUREG-0116. Washington, D.C.: Government Printing Office, October.

U.S. Nuclear Regulatory Commission. 1977. *Nuclear Power Plant Licensing: Opportunities for Improvement.* NUREG-0292. Washington, D.C.: Government Printing Office, June.

U.S. Nuclear Regulatory Commission. 1978. *Preliminary Statement of General Policy for Rulemaking to Improve Nuclear Power Plant Licensing.* NUREG-0499. Washington, D.C.: Government Printing Office.

U.S. Nuclear Regulatory Commission. 1978. *Program for the Resolution of Generic Issues Related to Nuclear Power Plants.* NUREG-0410. Washington, D.C.: Government Printing Office, January.

U.S. Nuclear Regulatory Commission. 1978. *Risk Assessment Review Group Report to the U.S. Nuclear Regulatory Commission.* NUREG/CR-0400. Washington, D.C.: Government Printing Office, September.

U.S. Nuclear Regulatory Commission. 1979. *Identification of Unresolved Safety Issues Relating to Nuclear Power Plants—A Report to Congress.* NUREG-0510. Washington, D.C.: Government Printing Office, January.

U.S. Nuclear Regulatory Commission. 1979. *TMI-2 Lessons Learned Task Force: Status Report and Short-Term Recommendations.* NUREG-0578. Washington, D.C.: Government Printing Office, July.

U.S. Nuclear Regulatory Commission. 1979. *TMI-2 Lessons Learned Task Force Final Report.* NUREG-0585. Washington, D.C.: Government Printing Office, October.

U.S. Nuclear Regulatory Commission. 1980. *Nuclear Regulatory Commission Action Plans*

Developed as a Result of the TMI-2 Accident. NUREG-0660. Washington, D.C.: Government Printing Office, May.

U.S. Nuclear Regulatory Commission. 1980. *Three Mile Island: A Report to the Commissioners and to the Public.* Prepared by Mitchell Rogovin et al. NUREG/CR-1250. Washington, D.C.: Government Printing Office, January.

U.S. Nuclear Regulatory Commission. 1980. *TMI-Related Requirements for New Operating Licenses.* NUREG-0694. Washington, D.C.: Government Printing Office, June.

U.S. Nuclear Regulatory Commission. 1981. *Identification of New Unresolved Safety Issues Relating to Nuclear Power Plants.* NUREG-0705. Washington, D.C.: Government Printing Office, March.

Index